Return to Aztlan

A book in the Latin American and Caribbean
Arts and Culture publication initiative.
Latin American and Caribbean Arts and Culture is
supported by the Andrew W. Mellon Foundation.

Return to Aztlan

Indians, Spaniards, and the Invention of Nuevo México

Danna A. Levin Rojo

university of oklahoma press : norman

Also by Danna A. Levin Rojo
(with Federico Navarrete) *Indios, mestizos y españoles: interculturalidad e historiografía en la Nueva España* (Mexico City, 2007)
(with Carlo Bonfiglioli, Arturo Gutiérrez, and Marie-Areti Hers) *Las vías del noroeste III: genealogías, transversalidades y convergencias* (Mexico City, 2011)

Library of Congress Cataloging-in-Publication Data

Levin Rojo, Danna.
Return to Aztlan : Indians, Spaniards, and the invention of Nuevo México / Danna A. Levin Rojo.
    pages cm. — (Latin American and Caribbean arts and culture)
    Includes bibliographical references and index.
    ISBN 978-0-8061-4434-4 (hardcover) ISBN 978-0-8061-9030-3 (paper) 1. Aztlan. 2. Aztec mythology.
3. Names, Nahuatl. 4. Names, Geographical—New Mexico. 5. Geographical myths—New Mexico. 6. Indians of North America—New Mexico—Historiography. 7. Indians of North America—New Mexico—Ethnic identity. 8. Spain—Colonies—America. 9. New Mexico—Discovery and exploration—Spanish. 10. Mexico—History—Spanish colony, 1540–1810—Historiography. I. Title.
    F1219.76.R45L49 2014
    978.9—dc23

2013035472

The paper in this book meets the guidelines for permanence and durability of the Committee on Production Guidelines for Book Longevity of the Council on Library Resources, Inc. ∞

Copyright © 2014 by the University of Oklahoma Press, Norman, Publishing Division of the University. Paperback published 2022. Manufactured in the U.S.A.

All rights reserved. No part of this publication may be reproduced, stored in a retrieval system, or transmitted, in any form or by any means, electronic, mechanical, photocopying, recording, or otherwise—except as permitted under Section 107 or 108 of the United States Copyright Act—without the prior written permission of the University of Oklahoma Press. To request permission to reproduce selections from this book, write to Permissions, University of Oklahoma Press, 2800 Venture Drive, Norman, OK, 73069, or email rights.oupress@ou.edu.

For Natalia, whom I love the most

Contents

List of Illustrations   **ix**

Acknowledgments   **xi**

Introduction   **1**

Part I

1. The Semantics of Place Names: New Spain and New Mexico   **15**
2. Mexican, Chichimeca, and Pueblo Indians   **36**
3. The Exploration and Conquest of Nuevo México   **60**

Part II

4. The Medieval Hypothesis   **89**
5. From the North We Came Walking: Traditions of Ancestral Origin among Nahuas   **108**
6. Your Past Is Our Future: Documenting a Cross-Cultural Loan   **173**

Conclusion   **196**

Notes   **205**

Bibliography   **263**

Index   **295**

Illustrations

Image Plates

1. Chicomoztoc, *Mapa de Cuauhtinchan no. 2*   **135**
2. Chicomoztoc, *Historia Tolteca-Chichimeca*   **136**
3. Chicomoztoc, *Codex Mexicanus*   **137**
4. Foundation of Mexico-Tenochtitlan, *Tira de Tepechpan*   **138**
5. Year-sign grouping, *Codex Aubin*   **139**
6. Aztlan, *Codex Mexicanus*   **140**
7. Aztlan, *Mapa Sigüenza*   **141**
8. Aztlan, *Codex Azcatitlan*   **142–143**
9. Aztlan, *Codex Aubin*   **144**
10. Foundation of Mexico-Tenochtitlan, *Codex Aubin*   **145**
11. Foundation of Mexico-Tenochtitlan, *Codex Mendoza*   **147**
12. Colhuacan, *Codex Azcatitlan*   **148–149**
13. Coatepec, *Codex Azcatitlan*   **150**
14. Teocalli de la Guerra Sagrada, engraved monolithic monument, Museo Nacional de Antropología e Historia   **151**
15. Tlatelolca troops under Vázquez de Coronado, and army commanded by Viceroy Mendoza in the Mixtón War, *Códice de Tlatelolco*   **153**
16. Terra Antipodv̌ Regis Castele, chart by Fernão Vaz Dourado, 1580   **154–155**

Figures

1. Chicomoztoc, *Codex Azcatitlan*   **165**
2. Chicomoztoc, *Selden Roll*   **166**
3. Chapultepec, *Códice Boturini*   **167**
4. Foundation of Mexico-Tenochtitlan, *Codex Azcatitlan*   **168**
5. Aztlan, *Códice Boturini*   **169**
6. Foundation of Mexico-Tenochtitlan, *Histoire mexicaine depuis 1221 jusqu'en 1549*   **169**
7. Breaking of the tree, *Códice Boturini*   **170**
8. Sacrifice of the *mimixcoa*, *Códice Boturini*   **171**
9. Cipolla (Cíbola/Zuñi), *Tlaxcala Codex*, in Diego Muñoz Camargo, *Descripción de la ciudad y provincia de Tlaxcala*   **172**

Maps

1. Spanish colonies in mainland North America   **158–159**
2. Mesoamerica, Aridamerica, and Oasisamerica   **160**
3. Central, western, and northern Mexico   **161**
4. Lake basin of Mexico in 1519   **162**
5. Map of Mexico-Tenochtitlan attributed to Hernán Cortés, Nuremberg, 1524   **163**
6. Sixteenth century exploration and conquest expeditions north of Mexico City   **164**

Acknowledgments

A book is never the work of just one person—at least not this book. Many people contributed in different ways across the years it took to turn a series of vague notes and ideas into the text it is today. I must mention first my family, always loving, patient, and encouraging: my mother and father, my siblings, and my daughter.

The book is based on my PhD research conducted as a student in the Department of Anthropology at the London School of Economics and Political Science. My research was supported by a scholarship from the Dirección General de Asuntos del Personal Académico of the Universidad Nacional Autónoma de México (1993–99), the institution where I studied for my first career as a historian and to which I owe all my professional education and first academic jobs. Without the scholarship, I would have not been able to pay for my postgraduate studies in London. It was precisely while working on a collective multivolume book as a research grant recipient at the Instituto de Investigaciones Históricas (UNAM) under the supervision of Rosa Camelo that I came across the first chronicles and historical documents that made me formulate the questions that are the basis for this book. I want to thank my supervisors in Mexico City and London for all their knowledge, support, and orientation throughout those formative years: Fenella Cannell, the late Alfred Gell, Peter Hulme, Alfredo López Austin, and Joanna Overing. Their guidance and criticism accompanied my initial research; they were always respectful of my ideas and encouraged me to engage in creative thought but demanded academic rigor. Also very helpful and encouraging was the input of my PhD dissertation examiners, Gordon Brotherston and Olivia Harris. Finally, I thank my fellow students and friends for their love and support during those years, particularly Henrike Donner and Maria Kaustrater, with whom I shared so many life experiences and also useful and interesting discussions that somehow made their way into my research. Cuauhtémoc Medina, my life companion for many years and the father of my daughter, deserves special mention as well. We shared many hours in archives and libraries and many academic discussions. He read different versions of my several manuscripts and produced useful comments, attentive in his own transit through libraries and bookstores to references and materials that could feed my research and writing process. Always a good friend and intellectual partner, he has a place in these pages.

Various friends and colleagues also contributed information, critical comments, and suggestions over the years, for which I am profoundly grateful: Deborah Cohen, Susan Deeds, Deborah Dorotinsky, Humberto Medina, Ethelia Ruiz Medrano, Federico Navarrete, Martha Ortega, Pablo Piccato, Cynthia Radding, and José Rubén Romero. Special thanks go to my friends and fellow historians Emilie Carreón and Cristina Montemayor Schivy, who helped me revise the complete manuscript and correct language mistakes, as I am not a native English speaker. In so doing, they also provided feedback on other historical issues. For language corrections I must also thank University of Oklahoma Press manuscript editor Emily Jerman and copyeditor Katrin Flechsig. Finally, Michelle Aguilar Vera, Gabriel Kruell, and Edith Llamas helped me during the last stages of preparation of the manuscript. Armando Égido drew the originals of the modern maps included in the volume, and Paula Arroio took care of getting publication permissions and pictures of the images contained herein.

Besides the universities that educated me, UNAM and LSE, other institutions must be mentioned. First, the Universidad Autónoma Metropolitana, where I have worked since 2001, has been very supportive, allowing me to take research leave and sometimes providing financial support to make research travel possible. My colleagues at the Posgrado en Historiografía (Unidad Azcapotzalco) where I am a professor have also helped in different ways to make this book possible. The Bancroft Library at the University of California, Berkeley; the Center for Southwest Research of the University of New Mexico, Albuquerque; the New Mexico State Records Center and Archives, Santa Fe; the Archivo General de la Nación, Mexico City; the Archivo General de Indias, Seville; the British Library, London; the Biblioteca Nacional de México, Mexico City; and the Biblioteca Nacional de España, Madrid, were all crucial in this research. Mexico North Research Network also gave me a grant to conduct research under the Transnationalism Studies Program (2004). Finally, I also received a grant from the Irwin Trust of the Central Research Fund of the University of London to conduct research in Spain during the summer of 1997.

Before continuing, a couple of clarifications are needed: (1) To distinguish the "imaginary world" this book deals with and the colonial province it gave birth to from the American state of the same translated name, I consistently use the Spanish name "Nuevo México" except when referring to the modern state of New Mexico; (2) all translations from sources originally written in Spanish are mine unless otherwise stated.

Introduction

This book explores the Spanish conquest of present-day New Mexico from a novel perspective, focusing on the impact that native Central Mexican myths of ancestral origin and migration had on Spanish representation, exploration, and conquest of the territory northwest of New Spain. It analyzes particular processes in the cross-cultural construction of geographic and historical knowledge insofar as they can be traced in sixteenth-century sources relating to that enterprise of colonial expansion. Until now, scholars have often depicted America's conquest history with little regard to the influence of native cultures on European perceptions and colonizing strategies.

Central to the argument developed in this book is the concept of "imaginary world" as defined by Peter Mason: an imaginary accretion referring to the configuration of the world perceived, but having no correspondence with any concrete empirical object. The imaginary world does, however, have "a certain reality effect" deriving from its linguistic expression as "an ensemble of names" that interlocks with other empirically grounded objectification systems (chronological, topographical, and so on). Imaginary worlds, Mason argues, have no concrete embodiment "in the material external world" but nevertheless inscribe specific attitudes toward the social and natural objects they address. Therefore, they are constitutive of the social practice of individuals within the world.[1]

The colonial "Kingdom of Nuevo México," *not* equivalent to the modern North American state of New Mexico, was established in 1598 as the northernmost Spanish possession in continental America (map 1). However, it had existed before as an imaginary world constructed by Spanish conquerors and settlers and their Indian allies throughout a period of approximately forty years after the fall of Mexico-Tenochtitlan. During this period, a long series of verbal reports suggesting the existence of seven rich and populous cities beyond the northern limits of New Spain were systematically connected to a widespread body of Central Mexican Nahua traditions concerning a distant land of origin: Aztlan-Teoculhuacan-Chicomoztoc. Toward the mid-sixteenth century this "worldmaking" process[2] gave birth to the chimerical realm of "Nuevo México," non-localized but conceived of as the original homeland of the ancient Mexicas (that is, Aztecs),[3] which successive parties of religious and lay adventurers then tried to locate. Finally, at the close of the century, this reified chimera turned into a concrete colonial province.[4]

The historical process outlined above, the central topic of this book, evolved in a vast territory that Mexican anthropologists divide into culture areas: Mesoamerica, Aridamerica, and Oasisamerica. Particularly important as the starting point is the lake basin of the Valley of Mexico, which became the main seat of government for the Viceroyalty of New Spain. The valley is located in Mesoamerica at the heart of Central Mexico, a region roughly coinciding with the maximum expanse of the so-called Aztec empire, primarily inhabited in the contact period by Náhuatl- and Otomí-speaking peoples (maps 2–4).[5]

Scholarly understandings of Nuevo México as a concept and as a territory have depended too much on imported Western paradigms and too little on local native tradition. Standard historiography disregards the importance of the Indian imaginary in conquest endeavors north of New Spain, and poses instead legendary marvels from European medieval lore. The latter, alongside pure ambition and evangelizing zeal, have been seen as the major sources providing Spaniards with goals for exploration and conquest. But the series of Nahua narratives that recount the ancestral Mexica migration from Aztlan-Chicomoztoc into the Valley of Mexico—commonly known as the "Aztec pilgrimage"—are far more important to explain the Spanish interest in the lands beyond the reach of Aztec control than the array of European fantastic motifs usually cited.

As a colonial province, Nuevo México comprised a variable portion of the territory of present-day New Mexico and Arizona. In the sixteenth century it was inhabited by linguistically diverse groups of sedentary, full-time farmers, today known as Pueblo Indians, and by increasing numbers of newly arrived hunter-gatherers. Various groups of conquerors, missionaries, and prospective colonists entered and competed over this region after the first sighting of the Pueblo villages by Friar Marcos de Niza in 1539. From that moment up to the 1580s, the Spaniards referred to the area as Cíbola, or the Seven Cities. Only then did it begin to be identified as Nuevo México and, most importantly, seen as the rich and populous original Aztec homeland that had been sought at least since the 1560s. A wide variety of early maps, colonial chronicles, soldiers' reports, private and official letters, and codices in native script indicate that conquerors saw in Nahua traditions of ancestral origin and primordial migration the promise of accomplishing their own particular ambitions. Moreover, the Spaniards represented and sometimes lived their conquest endeavors as a backtracking of ancient migration paths starting from Aztlan. Thus, the colonial appropriation of the area that eventually became Nuevo México must be understood as an

Indian-Spanish enterprise, not only because it involved the massive collaboration of Mesoamerican allies as troops, but also because the ideas these natives held about their own past, and perhaps also their political concerns, contributed significantly toward determining the destinations and routes that northward expeditions pursued after 1521. Indeed, attending to evidence reviewed in this book, it can be sustained that both Spaniards and Central Mexican Indians saw their participation in the search for and conquest of Nuevo México as a centuries-delayed "return to Aztlan."

This book, while neither a detailed reconstruction of New Mexico's politico-military conquest history nor a description of the social arrangements and culture of its original indigenous inhabitants, exercises the conjunction of history and anthropology promoted by Bernard Cohn, who more than two decades ago called for "an epistemology and subject matter common to the two disciplines." An anthropological history, he wrote,

> is not about a place being a place in the sense of being a bounded geographic location, or, for that matter, in the sense of what in the older anthropological literature was called a tribe, village, or category of people. We might choose to study in a certain place, but the unit of our study is not a place. Nor is it a segment of time as a sequence of empirical events. . . . The units of study in anthropological history should be cultural and culturally derived: honor, power, authority, exchange, reciprocity, codes of conduct, systems of social classification, the construction of time and space, rituals. One studies these in a particular place and over time, but the study is about the construction of cultural categories and the process of that construction, not about place and time.[6]

Accordingly, this book is not concerned with one specific community or category of people, but with many, as they are mutually related in the transforming, through categorical construction and colonizing practice, of abstract geographic space into a concrete socio-political place. I focus on the cross-cultural dealings between Spanish conquerors and native Mesoamerican Indian allies engaged in constructing Nuevo México as an imaginary and physical new territory. Santa Arias and Mariselle Meléndez recently observed that places, as the loci of daily social activity and interaction, are the spaces "where constructions of identities as well as differences can be recognized. . . . Consequently, they can be sites of appropriation, domination, solidarity, contestation, or liberation."[7] The history of Nuevo México uncovered herein is about the gradual definition of cultural identity and difference through cross-cultural epistemological negotiations involving appropriation and liberation, domination and contestation. It is the history of a nearly century-long, extraordinary episode in which, for the first time, a group of Western individuals was seduced by Native American historical memory.

Since the 1950s, history and anthropology, conceived of in the early twentieth century as opposed disciplines, have developed increasingly overlapping concerns, methodological insights, and theoretical worries. Particularly noticeable starting in the 1960s and 1970s with the development of historical anthropology,[8] this rapprochement rendered invalid the idea that historical research belongs to the realm of contingency and particularity whereas anthropological thought, allegedly less narrative and more classificatory, pertains to the sphere of structure and general abstraction.[9] Historians working from this new perspective shifted their attention from the institutional aspects of the state, economics, or public policy[10] to the wider study of past societies through their culture. Here they understood culture as the store of collective representations pervasive in everyday life, which pertain to the sphere of automatic, nonreflexive thought that implicitly regulates people's judgment and behavior in society.[11] This new breed of historical anthropologists pursued a micro-, qualitative research, methodologically based on what anthropologist Clifford Geertz defined as "thick description," to study specific cases and small communities in terms of the "structures of signification"[12] embedded in the apparently trivial routines that reinforce specific world views in unique historical settings. They approached such fragments of history as particular instances of things generally human rather than as constituting links in a causal chain of events.

Historical anthropology undergirds this book insofar as I share Robert Darnton's conviction that to conduct ethnography in the archives is possible as long as documents are treated as concrete expressions of a wide variety of comprehensive belief systems and are therefore taken to reveal socially shared responses to the world.[13] However, instead of a holistic perspective that views societies at any given moment as organic wholes, turning history to synchronicity, I adopt a fundamentally diachronic stance closer to more recent post-functionalist reflections in anthropology concerned with processual issues.[14] Like the post-functionalist anthropologists, I think the world is not divided into atomistic societies or peoples because, as Eric Wolf contended, every social or cultural formation exists within ever-changing extra-community webs of symbolic exchange, mutual dependence, dominance, and subjection.[15]

The conjunction between history and anthropology attempted in this book entails a double approach—at once processual and classificatory—to the complex social intersection between culturally diverse individuals. My aim is not to reveal how "cross-culture contact" upsets the structural coherence of particular economic, kinship, and belief systems, but to search for the meaningful transformations and continuities that make social and cultural change possible. Thus, despite exceeding the period and regions traditionally considered relevant for New Mexico's history and ethnohistory, the book has a narrow focus that may be described as the deconstruction of a toponym. That is, the detailed assessment of "Nuevo México's" encoded cultural meanings, the particular forms of social interaction its formulation reveals, and the theoretical challenge it poses to modern interpretations of the encounter between Europeans and the "others" they colonized in America.

Return to Aztlan is divided in two parts, each comprising three chapters. Part I presents the historical facts and contextual information regarding cultural geography upon which further interpretation is built. Chapter 1 analyzes the semantic import of Spanish toponymic practices exercised in the wake of the encounter with Mexico. Chapter 2 provides a preconquest ethnohistorical overview of the territory where the "quest for Nuevo México," as I call it, evolved. Chapter 3 is a narrative sequence of relevant expeditions in the sixteenth century aimed at the exploration, conquest, and colonization of the land located north of the Valley of Mexico.

Part II discusses why and how Nahua ancestral migration narratives, rather than European imaginary worlds, oriented the Spanish understanding of New Spain's human geography. In particular, it looks at how the "Aztec pilgrimage" story contributed to the articulation of cross-cultural conquest alliances in the north. Chapter 4 argues against traditional interpretations concerning the determinant role played by medieval motifs in the exploration and conquest of present-day New Mexico. Chapter 5 analyzes how Nahua forms of political organization in preconquest times articulated with traditions of ancestral origin and the configuration of local identities. Chapter 6 undertakes a systematic comparison of documentary evidence to bring the reader full turn to the argument that Spaniards would take native stories about the Mexica origin in Aztlan seriously and attempt to build their imperial hegemony through its reoccupation, just as their Central Mexican Indian allies did.

Based on the semantic analysis of the toponyms "Nueva España" and "Nuevo México," chapter 1 argues that the construction of Nuevo México, its later reification, and finally, founding are closely related to the Spaniards' early colonial intrusion into the Caribbean, initial navigation along the Mesoamerican coastline, and subsequent arrival in Mexico-Tenochtitlan. Unlike other colonies in the American continent that similarly came into being as imagined territories made real through the allocation of place names—Las Antillas or California, for example—the labeling of New Mexico developed in a way atypical of European colonial naming practices. After Hernán Cortés coined the term "Nueva España" for the territory he seized from the Aztecs (today Mexico's heartland), newly found American lands were designated through recapitulations of existing locations (Nueva Galicia, Nueva Vizcaya, New England). Nuevo México, however, is the only toponym formulated by Europeans in the early colonial period that reproduced the name of an Amerindian place, the indigenous metropolis whose destruction made possible the birth of New Spain itself: Mexico-Tenochtitlan.

This simple and apparently trivial fact, hitherto overlooked by scholars, suggests that the interpretation of New World colonial experience should pay more heed to the Europeans' cognitive response[16] to human difference and the practical implications this had for the design of territorial expansion strategies.[17] The surprise that the conquerors experienced on witnessing an apprehensible difference between their own society and the complex, urban societies of Central Mexico had enormous consequences. For the first time since their arrival in the New World, conquerors could use the same categories applicable to their own society and its material artifacts (books, temples, idols, vassals, lords) to describe the universe that lay before them. This compatibility allowed them to see Native Mesoamerican and European historical discourse as analogous forms of knowledge. As a consequence, they granted credibility to Nahua migration stories and acted accordingly, searching for the land of origin found in these narratives.

Chapter 2 is organized as an assessment of key academic debates concerning the boundaries that scholars have drawn to divide North America into "culture areas," particularly Mesoamerica and the overlapping areas labeled under the categories of the Southwest, Aridamerica, and Oasisamerica. Its purpose is to illuminate the conditions under which European conquerors and settlers, Mesoamerican conquered and conquerors, and local Amerindian populations in the extreme north of New Spain interacted. Of particular importance is the description of pre-Columbian cultural corridors traversed by routes of migration and commercial and ritual exchange that conquerors could later follow. The chapter also discusses the ambiguous and polyvalent meaning of the Náhuatl term "Chichimeca" adopted by Spaniards to label resisting tribes of unsettled hunter-gatherers who hindered their colonial advance in the north. For many Mesoamerican Indians who acted as "allied troops," Chichimeca was also a self-defining term, applied to their own ancestors, which may partly explain their willingness to engage in northbound Spanish expeditions. For these discussions I draw on several recent studies concerning the pre-Columbian Mexican north and its relations to both Mesoamerica and the southwestern United States. This literature, best represented by Beatriz Braniff, María Teresa Cabrero, Marie-Areti Hers, and Patricia Carot, proposes a new reading of ethnohistorical sources illuminated by archaeological evidence obtained in present-day Michoacán, Jalisco, and Durango. These studies show important historical and cultural continuities between the agrarian societies that evolved in those regions and the civilizations that flourished in Central Mexico in the Classic and Post-Classic periods, thereby modifying traditional views on preconquest Mesoamerican origin "myths" and their connection to ancient migration.[18] The exploration and conquest routes followed by expeditions aimed at discovering Nuevo México, and the involvement of Mesoamerican Indian conquistadors in such expeditions, support the revisionist arguments these authors develop.

Nuevo México's existence as an "imaginary world" predates Friar Marcos de Niza's 1539 journey to Cíbola. Chapter 3 therefore expands the geographic and temporal scope of standard narratives on New Mexico's early colonial history. Besides the famous odysseys always drawn on (that is, Alvar Núñez Cabeza de Vaca, Niza himself, Francisco Vázquez de Coronado, Juan de Oñate, and a few others from the 1580s), the chapter examines a set of conquest endeavors from the 1560s that did not aim to reach Pueblo Indian country but were inspired by the conquerors' personal memories of Mexican splendor (from the time they first saw Tenochtitlan) and indigenous versions of ancestral Aztec past. It explores the early conquest (1520s and 1530s) of Central Mexico and Nueva Galicia as well, because it was then that empirical evidence started to belie the fantastic baggage that conquerors brought from Spain, which was soon displaced by native reports gathered precisely in that period.

As conceived in this book, the sixteenth century quest for Nuevo México challenges the widespread historiographic tendency to present the conquest of New Mexico as yet another instance of the simplistic transplant of European classical and medieval imageries to America, specifically the legend about the Seven Cities, supposedly founded by seven Portuguese bishops who had escaped from the Arab invasion of the Iberian Peninsula. This interpretation, based on an equivocal identification between the Seven Cities of Cíbola and those established by the fleeing Portuguese bishops,[19] is proved wrong in chapter 4. Unfortunately, standard narratives of New Mexico's colonial history continue to emphasize the transfer of European mythic and legendary motifs while neglecting the role of native Central Mexican culture in the Spanish conquest of the American Southwest. The Eurocentric discourse of classical works by such authors as Hubert H. Bancroft or Herbert E. Bolton has thus been kept alive.[20]

Twentieth century models for assessing cross-cultural interaction between European and non-European societies are of two kinds. Some, focused on the European experience of "the other," stress the imposition of Western cosmological premises on the alien worlds with which Europe interferes. Other models, more interested in the response of non-Western societies to the European presence, look at how native peoples perceive and represent the West, or how they accommodate to, and resist, colonial intrusion. The most influential in the first group was perhaps the model defining "Western systems of alterity"; that is, the systematic store of images and discourses that individuals of Western culture deploy in constructing images of otherness.[21] Research undertaken from this perspective is primarily concerned with the political significance and epistemological basis of difference and considers Western images of otherness as a domination strategy of disempowerment that operates through categorical inferiorization and exclusion.[22]

The Western systems of alterity model draws from Michel Foucault's concept of knowledge as power tactics and Emmanuel Levinas's reflections on the definition of alterity as the reverse side of identity.[23] Its central argument sustains that the "self-other" opposition in Western cosmology is comparable to the "reason-unreason" division Foucault studied, insofar as "the other," like "unreason," is often defined in purely negative terms that express the absence of the qualities attributed to the defining self (reason). As a consequence, the properties of "the other," thus deprived of a positive identity, are perceived as strange, hidden, frightful, and menacing; reasons for which they invite physical suppression, confinement, and marginalization.[24]

The analysis of early European perceptions of Amerindian civilizations has been particularly important for alterity theory. Johannes Fabian and Bernard McGrane, for example, categorized the New World encounter as the quintessential experience of absolute human and geographic alterity and asserted that, paradoxically, it prompted a unifying conception of the universe that reduced the menacing properties of otherness to controllable intelligibility. For, just as the theological heavens were transformed into astronomical space, turning the earth into just another planet, Europe became simply another continent, which allowed Europeans to bridge incommensurability by applying familiar notions of the unknown to unfamiliar settings that could then be subjected to physical appropriation.[25] Authors working from such an "alterity-taming" perspective set out to demonstrate that physical conquest entails suppressive definition. In colonial discourse, they observed, Amerindians appeared as the exotic and pathological antithesis of what conquerors thought themselves to be, Juan Ginés de Sepúlveda's position in his debate with Bartolomé de las Casas (1550–51) being the prototypical example of this kind of representation.[26] Authors like Anthony Pagden, Peter Mason, and Peter Hulme noted that early depictions of New World peoples made ample use of the monstrous and fabulous races of ancient travel lore and cosmography, derogatory references the Greeks and Romans had devised to describe social groups standing outside the scope of hegemony. Thus, according to Mason, the imagery of the exotic that was applied to the American Indian was a well-developed language for alterity already in use by the European upper classes to define their own internal "others." In America it allowed for the fixing of Indian status at the lower echelons of the conquerors' own society, alongside the Jew, the mad, the child, and the peasant.[27]

Despite its illuminating contributions, this literature tends to reproduce a colonialist image of self-other relations in the conquest of America because it portrays indigenous peoples as the silent object of European self-inscription.

The Euro-American encounter appears in its pages frequently pictured as an endless monologue that allowed Europeans, through the representations (discourses) they formulated, to maintain the asymmetric situation and remain fundamentally European, while Amerindians increasingly adopted the ways and perspectives of their super-powerful conquerors. Furthermore, in stressing the asymmetry between Indians and Europeans, authors such as Mason propounded that while examples abound of Indians who perforce adopt the values of their conquerors, there are few instances of the reverse.[28] As shown in chapters 5 and 6, the quest for Nuevo México provides, precisely, one such example. The problem, perhaps, is that instances of the reverse have simply escaped the eye of scholars who consider Western attitudes toward Native America as totally permeated by a logic of exclusion and inferiorization, not to mention more traditional historians who are unused to considering post-conquest Indian agency as a possibility.

Early twentieth-century studies of the Euro-American encounter discussed in chapter 4 presented Spanish conquerors as little more than a mystified and lustful lot, unable to see beyond their own fantastic medieval imagination. This kind of interpretation neglected the impact that local indigenous knowledge and cosmology had on the conquerors' understanding of America's geographic and cultural reality. More recent literature dealing with the colonial representation of otherness, written after the fundamental work by Edmundo O'Gorman reformulated the discovery of America as a process of invention,[29] has also tended to view the conquest in a teleological light, as if the colonizers' dominant position had never been at stake and their world views had remained always the same. Thus the unlikely assumption that dominant subjects in colonial encounters undergo little cultural change has been implicitly reinforced.[30] I show that, in fact, the Spaniards' mental framework did experience a significant transformation through their engagement and interaction with native peoples during the conquest of New Spain. To demonstrate it, chapter 5 undertakes a detailed assessment of Nahua migration stories and the social and political functions they fulfilled before the conquest, and chapter 6 traces such stories in colonial documents concerning the search for, exploration, and conquest of Nuevo México.

In 1994 Nicholas Thomas warned scholars against lapsing into the illusion "that prospectively or already colonized places are *tabula rasa* for the projection of European power and European representations."[31] Since then, an increasing number of studies concerning colony-metropolis relations all around the world have questioned the alleged imperviousness of colonial discourse and the homogeneity traditionally attributed to colonizers and colonized. Homi Bhabha's notions of ambivalence, mimicry, and hybridity are good examples of this development,[32] like

John Comaroff's or Ann Laura Stoler's examination of internal diversity and competing agendas in both social fields confronted in colonial situations.[33] Also in the Americanist field, a wealth of ethnohistorical studies has appeared that emphasizes indigenous agency, both during conquest and under Spanish rule.[34] However, intersubjective arenas wherein the emergence of new culture involves the colonizer's embrace of the colonized's wisdom and ideas have rarely been addressed. Among the few examples of research heading in that direction are the exceptional works by James Lockhart and, more recently, James Brooks.[35]

The successive epistemological ruptures and cognitive negotiations my research has identified in what I call the quest for Nuevo Mexico show that Spaniards did not simply experience the New World as the passive scenario for the enactment of their own power games and prejudices. On the contrary, just as Native Americans changed as they adapted to foreign domination, Spaniards underwent a process of self-transformation through their engagement with the unknown realities they intruded upon. Of course this is not to say that colonized and European cultures in America were dialectically integrated in a harmonic synthesis. Debates around the Columbian quincentenary demonstrated that such argument, implicit in the notion of an "Encounter between the Old World and the New," is, at least, questionable, since Europeans and Amerindian peoples took part in these events in conditions of inequality.[36] Nevertheless, when asymmetric power relations are inscribed in situations of cultural difference, the oppressors, like the oppressed, often inhabit the alien discourse of the opposing "other," building up hybrid representations that become the basis of much of colonial practice. This is why a reassessment of New World documentation, paying attention to non-state-determined forms of power and non-power-conditioned forms of perceiving and organizing experience, is fundamental in order to advance the discussion of how cultural difference has been dealt with "colonially." Methodologically, this would amount to bringing the European colonist and the "indigene," as Cohn advised, "into the same analytic field."[37]

Among the models most frequently applied to assess non-Western experiences of incoming Europeans is one that treats indigenous responses in terms of acculturation.[38] Anthropologists—since Redfield, Linton, and Herskovitz's 1936 definition—use "acculturation" to designate all processes of culture change evolving from the contact between two or more autonomous cultural systems that result in increased mutual similarity. Although implying heterogeneity, the model, more recently reformulated as occidentalization,[39] focuses on situations of inequality, emphasizing forms of social reorganization and cultural adaptation that involve the assimilation of the weaker by the stronger contact group(s). The model, however, neglects the production of distinctive successor cultural forms. Moreover, applied to the imposition of European hegemony in America, the concept has been frequently used to suggest that individuals or groups who took on the new culture necessarily compromised their own identity while rarely enticing their dominant counterpart into significant cultural adjustment.[40]

The major concern of this book is the opposite of that addressed by the classic concept of acculturation. Rather, it considers the cultural transformation of dominant parties in colonial contexts as they are impacted by the culture of the colonized. Instead of looking at the forced accommodation, or open or concealed resistance, of conquered Native Americans, or the wealth of routines imposed and representations displayed by European colonists, it describes one among many ways in which the Spaniards who came to stay in the New World became culturally "naturalized." This book therefore builds on the concept of transculturation that Fernando Ortiz coined in 1940 to express the varied phenomena resulting from the confrontation and intermeshing of cultures as different human streams, some forcibly dislocated, some migrants of their own will, and some local, converging on the island of Cuba:

> The word *transculturation* better expresses the different phases of the process of transition from one culture to another because this does not consist merely in acquiring another culture, which is what the English word *acculturation* really implies, but the process also necessarily involves the loss or uprooting of a previous culture, which could be defined as a deculturation. In addition it carries the idea of the consequent creation of new cultural phenomena, which could be called neoculturation. In the end . . . the result of every union of cultures is similar to that of the reproductive process between individuals: the offspring always has something of both parents but is always different from each of them.[41]

The term "transculturation" is particularly pertinent to an understanding of the cognitive process that the imaginary construction of Nuevo México entailed because, as Fernando Coronil expressed, it apprehends at once "the destructive and constructive moments in histories affected by colonialism and imperialism," making operative the premise that culture contact affects all the groups engaged in cross-cultural interaction, whether hegemonic, marginal, or subservient.[42]

The challenge that the concept of transculturation poses to the sharp distinction traditionally drawn between colonizer and colonized has been taken up in the last twenty years by authors who adopt a dialogic perspective,[43] also fundamental to the argument developed in this book. Dialogue, as Mikhail Bakhtin makes clear, is the primordial condition of human subjectivity; and meaning, like practice, is therefore always contextual, heterogeneous, and contested.[44] Walter Mignolo's concept of "colonial semiosis" and some recent disquisitions on hybridity and the dynamics of mimicry in colonial "first encounters" also offer powerful theoretical instruments to address the creativity of cross-cultural interaction.[45] Both perspectives deal with localized, day-to-day ways of negotiating power through representation and facilitate the formulation of dynamic models to understand how colonial societies live their cultural predicament, defying the hierarchical structure of what I shall call the "imposition-resistance-conformity" complex.

The goal of this book is to contribute to current debates on colonialism and postcoloniality by using the case of the Spanish in New Mexico to challenge the widespread assumption that colonizers and colonized operate in worlds unknowable to each other. Through a detailed analysis of the social and cultural meanings codified in place names, the book uncovers the particular forms of social interaction embedded in toponyms and thus reveals what was at stake in the Spanish—and Native Mesoamerican—expansion from Central Mexico to New Mexico. In using this sixteenth century case to disclose the negotiation of the knowledge frames and logics that the Spanish brought to their dealings with Central Mexican Indians, and the repercussions of that negotiation, I question reigning interpretations of colonial encounters and the models that scholars have constructed for the analysis of the interaction between European and non-European societies. Finally, this book contributes to the currently changing field of United States–Mexico borderland studies[46] by broadening the recent focus on the cross-cultural dealings between European colonists and local native societies to include the cultural input of Mesoamerican Indians in the conquest and post-conquest history of the region.

Part I

CHAPTER ONE

The Semantics of Place Names

New Spain and New Mexico

Early in November 1519, a few hundred Spaniards led by Hernán Cortés entered Mexico-Tenochtitlan, capital of the ancient Aztec empire. The invaders came from Cuba, following the trail to a gold-rich, populous land that lay—according to previous explorers—somewhere to the west of the recently colonized "Islands of the Ocean Sea." While the astonishment they experienced on sighting the city has been widely noted, its expression in the toponyms they formulated at the time has received little attention. The issue is of no little importance, considering that, as Edmundo O'Gorman demonstrated in *La invención de América* (1958), toponyms are endowed with more semantic attributes than is usually acknowledged. Created by people as a means to relate to geographic space, toponyms are not merely arbitrary signs to distinguish between places. Nor do they necessarily denote particular landmarks, physical characteristics, or contingent events. Often, toponyms encode political arrangements and project onto the signified terrain all sorts of representations of the social and cosmic order, therefore constituting empirical traces of the political and cognitive operations whereby people shape and make sense of the world.[1]

This chapter analyzes the epistemological import of geographic naming practices performed by Europeans in the wake of the encounter with mainland America. It focuses specifically on the formulation of two toponyms, Nueva España and Nuevo México, as well as on these toponyms' historical and semantic connections. I revisit a series of well-known passages from early colonial documents and compare the physical and social descriptions the conquerors made of Central Mexico with the previous and later perceptions they expressed about other lands and peoples in the Caribbean and North America. My purpose is to underscore the semantic transference that occurred when conquerors named a remote region inhabited by village-dwelling farmers after the city of Mexico-Tenochtitlan, the hegemonic center of what they considered to be the first "civilized"[2] territory in America they had subdued, which in turn they had named Nueva España. The naming choices are extraordinary on two counts: First, both toponyms represented significant ruptures in Spanish colonial naming practices.

Second, although both names enunciate a "New *Something*," one has its referent in Europe (Spain), while the other has it in America (Mexico).

Following O'Gorman's argument that America was "invented," not "discovered," a wealth of late twentieth-century literature interpreted New World colonial place-names as part of a linguistic strategy of appropriation and cultural obliteration of imperialized native populations who, according to this perspective, were cognitively constructed from a European standpoint to make of them suitable objects of rule.[3] It is certainly true that, as noted by Raymond Corbey and Joseph Leerssen, European expansionism went "hand in hand with an attempt to subdue the strangeness of 'the Other' in cognitive terms."[4] However, comparative analysis of regional place-names and testimonies about local human geography indicates that in sixteenth century Mesoamerica, the opening of a space for cognitive negotiation between indigenous and Spanish thinking was also integral to the process of colonial appropriation.

Spanish conquerors perceived multiple similarities between their own society and those societies they came across in Central Mexico. This allowed for the incorporation of native categories into transcultural frames of conceptual reference, which the Spanish soon adopted for the subsequent assimilation of New World realities, thereby making indigenous knowledge their own. Like the change in the order of knowledge that Foucault recognized in the transformation of folly into madness, or the birth of a medical science based on clinical rather than classificatory methods,[5] this cognitive negotiation—which the emergence of new geographic naming conventions reflects—transformed the principles under which experience was codified, giving rise to novel forms of practice in a wide variety of colonial affairs. For example, native views and artifacts became frequent in the administration of justice for Indian subjects, as recently shown by Ethelia Ruiz Medrano,[6] and they also cropped up in the production of geographic knowledge and territorial representation. The terms "Nueva España" and "Nuevo México" are an index of this phenomenon, which is defined by Walter Mignolo as colonial semiosis: "A network of semiotic processes in which signs from different cultural systems interact in the production and interpretation of hybrid cultural artifacts [and concepts]," the meaning of which no longer depends on their "original cultural context . . . but on the new set of relations generated by communicative interactions across cultural boundaries."[7]

Before going any further, a brief reminder of early routes of conquest is in order. The itinerary the conquerors followed from the Caribbean to Mexico helps explain Spanish reactions to local indigenous discourse as well as to regional variations in the native social order, material culture, and landscape. The subjugation of mainland America was accomplished by military forays beginning with Hispaniola (today the island of Santo Domingo), where Christopher Columbus established the first European colony in the New World. Native populations soon declined due to new epidemic diseases and a pattern of extreme exploitation the colonists enforced. As a consequence, slave raiding moved to the islands of Puerto Rico and Cuba, and then to the continental shoreline. Between 1492 and 1550, indigenous peoples were virtually extinguished in the Caribbean, a demographic catastrophe that was repeated elsewhere. It has been calculated, for example, that in Central Mexico the Indian population dropped from around 25,200,000 in 1519 to 1,069,225 in 1608.[8]

Beyond the Antilles two major lines of conquest can be identified. One, organized from Cuba, swept through Mexico between 1519 and 1522 and then extended both north and south of the Mexican Central Plateau. The other started in Panama in 1522 and, after moving briefly up to Nicaragua, took the Pacific route southward as the Spanish conquered the Inca empire (1531–33), the Amazon basin, and Chile (1525–49).[9] The events addressed in this book fall within the Cuba-Mexico path, and can be divided into two phases. The first ended in 1542 with a fruitless expedition led by Francisco Vázquez de Coronado to the heart of the present-day American Southwest (Arizona and New Mexico). The second began in the 1550s and was over by 1598 with the precarious consolidation of Nuevo México, the northernmost Spanish possession in the Western Hemisphere.

Also important for further discussion, the administrative structure of the Spanish empire overseas consisted of two government agencies in the Spanish metropole and an increasing number of local governorships later subjected to intermediate agencies of control. The Casa de Contratación de Sevilla, established in 1503, "was responsible for organizing and controlling the passage of men, ships and merchandise between Spain and America,"[10] whereas the Real y Supremo Consejo de Indias, founded in 1524 to assist the king in the formulation and enforcement of global policies for the colonies, was vested with legislative and judicial powers. As time went on, the spontaneous leaders of the early years, who acted as governors of the lands they had conquered, were subjected to a complex bureaucratic apparatus consisting of a number of permanent tribunals or *Audiencias,* on which all regional governorships became dependent. The first Audiencia, established in the city of Santo Domingo in 1511, was followed by eight more Audiencias as colonial domination extended over new regions. The system—with its higher officials appointed by the Consejo de Indias—was completed with the creation of two viceroyalties, New Spain in 1535 and Peru in 1546. Thus, the Crown managed to consolidate its hegemonic control overseas, temporarily threatened by the entrepreneurial model characteristic of early conquest endeavors.[11]

At the end of the fifteenth century, the Spanish monarchy had handed over the responsibility of overseas expansion to private individuals who volunteered to fund, organize, and carry out conquest expeditions based on contractual relations, formally stipulated in documents called *capitulaciones*. These documents endowed each captain who volunteered for an expedition with a number of privileges and the lifetime title of governor of the lands he might subdue, reserving for the king ultimate sovereignty over the provinces thus established and a percentage of the booty and wealth they produced. However, later bureaucratization transformed governorships into short-term posts. Capitulaciones continued to exist, but governors began to be periodically shifted, as were judges of the Audiencias and viceroys. A permanent system was set up to monitor the performance of every functionary in America: independent judges conducted periodic inquiries (*visitas*) and everyone in public office was subjected to a *residencia* trial at the end of his term. Written allegations flourished under this highly legalistic and bureaucratic regime. The abundant testimonies and reports the colonial bureacracy produced, filled with elaborate arguments and minute descriptions that frequently manipulated concrete information to suit the interests of the individual or group concerned, are the source of the information used for most of the arguments this book develops.

Identification: The Mexican Paradox

The establishment of the municipality (*ayuntamiento*) of Veracruz and the subsequent fall of Mexico-Tenochtitlan on August 23, 1521 under forces led by Hernán Cortés, were the first steps in the creation of a Spanish colony in North America. The colony received the name "Nueva España" and, in due course, became the political center controlling the kingdoms and provinces later established to the north (map 1). While this was certainly not the first place in the New World named after one in the Old, the character of the reference inscribed in the term "Nueva España" is entirely original and reflects the unusual circumstance of its formulation. The earliest known document to use the term "New Spain" is a certificate that Hernán Cortés signed on August 6, 1520, empowering Juan Ochoa de Lejalde to act as his attorney before the metropolitan authorities when Cortés had been temporarily expelled from Mexico-Tenochtitlan. Given the official way in which it appears in this document—"I, Hernando Cortés, Captain General and Chief Justice of New Spain of the Ocean Sea"[12]—one may assume the name was formulated before this date. In the "Carta del Cabildo," an earlier document dated July 10, 1519, and signed by the authorities Cortés had designated to report on events after the army's departure from Cuba, the toponym does not yet appear.[13] Therefore, it was probably coined between July 10, 1519, and August 6, 1520. Friar Juan de Torquemada asserts that it was Captain Juan de Grijalva who came up with the toponym in 1518 while sailing along the coast from Yucatan toward Veracruz and seeing many things that resembled the Iberian Peninsula.[14] There is no direct evidence, however, to corroborate his statement. The chaplain on that expedition, Juan Díaz, does not mention such an episode or place name in his report, the only surviving contemporary testimony concerning Grijalva's exploration.[15] The name also appears in the "Merced a los caciques de Axapusco y Tepeyahualco," supposedly written by Cortés on May 20, 1519, shortly after landing in San Juan de Ulúa and before he wrote the power of attorney quoted above. This document, however, is a forgery, as José Luis Martínez has demonstrated.[16]

In any case, Cortés himself explains at the end of his second letter to the king (October 30, 1520) why he chose the name: "Judging from all I have seen and understood about the similarity between this land and Spain, both regarding its fertility and grandeur and its cold climate, *and many other things which make them alike*, it seemed to me that the most suitable name for this said land was that of New Spain of the Ocean Sea; therefore, in Your Majesty's name I called it thus."[17] Reading between the lines, one realizes that—beyond the physical resemblance the passage remarks on—the extraordinary nature of the situation encoded in the toponym resides in those "many other things" that make Spain and New Spain alike. These similarities are not explicit in the paragraph because Cortés reviews them in detail in previous sections of his letter.

To discover where the singularity of the encounter with Mexico lies, one may also consider additional accounts by the soldiers involved, as well as the impressions of those who saw the New World at a distance through the news and objects sent to Europe. Contrasting with previous experiences in the Caribbean, the conquerors' feeling of alienation before native peoples was here attenuated by partial recognition. Some features of indigenous attire and way of life resembled, however superficially, the Spanish universe of things and habits, as the private letter of a member of the Spanish court, Pedro Mártir de Anglería,[18] states: "They have brought numerous and magnificent presents for the king from Coloacana, Olloa, and Cozumela, where . . . people live in a civilized manner, under the rule of law."[19]

It is true that when Pedro Mártir wrote these lines in March 1520 he was still unaware of the marvels of Mexico-Tenochtitlan, the messengers who carried the presents back to Spain having already embarked from Veracruz when the Spanish party entered the Aztec capital at the beginning of November 1519.[20] Yet his words reveal an early awareness of the radical contrast between Caribbean and mainland North American peoples, and show that even before Tenochtitlan came into view, soldiers in the field and politicians in Europe regarded the societies just encountered on the mainland as comparable to their own. Like Spain, these peoples had a ruling class that exercised full sovereignty, something Cortés made clear when he remarked on the wide scope of Moctezuma's authority: "The dominion this Moctezuma had over these lands is as yet unknown, because in none of the places where he sent his messengers, two hundred leagues from his magnificent city in either direction, was his command disobeyed; even though he was at war with some provinces in the area."[21] Likewise, their numerous institutions and administrative procedures surpassed the apparently simple structures characteristic of the small chiefdoms on the Caribbean and the North Atlantic coast of South America, as briefly described in early accounts.

Conquerors made few comments on the social and political organization of the first peoples they came across before discovering Yucatan. Their reticence indicates how far removed they felt from those societies. Generally speaking, chronicles from the Caribbean phase describe nature and geography in detail, but when it comes to beliefs and customs, they focus on people's "superstitions," the objects they worshipped (*zemes* or *cemís* in the Spanish transliteration of the local language), nakedness, and cannibalism.

Native kings (*reyes* or *reyezuelos*), rulers (*régulos*), and principal men (*hombres principales*) whom the Indians called "caciques" are mentioned constantly in early accounts such as the first *Decade* of Mártir de Anglería's *De Orbe Novo Decades* (1530),[22] and the writings of Columbus, Friar Ramón Pané (ca. 1498), and Hernán Pérez de Oliva (1525–28). Columbus's diary, for example, records under the heading for December 17, 1492, that on the island of Hispaniola "they saw a man the Admiral took to be the governor of that province, whom [the natives] called *cacique*." The next day's entry reiterates: "The Admiral learned there that in their language they called the king *cacique*."[23] Pérez de Oliva glossed the episode as follows: "Columbus pondered the customs of that people as best as he could and he knew from their gestures and indications by sign that the island was governed by kings, one of whom was present at the time."[24] In these early chronicles the lack of a proper description of the functions kings or caciques were meant to fulfill suggests that the Spaniards assumed a shared definition. Whether they simply could not tell the difference or were not sure of the equivalence; they were in the habit of pairing the words "cacique" and "king" or "governor" in the same sentence when not preferring *hombres principales* or *régulos*, terms with a more general and ambiguous meaning.

The Spaniards' difficulty in interpreting the Caribbean world is manifest in a letter Columbus addressed from Juana (Cuba) on March 4, 1493, to the Spanish monarchs. He presumes that the inhabitants lack a political or social regime: "I came to a very good harbor, from which I sent two men inland . . . so that they could see and determine if there were any cities or large settlements, and which land it was and what there was in it. They found many settlements and innumerable people, but no government of any importance." "Nowhere in these islands," he asserts, "have I known the inhabitants to have a religion, or idolatry."[25]

The letter establishes a connection between the lack of political order and the lack of religion, a connection also found in other contemporary documents.

Accordingly, the writers exclusively use the indigenous word *zeme* for all sorts of objects of worship in the Caribbean context. The phenomenon stands in contrast to the proliferation of "vassals," "lords," and "idols" we see in most eyewitness accounts of the conquest of Mexico and the two expeditions along the Mesoamerican coast that preceded Cortés, the first led by Francisco Hernández de Córdoba (1517), the second by Juan de Grijalva (1518).

Like the word "fetish" in Portuguese accounts of their sixteenth and seventeenth century forays along the West African coast, the Caribbean word "zeme" in Spanish accounts escaped the definition of "idol," a word that implied, according to William Pietz, a "relation of iconic resemblance to some immaterial model or entity." The fetish, distinguished from other objects of worship by its "irreducible materiality," was a god-object in itself, a material embodiment of a particular force or natural property.[26] Zemes were also nonfigurative, venerated objects of direct worship that exerted no moral authority and entailed no institutionalized ritual but were used to induce beneficial effects, such as health or abundant crops.[27] Conquerors therefore perceived them as the devotional counterpart of a lawless and disjointed society.

Friar Pané lived among Taínos of Hispaniola for nearly three years, but his report on indigenous culture refers only twice to the sociopolitical order. First he asserts that "their law is contained" in ancient songs, which they govern themselves by; and when they want to sing these songs they use a musical instrument ... which the *hombres principales* play."[28] Pané next describes the secret consultations held by these men, who inhaled a certain vegetable powder called *cohoba* to induce visions through which they could foresee the results of war.[29]

Pérez de Oliva wrote his *Historia de la invención de las Indias* in Spain between 1525 and 1528, based on his readings of Pané and Pedro Mártir. Like the latter, Pérez de Oliva had never been to America and found it all too easy to render all the caciques, régulos, and hombres principales into "kings," while contradictorily stating that the Caribbean people knew neither law nor literacy but were guided only by custom.[30]

In New Spain things were different. Sociopolitical comparability was incontestably signaled by the presence of cities, stone-and-mortar buildings (*edificios de cal y canto*),[31] and markets set up in large plazas, where people gathered periodically to "buy and sell" everything they needed.[32] Idolatry was visible as well, identifiable by "towers" that served only for devotional purposes.[33] But as Carmen Bernand and Serge Gruzinski contend, to say "idolatry" in sixteenth century Spain was to say "civilization," albeit civilization plus the devil, or minus the true God. In contrast with the Caribbean, conquerors advancing through coastal and inland Mexico immediately identified the presence of religion, which they compared to Islam and defined as idolatry. In both Mexico and Peru the conquerors assumed that idolatry, being a corrupt form of religion, could only exist in civilization. The Spaniards felt that no matter how distorted a religion idolatry was, it supplanted chaos and appeared only in conjunction with a constituted, superior authority to centralize power.[34]

The terminology employed in eyewitness accounts of the first three mainland expeditions is revealing. The stated purpose of the Carta del Cabildo (July 1519), for instance, was for Cortés to inform the Spanish monarchs of the things and wealth found in the discovered land, "the people who possess it, and the *law* or *creed*, rites and ceremonies they live by."[35] In contrast with previous reports on the Antilles, it was in Mesoamerica—soon to be New Spain—that for the first time, native societies were described using words like "palace" (*palacio*), "marketplace" (*mercado*), "priest" (*sacerdote*), "street" (*calle, calzada*), "law" (*ley, administración de justicia*), "ally" (*aliado*), "governor" (*gobernador*), "vassal" (*vasallo*), "lord" and "lordship" (*señor, señorío*).[36] Not merely a coincidence, this was the linguistic expression of an awareness of similarity that made Spaniards more open to indigenous views, a first step toward the establishment of cross-cultural communication.

Paradoxically, the possibility of classifying what they saw after landing in Yucatan according to their own categories gave Spaniards a clearer idea of what they had seen earlier, which made their linguistic appropriation a stronger cognitive resource. For example, the word "cacique" (from the Arawak *kassiquan*, to have or maintain a house),[37] which the Spaniards initially used as a synonym for "indigenous ruler" in general,[38] acquired a more precise meaning in New Spain. Here "cacique" gradually became the specific term to designate local chiefs with circumscribed power. While the Carta del Cabildo called all types of indigenous rulers "caciques," none of the subsequent *Cartas de relación*, written after the Spaniards arrived in Tlaxcala, repeats the term. Instead, the *Cartas de relación* consistently refer to rulers as "señores" (lords) and to Moctezuma as "gran señor" (great lord).

Statements by Bernal Díaz del Castillo also reveal this increased precision. He records that on the way from Cempoala to Tenochtitlan, the Spaniards explained to Olintecle, "a cacique from Zocotlan," that they came "from faraway lands by order of our King and Lord, the great Emperor Don Carlos, who has many great princes as his vassals."[39] Later, mentioning the greeting Moctezuma had arranged on the outskirts of Tenochtitlan, Bernal Díaz declares: "Thus we stopped for a long time, and thence the *Cacamatzín*, lord of Tezcuco, and the lord of Iztapalapa and the lord of Tacuba and the lord of Cuyoacan approached to meet the great Moctezuma, who came near . . . accompanied by other great lords and caciques who also had vassals."[40]

In these excerpts, the terms "lord" and "vassal" describe both native and Spanish categories, while "emperor" applies only to the European context and "cacique" refers exclusively to the local Indian context. Furthermore, "emperor," "lord," and "cacique" neither substitute for one another as synonyms nor are they used reiteratively together, as had occurred in the Caribbean. Instead, they are clearly differentiated as three positions in the hierarchy of power.

Robert Haskett has explained that Spaniards adopted the word "cacique" early in the Caribbean and then applied it to the *tlatoque* and other high nobles of Central Mexico. Men described as caciques—he says—held the governorship with great frequency in sixteenth century New Spain, but by the mid-seventeenth century it was rare to find caciques in high public office because their status had been progressively eroded in the face of competition from aggressive figures of lesser status.[41] Nonetheless, if seventeenth century documents do not speak of high public officers as caciques, this may also be attributed—at least partially—to a modification in the meaning of words. Men that the Spaniards called "caciques" in sixteenth century Central Mexico may have been ruling *tlatoques* before the conquest, but once integrated into the colonial administration, they occupied lesser positions within the overall scale of rule. Indian rulers of high rank in Mesoamerica, in fact, were initially called lords, not caciques. As a concept in the Spanish language, "cacique" implied circumscribed authority from the moment the conquerors arrived in Central Mexico. The fact that Moctezuma and, later on, the *cazonci* (Tarascan overlord) were never called caciques is otherwise inexplicable.

Recognition of familiar concepts and forms to organize practice in the spheres of politics and religion allowed the Spaniards to bridge incommensurability because these spheres were precisely the cornerstones of their own identity. Indeed, they regarded native dealings and cultural achievements—including idolatry—as signs of civilization in the Roman-derived sense of a civic-oriented community life. If only these natives were introduced to the Catholic faith, they would soon embrace the true God, since they are politically organized, the Carta del Cabildo remarks, asking for the monarchs' support. "We believe that by the aid of interpreters and people who would clearly explain to them the truth of the Holy Faith and the error in which they live, many, and even all of them, would come to embrace true knowledge, because they live in a more political and reasonable manner than any of the peoples seen up to now in these parts."[42]

Many soldiers of Cortés had already spent some years on the islands of Hispaniola and Cuba and were now awestruck by the presence of fortified cities, formal marketplaces, cotton clothing, and book-like documents. Cortés himself wrote that Tlaxcala had "buildings as good as did Granada and many more people than that city had when it was taken."[43] Government in the province, he said, was "almost like in the lordships of Venice, Geneva or Pisa" because rather than "one overlord there were many lords," all of whom lived "in this city" and had the "peasants" of the surrounding villages as their "vassals."[44] Cortés wrote that in Churultecal (Cholula) every piece of land was cultivated, and yet in many quarters people suffered from scarcity, with many poor "who beg among the rich in the streets, the houses and markets as the indigent do in Spain and other places where there are people of reason."[45]

Examples are multiple but the previous will suffice to show that the amazement the conquerors experienced did not result from facing absolute oddities in the form of unrecognizable objects. Their awe derived from the consonance with a human order they found readable, even with negative aspects like the presence of beggars. At least, this is what conquerors believed: "In the services they have and the manners they follow," said Cortés of Tenochtitlan, "there is almost the same way of life as in Spain, with the same concert and order."[46] The paradox entailed in this particular combination of surprise and familiarity makes the Spanish arrival in Central Mexico extraordinary, both for us (analytically) and for the individuals involved (in terms of historical actuality).

Two propositions derive from this discussion. First, this "Mexican paradox" established an epistemological precedent: the apprehension of exotic human realities by means of their assimilation to familiar notions applicable to European society. Second, the name "Nueva España" entitled the cognitive process herein described.[47] Both arguments are consonant with the concept of "double mistaken identity" James Lockhart has developed to define a mechanism at the root of cultural interaction between Nahuas and Spaniards. Both arguments are pitched against traditional interpretations of the European cognitive response to New World oddity. The classic view persistently describes European attitudes toward, and representations of, America either as a strategy of symbolic domestication to achieve political and economic control over its population and resources, or as a form of linguistic appropriation through labeling. Such conceptual strategies were based, according to this view, on projecting European names and preconceived notions of alterity, derived from the Classical and Christian traditions, on American realities. In contrast, Lockhart contends that the massive contact between indigenous and immigrant Spanish populations in Central Mexico entailed a good deal of misunderstanding between the members of two societies that surprisingly, though superficially, resembled each other. Each side in this process assumed that certain forms and concepts of the other were also part of its own tradition and that they operated in much the same manner in either context, allowing both cultural patterns to affect each other and be partially preserved. Thus, the Spanish conquest of Central Mexico was possible, in a sense, precisely because there was a certain degree of perceived coincidence between native and Hispanic practices and institutions.[48] This, rather than appropriation, is what the name "Nueva España" connotes.

Naming Places: A Process of Homologation and Transference

Toponymic practices during the initial Caribbean phase of colonial expansion were heterogeneous. Sometimes colonists simply endorsed what they thought to be the indigenous name of a given place (Cuba, Paria, Urabá) seldom realizing that, as in the case of Yucatan, the word they took to be a territorial denomination actually conveyed quite a different message. "Yucatán," according to Alonso de la Cruz, Mártir de Anglería, and Francisco López de Gómara, was a mishearing of the Mayan expression *tectetan,* meaning "I do not understand you."[49] Another custom, used in the Caribbean, mainland, and trans-Pacific expeditions, was to name places after Spanish monarchs and viceroys as in the case of the Philippines and Cape Mendocino, California, for example, or the early names for Cuba—Juana and Fernandina.[50] Perhaps more frequent was to name places according to the dates of the Christian calendar on which they were "discovered" or their inhabitants reduced to political obedience (for example, San Salvador, Santo Domingo, Trinidad, and Corpus Christi). Finally, some places were named after a province or other location back in the Old World in accordance with the provenance of the conquerors, or the perception of a certain geographic similarity (Mérida, Cartagena de Indias, Castilla del Oro).[51] Applying a grammatical analysis, one can say that in this last instance a name, which particularizes, almost becomes a generic noun; that is, a word syntactically functioning as the subject in a sentence, and therefore, cities such as Mérida have three or more different embodiments in Spain and its colonies. Like "dogs," or "houses," there can be as many Méridas as there are cities in the world.

Strange as it may appear, "Nueva España" does not fit this latter toponymic logic. There is a fundamental difference between the representational value of the individual words in this name, and others that at first glance seem equivalent. "Cartagena de Indias," for example, takes the name of a city in the Iberian Peninsula (Cartagena) and adds a modifier specifying its location (de Indias). The same can be said of Castilla del Oro: the name of a European territory followed by a naturalistic qualifier (del Oro). In both instances the modifier differentiates the Old World referent from the place it designates in the New.

"Nueva España" works under a different principle. A European name is again reproduced, this time that of the motherland itself. A qualifying particle (Nueva) is again added to distinguish the double from the original. But "new" only allows a distinction between *two* entities, not many. The word "España" does not become a *noun* but remains a *name* with two referents related almost in a symmetrical fashion. Thus, the distinguishing particle in this toponym does not function as a modifier that changes the original meaning of the term. On the contrary, the adjective "Nueva" emphasizes the meaning of "España," drawing toward the new territory the essential semantic content of the concept. Compared to an example like Cartagena de Indias, it works through displacement and replication rather than by modification. This is confirmed by the fact that "España" signified a political entity that articulated a number of different communities, and even peoples, under the same sovereignty,[52] as the empire ruled by Moctezuma apparently did in the eyes of the labeling intruders. In conclusion, the link between this newly coined toponym (Nueva España) and its referent (the lands and peoples formerly subjected to, or contesting, Mexica state domination) is not restricted to the previous praxis, which highlighted the resemblance between certain features of the Spanish and American geography. In this case the signifier, though altered by the new context, carries the full connotations of its previous meaning, drawing a relation of homology between Spain and New Spain.

The term "Nueva España," first of its kind in America (that is, "New *Something*"), marks the emergence of a global and normalized naming practice, applied thereafter in the colonial world overseas alongside the consideration of incidental and limited resemblances evocative of the explorer's homeland, the spirit of commemoration, or the mere acceptance of a native name. Indeed, the coinage gave rise to the centenary practice of mirroring the names of European sovereignties in their American dependencies. New France, New England, New Holland; the formula established rights of conquest across the Atlantic Ocean.

However, despite the importance of New World toponymy as a discursive practice tied to the imperialist career of the European nations, the colonialist pattern of naming is not central to this discussion. More important is the cultural predicament from which the toponym "Nueva España" sprang. That its coinage established a labeling code for imperialist endeavors is undeniable, yet this does not mean that the New Spain designation was primarily conceived as a signal of colonial appropriation. In this sense, "Nueva España" stands in sharp contrast to that other name that Christopher Columbus devised for the first island he claimed in favor of the Spanish Crown: Hispaniola (La Española).[53] "Española" is a genitive grammatical form literally meaning "that which belongs to Spain," actually the abbreviated form of "La Isla Española" (The Spanish Island).[54]

The linguistic overtones of the imperialist competition are so evident in geographic naming that historians frequently dismiss the cognitive value inherent in the place names formulated by the conquerors, and they take their meaning for granted as if the name had a straightforward relation to the signified place. But the semantic constitution of the toponym "Nuevo México," at least, testifies to a linguistic process that runs parallel to, yet is not fully encompassed in, that of Spanish colonial hegemony. Even if "Nuevo México" fits the same mold as "Nueva España" and other similar place names, its referential structure diverges from the toponymic encoding of Indian subjection to the European empires.

The implied homology that the name "Nuevo México" draws between the old and new referents does not involve the projection of anything European; instead, "Nuevo México" reproduces the name of a part of the land being colonized. Thus, if conquest and domination are not proposed as the main, or sole, explanation for cross-cultural concepts like the two toponyms under discussion and both are interpreted, instead, as related to the cognitive process whereby they came into being, a different picture of the interaction between the parties involved in the Euro-American encounter (intruders and natives) comes to light.

The semantic correlation between the terms "Nueva España" and "Nuevo México" indicates that in Central Mexico the Spaniards had endorsed indigenous knowledge as valid and trustworthy. This epistemological transformation in Spanish attitudes toward the native culture resulted in the practice of conceiving "self" and "other" in homological terms as a methodological operation to mediate between *certitude* and *surprise,* two elements that characterize Cortés's enterprise and make it unique compared with previous and posterior experiences in the New World. At the same time, this transformation brought about an increasing recourse to analogies—not only to Spanish institutions and customs, but also to their newly recognized aboriginal correlates—in constructing knowledge. Indeed, after the encounter with Central Mexico, the Spanish conquerors often measured the exotic against the self-constitutive: they perceived the region as a "new" Spain, mistaking, as Lockhart observed, superficial similarities for evidence of a systemic equivalence in concepts and institutions. The authoritative status they granted to local culture, evident in the remarks reviewed below, made possible the interethnic collaboration between Spaniards and natives in the search for and conquest of Nuevo México.

According to their own testimony, the first emotion that held Cortés and his men in its thrall when they reached Mexico-Tenochtitlan was that of surprise. Diego de Ordaz, the first soldier to catch a glimpse of the whole Valley of Mexico during a scouting mission to the Popocatepetl volcano in September 1519, declared himself "thunderstruck (*espantado*)[55] by what he could see" from the summit: "Another new world of large settlements and towers, and a sea, and in it a huge city built, which, in all truth, provoked fear and *espanto.*"[56] Cortés himself wrote that Tenochtitlan was as big as Cordova or Seville, two of Spain's largest urban settlements of the time. But if its size seemed overwhelming, its location—amid the waters—was no less disturbing, as indicated by Ordaz's testimony and the ephemeral nickname, "Venecia la Rica," the conquerors initially used.[57]

Tenochtitlan stood on an island in a lake basin in the center of a broad valley nearly five thousand square kilometers in size (map 4). Over time, the natural island, located near the juncture of the salt and fresh waters of lakes Tetzcoco and Xochimilco, had been enlarged by a technique of reclaiming land from marshy areas.[58] At the time of the Spanish arrival, most of the city was built atop a collection of artificial square plots (*chinampas*) laid out in a grid pattern and crisscrossed by a system of streets and canals leading toward the four cardinal points from a central, walled precinct (map 5).[59] Most of the seventy-eight buildings within this precinct, according to Friar Bernardino de Sahagún, were sacred.[60] Most important were the great twin temple-pyramids dedicated to Tlaloc and Huitzilopochtli; but also included were the multiroomed palaces of rulers and nobles, the scene of the luxurious court life that chroniclers so vividly described. Moctezuma's palace, for instance, was said to have a hundred rooms including bedchambers, salons, and granaries, plus a number of magnificent gardens.[61] A series of causeways connected the island with three major cities ashore—Tlacopan, Tetzcoco, and Colhuacan—dividing the city in four cardinal sectors, or boroughs. Together with a dike that separated fresh and salt water, the causeways also served to control the currents and prevent floods. All five lakes constituting the basin of Mexico were constantly navigated by canoes transporting people and goods to the many towns and small cities that ringed the lakes, each settlement with its own civic and ceremonial center.

Archaeological evidence for the preconquest urban complex encircling the lakes is scarce, because Mexico City is now built atop the main settlements of that period. For the central hub—the original island—a few isolated but significant archaeological finds demonstrate the accuracy of most of the descriptions recorded in the early 1500s regarding the extension and physiognomy of the urban area, the number of its inhabitants, and their occupations.[62] One of Cortés's companions, known as the "Anonymous Conqueror," observed: "this city may be . . . more than two and a half leagues or almost three, approximately, in circuit."[63] Based on this and other testimony, and projecting the ancient boroughs onto a map of the modern city, José Luis de Rojas has calculated its size at approximately 13.5 square kilometers.[64]

The lengthy descriptions found in Cortés's second letter to the king and the accounts by other men in his party, such as Andrés de Tapia, Francisco de Aguilar, and Bernal Díaz del Castillo, hint at the features that attracted the Spaniards' attention.[65] They admired the city's layout as much as its cultivation techniques, but two aspects of the political economy amazed them the most: commercial activities and material markers of the prestige structure of native society. This is clearly attested to by the unusually long passages they devoted to marketplaces and ruling class etiquette. Díaz del Castillo wrote that his fellow soldiers were deeply impressed by the market square of Tlatelolco: "We turned to see the great plaza and the multitude assembled there, some buying and some selling. . . . And there were among us soldiers who had been in many parts of the world, in Constantinople, Italy, and Rome, who said nowhere had they seen such a well-organized and large plaza, and one so full of people as this one is."[66] Equally impressed, Francisco de Aguilar noted that Moctezuma behaved at every moment "with much authority" and was served "like a great prince and lord."[67]

The enthusiasm that the Anonymous Conqueror displays in his description of Tlatelolco's main square shows that the Spaniards found marketplaces appealing because they resonated with their own world. Further, they could be seen as microcosms revealing the complexity of the indigenous society at large. Like courtly routine, markets revealed the prevailing degree of specialized production and concomitant social stratification. They therefore stood as reminders of things left behind in the Iberian Peninsula:

> There are very large and beautiful plazas in the city of Temistitan México, where everything this people use is sold; especially the great plaza they call Tutelula [Tlatelolco], which may be three times the size of the great square of Salamanca, and is all surrounded by porticoes; from twenty to twenty-five thousand people gather every day in this place to buy and sell; and on market days . . . forty to fifty thousand people. They are well organized, both in that each type of merchandise is separate in its own section, and in their transactions. On one side of the plaza they sell gold; and in a nearby area . . . various classes of precious stones mounted in gold in the shape of different birds and animals. In another section they sell beads and mirrors; elsewhere feathers and tufted crests of birds of every color to adorn the clothes they wear at war and in festivities. Farther away they are busy turning stones into knives and swords. . . . Here the grain they eat is sold, there several kinds of bread; in one spot they sell cakes, in another, hens, chickens and eggs, and nearby, hares, rabbits, deer, quail, geese, and ducks. . . . Then, in a different area they sell wine of various classes, and in yet another all kinds of vegetables.[68]

Regarding the city's population size, the Anonymous Conqueror stated that most soldiers "calculate it has more than sixty thousand inhabitants, rather more than less."[69] Because other chroniclers mention some sixty thousand houses, not individuals, it seems that the Italian editor of the now lost anonymous report mistranslated *vecinos* as *personas*, which is incorrect because in the Spanish usage of the period, *vecinos* generally meant householders.[70] Twentieth century academics have engaged in lengthy demographic debates. Total figures that have been suggested vary widely, but according to Rojas's 1986 pondering of all past estimates, total numbers for the time of Cortés's arrival in 1519 are most likely to fall in the range of two to three hundred thousand inhabitants.[71] In any case it is clear that Tenochtitlan was the largest city in the Americas, and it was also unusually large by European standards.[72]

Whatever the precise figures may be, the amount of labor and resources visibly invested in the city, and the large quantity and variety of goods its inhabitants consumed exceeded the productive capacities of the valley. That such a concentration of wealth and people required some sort of imperial control was as clear to the Spaniards as it is to modern scholars, even if the former did not entirely understand the particular structures that articulated the relations of economic dependence between Tenochtitlan and its sustaining hinterland.

These articulations have been thoroughly studied by Ross Hassig (1985). The so-called Aztec empire was a military tribute state constituted by numerous heterogeneous, self-contained polities. These polities were subject to the domination of a confederation of three city-states in the Valley of Mexico: Tlacopan, Tetzcoco, and Mexico-Tenochtitlan, linked in a triple alliance under the leadership of the latter. Unlike that of the late Roman empire, the Aztec system of domination entailed no physical occupation of conquered territories or the replacement of local officials. It was a hegemonic empire that attained political dominance via clientelism, the imposition of tribute, and military threat.[73] In November 1521, Alonso Zuazo, a colonial judge appointed to oversee Cortés's government, described the Aztec political structure as follows: "Among the lords of these cities, villages and places there are some more important than others who pay tribute to each other . . . and enter each other's councils and assemblies, and hold consultation meetings, mainly regarding war."[74]

In the ninety years before Spanish contact, the Aztec state had secured its growth and material well-being through war and forced alliances but did not destroy the political autonomy and local customs of defeated opponents. Instead, it subjected them to the payment of annual tribute, usually consisting of products of the land. The supplying of auxiliary troops and the obligation to provide "peripheral security against low-intensity threats" were sometimes substituted for payments.[75] The system, therefore, was organized to secure regular access to the same varied resources the Spanish conquerors saw in the marketplace, rather than as a means of strict political control. Tribute to Tenochtitlan, itemized in the *Codex Mendoza,* included farming, hunting, and mineral products including raw materials such as maize, beans, chili, cacao, amaranth, honey, *maguey* syrup, wooden planks and beams, cotton, rubber, amber, lime, salt, gold, turquoise, animal skins, and feathers. The tribute also included various manufactured items, among others, featherwork dresses, tunics, standards, shields, and headdresses; cotton cloaks and clothing; gold, jadeite, and turquoise shields, diadems, and necklaces; pottery and gourd bowls; and *maguey* and *amatl* paper.[76]

Hernán Cortés was well aware of this tributary network almost from the time he disembarked, and he took advantage of it when he occupied the position of ruling lord. More than the brilliant mind of the "hero," his attitude (repeated by subsequent administrators) illustrates the Spanish conviction that native Central Mexican arrangements were efficient and therefore worth reusing.

As seen above, physical resemblance to the Iberian Peninsula was, from the start, determinant in the Spanish conceptualizing of mainland North America, but the significant similarity expressed in the toponym "Nueva España" did not pertain to the realm of nature. Despite remarks concerning landscape, climate, plants, and animals contained in the Carta del Cabildo, Cortés's second report letter, and other early accounts, more consequential was the recognition concerning urban life and politics. In Yucatan, coastal Veracruz, Tlaxcala, and Mexico the Spaniards found societies they considered analogous to their own. Unlike any they had seen before in the New World, these societies evidenced a high degree of labor specialization and a ruling class totally detached from productive activities. Nowhere before had the Spaniards come across an administrative apparatus that linked such a number of distant lands and villages. Not a single path in their previous Caribbean experience had led them to proper urban centers where people dressed in handsome garments lived in houses as permanent as brick and stone can guarantee. This is attested to by the concluding paragraphs of Juan Díaz's "Itinerario de la armada," referring to the land of Ulúa, that is, the coastal area where Cortés later founded the first municipality in New Spain: "people are found who go about dressed in cotton, display great civility and live in stone houses, and they have their laws and ordinances, and public places reserved for the administration of justice."[77]

Repetition: Cíbola as a New Mexico

Unlike Columbus twenty-seven years before him, Cortés and his men had a fairly clear idea of what they would see when they first headed inland from Veracruz toward the Valley of Mexico. This is hardly surprising. They had two enormous advantages over Columbus: the means to establish efficient communication with the aboriginal population, and the precedent of earlier experiences that had secured significant knowledge about the land.

Columbus's attempt to reach Asia by heading west across the Atlantic Ocean rested upon geographical knowledge derived from the opposite route of the one he chose. Luis de Torres, his only interpreter, spoke Hebrew, Amharic, and Arabic,[78] languages that were no help before Amerindian interlocutors. No wonder both in his diary and the annotations he wrote in the books he brought along (Pierre d'Ailly's *Imago Mundi*, an Italian version of Pliny the Elder's *Historia Naturalis*, a copy of Aeneas Sylvius's *Historia Rerum Ubique Gestarum*, and a Latin version of *The Travels of Marco Polo*), the Admiral consistently related his findings to kingdoms known from antiquity; the Bible; or Marco Polo's voyages, such as Tarshish, Ophir, Sheba, Cathay, Mangi, and Cipangu.[79]

Cortés, in contrast, followed the lead of previous explorers in Yucatan and the coast of the Gulf of Mexico, both accidentally discovered in 1517 by a small party under the command of Francisco Hernández de Córdoba that was driven astray by rogue currents during an Indian slave-raiding expedition in the vicinity of Cuba.[80] Despite having been violently expelled by the natives, the small taste of the land these adventurers had was enough to engage the governor of Cuba in the preparation of a second journey (1518), entrusted to Juan de Grijalva, and a third, entrusted to Cortés.[81] As for the language, Cortés could rely at an early stage on the services of four translators: two Maya Indians captured by Hernández de Córdoba, a Spanish survivor of a 1511 shipwreck—Jerónimo de Aguilar—rescued in Cozumel, and a bilingual (Mayan/Náhuatl) woman—Malintzin—whom he received in Tabasco as part of a peace settlement.[82] Thus, if exploration in Columbus's day was based on the systematic translocation of concepts that forced empirical data to fit into a preconceived scheme of the world, as several authors insist,[83] direct observation and personal dialogue with indigenous individuals were far more important in conceptualizing "otherness" twenty-seven years later, once the identity of the newfound lands was established as a theretofore unknown continent.

As Cortés and his men traversed the lands of soon-to-be New Spain for the first, second, or third time—many had participated in Grijalva's expedition, and some, like Bernal Díaz, even Hernández de Córdoba's expeditions[84]—they came across peoples involved in different types of relations with the Aztecs, from total independence and perpetual confrontation to partial or complete subjection. In fact, Cortés already possessed valuable firsthand information on regional conflicts and allegiances when he came in touch with Moctezuma's ambassadors in Veracruz in April 1519. He knew that numerous peoples were subjects and paid tribute to Moctezuma, whose domination many resented. He also knew that an extraordinary commercial network allowed Aztec merchants to reach faraway places to the south. He knew, in short, that he was heading for a densely populated and highly urban settlement, the heart of a complex society with centralized administrative structures. But even if the conquerors could anticipate some of the things to be found in the Aztec capital, its actual appearance surpassed any expectation they might possibly have held, and this reemergence of the unprecedented resulted in a complete epistemological rearrangement. From then on, Mexico and the Caribbean frequently substituted for Spain, Europe, or the Far Eastern empires as the touchstone with which to compare new geographic and ethnic realities.

Names are not always fortuitous. Forty years after the Spaniards bracketed Mexico-Tenochtitlan and the territory subject to Aztec hegemony under the name "Nueva España," a series of expeditions were mounted in what may be called the quest for Nuevo México, an ill-defined entity which as yet existed only in the imagination but by the 1590s had materialized in the form of an actual province.

The expansion of territory effectively under Spanish control in mainland North America was conditioned by the presence of different types of indigenous sociocultural complexes in the sixteenth century. Most propitious for Spanish interests was the agricultural and mercantile economy that prevailed in northern Central America and southern central Mexico, where urbanization had developed hand in hand with intensive agriculture, a hierarchical social organization, and aggressive forms of hegemonic domination. This type of indigenous system accounted for a relatively small geographic area but had great demographic significance. The other sociocultural complexes were combinations of hunting-gathering, part-time farming, and fishing economies practiced by the more loosely organized and sparser population of the steppes and deserts of present-day northern Mexico. The Spaniards mistakenly called many of these northern groups "Chichimecas" and came to regard them as crude "savages," whom they likened to the Caribs and Arawaks of the Antilles.[85] Once the conquerors entered the northern territories, the rhythm of penetration slowed down and became almost stagnant by the 1550s in spite of the extensive reach of the northwestward explorations conducted between 1529 and 1542.

Most of the geographic imagery that led to the notion of Nuevo México as a land of wonder was amassed precisely during these thirteen years of hectic exploration. Rumors and eyewitness reports spoke of seven marvelous cities to the far north, with multilevel stone houses and cotton-garbed people rich in gold and turquoise. Probably referring to the settlements of the so-called Pueblo Indians of present-day Arizona and New Mexico, the reports were first heard by Nuño de Guzmán around 1529. But the most influential story of wealthy and distant countries to the north reached Mexico City only in 1536 with Alvar Núñez Cabeza de Vaca and other survivors of a shipwrecked expedition to Florida.[86] A Franciscan friar, Marcos de Niza, commissioned in 1539 to verify these rumors, reported the existence of a province with seven cities, one of which—Cíbola—he claimed was larger than Mexico City and the gateway to other provinces of no less grandeur farther ahead.[87] On this basis, Viceroy Antonio de Mendoza launched an elaborate conquest expedition (1540–42) that he entrusted to Francisco Vázquez de Coronado, but since it failed completely, official, systematic efforts to penetrate the far north were abandoned until around 1560. From then on, several prospectors, stimulated among other things by the expansion of the mining frontier triggered by spectacular discoveries of silver in the 1540s, formulated the explicit purpose of discovering the original Aztec homeland, also called Nuevo México and ultimately identified with Cíbola in 1581.

An overall pattern of projection and duplication harkening back to Cortés's early experience in Mesoamerica stands out in this chain of events. The toponym "Nueva España," it will be remembered, was devised sometime between June 1519 and August 1520. About four decades later a Franciscan friar named Jacinto de San Francisco set out from Mexico City in search of Nuevo México, an enterprise that other Spaniards soon replicated. It was as if a semantic void befell Mexico when it was baptized "New Spain," prompting the longing for a "New

Mexico." Moreover, nurtured by native historical records and testimonies that promised reiteration, this nostalgic desire eventually blurred the motherland's image.

The landmarks of the two conquest periods under discussion follow a repetitive pattern:

> (1) the Spaniards settle in the Caribbean;
> (2) Indian voices spread vague rumors about more sophisticated societies to the west (that is, mainland Mesoamerica);
> (3) verbal rumors are confirmed empirically by expeditions to the Yucatan Peninsula and the coastline of the Gulf of Mexico, where the conquerors gather information regarding more fabulous provinces to the west;
> (4) the Spaniards establish a small settlement in Veracruz and head on to Central Mexico;
> (5) as had happened with rumors gathered in the Caribbean about mainland Mesoamerica, information provided by native informants is verified when Cortés and his men arrive in the Valley of Mexico; and
> (6) once settled in Tenochtitlan, the Spaniards hear abundant news of magnificent cities and kingdoms to the north.

The latest rumors, again spread via Indian voices, convinced individual adventurers, state officials, and missionaries to attempt new journeys to verify the stories. Needless to say, they expected the province to the north to be substantially similar to, almost a replica of, Mexico / Nueva España, but perhaps one that would even surpass their expectations, as had occurred when they first came to Tenochtitlan.

Repetition also surfaces in the ethnic categories the Spaniards used. A number of late sixteenth-century documents literally describe Chichimecas as being "Caribs."[88] A grammatical perspective is once again illuminating: north of New Spain, the ethnonym "Caribe" became an adjective conveying a sense of uncontrolled aggressive instincts, disorderly customs, and duplicity. The taxonomic connection thereby drawn between Caribbean peoples and natives living north of New Spain points to the use of analogy as a fundamental epistemological tool.

It is difficult to know whether Spaniards realized that Caribs and Chichimecas were culturally very different. It is clear, however, that in calling the Chichimecas "Caribes," conquerors not only drew an analogy concerning the people they were comparing (Carib is to European as Chichimeca is to Mexica); the operation also referred to their own experience. Many Spaniards (or their kin) who led expeditions heading north from Mexico City had also performed as conquerors in the Caribbean and no doubt perceived similarities in the two circumstances. In both instances, conquerors confronted societies they considered uncivilized compared with the world they had left behind—Spain and Mexico-Tenochtitlan respectively. On both occasions these barbarians had emphasized the existence of much more sophisticated societies farther ahead. Such mounting repetitions convinced the Spaniards that, if rumors gathered from the islanders found confirmation in Mexico-Tenochtitlan, they could expect the same of similar Indian reports collected in New Spain among peoples who had a sophisticated culture.

Ironically, once it became a subject of the Spanish Crown in 1598, Nuevo México turned out to be a difficult place to live. Sparsely populated by self-sufficient, autonomous communities who stubbornly resisted submission, and lacking in gold and silver, it did not produce much wealth that idle intruders could appropriate. Although the settlers' disenchantment was temporarily overcome by the prospect of further military conquests, growing difficulties with the natives and grievances between the colonists and their captain convinced them that a place where individual prosperity demanded the investment of hard personal labor was not worth staying. Therefore, by 1602 they began to abandon the land, taking along their few belongings as they returned south.

The gap between fact and fantasy in the New Mexican adventure raises serious questions about the cornerstones on which the dreams of the Spaniards rested. Expectations based on their experience of astonishment in the Valley of Mexico do not provide a complete answer. To develop into feasible-sounding projects, mere aspirations needed to be supported by reputable evidence to counterbalance the risks implicit in the pursuit of a dream. Aztlan-Chicomoztoc, the "mythic" place of ancestral origin of the Mexica and other Náhuatl-speaking peoples, worked as the principal catalyst in the formulation of imagined geographies explored in this book, because conquerors perceived as history what is now considered "myth." This was only possible because the Spaniards fully recognized in Central Mexican societies a civilization similar to their own and were consequently convinced that the historical and geographic knowledge the natives produced, even if distorted by the hand of the devil, was one they could generally trust.

CHAPTER TWO

Mexican, Chichimeca, and Pueblo Indians

The southwestern portion of North America where the sixteenth century "quest for Nuevo Mexico" unfolded is characterized by an overwhelming human and natural diversity. From a geographic perspective it is dominated by an almost unbroken cordilleran system running from Alaska south to Central America and branching into five massive mountain ranges. Biotic and climatic microzones within the region are largely dependent on variations in altitude. The terrain forms a series of more or less parallel ridges with elevations ranging from near sea level to approximately 5,700 meters above sea level, alternating with valley basins and fairly flat highland mesas.[1]

The northernmost range in this continental system, the Rocky Mountains, has always been sparsely populated because it has little arable land and a short growing season. Its heavy winter snow contributes much of the water for the Colorado, Rio Grande, and Pecos rivers. Toward the west the forested ranges of the Rockies descend into the high desert of the Colorado Plateau, with its numerous deep canyons and steep-walled mesas of volcanic origin. Except for the Colorado River, flowing through the Grand Canyon, this area has few permanent streams. Toward the east are the vast High Plains, covered with grass and scrub, that include the drainage of the Pecos River in central New Mexico. As elevation decreases north and southwest of the Colorado Plateau, short, isolated mountain chains scattered throughout basin areas that once contained shallow lakes mark what physiographers call the Basin and Range Province. The province is divided between a higher, cooler section in Utah and Nevada—the Great Basin—and a lower, hotter, desert stretching from southern Arizona and New Mexico across the Mexican border to flank both sides of the Sierra Madre Occidental. The Rio Grande flows from the Rocky Mountains into the Gulf of Mexico, demarcating the border between Texas and Mexico. On the western rim of the Sierra Madre Occidental large rivers (Sinaloa, Fuerte, Yaqui, and Sonora) flow across the desert, creating narrow and fertile valleys. East of these mountains the environment is harsher, combining extremely hot days, cold nights, and very low rainfall.

Farther south rises the Mexican Central Plateau, flanked on the east and west by the Sierra Madre Oriental and Sierra Madre Occidental. Its low, hilly areas and wide basins of volcanic origin contain shallow lakes such as Chapala, Pátzcuaro, Yuriria, and Cuitzeo, as well as the dry beds of extinct lakes such as those of Mexico, Puebla, Toluca, and Guadalajara. Thanks to its plentiful arable land and fertile soils, the Mexican Central Plateau is, and perhaps always was, the most densely populated region in North America. Its southern rim is formed by the Cordillera Neovolcánica, dominated by a row of volcanoes ranging from 3,800 to 5,747 meters above sea level that include Popocatépetl and Iztaccíhuatl. Much of the central plateau lies in a temperate zone, but the climate is cold in its higher elevations. Rivers are few, although the plateau is drained by three major systems: the Pánuco-Moctezuma, running from the northeastern edge into the Gulf of Mexico; the Lerma-Santiago; and the Balsas, both flowing west into the Pacific. Along the Pacific coast and the Gulf of Mexico lie narrow lowland strips of hot climate where moisture, soil fertility, and vegetation vary widely. Other mountain chains continue south, forming the highlands of Oaxaca and Guerrero, and separated by the Isthmus of Tehuantepec, the Chiapas-Guatemala highlands that descend into the Yucatan Peninsula.

Aside from its topography, this enormous territory is also diverse in ethnology. The model most often used to explain the correlation between its environmental and cultural diversity was developed by classifying characteristic socioeconomic features and noting their geographic distribution. This method allowed researchers to draw analytic boundaries that divide the land into different "culture areas." Mexican anthropologists typically adopt the scheme that Paul Kirchhoff proposed, which defines three culture areas in this region: Mesoamerica, Aridamerica, and Oasisamerica,[2] though scholars in the United States regularly enfold the latter two into a larger area they call the American Southwest or Greater Southwest. Both schools attribute primary importance to settlement patterns (temporary camps, permanent or semi-permanent villages, or cities), forms of food procurement and production (hunting, farming, fishing, or gathering), and sociopolitical orders (clans, tribes, simple or complex chiefdoms, or states).[3]

Though one must be aware of the risks of oversimplification via geographic and economic determinism, the interaction between European conquerors-settlers, Amerindian conquered-conquerors, and local native communities subdued by Europeans and their Indian allies as the conquest progressed in early colonial North America indeed varied according to regional specificities in culture and economy as well as to environmental constraints. Recent research has certainly shown that the classic distinction between two basic forms of livelihood—nomadic and sedentary—does not capture the complexity that existed at the time of European arrival, nor does it entirely explain the response of Spaniards and Indians to their mutual confrontation.[4] As Susan Deeds remarks, the idea that the arid regions north of New Spain right before the time of contact had a relatively small population of loosely organized, dispersed communities may be a misconstrual derived from worsened conditions observed later in the sixteenth century. Spanish statements noting the prevalence of the *ranchería* pattern in Chihuahua, Durango, and Sinaloa in the seventeenth century upon which the standard view of this northern prototype was built, she explains, probably reflect "varying stages of disorienting sociopolitical transformations" underway in those areas, caused by the precipitous demographic decline that the earlier European introduction of new diseases in Central Mexico had provoked.[5]

Nevertheless, when Cortés arrived, the area known as Mesoamerica was packed with centralized, urban societies with farming economies and varying degrees of institutionalized sociopolitical organization, in sharp contrast with most northerly communities. In the sixteenth century, at least, people living beyond the northern reach of Aztec and Tarascan control had less-permanent settlements and subsisted on some combination of hunting, fishing, gathering, and small-scale agriculture. In some ecologically suitable areas, however, they regularly cultivated the land and built more-permanent villages. Such different modes of subsistence, and their associated political structures, entailed varying degrees of resistance and collaboration on the part of the Indians, forcing Spaniards to develop multiple domination strategies and enticing them variably into cultural borrowing. The concept of Mesoamerica, Aridamerica, and Oasisamerica may only reflect the particular moment immediately after Spanish contact and rests, no doubt, on gross generalizations. Still, it illuminates Spanish-Amerindian negotiations and alignments, better understood in the framework of a long period of preconquest autochthonous development. This chapter addresses that development through an assessment of key academic debates regarding how to define the relevant culture areas.

The "Meso-Arid-Oasisamerica" classification of native Amerindian cultures rests on the "colonial knowledge" produced by European invaders. Despite its extensive incorporation of archaeological evidence, this classification is mainly based on the features that sixteenth century observers chose to emphasize. But the value-laden taxonomy resulting from the academic reproduction of "colonial knowledge," biased as it is, permits an adequate appreciation of how Spanish conquerors conceived of the people living in the territory they intended to occupy.

"Colonial knowledge" is seldom entirely detached from "local knowledge." The 1860s bureaucratic classifications of people, leading to fixed notions of caste in the British Raj and of tribe in Africa, were colonial constructs that defined the members of colonized societies according to static categories to facilitate the control of otherwise fluid and confusing social and political relationships. Yet, rather than a whole-cloth invention of astute European bureaucrats, both were reelaborations of preexisting local categories collected from elders or local law officers (*pandits*).[6] Something similar had occurred in New Spain three centuries earlier: the distinction that Náhuatl-speaking sedentary farmers from Central Mexico drew between themselves and the peoples they called Chichimecas, though grossly misunderstood by Spaniards, became the template that the colonial administration used to classify the aboriginal population. The term Chichimeca, originally alluding to both hunter-gatherer lifestyles and peoples of northern provenance, already carried a great deal of ambiguity in the preconquest era.[7] This semantic fluidity was lost in its colonial definition, which, like so many other instances of colonial labeling, set up those to whom it was applied for physical abuse and spoliation.[8] But my goal here is not to provide yet another example of how, under colonialism, social taxonomies function to allow for different intensities and specific forms of violence. Rather, my purpose is to stress how "ethnological" categories are successively transferred from preconquest folk taxonomies to colonial representations to modern culture-area classifications. The phenomenon counters easy depictions of colonizing-dominant-ruling groups as internally coherent and impervious to tensions and influences emanating from the encounter with the colonized other.

Since the 1980s, extensive appraisals in anthropology, history, and literary studies have increasingly concerned themselves with the intricacies of colonial relations. They have begun to reformulate the extent and manner in which particular colonizing projects are inflected by the indigenous societies they rule over; and the degree of accord and efficacy attributable to colonizers' agency.[9] Many scholars would now endorse the affirmation that European states were not "self-contained entities that at one point projected themselves overseas," while their colonies "were never empty spaces to be made over in Europe's image or fashioned in its interests."[10] Yet, many of these scholars continue to focus on how particular colonial regimes and the success or failure of their projected aims are conditioned by native reactions to European dominance. These scholars also dwell on the existence of competing agendas and strategies of control among the colonizers, or the unforeseen, disruptive alignments resulting from policies originally devised to maintain the hierarchies of rule.[11] So far, little attention has been paid to the naturalizing transformation of colonizers through cross-cultural interchange with natives at the level of everyday, personal experience; that is, beyond (or better said, beneath) the grand level of metropolitan politics and colonial project enforcement.

This chapter sketches out an ethnohistorical overview of the local conditions that led Spanish conquerors to become culturally naturalized in the process of constructing Nuevo México—alongside their Indian allies—as the place of ancestral Aztec origin. Therefore, instead of providing an itemized inventory of the human groups living in sixteenth-century New Spain, this chapter outlines regional sociocultural contrasts that were decisive for the transcultural design of northbound colonizing expeditions.

The quest for Nuevo México began in the heartland of Mesoamerica around 1540 and ended more than half a century later in the core of the area that Paul Kirchhoff called Oasisamerica, roughly comprising New Mexico, eastern Arizona, and portions of Chihuahua and Sonora.[12] Expeditions across this vast terrain followed pre-Columbian routes of migration, commerce, and ritual exchange that resulted from centuries-long population movements, which explains to some degree the ethnic pattern of Mesoamerican involvement in the northward colonizing enterprise. The expeditions came across the ruins of ancient settlements, which the Spaniards interpreted as sound evidence that Pueblo Indian villages along the Rio Grande were in fact Aztlan. These ruins likewise figure among the evidence used to model culture areas in twentieth century anthropology. Deliberately artificial, culture-area classifications do not necessarily reflect Native American identity definitions. However, the boundaries Kirchhoff drew over the territory herein concerned do reflect the geographic scope of certain "ethnologic" categories, such as "Chichimeca" and "Pueblo," that preconquest indigenous or Spanish colonial folk taxonomies had already applied. A brief review of the principles that articulate culture-area debates will illuminate why this is so.

The concept of "culture area," defined as a distinct geographic region wherein a number of individual societies share a set of common traits, was coined in 1917 by anthropologist Clark Wissler. The culture-area principle was an alternative to earlier categories for the study of Native American societies and was grounded in a systematic comparison of the copious amounts of new ethnographic and archaeological evidence available to researchers in the early twentieth century.[13] Late nineteenth-century models such as Edward Tylor's popular comparative method, which had promoted the notion of a unitary human civilization supposedly developing along a uniform pattern across the globe according to universal laws of cultural evolution, was supported by a weak empirical foundation and lacked historical and geographic specificity. Wissler intended to create a methodology that allowed for sufficient generalization without lapsing into the extremely loose abstractions typical of these unitary theories. He also wished to overcome the unquestioned adoption of the boundaries that geographers had set for the classification of human groups, the tendency then all too common to explain cultural difference in terms of race and biology, and the classification of people according to language differences and interconnections.[14]

If North American peoples seemed overwhelmingly diverse on the basis of number of languages alone,[15] Kirchhoff reasoned, certain cultural patterns and modes of social and political organization cut across language boundaries. These patterns and modes justified grouping societies into large analytic units, albeit spatially grounded in concrete geography. Kirchhoff clearly expresses this theoretical stance in his assertion that individual societies occupying contiguous geographic settings usually share "so many cultural traits and are organized along such similar lines that they appear as variants of one regional culture or culture area."[16] Some anthropologists, including Daniel G. Brinton, had preceded Wissler in discarding racial and biological criteria—cranial shape, height, or skin color—as relevant categories for the assessment of cultural diversity. Still, the continental super-areas that Brinton's (1891) ethnography-based classification established for the Americas, though subdivided according to language distribution and modes of livelihood, corresponded to basic directional indications and geomorphology: North Atlantic, North Pacific, Central America, South Pacific, and South Atlantic.[17] Though never completed, the gradual replacement of continental boundaries and topography with economic, institutional, and cosmological criteria owes a lot to Wissler's ideas, significantly refined after Alfred Kroeber (1939) underlined the need to emphasize the historicity of culture-area configurations.[18]

Although no general agreement exists concerning the number and limits of the culture areas into which America should be divided, and while culture-area classification has been almost abandoned as a primary goal and methodology,[19] some of its legacies, such as the definition of Mesoamerica, still frame ethnohistorical and archaeological debates.

Mesoamerica and Its Movable Frontier

The literal meaning of the term Mesoamerica, proposed by Kirchhoff in 1943, refers to the geographic position of a vast area roughly comprising the southern half of present-day Mexico, the complete territory of Guatemala, Belize, and El Salvador, and some portions of Honduras, Nicaragua, and Costa Rica (map 2). Rather than a fixed piece of land, the Mesoamerica concept originally denoted a cultural-territorial complex occupying a variable geographic span. It defined a particular kind of civilization expressed in the aggregate of objects, beliefs, and practices that a number of farming peoples, organized in multiple sociopolitical units of variable extension and duration, used and entertained between the second millennium b.c. and the sixteenth century a.d.[20] Later, some authors also applied the term to postcolonial and modern communities of indigenous and mestizo composition that manifested obvious continuities with the traditions established in that early phase of history.[21]

Agriculture is the first element quoted in every definition of Mesoamerica, with maize, beans, and squash as the basic food crops, adapted through domestication to flourish in nearly every type of soil and weather.[22] Around ninety additional plant species, some of which only grew under certain environmental conditions, were also cultivated locally, fostering cross-regional complementarity as they were exchanged as important trade and tribute articles. Farming techniques included the systematic fallowing of permanent fields, terracing, and irrigation, although migratory slash-and-burn cultivation was the most extended tillage system, and farm implements were rudimentary. Other means of livelihood identified as Mesoamerican features are the widespread breeding of dogs and turkeys, and, depending on local conditions, supplementary fishing, hunting small prey, and gathering insects and their larvae.

While most of these elements were present elsewhere in the Americas, the combination of certain attributes, such as organized trade and markets, centralized political structures, organized religion with an elaborate priesthood, and a mixed pictographic and phonetic writing system, is to all appearances uniquely Mesoamerican. Other features found elsewhere on the Americas, such as matrilineal clans and poisoned weapons, were completely absent in Mesoamerica. In South America, of course, the Andes were the other major center of plant domestication in the New World; and just before the Europeans arrived, Andean societies also had a well-developed agriculture capable of supporting large populations, as well as compact urban settlements and a sophisticated social fabric. However, formal market exchange and written screenfold books did not exist in that region before the establishment of the colonial regime.[23]

In sum, the principal attributes that Kirchhoff listed as characteristically Mesoamerican are full-time farming societies; large ceremonial centers with truncated-pyramidal temple-bases, ball courts, and palaces built of stone, lime, and mortar; restricted metallurgy primarily used for the production of luxury articles; combined pictographic and hieroglyphic writing systems that had some phonetic elements but never turned into full alphabetic script; a calendar based on the juxtaposition of two major cycles, one composed of a combination of thirteen numbers and twenty day-names intermeshing to create a 260-day sequence, and another of 365 days; and a distinctive social organization based on self-contained kinship-territorial units, often patrilineal in descent, whose members shared a residential quarter, an economic activity, and a tutelary god.[24] This last, a microcommunity only comparable to the *ayllu* of Andean societies, was called *calpulli* (plural *calpoltin*) in Náhuatl, *siqui* in Mixteco, and *amak* in Maya Quiché.[25]

This definition of Mesoamerica, abstracted from colonial reports on conditions existing at the time of Spanish arrival, was significantly enriched as archaeology yielded more precise and abundant data. A simultaneous shift in focus from the search for common traits to the analysis of local peculiarities resulted in the adoption of different theoretical models to explain how regional specificities interlocked. Eduardo Matos, for example, applied Marxist theory to address the long-standing presence in the area of complex, stratified societies with reduced ruling classes.[26] He proposed that this mode of production, which involved dual exploitation—one class over another within a society, and the ruling class of one society over other societies—appeared on the coast of the Gulf of Mexico with the consolidation of the Olmec civilization (circa 1200–400 b.c.) and expanded gradually until reaching the boundaries Kirchhoff marked off for Mesoamerica in the sixteenth century. Based on Immanuel Wallerstein's (1974) "world system theory," other authors claimed that Mesoamerica, like Renaissance Europe, could be defined as a diverse but integrated, stratified world because the links of domination and dependence between its multiple societies did not involve a common political governing structure.[27]

Scholars of late have discarded the idea that Mesoamerica was a unit because the societies therein shared a list of common traits. They prefer to stress that *difference* is what interconnects individual societies through peaceful exchange and collaboration, or through violent confrontation or forced dependence. Today Mesoamerica is understood as the territorial embodiment of a complex network of intergroup relations developed via a common historical process, which has been shaped by ecological, cultural, and political factors.[28] Its extension varied from time to time according to the changing scope and nature of those relations, but it had a fundamental core that remained fairly stable in size.

By the time of Spanish contact, regional dynamics had given way to the formation of various sub-areas within Mesoamerica, each characterized by a predominant language and a distinctive cultural pattern promoted by regionally hegemonic groups. These groups were articulated in complex networks of transregional relations through ceremonial gift-giving, mediated trade, outright conquest, and the imposition of tributary demands.[29] Two sub-areas are particularly relevant here: Central Mexico and Western Mexico. Central Mexico comprised the modern states of Hidalgo, México, Tlaxcala, Morelos, Puebla, and the Federal District. It was culturally rather homogeneous, with the Oto-Manguean linguistic family fairly well represented by Otomí, Mazahua, and Matlatzinca, although it was numerically dominated by peoples who spoke Náhuatl, the most extended of the Uto-Aztecan family, which includes languages from the southwestern United States and northwestern Mexico.

In contrast, the Western Mexico sub-area, comprising present-day Sinaloa, Nayarit, Jalisco, Colima, Michoacán, and Guerrero, was culturally and perhaps linguistically the most heterogeneous Mesoamerican region,[30] with numerous unclassified languages, today extinct, spoken alongside others of the Uto-Aztecan family, plus Tarascan, apparently unrelated to any other tongue.[31]

Nowadays it is clear that the equation "Mesoamerica / sedentism / agriculture versus Aridamerica / nomadism / hunting-gathering" ingrained in Kirchhoff's model is a gross simplification, because agricultural knowledge and practice do not invariably correlate with sedentism. Archaeologists have documented examples of non-farming but sedentary communities in what is now Mexican territory, as well as instances of hunter-gatherer groups sufficiently acquainted with plant germination as to cultivate certain species during seasonal periods of rest. Permanent settlements belonging to mollusk gatherers have been found in coastal areas, and in the lake basin of Mexico an incipient development of sedentism before agriculture was practiced with any regularity has also been detected.[32] Conversely, remains of domestic squash dated at about 8000 years b.p. appeared in shelters occupied by nomadic hunter-gatherers in Oaxaca.[33] Nevertheless, the domestication and successive general adoption of maize, a plant that yields abundant storable crops but demands regular, intensive work all year round was decisive for the integration of Mesoamerica, as it led to an entirely new form of settled village life.[34] Domestic maize provided the foundation for sustained demographic growth resulting in high population densities that no pre-agricultural society could have achieved, let alone the groups of hunter-gatherers who occasionally cultivated short-term vegetables such as squash.

The purported antiquity of existing samples of the earliest cultivated maize, recovered in the 1950s and 1960s from sites in Tehuacán (San Marcos Cave) and Tamaulipas (Romero's Cave and Valencia's Cave) has been significantly reduced. Originally dated at around the years 5000 to 3500 b.c., they have now been proven not to date back beyond the year 2700 b.c.[35] The earliest evidence of maize domestication, however, consists of three cobs of domesticated *teosinte* (*Zea mays* ssp. *parviglumis*), the wild predecessor of maize, uncovered in Guilá Naquitz in present-day Oaxaca and considered to be 6,250 years old. Recent ethnobotanical research has led to the consensus among specialists that initial domestication arose from the accidental discovery of a rare mutation of teosinte by a group of hunter-gatherers with semi-permanent habitation who already used the plant, though not its grains, as a dietary supplement.[36] They estimate this occurred around 9000 years b.p. somewhere in the Central Balsas River drainage, where this wild predecessor of maize grows abundantly. This time frame has been calculated by considering genetic changes, as well as the subsequent spread of the domesticated variety into Oaxaca, and of the fully developed maize into Tehuacán and Tamaulipas, where no trace of wild teosinte has been detected.[37]

No matter how domestication occurred, the earliest evidence showing a clear association between maize cultivation and sedentism corresponds to the remains of permanent preceramic settlements found in the lowlands adjacent to both the Pacific and Atlantic coastlines, dated at about 3000 to 2500 b.c.[38] One can only begin speaking of Mesoamerica from around half a century later, when a firmly established farming tradition could sustain permanent forms of exchange, alliance, and domination among permanent settlement dwellers, from the Mexican Central Plateau to Central America.

For the purposes of my argument concerning long-term historical memories of migration and ancient trails as two factors explaining the overall direction of early Spanish conquest enterprises north from the Valley of Mexico, and the involvement of Mesoamerican Indians in these enterprises, the next relevant historical landmark is the emergence of state societies at the beginning of the Classic Horizon (a.d. 200–900/1000). This milestone is visible archaeologically in the growth of villages into large urban centers with public architecture of unprecedented dimensions, significantly expanded irrigation systems, and the concentration of items of regionally circumscribed production (tools, ceramics, and textiles) indicative of well-organized, wide commercial and perhaps tributary networks. Two civilizations dominated the Classic world: Teotihuacan in the Valley of Mexico, and the Mayas in Guatemala, Yucatan, and Chiapas. The specific nature of their political systems is obscure, given the paucity of written sources, but according to López Austin, in the early Classic Horizon leadership was probably based on ethnic or lineage affiliation, and political organization did not involve the imposition of state controls such as tribute or centrally designated rulers as a means of territorial integration. However, it is clear that the dynamic of trade, war, and migration that characterized the last period of the Classic Horizon, known as the Epiclassic for Central Mexico (a.d. 650/800–900/1000), eventually gave way to political fragmentation.[39]

After the largest Classic polities collapsed due to causes still unclear, numerous small communities took over and created forms of local and pan-regional organization that, in López Austin's opinion, were characterized by the gradual replacement of lineage-based authority with state mechanisms of political legitimacy, domination, and territorial control.[40]

A broadened network of sustained interactions among smaller polities is the hallmark of the Post-Classic Horizon (a.d. 900/1000–1519), a period that is fairly well known in contrast to former periods of Mesoamerican history. Indigenous historical traditions contained in sixteenth century chronicles and pictorial documents of Indian and Spanish authorship, combined with archaeological evidence, draw a picture of great instability and extreme population mobility. Complex multi-ethnic aggregation and disaggregation within fairly centralized political units ranging from chiefdoms to city-states were accompanied by the constant alternation of city-state confederations as regional powers. Thus in Central Mexico the Post-Classic began with the rapid growth of Tula to a position of hegemony; Tula was a city-state north of the Valley of Mexico, composed of a mixed population that included local groups and immigrants from the north. Tula then fell and was abandoned, while new migrant groups from the north, establishing themselves in the valleys of Mexico, Puebla, and Tlaxcala (circa a.d. 1250–1350), founded the city-states that would dominate the final phase of pre-Hispanic history in the area. Náhuatl-speaking peoples, who claimed to be Tula's cultural and ethnic heirs,[41] dominated a large part of Mesoamerica starting in the late fourteenth century. In the west, the Tarascan state, one among several minor polities that grew to control small irrigation systems, developed a fairly wide hegemonic sphere that was beginning to collide with the so-called Aztec empire when the Spaniards arrived.

Some diagnostic elements of the material culture that characterized Mesoamerican civilizations of the Classic Horizon have also been found in the archaeological remains of large settlements built in the same period in north and northwest Mexico. The discovery of these urbanized elements, usually associated with farming societies, in a region where Spaniards centuries later found only hunter-gatherers and part-time farmers, has been the subject of diverging interpretations, outlined below.

The northern frontier of Mesoamerica, traced in detail by Pedro Armillas for the early sixteenth century, roughly followed the course of the Moctezuma and Lerma rivers southwest across the Sierra Madre Oriental and the Mexican Central Plateau, and after making a turn to the northwest near Lake Chapala, it continued along the Sierra Madre Occidental to meet and thence follow the Sinaloa River down to its drainage in the Pacific Ocean.[42]

At that time and during the preceding three or four centuries, most of the land north of this line and extending into the present-day southwestern United States was primarily inhabited by specialized hunter-gatherers dwelling in small, semi-permanent settlements. Scholars refer to their foraging forms of livelihood and simple material culture, suitably adapted to the predominantly dry environments of the region, with the term Desert Culture.[43] Indeed, in most of that territory, environmental conditions and difficult irrigation made seasonal agriculture unfeasible with available technologies. Nevertheless, in a few reduced ecological niches, people did cultivate the land,[44] at least since the end of the third millennium b.c. in present-day New Mexico and Arizona, when agriculture was introduced from the south,[45] and from about a.d. 600 in the present northern Mexico.[46] Both farming and non-farming societies in the overall area exhibited a particularly low degree of centralization and knew no wide structures of domination.[47] Neither the Tarascan nor the Aztec states extended their sway over the region, presumably because it produced few prestige goods and scarce accumulative surplus.[48]

Cultural frontiers, however, are neither solid nor unchanging. Throughout most of the Classic Horizon, the northern edge of Mesoamerica, as denoted by the practice of permanent agriculture, lay about 250 kilometers *north* of the Lerma and Sinaloa rivers, draining respectively on the eastern and western coasts of Mexico. This line cut across the Mexican Central Plateau through the northeastern extreme of present-day Durango, central Zacatecas, and San Luis Potosí from the mouth of the Mayo River in Sonora to the Tamesí and Pánuco rivers in Tamaulipas.[49] Its central portion was thus some six hundred kilometers north of the demarcation line that Kirchhoff and Armillas drew for Mesoamerica for the sixteenth century (map 2).[50] As they themselves acknowledged, the line they drew merely represents the final position of a frontier that had moved southward in the process of contraction of an area occupied, between the first and eleventh centuries of the Christian era at least, by groups with Mesoamerican culture. Specialists call the area stretching between the two boundary lines "Marginal" or "Northern" Mesoamerica. Interpretations concerning the cause and dates of this oscillation in the northern limits of Mesoamerica vary, but there are some agreements:

> (1) The initial spread of agriculture-based civilization into the Desert Culture that had prevailed beyond the Lerma and Sinaloa rivers for several millennia was the result of migrant flows from the south.[51] These southern people probably originated in such diverse regions as the lowland coast of the Gulf of Mexico,[52] southern Guanajuato, the Teuchitlán-Etzatlán area of present-day Jalisco, and Zacatenco and Cuicuilco in the Valley of Mexico.[53]
> (2) The strip of land thus overlaid with farming village life reached its point of maximum expanse and efflorescence between the third and ninth centuries a.d.
> (3) Waves of southward immigration that marked the beginning of the Post-Classic Horizon in Central Mexico were part of the final retreat of full-time farmers from Marginal Mesoamerica.
> (4) Some characteristic features of New Mexico and Arizona Puebloan cultures originated in Marginal Mesoamerica at this time.[54]

Debates concerning the changing position of this frontier in its central and western portions center around the so-called "Chalchihuites culture," a chain of farming societies that developed between the first and thirteenth centuries of the Christian era along the eastern rim of the Sierra Madre Occidental from southwest Zacatecas to the Durango-Chihuahua border.[55] Archaeologists in the first half of the twentieth century considered this area a transitional zone where central Mexican and Puebloan influences combined with local developments. Others later formulated the hypothesis that Chalchihuiteño settlements, established by migrants from Mesoamerica, constituted the major channel through which farming village life and ceramics were introduced in the Pueblo area.[56] Research conducted over the past decade, however, shows that while the spread of both elements probably followed the same geographic corridor, it occurred long before the Chalchihuites culture evolved.[57] An earlier, very popular, view of Chalchihuites culture defined it as the product of either Tarascan or Toltec expansion in the early Post-Classic Horizon, but by 1960 it was clear that peasant communities and stone architecture in the area predated the consolidation of the Tarascan and Toltec states. That suggests that Tula was the *recipient* of influences from the north rather than the center from which cultural patterns radiated northward.[58]

New interdisciplinary research to clarify the situation was carried out along the north-central Mesoamerican frontier under the supervision of Charles Kelley, Pedro Armillas, Román Piña Chan, and Walter Taylor in the 1960s. Armillas gathered evidence at La Quemada, presumably one of the largest pan-regional sanctuaries in Marginal Mesoamerica, situated in the modern state of Zacatecas.[59] To make sense of his discoveries, Armillas proposed that major climatic changes, roughly coinciding with the collapse of Teotihuacan (a.d. 500–600) and later the collapse of Tula (circa a.d. 1300), caused the successive enlargement and shrinkage of Mesoamerica. From this perspective a modified version of the farming culture initially introduced to the north by immigrant Mesoamericans could easily have been imported into the Valley of Mexico many generations later. It was Armillas's view that after the collapse of Teotihuacan, entire groups of sedentary farmers poured north into an—until then—extremely arid territory that, for meteorological reasons, became transitorily suitable for agriculture (ca. a.d. 600–1200). As a result, peasant communities took root in the area of La Quemada under the military protection of local lords. Meanwhile, in the Valley of Mexico, the position of the regional center of power shifted slightly north when Tula emerged as a dominant state around a.d. 800–950. Between the twelfth and fourteenth centuries, however, a climatic reversal caused the aridity index to rise dramatically, thereby prompting a massive southern exodus of full-time farmers from Marginal Mesoamerica, possibly followed by the resumption of former hunting-gathering lifestyles among the people who did not join the southward flight.[60]

Today most specialists accept the general lines of this oscillatory frontier thesis, although chronological and other related aspects of it have been adjusted to fit new radiocarbon datings and archaeological evidence obtained north and south of La Quemada. Excavations by Román Piña Chan and Beatriz Braniff in 1962 indicated, for instance, that in the Mexican Central Plateau the initial expansion of Mesoamerican culture occurred *before* the fall of Teotihuacan, earlier than Armillas had suggested. On the other hand, Charles Kelley and Ellen Abbott demonstrated that Mesoamerican features had disappeared almost completely from Zacatecas by a.d. 950. This end date is valid even at La Quemada, for it turns out that the site's reputed flourishing period—a.d. 900–1000—was initially miscalculated by mixing evidence from various construction phases and later reoccupations.[61] The current consensus is that Mesoamerican occupation in the Chalchihuites culture area started around the beginning of the Christian era, whereas sedentary farmers had nearly deserted the central and eastern portions of Marginal Mesoamerica—Chalchihuites included—by the early eleventh century, persisting until a.d. 1250–1300 only in some mountain areas such as the eastern valleys of the Sierra Madre in Durango.

This whole complicated story of the northern fringe of Mesoamerica is relevant here because the Chalchihuites culture corridor was also a major passageway, if much later, for Spanish colonists heading north, which indicates that they followed ancient migration trails. In 1529–30, during his conquest of the future province of Nueva Galicia, Nuño de Guzmán subdued southwest Zacatecas and northern Jalisco.[62] He found it impossible to proceed beyond La Quemada and El Teúl, however, by these inland trails because they had been interrupted long before, when farmers of Mesoamerican culture deserted Zacatecas-Jalisco (circa 850–900) and most of eastern Durango (circa 1250–1300). Therefore, he had to turn west toward the Pacific and take a coastal route that had been opened in the ninth century with the development of the still poorly understood Aztatlán cultural complex, which extended the northwestern Mesoamerican frontier up to the Río Fuerte in present-day Sinaloa for a short period.[63] In fact, the first trail that Spanish conquerors took to Pueblo country went along this coastal corridor; only around the last quarter of the sixteenth century were they able to reestablish the inland roads.

Most important for us, however, is the fact that early Spanish missionaries and explorers who came across vestiges of architecture left over from the temporary enlargement of Mesoamerica did not hesitate to attribute their construction to the ancestors of "civilized" Indians from Central Mexico. Friar Juan de Torquemada wrote in his *Monarquía indiana* that seven leagues south of the city of Zacatecas he had seen very old ruins of magnificent buildings (undoubtedly La Quemada)[64] which, he affirmed, were certainly the work of the Aztecs and other Náhuatl-speaking tribes who had migrated into the Valley of Mexico from a northerly country, according to ancient pictographic records and oral traditions.[65] The same opinion regarding the presence of sophisticated architecture amid a territory mainly occupied by nomadic hunter-gatherers appears in the writings of Friar Antonio Tello and Francisco Javier Clavijero,[66] as well as other colonial documents.

Archaeological evidence and reinterpretation of sources produced by Marie-Areti Hers in the 1980s show these opinions were somewhat correct. Not, of course, that wandering Aztecs actually built La Quemada on their way down to the Valley of Mexico. To the present day, despite all efforts, the place of origin of Náhuatl speakers has not been located. Moreover, the first construction phases of La Quemada predate by several hundred years the start of the Aztec migration, according to the same historical traditions quoted by Torquemada, Tello, and Clavijero. Nevertheless, the excavations Hers conducted in the Sierra del Nayar between 1974 and 1981 corroborate that some of the groups who forsook the Chalchihuites area were indeed the creators of the Toltec culture, together with the Nonoalca—a Mesoamerican group long established in Central Mexico.[67] Hers confirmed that some of the most characteristically Toltec elements existed in Chalchihuiteño settlements at least five hundred years before they appeared in Tula and other Post-Classic Mesoamerican sites, such as Chichén Itzá and Mexico-Tenochtitlan; specifically pseudo-cloisonné-type ceramics, copper and turquoise objects, rectangular precincts with colonnades, enclosed by surrounding walls, and, most important, two types of structures associated with human sacrifice. One is the *tzompantli,* a skull rack for the public exhibition of heads of sacrificed warriors; the other is an altar commonly known as *chacmool,* carved in the shape of a semi-reclining human figure, apparently used to place braziers with the burning hearts of sacrificial victims. All these elements—she contends—were brought along by the migrant farmers who poured back into Central Mexico, causing Mesoamerica to shrink.[68]

Aridamerica and Oasisamerica

While the concept of Mesoamerica is almost universally accepted, categorization of the territory extending north across the United States–Mexico border is controversial. North American scholars use two different terms for the area: Southwest and Greater Southwest, the first encompassed by the second as a sub-area to the north where "primitive" part-time farmers and late-arriving tribes of hunter-gatherers coexisted with unstable horticulturist societies of segmentary lineage, settled from about 500 b.c. near natural wells and rivers. Mexican scholars, following Kirchhoff, generally prefer the term Oasisamerica for the farming complex developed in the Southwest and Aridamerica for the hunter-gatherer cultural complex that continued to prevail in the remaining portion of the Greater Southwest until the late colonial period.

Not merely two sets of terminologies referring to one and the same empirical object, Southwest/Greater Southwest and Oasisamerica/Aridamerica are two analytic models with divergent assumptions and implications and do not even apply to the same geographic space. Both, it is true, refer at least to the dry lands extending over Sonora, Chihuahua, Sinaloa, Durango, Coahuila, Nuevo León, and Tamaulipas on the Mexican side; and nearly all of Arizona and New Mexico, the southern and western extremes of Texas, and southern California, on the U.S. side. Yet scholars who speak of the Southwest, or even the Greater Southwest, usually mean the southwestern fringe of the United States and a rather small portion of the adjoining Mexican regions.[69] The Aridamerica/Oasisamerica model, on the other hand, includes Baja California and the middle part of the Mexican Central Plateau that comprises the states of Zacatecas, Guanajuato, San Luis Potosí, and Querétaro.[70]

Although not all of this land is a desert and, geographically, it is certainly diverse, the Aridamerica/Oasisamerica model escapes at least the implicit burden of the nation-state that characterizes its Southwest/Greater Southwest counterpart. Instead of defining its terms in relation to modern political units, it considers the contrast between local forms of livelihood and their relation to environmental constraints. A review of the principles articulating each of these models will bring to the fore the human mosaic that sixteenth century Spaniards dealt with as they ventured northwest of Mesoamerica.[71]

The initial definition of the Southwest as a culture area was based on evidence drawn from peoples north of the U.S.-Mexico border who became the subject of modern ethnographic and archaeological interest only when Texas, Arizona, New Mexico, and Upper California were incorporated into the United States at the end of the 1846–48 Mexican-American War. Extensive governmental inspections aimed at measuring, mapping, and classifying the acquired land, its resources and inhabitants became imperative for U.S. federal authorities in order to implement the Indian Reservation policy already being enforced elsewhere in the national territory.[72] But if the comprehensive scope of this official survey covered most of the newly acquired territory to furnish policymakers with sufficient information to work with, the focus was certainly narrower in academic circles.

Late nineteenth and early twentieth century scholars paid particular attention to the more or less tightly organized groups of horticulturists living in what Otis T. Mason and Pliny E. Goddard called the Pueblo Indian country,[73] roughly comprising southern Utah and Colorado, and most of Arizona and New Mexico.[74] As an area of scholarly research, the Southwest was initially restricted to this area, the only region in the present-day United States where Europeans encountered still-inhabited, compact masonry settlements of native manufacture.[75] Spanish colonists had called these settlements "pueblos" because, unlike the rather diffuse and mobile "rancherías" of neighboring hunter-gatherers and part-time farmers, they resembled the towns Spaniards inhabited back in the Iberian motherland and in New Spain; hence the misinterpretation that Mason and Goddard incurred by using the word "Pueblo" as an ethnonym.

The first Europeans to arrive in the Pueblo area (1539–40) found some seventy inhabited towns and the ruins of several others.[76] Each town was a self-contained, autonomous community with its own governing chiefs and internal organization. According to colonial sources, the Pueblo villages maintained fairly regular trade relations[77] but made no political alliances except temporary ones for extraordinary defense reasons. Spanish observers perceived all Pueblo Indian groups as having more or less "the same rites and customs."[78] They all grew maize, beans, chili, squash, cotton, and tobacco in irrigated fields and kept domesticated turkeys and dogs; they dressed in cotton blankets and animal skins; they resided in compact stone and adobe houses that were clustered together in compounds of several stories centered around open plazas; they were monogamous and had no legal systems or governing lords, although they did have priests and followed the elders' advice.[79]

Modern scholars, too, consider that, compared with their neighbors, Pueblo Indians "form a unit," even when closer examination reveals differences regarding language and social organization. The basic division generally recognized is between the western Pueblos of New Mexico and Arizona and the eastern Pueblos of the Rio Grande and its tributaries. The most conspicuous contrast between them concerns their kinship systems and attendant social structures.[80]

Pueblo peoples represent four different linguistic stocks, three of which correspond to the western Pueblos: the Hopi (or Moqui) of the Tusayan province in northeast Arizona, located between the San Juan and Little Colorado rivers, speak a language of the Shoshone family; the Keres (or Queres), some living in Arizona and western New Mexico, and some in the Rio Grande valley, speak a language with no known affiliations; and the Zuñi (in the province of Cíbola in western New Mexico) speak a language distantly related to the Penutian language family of California. The fourth linguistic stock corresponds to the eastern Pueblos: the Kiowa-Tanoan, represented in the Rio Grande by three subgroups, Tiwa, Tewa, and Towa, each comprising several dialects. Both the Shoshone and Tanoan languages, like Náhuatl, belong to the Uto-Aztecan family.[81]

At the time of Spanish contact, Athabascan-speaking groups of hunter-gatherers, generally known as Apaches, also lived in Colorado, Texas, Arizona, and New Mexico. They had migrated south from the Mackenzie River basin in Canada, following the slopes of the Rocky Mountains, and had arrived in the southwestern United States around a.d. 1400.[82] Early in the twentieth century they, too, received much scholarly attention, completing the image of the Southwest as a combination of sedentary farmers and roaming hunter-gatherers living close to each other in a semi-arid environment.

The nationalist bias of the Southwest/Greater Southwest model is noticeable in that groups of farmers similar to the Pueblo people but south of the international border, such as the Cahitas, Pima-Opatas, and Tarahumaras, were initially disregarded. Alternatively, they were lumped together with north Mexican hunter-gatherers and Mesoamerican peoples in a different area—Middle America—also comprising Central America. Nevertheless, as the native peoples and archaeological remains of northwest Mexico began to be studied early in the twentieth century, a redefinition of the original Southwest seemed imperative. Subsequent reformulations included portions of the Mexican states of Sonora, Durango, Sinaloa, and Chihuahua, where a preconquest Puebloan culture had left impressive ruins: the large city of Paquimé (Casas Grandes), with its well-laid-out, multistory, adobe-walled buildings, ball courts, and plazas, that flourished as a regional trading center between a.d. 1200 and a.d. 1490.[83]

The paramount criterion defining the Southwest in late nineteenth and early twentieth century scholarship was intensive agriculture. Wissler and Kroeber had argued that the presence of a few late-arriving hunter-gatherers did not change the fact that farming was the predominant form of livelihood in the region.[84] Yet once the definition of Southwest was extended to include Sonora, Durango, and Chihuahua, the agricultural versus nonagricultural split ceased to be pertinent. Hunter-gatherer and farming societies of New Mexico and Arizona shared important attributes such as pottery styles or weaving techniques. At the same time, many gatherers and hunter-gatherers in northern Mexico showed striking similarities with the Sonora-Chihuahua farmers whose existence had prompted the revision. It was in 1943 that Ralph L. Beals came up with the concept of the Greater Southwest, a super-area that encompassed the North American states traditionally included in the Southwest, plus north-central and northwest Mexico, southern California, and most of Texas.[85]

More recent debates on the classification and history of American peoples have challenged the utility and validity of the notion of "culture area" altogether.[86] Nevertheless, I still consider the Aridamerica/Oasisamerica model useful in our understanding of long-term historical processes and their connection to the natural environment. It is particularly helpful if one does not take its basic categories as denoting fixed geographic areas but as cultural-economic complexes. Seen from this perspective, the Aridamerica/Oasisamerica model acknowledges the homogeneity in cultural features—besides modes of food procurement and production—that, according to Beals, is likely to have prevailed in the southwestern United States and north-central and northwest Mexico prior to the full adoption of agriculture in some regions within this area. The model also accords importance to the fact that, for nearly two thousand years before European penetration, the social structures, settlement patterns, and daily customs of one portion of its inhabitants developed around farming as the primary basis of subsistence, thus giving way to the emergence of a separate cultural complex—Oasisamerica—in certain enclaves, such as the Pueblo Indian country—within the territory occupied by Aridamerican cultures.[87] In spite of its general geographic correspondence with the initial renditions of the Southwest, the term Oasisamerica is not fundamentally a spatial category; instead it denotes a cultural form, scattered in a series of geographically disconnected spots throughout present-day Utah, Colorado, Arizona, and New Mexico in the United States; and Chihuahua, Sonora, and Durango in Mexico.[88] Similarly, Aridamerica comprises cultures that evolved from a prehistoric "desert tradition" in the dry lands extending on both sides of the current international border; people who belonged to these cultures practiced no agriculture and built no permanent settlements until Europeans arrived.[89] Once geographic boundaries are blurred, a more flexible approach is possible, making it easy to think of places where

Arid and Oasisamerican cultures overlap without having to circumscribe them within fixed and separate territories (map 2).

The main features indexed in academic literature to typify Oasisamerica are sedentism; intensive dryland agriculture; compact villages with stone and adobe houses clustered together to form unitary compounds; and a kin-based social structure of segmentary lineages cross-cut, in some places, by a network of associations for ritual and labor-organization purposes, superimposed as a means to foster town-wide integration.[90] Pueblo societies, the archetypal Oasisamerican example that survived into the colonial and modern eras, are described in colonial sources as collections of clans or extended families with no hereditary rulers.[91] Perhaps this is why, though considered civilized, they did not match Spanish ideas of Aztec ancestry.

The prototypical Oasisamerican societies that flourished in the modern state of Chihuahua, the southernmost extreme of this "culture area," had disappeared by the sixteenth century. However, groups of farmers practicing migratory slash-and-burn cultivation subsisted in some regions contiguous with Mesoamerica up to the time of Spanish contact, from the Pacific coast to the western edge of the Mexican Central Plateau. The largest groups among them were the Tarahumara and Tepehuan, scattered in seasonal dwellings in the Sierra Madre Occidental and relying mostly on hunting and fishing, whereas the Cahita, Yaqui, and Papago, less numerous, were living in small, permanent villages on the coast. In contrast, Mesoamerican farmers who lived along the frontier on the Mexican Central Plateau were in direct contact with nomadic and semi-nomadic tribal peoples such as the Zacateco, Pame, Guachichil, as well as some Apaches who were specialized gatherers rather than primarily hunters.[92] It is true that farther north, in Chihuahua and Coahuila, lived other seasonal farmers such as the Concho Indians,[93] but outside of the Pueblo area, Oasisamerican irrigated fields and terraces only survived Mesoamerica's contraction among the Pima and Opata in Sonora, many kilometers away from Kirchhoff's demarcation line.[94]

Settled Mesoamericans versus Unsettled Chichimecas

To round out this chapter, let us examine a polysemic ethnologic category that, in classifying native populations of the North American continent, the Spaniards borrowed from Mesoamerican Náhuatl speakers. A self-defining term for many farmers in preconquest Central Mexico, this category—Chichimeca—was later used to label all resisting tribes of unsettled hunter-gatherers who hindered Spanish colonization in the north. A close examination of its changing and multiple meanings can illuminate the willful involvement of Mesoamerican Indians in expeditions aimed at discovering Nuevo México. Colonial historical sources subsume most Aridamerican groups under the general label of "Chichimeca." The term was in current use in Central Mexico when the Spaniards arrived, but even then its original meaning was obscure. Semantic layers acquired in the colonial context have only added to its ambiguous character. Náhuatl-speaking Indians in the basin of Mexico often referred to their own ancestors as Chichimecas, whom they proudly defined as immigrants from the north. They were thought of as expert hunters who also cultivated the land and who were ruled by sovereigns called *tlatoque* (plural of *tlatoani*),[95] whereas the Spaniards always spoke of Chichimecas in a derogatory tone, as unsettled and "primitive" savages.[96]

As early as 1525, for example, a Spanish soldier reported hearing from Indians in Aguacatlán that peoples living farther north were Otomís, or even *"Teules Chichimecas, who are like beasts."*[97] Much later (1574) a settler in the mining town of Llerena, Nueva Galicia, used the word Chichimeca similarly in a petition addressed to the king: "I, Melchor de Alava, resident of the village of Llerena and mines of Sombrerete . . . declare that I have been for a long time at Your Majesty's service conquering and subduing the Chichimeca Indian bandits who roam the outskirts of the said village . . . and many other places and royal roads, who have done and are doing very great harm."[98] Viceroy Martín Enríquez wrote a similar complaint in 1580:

> Some Indians that around here they call Chichimecas, together with others from different nations, all of whom remain to be conquered . . . have been a plague that has given a good deal of trouble to these kingdoms, because they inhabit the largest and roughest of all territories in this land, for which reason it is understood that not even all the Spaniards living here joining together to punish them would be sufficient because [those Indians] have no permanent residence, nor a place to be found with certainty, rather, with bows and arrows, which is the weaponry they use, they constantly wander from one place to another, and they live like deer, feeding only on herbs and roots and ground-up animal powders that they keep in gourds.[99]

In Spanish usage, the category Chichimeca embraced several different language groups, as exemplified in the above quotations. It was particularly used as an epithet for Guachichiles, Guamares, Zacatecos, and Pames, against whom the Spaniards waged a prolonged series of wars in the mid-sixteenth century with the aid of vast numbers of Otomí, Tarascan, and Tlaxcaltecan troops.[100] Using the term in this manner to identify the nomadic part-time farmers and hunter-gatherers of Aridamerica, as opposed to Mesoamerican sedentary farmers, was not a mere Spanish whim. This was one of several meanings of the word in Indian discourse at the time of the conquest.

The following review of a few passages from chronicles reputed as privileged sources for Náhuatl culture and cosmology will bring such meanings to the fore. In his *Historia de los indios de la Nueva España* (1565), Friar Toribio de

Benavente, known as Motolinía, noted that before the conquest, Indians from Mexico-Tenochtitlan kept their history in a pictographic book they called the "Year-Count Book" (*Libro de la cuenta de los años*). In Motolinía's interpretation, the Chichimecas were the first and most ancient of three kinds of people to inhabit Central Mexico. Unlike "Colhuas" and Mexicans—the other two kinds he mentions—the Chichimecas "had no literacy because they were barbarians who lived like savages," and for this reason, "nothing is known about them except that for eight hundred years they have dwelt in this land, though it is taken for certain that their antiquity is even greater." Motolinía also observes in this passage that Chichimecas were monogamous and recognized one leader to whom they rendered complete obedience, yet "they had no permanent residence, nor clothing nor corn or any other kind of bread or seeds." "Rather, they lived in caves and hills, feeding on wild roots, deer, hares, rabbits, and serpents; and even today there are people who live in the same manner." These descriptions, clearly corresponding to nomadic hunter-gatherers, include the fact that Chichimecas did not perform bloody sacrifice and had no idols as proof of their primitive simplicity.[101] It is remarkable that Motolinía's distinction between Chichimecas, Colhuas, and Mexicans is based on cultural and historical considerations; it implies a differentiation between three human groups that, having attained different cultural achievements, successively migrated into Central Mexico. Note that Motolinía's description of the ancient Chichimecas stems from his own comparison between Chichimecas depicted in Indian documents and certain groups known by the same name in his day; in consequence, it does not necessarily reflect with accuracy Indian conceptions of the term Chichimeca. This becomes clear when comparing Motolinía's passage to chapter 29, book X of Friar Bernardino de Sahagún's *Códice Florentino*,[102] devoted to describing New Spain's native population.

Sahagún's account seems to voice no personal interpretation; he describes nine groups of people, each in a separate section, organized in such a way that the principle of classification can hardly be discerned, which suggests that Sahagún was faithfully reporting his informants' taxonomy rather than trying to make sense of the people he observed. Toltecs occupy the first paragraph and are categorized as highly cultured peoples who spoke Náhuatl and were the first to arrive in Central Mexico. Paragraphs 2 to 4 are devoted to the Chichimecas, divided into three main types: the Otomí, farmers of a relatively low cultural development; the Tamime, meaning "arrow shooters," mainly hunters who built no towns but occasionally cultivated the land and had some sort of organized rulership; and the Teuchichimecas, or "authentic Chichimecas," completely wild and uncultivated peoples who practiced no agriculture at all, lived on hunting, and had no fixed places of residence. Ensuing paragraphs are devoted to other peoples; some, characterized as advanced farmers with complex forms of social organization, are also said to have been Chichimecas; namely, all the Náhuatl speakers (paragraphs 5, 11, and 14), the Mazahuaque (paragraph 9), and the Micchuaque (paragraph 13).

Without going into detail, we can summarize the conclusions scholars have drawn from these and other accounts as follows: In a general sense, Chichimeca—a Náhuatl word—was a broad cultural category frequently used to denote the unsettled lifestyles of hunter-gatherers. Their way of life stood in opposition to archetypal forms of civilization represented by the Toltec society of bygone times and understood as the sum of arts, urbanism, institutionalized rulership, and ritual (including human sacrifice).[103] This characterization seems to cover the ancient Chichimecas mentioned by Motolinía as well as Sahagún's Teuchichimecas and Tamime. In a more specific sense, the term was applied to the descendants of those farming groups that moved temporarily north to Chichimeca lands during the period of an enlarged Mesoamerica and moved back south at the beginning of the Post-Classic. This more specific usage of "Chichimeca" includes the Otomí, Mazahuaque, and Micchuaque, together with all Náhuatl-speaking peoples including the Mexicans and even the Toltecs (or at least one of their constitutive branches, the Tolteca-Chichimeca).[104] As Hers demonstrated in *Los toltecas en tierras chichimecas*, the forebears of some of the groups that constituted the Toltec society, farmers in a long-standing Mesoamerican tradition, lived for generations in Marginal Mesoamerica under constant threat, struggling to defend their settlements from the attacks of hunter-gatherers whom they had displaced. Consequently they developed a war-centered culture that became generalized in the Mesoamerican heartland when their descendants returned. Contrasting with both types of Chichimecas were the Olmecas, the Huixtotin, and the Nonoalcas, who, according to Sahagún's informants (paragraph 12), never received the name of Chichimeca.[105]

Measured against the documents quoted above, this interpretation posing at least two native meanings for the term Chichimeca (northern farmers of Mesoamerican culture retreating south in the late Post-Classic Horizon, and hunter-gatherer lifestyles) seems correct. As confirmed by the expression "Teules Chichimecas," which a Spanish soldier distortedly recorded in Aguacatlán, present-day Nayarit, in 1525, Sahagún's category of Teuchichimeca comprised all northern hunter-gatherers living beyond Mesoamerica up to the moment of Spanish arrival, who never adopted the farming culture prevailing south of their territory.[106]

Motolinía's "ancient Chichimeca" are more difficult to identify but may comprise the first invading groups of hunter-gatherers from the north who were not originally from Mesoamerica and who spoke languages other than Náhuatl; for instance, the group that swept down into the Valley of Mexico led by a chief called Xólotl in the early thirteenth century.[107] These Chichimecas were indeed the first immigrants to reach the basin of Mexico after the collapse of Tula, preceding all Náhuatl speakers except the Tolteca-Chichimecas.[108] However, other similar groups of non-Mesoamerican ancestry had established themselves elsewhere in Central Mexico long before, when the frontier of permanent agriculture began to shrink (circa a.d. 850–900), and they may be among those Motolinía invoked.[109] By the sixteenth century all these groups had adopted a Mesoamerican culture, and once integrated with the local population via marriage exchange, had even dropped their own languages, taking up Náhuatl instead.[110] An exception would be the Tamime, probably also recently arrived hunter-gatherers, who did not completely adopt Mesoamerican lifestyles and still spoke their own language. The same might hold true as well for the Otonchichimeca, the Nahuachichimeca, and the Cuextecachichimeca briefly mentioned in paragraph 4 of Sahagún's text as acculturated hunter-gatherers who spoke their own Chichimeca language but had also learned that of their new neighbors: Otomí, Náhuatl, and Huasteco, respectively.[111]

Charles Di Peso and Beatriz Braniff coined the term "Gran Chichimeca" for the area that Kirchhoff, on the basis of its ecologic diversity, called Arid and Oasisamerica. Phil Weigand, on his part, proposed an extended notion of Mesoamerica that includes the Pueblo Indian country and the trading corridor stretching along the Sierra Madre Occidental between both regions.[112] I believe the Arid, Oasis, and Mesoamerica triad continues to be useful for certain discussions, as long as one does not insist on rigid geographic boundaries or historically undifferentiated lists of attributes. Spaniards drew clear distinctions between the peoples living in each of these culture areas, and from their perspective, Pueblo Indian country was indeed an oasis amid "barbarians," this being an important reason they called it Nuevo México.

Culture-area taxonomies are useful as theoretical constructs, even if they often find no equivalent on the ground among the societies they classify. But regional historical memory and local discourse sometimes do endorse academic classificatory schemes. The limit between Mesoamerica and Aridamerica was meaningful for Central Mexican sedentary peoples in preconquest times; its late Post-Classic position coincides vaguely with the geographic scope of such categories as Chichimeca, which, as seen above, appears to have had some relation to the changing span of permanent agriculture. This was a frontier of remarkable importance throughout the colonial period and remained perceptible as a transition zone between the predominantly European and Mestizo north of Mexico, and the culturally Indian and Mestizo south. This ethno-cultural contrast between north and south continued to be relevant partly because European colonization of Aridamerica, with its frequent policy of Indian extermination, accentuated the already extant pattern of demographic dispersal and relatively low population density.

On one level of analysis, the contrast distinguishing Mesoamerica from Arid and Oasisamerica determined the pace of Spanish advance in the north, as well as the general direction and routes the conquering parties followed. Particular forms of indigenous civilization required different types of warfare. On the other hand, peoples living outside the areas controlled by aboriginal "high cultures," whether small-scale farmers, or regular or seasonal nomads, represented almost insurmountable difficulties for Spanish conquerors, as they had a flexible relation with the territory they occupied, and the loose political structures that bound them together were not based on permanent subservience.

Spanish northward expansion was anchored on the manpower and local knowledge of already conquered Indians from Central Mexico, massively recruited as troops, guides, scouts, and interpreters. Indigenous perspectives, therefore, were inevitably adopted when strategic decisions were to be made, as shown by the statement Nuño de Guzmán made in a letter to the king in July 1530: "From Michoacán I wrote to Your Majesty . . . to tell how I came with one hundred and fifty horsemen and foot soldiers in similar numbers . . . and also seven or eight thousand Indian friends to discover the land and conquer the province of the *teules chichimecas* that is contiguous with New Spain."[113]

This is one among many examples of the recruitment of native warriors. The decisive collaboration of Tlaxcalan allies to topple Moctezuma in 1521 had set a precedent for a practice that continued throughout the sixteenth century.[114] Beyond the indisputable practicalities this co-participation entailed, Spanish expectations regarding further lands to be conquered were significantly shaped by Indian notions, including information on land and people, cosmological conceptions about the world at large, and local historical traditions. In the letter quoted above, Guzmán adopted, however distorted, the term that his Mesoamerican warriors used to identify the local groups he fought against: "*teules chichimecas.*" The operation reveals that information flowed between the Spanish captain and his Indian "friends," and points to the possibility that, alongside ethnic taxonomies, the Spaniards absorbed other indigenous views and customs through their tireless ventures in the north.

CHAPTER THREE

The Exploration and Conquest of Nuevo México

History is usually written—at least since the rise of the nation-state—in terms of political geography. New Mexico's past is no exception: historians and anthropologists have spun a coherent narrative based on institutional and military events occurring within the boundaries it acquired as a state of the United States.[1] Their narrative concentrates on the scores of Spanish adventurers who, since 1539, penetrated (or attempted to penetrate) the Pueblo Indian region where Juan de Oñate founded the colonial kingdom of Nuevo México in April 1598. Their limited focus obscures a clear perception of relevant historical processes beyond the state borders or not strictly tied to state affairs. The usual version of New Mexican history is thus built on a retrospective projection of modern political frontiers.

Sixteenth century sources that mention "Nuevo México" do not necessarily refer to the territory comprised within the nebulous limits of the colonial province of that name, an area that Spaniards initially called Cíbola, in accordance with the report of its first Spanish visitor, Friar Marcos de Niza (1539).[2] The name "Nuevo México" was applied to other places in mid-sixteenth century documents as colonial expansion progressed, each place in turn mistaken for the Aztec homeland of Nahua origin myths, but it was only in the 1580s that people applied the name to the region theretofore known as Cíbola. Accordingly, Nuevo México might be termed a "transcultural imaginary world," not corresponding before that moment to any concrete place. In consequence, the temporal and geographic scope of New Mexico's early colonial history must be expanded to include several expeditions that never set foot in the confines of Pueblo Indian country, or even aimed at reaching it, but were nevertheless fundamental in cementing the "imaginary construction" that Oñate's foundational act transformed into the northernmost Spanish possession in North America.

Most New Mexico histories, from the nineteenth century on, start by recalling the famous odyssey of Alvar Núñez Cabeza de Vaca and three other survivors of the lost expedition that Pánfilo de Narváez led to Florida in 1528, particularly the reports they produced concerning large cities near the route they followed in search of other Spaniards. The episodes traditionally mentioned next are the 1539 scouting journey that Friar Marcos de Niza conducted to the vicinity of

Zuñi and the conquest expedition under the command of Francisco Vázquez de Coronado over the whole Pueblo area between 1540 and 1542.

No doubt these expeditions were the first to bear a strict relation to the physical territory later named Nuevo México. It is clear that Viceroy Antonio de Mendoza commissioned Niza's excursion to verify the rumors spread by Cabeza de Vaca, thereby heading off the intrusion of other possible claimants such as Hernán Cortés. It is also clear that the friar's description of his findings—an urban settlement "larger than Mexico City" situated amid a province that "in my opinion is the largest and best among the lands hitherto discovered"[3]— prompted a colonizing frenzy with few parallels. As a personal letter by Bishop Juan de Zumárraga shows, numerous volunteers to follow up on Niza's discovery enthusiastically enrolled in the army that Mendoza put under command of Vázquez de Coronado.[4] The prospective colonists, however, soon deserted the place as they realized that Pueblo villages were insignificant compared to ancient Mexico-Tenochtitlan.

Standard historiography remarks on the several decades during which the Pueblo land was almost forgotten, reappearing under the name "Nuevo México" only by 1581. However, the dream of discovering another Mexico was not extinguished. Rather, it became more complex as it intertwined with indigenous traditions. By the decade of 1560, Spanish explorers did not simply aspire to find a place that equaled the abundance, population density, and sophistication of ancient Mexico; they also hoped to locate its original source. Conquistador Francisco de Ibarra and his uncle Diego—a rich and prominent settler of the mining district of Zacatecas—for example, searched for the "original homeland of the culgua mexica" throughout the region they named Nueva Vizcaya, which corresponds approximately to the modern Mexican states of Durango, Chihuahua, and Coahuila. A soldier in Francisco de Ibarra's army, Baltasar de Obregón, stated in a chronicle he wrote in 1584 that Diego de Ibarra was determined to "discover and conquer the New Mexico," generally suspected as the place where "the ancient *culguas mexicanos*" had come from. For this purpose, Diego agreed to provide his nephew Francisco, appointed captain for the enterprise by Viceroy Luis de Velasco, with all the support and means he needed.[5]

Other reports, discussed below, point in the same direction, but historians frequently dismiss the Nueva Vizcaya episode, jumping directly from the discovery of mines in Nueva Galicia in the 1540s and 1550s to the three or four unauthorized excursions carried out into the Pueblo area during the 1580s.[6] Particular importance is attributed to Friar Agustín Rodríguez and Juan Sánchez Chamuscado's 1581 expedition because they were apparently the first Spaniards to visit Cíbola since 1542, but also because it was they who called that region Nuevo México for the first time.[7] Thus, for traditional historiography, Vázquez de Coronado represents a transitional figure between the fantasizing ventures of early times and the supposedly more realistic endeavors of the 1580s and 1590s. He is presented as the demystifying hero who "discovers" the true character of the land Sánchez Chamuscado later renames.

Such a distinction between a fantasy-dominated period and a reality-oriented one is misleading. The toponym Nuevo México, formulated after Vázquez de Coronado abandoned Cíbola and before Rodríguez and Sánchez Chamuscado revisited and renamed it, resulted indeed from the reification of an imaginary world: the Aztec original homeland. As will be shown in chapter 5, however, this imaginary world was not completely unreal. The process of its construction involved the combination of truth and fantasy throughout a long history of cross-cultural representation, starting with the adventure of Hernán Cortés in Tenochtitlan and ending with Juan de Oñate's 1595–98 conquest of Nuevo México. It is a foundational history of cognitive and political negotiations with strong mythic overtones that have lasted up to the present day.

Early Settlement and Exploration of New Spain: The Emergence of Cíbola

Most of Mesoamerica was thoroughly explored between the time of Cortés's landing at Veracruz in April 1519, and 1524. Mesoamerican towns were relatively easy prey for the Spanish conquerors due to the existence of long-established and densely settled *señoríos* ruled by noble lineages, often supported by tribute exacted in kind and labor. In this period nearly all the states tributary to the Aztecs and some important independent ones like Tlaxcala and Michoacán accepted the Spaniards as their new rulers, although subsequent uprisings occurred, forcing further consolidation campaigns.[8]

To a great extent the velocity of this expeditionary assault can be attributed to the information and support the invaders received from the Aztec emperor. This is made clear by questions 97–99 of a 1534 questionnaire Cortés formulated for the defense witnesses in his residencia trial. Could the respondents confirm that Cortés cordially sought Moctezuma's advice regarding the best way to secure the submission of his subject states? Would they testify that Moctezuma summoned the local rulers to request their acceptance of the Spanish overlordship, and that his messengers then departed in all directions, taking five or six Spaniards along, to spread the news and view the resources of the land?[9] Witnesses who had participated in such excursions, including Andrés de Tapia, answered affirmatively, adding that the Spanish captains personally collected the gold that local people gave as a present, while Moctezuma's messengers negotiated a peaceful surrender.[10] Thus the particular interest that Cortés and his men showed from the beginning in visiting the gold-producing districts—the existence of which they partly figured out through Moctezuma's tribute records[11]—was almost immediately satisfied, just as their need to locate ports other than Veracruz along the Atlantic shoreline. In his second letter to the king (October 30, 1520) Cortés reports that the Aztec emperor not only ordered his officers to draw him a map of the eastern coast but also offered several escorts to show the Spaniards the gold mines and gold districts of the south.[12]

As is well known, the massacre that Pedro de Alvarado ordered in the Great Temple of Mexico-Tenochtitlan (May 1520) and Moctezuma's subsequent death (June 1520) brought the Indian collaboration to a violent end. Forced into a precipitous flight from the Aztec capital, Cortés interrupted the surveys he had initiated in areas today embraced within the Mexican states of Veracruz and Oaxaca.[13] Nevertheless, by the time the Spaniards recaptured the city in August 1521, the scope of their domination was considerably enlarged, and once they controlled the heart of the ancient Aztec empire, they resumed exploration in more distant areas, which fell one after the other before the conquerors' sweeping campaigns.

On the western front Cortés had the coast of the Pacific Ocean (Mar del Sur) explored between 1521 and 1522. Later on he planned to engage in maritime exploration from the ports of Zacatula and Tehuantepec, which had been located in that period. In 1521 the Tarascan state of Michoacán received its first Spanish visitor in the person of Antonio Caicedo. His friendly encounter with the local ruler, Tangaxoan II, the Cazonci, encouraged Cortés to dispatch a much larger expedition under the command of Cristóbal de Olid in summer 1522.[14] The *Relación de Michoacán* and Cortés's fourth letter to the king (October 15, 1524) show that despite the Cazonci's rapid submission, plans for a Spanish settlement in Pátzcuaro died out when Olid learned that not a gram of the gold he confiscated was locally produced, although gold and silver mines were later discovered in the Tarascan territory.[15] Early in 1523 one of the captains in Olid's army, Juan Rodríguez Villafuerte, apparently ventured an unauthorized assault on the bountiful and autonomous province of Colima that was conquered by Gonzalo Sandoval later that year.[16] North of Colima, Juan de Avalos, Hernando de Sayavedra, and Francisco Cortés conducted the first incursions into present-day Jalisco and Nayarit (1523–25),[17] a region that only the following decade was effectively occupied by Nuño de Guzmán.

While the north and northwest limits of New Spain expanded periodically throughout the sixteenth century, the northeast frontier was fixed early on at the province of Pánuco (northern Veracruz, southern Tamaulipas, and southeast San Luis Potosí), a territory over which successive disputes arose between Hernán Cortés and other captains.

Northeast of Pánuco lay the Florida peninsula; from its northern extreme on the Atlantic side (Punta de Santa Elena, today Port Royal in South Carolina) the coast ran up to the Land of the Bacallaos (Cape Breton in modern-day Nova

Scotia). Many thought this shoreline hid the mouth of the Strait of Anian that was presumed to connect the Atlantic and Pacific oceans. Because Punta de Santa Elena could serve as the starting point to search for the strait, and the Bahama Channel that separates Florida from the Caribbean islands was the route every vessel took on its way back to Europe,[18] the area became the object of much imperial competition, and the Spaniards very early tried to secure its control against any possible European rival.

Florida, discovered in 1512 or 1513 by Juan Ponce de León, governor of Puerto Rico, was taken for an island until Francisco de Garay demonstrated it was a peninsula in 1521. Several conquest attempts in succession were made, but fierce indigenous resistance, isolation, and harsh natural conditions thwarted all colonizing efforts,[19] harboring instead the looting activities of English and French pirates; whence the strategic importance of Pánuco, which for many decades was the main barrier against prospective French colonists.[20] In fact, Francisco de Garay had commissioned several expeditions in the Pánuco area since 1519, hoping to establish a colony under his own independent government. In 1523 he even took up the personal lead of a military campaign, but when Garay reached Pánuco, Cortés had already established a municipal council there, calling it Santiesteban del Puerto, and soon endorsed by the authority of a royal charter, he forced Garay to withdraw.[21] This victory of Cortés over the control of Pánuco marks the closure of the first stage in the creation of New Spain, a colony that conquerors assumed comprised the whole of continental North America, whatever its extension. Pánuco's importance for the history of New Mexico rests on the fact that the native residents provided early reports, prior to Cabeza de Vaca, concerning urban settlements to the north.

By 1524, New Spain's effective boundaries reached south to El Salvador and Honduras, northeast to the Huasteca, and west to Colima. The irregular pattern that characterized its sixteenth century growth was determined by a combination of the conquerors' ambition and local demographic and natural conditions. If, at the beginning, exploration pursued, above all, the discovery of gold and silver, a port suitable for transpacific navigation, and the Strait of Anian, as it became clear that precious metals were not available for immediate appropriation and the transcontinental strait proved elusive, conquerors gave priority to founding Spanish villages in well-off agricultural districts that offered abundant indigenous labor.[22] Nearly fifty-seven thousand Spaniards lived in the central highlands and the west by 1570, according to Woodrow Borah.[23] Both areas were highly productive and had an extremely dense Indian population that was accustomed to a dominance system based on the exaction of tribute and personal service. Spanish colonists also intensively settled Colima and the Tarascan plateau, attracted by their abundant resources and large population,[24] even though Cristóbal de Olid had initially refused to settle in the gold-lacking core of the Tarascan domain. But expansion could not proceed at the same pace in areas where no political structures of subservience existed, where hostile populations proved a formidable enemy and colonization revealed itself a more difficult enterprise than simply Indian military defeat.

The conflicts of power that evolved between imperial and local interests and between competing conquerors also contributed to slowing down colonial expansion. Toward the end of 1525 the Crown adopted two administrative measures aimed at achieving control over its newly acquired colonies in mainland North America, thereby arresting the hegemonic position that Cortés hitherto occupied in New Spain. On the one hand, the Crown appointed Luis Ponce de León visiting judge to inquire about Cortés's administration; on the other, it granted Nuño de Guzmán an independent command at Pánuco.[25] Although Ponce de León's unexpected death in July 1526 delayed the legal proceedings against Cortés, the latter had to renounce the office of governor of New Spain and preserved only for a short period his assignment as captain general and administrator of the Indians.[26] Nearly two years later, on April 5, 1528, Guzmán acquired jurisdiction over the whole colony as president of the first Audiencia of Mexico,[27] a post that from 1535 on was assigned to the newly created office of viceroy.

From the moment Guzmán disembarked in Pánuco in May 1527 he confronted the enmity of Mexico City's *cabildo*,[28] the administrative head of New Spain, still controlled by partisans of Cortés who were not willing to recognize the Pánuco government's autonomy.[29] Guzmán was an ambitious character, though, so taking no heed of this hostility, he ruled the province at will until he left for Mexico City in December 1528 to take possession of the Audiencia presidency.[30] Later on Guzmán was dismissed from both positions under several charges. In the meantime, however, he conducted the first wide-ranging conquests attained beyond the northwest limits of the bygone Aztec empire. "Espíritu Santo de la Mayor España" was the name he chose for the territory he then subdued, though in appointing him governor of this now independent province, the empress (Queen Isabel of Portugal, then acting empress in the absence of her husband, Carlos V) stipulated it be called Nueva Galicia.[31]

Primary sources concerning the comprehensive enterprise of subduing Nueva Galicia (the current states of Aguascalientes, Colima, Nayarit, Jalisco, and Colima) are relatively abundant: Besides a couple of letters of report that Guzmán addressed to the monarchs, the *Memoria* he prepared in 1538 or 1539 to base his defense on in his residencia trial, and other documents derived from the lawsuits to which he was subject,[32] some captains under his command wrote accounts relating their own actions.[33] Also, ten of the 168 *Relaciones geográficas* existing for New Spain, compiled from local witnesses in the second half of the sixteenth century, provide independent information on the subject.[34] Finally, there is Friar Antonio Tello's chronicle (1651), the first history ever written on the conquest of Nueva Galicia.[35]

According to Captain García del Pilar, Nuño de Guzmán set out from Mexico City on December 21, 1529, leading an expedition toward the west composed of a few Spaniards and plenty of Indian auxiliaries, mainly Tlaxcalans.[36] Guzmán himself provides no date for his departure but specifies that he took 150 Spanish horsemen, 150 Spanish foot soldiers, and seven or eight thousand "Indian friends."[37] His captain, Francisco de Arceo, counts 250 Spaniards and only fifteen hundred Indian allies;[38] similar though smaller numbers are provided by one of the three anonymous accounts regarding these events.[39] The composition of Guzmán's army was similar in terms of the proportion of Indian and Spanish men at service in most north-going expeditions and many conquering parties in the earlier, Central Mexico stage. We can therefore infer that the goals, routes, and strategies were not only determined by Spanish aims and unfounded imaginings, but in many ways responded to Indian agency, knowledge, and interests.

Historian Donald Chipman argues that Nuño Guzmán set out on this expedition because he was trying to avoid the residencia trial concerning his administration of Pánuco,[40] but Pedro de Castañeda Nájera, a soldier in the army that Vázquez de Coronado later led to Cíbola, attributed the undertaking to certain reports that Guzmán had received in Pánuco from an Indian captive from "Oxitipar":

> In the year 1530, while serving as president [of New Spain], Nuño de Guzmán owned an Indian who was a native from the valleys of Oxitipar. This Indian said that he was the son of a merchant who was then deceased, but when he was a little boy his father used to travel inland to trade precious feathers, and when he returned, he brought gold and silver in great quantities. . . . [He also said] that once or twice he went along and saw very large settlements, comparable to Mexico and its surrounding district. [He also said] that he had seen seven exceedingly large towns with streets paved in silver. . . . It was under [the promise] of this report that Nuño de Guzmán enlisted almost four hundred Spanish men and twenty thousand friends from New Spain [to go in search of them].[41]

The great number of "Indian auxiliary troops" or "Indian friends" and the nature of their participation in conquest expeditions is, of course, a delicate issue. Several testimonies assert that they were forced to go along, to the point that they went in chains. Nevertheless it is difficult to believe that warriors could be forced to fight in chains, while it seems clear that warriors, bearers, and servants did not share the same status. The extremely divergent figures given by Spanish captains and eyewitnesses quoted above may reflect this situation. But what is most remarkable about the last quote is that even if Guzmán wished to escape his residencia trial by engaging in a broad expedition that would outdo Cortés's achievements,[42] his faith that toward the north he would accomplish fruitful conquests rested on the hearsay of a native. None of Guzmán's own testimony, it is true, mentions an "Oxitipar" informant. Nevertheless, he does affirm in his "*Memoria*" that before leaving Pánuco to assume the presidency of the Audiencia, he commissioned the conquest of the valleys "that people call Ogitipa (*que dicen de Ogitipa*)," where he later founded the village of Santiago de los Valles.[43] Furthermore, Pedro de Guzmán and the second anonymous *relación* on the conquest of Nueva Galicia assert that the expeditionaries did search for the "Seven Cities," the existence of which they were aware before leaving Mexico.[44]

Located in the Huasteca Potosina, Oxitipa was indeed one of the most populous and lucrative towns in Pánuco. When the Spaniards arrived, Oxitipa numbered among the most important polities in the region, and although it is not mentioned in any of the extant records that list the conquests of the Triple Alliance, it does appear in *Codex Mendoza* (plate 55r) among the communities paying the richest tribute to Moctezuma II.[45] The polity, conquered by the Mexicas at the beginning of the sixteenth century, was early on assigned to Cortés—it is included in the list of the *encomiendas* he planned to request, contained in a letter to his father dated September 1526[46]—but due to the significant tribute it rendered, Guzmán actually took it away from Cortés on the grounds that it belonged to the governor's office rather than any particular individual.[47]

It is worth noting that Castañeda Nájera, the soldier who first mentioned the Indian from Oxitipa, wrote his chronicle between 1560 and 1565, more than twenty years after he joined Vázquez de Coronado's expedition, and did not take part in any of Guzmán's excursions. His purpose was to prove that Cíbola was still worth conquering because rumors of its grandeur—which he documented—had reached the Spaniards from early times, drawing their steps toward the north but eluding them repeatedly. Therefore it is not surprising that he mistakenly dated the incident as taking place in 1530, after Guzmán had actually departed from Mexico City, and that he highlighted hearsay incidents that Guzmán himself had not considered worth reporting, in view of the particular purpose he then pursued. That a captive from Oxitipa could have been to the Zuñi area with his merchant father to trade feathers and describe it as seven wealthy cities is plausible, considering extant evidence on the Huaxteca's feather production and certain references suggesting the existence of a small-scale trade route between the two places.

Moreover, Guzmán's conviction concerning rich, urban provinces northward probably rested on other sources as well. On the one hand, in Mexico he may well have seen the reports of the expedition that Francisco Cortés had led to Aguacatlán and Xalisco (1524), which described a series of rich and densely settled territories.[48] On the other, he no doubt obtained valuable information about the land beyond Michoacán from the Cazonci he captured in Mexico City to procure, though unsuccessfully, his purported knowledge about gold and silver mines.[49]

Nuño de Guzmán spent the first months of his journey gathering supplies and additional Indian recruits in Tzintzuntzan, the Tarascan capital. At the Lerma River (which he named Nuestra Señora de la Purificación de Santa María) he tormented the Cazonci and had him executed, before heading north in February 1530.[50] Then he sent Peralmíndez Chirino and Cristóbal de Oñate ahead and led his army to Cuitzeo.[51] By July 1530 Guzmán had taken over present-day Guanajuato and southern Jalisco. He ravaged the rich farming district around Lake Chapala ("Chapetela") and Tonalá, claiming jurisdiction over it from already settled Spaniards because he believed gold was abundant there and in nearby Contla and Nochistlán ("Michitlan").[52] Unfortunately for him, the silver veins extending through the Sierra Madre Occidental to Sinaloa, and from San Luis Potosí through Zacatecas to Chihuahua, remained hidden for several years.[53] Yet he came across the magnificent ruins of La Quemada and El Teúl[54] and saw people wearing gold ornaments in Tepic and Centicpac ("Centiquipaque") before temporarily establishing himself in Omitlán to prepare the attack on the lake district of Aztatlán that Gonzalo López had discovered on a scouting mission.[55]

In December 1530 Guzmán subdued the towns of Chametla and Piaxtla, reaching present-day Culiacán by Easter 1531. The village of San Miguel that he later established in there remained the farthest outpost of Spanish occupation for the following sixty years,[56] but Guzmán was soon convinced that nothing of interest existed beyond this point, based on reports by two captains who explored the land up to the Petatlán and Nazas rivers.[57] Therefore, in December 1531 he sent Cristóbal de Oñate southeast to establish the village of Guadalajara[58] and he himself moved south toward Espíritu Santo (later called Compostela), a village he had earlier established in the region of Tepic. Emulating Cortés, he had founded the village as the provisional seat for a municipal council with jurisdiction over the lands he had occupied thus far. He received official notice of his appointment as governor of Nueva Galicia there on January 16, 1532.[59]

Now that he nominally held the government of all known lands north of New Spain from coast to coast, Guzmán pursued their effective occupation. Heading east from Compostela early in 1533, he followed the Lerma River to the Huasteca Potosina, and as a waystation between Pánuco and Nueva Galicia, he founded Santiago de los Valles de Oxitipa (later known as Ciudad Valles). Despite being dismissed as governor of Pánuco on April 20, 1533, he retained his post of governor of Nueva Galicia until January 1537, when he was put under arrest and remanded to Spain.[60] From then on, Viceroy Mendoza took over the exploration and conquest of the north, using Compostela, Culiacán, and Guadalajara as departure stations for new expeditions. In less than two years (February 1530–September 1531), Guzmán had put an enormous territory, nearly half the size of New Spain, under the Spanish Crown (map 1), but his military strategy—entering settled villages, taking control of their wealth and destroying the remains so no counter-offensive could be organized—eventually proved counterproductive for the overall colonizing enterprise.

Between 1540 and 1542, southern Zacatecas and Jalisco became the theater of several revolts, the most famous being the Cazcán rebellion, or Mixtón War, because it represented such a threat to Spanish domination that the viceroy personally arrived to put it down. Even if, according to the third anonymous *relación* on the conquest of Nueva Galicia, this uprising began as an Indian refusal to pay tribute to the Spaniards living in Guadalajara and Compostela,[61] and therefore, Guzmán was not directly responsible for its eruption, the bitter resentment he had left behind certainly fostered native defiance. Some captains such as Gonzalo López and Juan de Sámano acknowledged that they had occasionally taken the food and burned the towns before leaving, but just as Guzmán and his captain Arceo did, they blamed this destruction on the Indian allies.[62] Other accounts are more critical of the governor. Pedro de Carranza, for instance, asserts that in the town of Cynan and elsewhere, allies went about burning everything, but at least in Xalisco and Chametla, it was Guzmán himself who delivered such orders.[63]

While Guzmán conducted his brutal exploits in Pánuco and Nueva Galicia, Pánfilo de Narváez, another ambitious captain, attempted without success the conquest of the territory between Las Palmas River and the cape of Florida. He had participated in the conquest of Cuba in 1511 and had been waiting for the opportunity to try his fortune since 1520, when he returned to Spain as a prisoner after having failed to reduce Hernán Cortés to the obedience of the island's governor. On November 17, 1526, Narváez finally signed a capitulación, believing he would become the master of lands that, like others before him, he imagined to be as rich and wonderful as those Cortés had subdued. Yet when he set sail from Spain on June 17, 1527, leading some six hundred men aboard five ships, he did not suspect how disastrously this adventure would turn out. Neither could his treasurer, Alvar Núñez Cabeza de Vaca, foresee the importance that his personal memoirs would acquire.

In April 1528 the ships Narváez commanded went down off the coast of present-day Texas. The captain sent a small party by sea to locate the mouth of Las Palmas River and took the rest inland to search for wealth and people, but disease, starvation, and Indian arrows dramatically reduced the expeditionary group. On September 22, those who remained alive set sail again aboard five precarious rafts they had built themselves, only to suffer by November yet another shipwreck on the island they called Mal Hado. The few survivors fell prisoner and were apportioned as slaves among different Indian groups. One, at least, became assimilated to the culture of his captors—Hernando de Soto found him and received his help in 1539—but the majority certainly perished. Only four managed (or wanted) to escape and return to their fellow countrymen.[64]

The amazing story of how Alvar Núñez Cabeza de Vaca, Andrés Dorantes, Bernardino del Castillo Maldonado, and the Moorish slave Estevan escaped (in 1533 or 1534) and traveled westward until they reached the frontier settlements of New Spain, managing to survive as healers and merchants, is told by Cabeza de Vaca in a *relación* today known as *Naufragios,* first published in Zamora, Spain, in 1542.[65] A shorter account based on another manuscript that Cabeza de Vaca, Dorantes, and Castillo Maldonado supposedly wrote and sent to the Audiencia of Santo Domingo in 1539 is summarized in chapters 1–7 of Gonzalo Fernández de Oviedo's *Historia General y Natural de las Indias* [1535–52].[66] Most sixteenth and seventeenth century chroniclers also include a section on this expedition, certainly based on the *Naufragios.*[67]

Cabeza de Vaca and his companions arrived at San Miguel de Culiacán in May 1536 escorted by a soldier who while conducting a slave raid spotted them near the Petatlán River. After meeting Governor Guzmán in Compostela they continued down to Mexico City and met Viceroy Mendoza and Hernán Cortés on July 23.[68] Modern scholars have engaged in numerous controversies concerning the truthfulness and accuracy of the stories they told, the route they followed from Mal Hado to Petatlán,[69] and more recently, the character of the *Naufragios* as a particular form of colonial discourse;[70] but the skepticism that has surrounded these reports since the nineteenth century was absent in the sixteenth. The seven populous cities the adventurers heard about but did not see seemed to confirm the rumors that had put Guzmán on the road in 1529 and therefore gave rise to a new, frenzied exploring activity.[71] Whether or not the Pueblo settlements are the cities these men referred to, as is generally sustained, their amazing stories did trigger the general belief that a promising urban world lay hidden north of New Spain.

Friar Gerónimo de Mendieta wrote that in January 1538 Antonio de Ciudad Rodrigo, provincial of the Franciscan order, sent three friars by sea to explore the north Pacific coast, and other friars overland across Nueva Galicia.[72] One of them, he asserted, heard tell of a remote land where cotton-garbed people lived in houses several stories high, a clear index of farming civilization from the Spanish perspective. That, he affirmed, is why Friar Marcos de Niza, who had just arrived from Peru and Guatemala to succeed Ciudad Rodrigo, set out in 1539 to trace the oft-mentioned urban region. The same episode is retold with less detail in a *relación* that a Jesuit friar, Gerónimo de Zárate Salmerón, wrote around 1629,[73] and it is repeated in a 1792 chronicle by Friar Juan Domingo Arricuita, though the latter names only two traveling friars—Juan de la Ascensión and Pedro Nadal—and names Viceroy Mendoza instead of Ciudad Rodrigo as the one sending out the party.[74] No firsthand testimony concerning these excursions has come to us. Nor does the chronicle by conqueror Pedro de Castañeda Nájera, the most detailed account of Vázquez de Coronado's journey and its precedents, mention any such expedition.

The first well-documented undertaking aimed at reaching the "Seven Cities" is that of Marcos de Niza, commissioned by Viceroy Antonio de Mendoza. His "Relación" (1539) and the instructions he received have been published many times and are preserved in the Archivo General de Indias, together with several letters and other related, minor documents. Vázquez de Coronado had replaced Guzmán as governor of Nueva Galicia late in 1538, and his most immediate commitment was precisely the detailed organization of Niza's excursion.[75] Like the viceroy, he was deeply interested in discovering the wondrous universe the north apparently concealed. After dispatching the friar from Culiacán on March 7, 1539,[76] Vázquez de Coronado led an ambitious though failed expedition to Topia (Topira), another reputedly wealthy province northeast of Culiacán.[77] Back in Compostela, in September he received Niza's reports about four neighboring kingdoms never before visited by Christians. Niza was indeed the first European ever to reach the Pueblo area, and in fact, his report is the first document to contain the word "Cíbola"—a phonetic transcription of the name the Zuñi Indians called themselves: *Shi-wi-nah*.[78]

Friar Niza only mentions in his *relación* some of the names of the places he visited, although he could have learned more, as he took along natives from Petatlán, together with Estevan and various Indians who had followed Cabeza de Vaca back to New Spain. He followed roughly the coastal route opened centuries earlier along the corridor established by the Aztatlán cultural complex through Sinaloa, Sonora, and Arizona, stopping first at Petatlán, where he left Friar Onorato, his only Spanish companion. After meeting some Indians from the "island" where Cortés had recently been (that is, Baja California),[79] nothing remarkable happened until he trekked for four days across an uninhabited area (*despoblado*), after which he came across people who had never seen or heard of Europeans. These people indicated that five days' journey heading inland, the mountains gave way to a country with huge settlements, but the friar preferred to stick to the coast and visit the place on the way back. From the "reasonably large" village of Vacapa that he stumbled on next, Niza sent messengers to the seashore while Estevan rushed ahead to reconnoiter the country, promising to mark his path with crosses of varying sizes to indicate the magnitude of his discoveries. A few days later Estevan's envoys returned, bringing crosses the size of a man, and for the first time, news alluding to "the land people call Cíbola."[80] From that moment on, natives would not cease to provide glowing reports of wealthy provinces teeming with cities of multistory stone houses inhabited by people who dressed in cotton and wore turquoise jewelry: Cíbola, Marata, Acus, and Totonteac.

Accompanied by an ever-growing Indian escort, Niza traversed densely populated lands and a couple of despoblados, making a brief detour to take a look at the coast. One day's distance from Cíbola he encountered a group of Estevan's companions hastily running away, as the ex-slave and most of his vanguard party had been killed. Despite the implied danger, the friar pushed forward until he saw Cíbola from afar in June 1539; he took possession of the land and turned back immediately, stopping just outside Vacapa to cast a quick glance at the cluster of settlements he had heard about, before he first reached Vacapa on his way north.

Marcos de Niza's report was favorable enough to renew the viceroy's determination to colonize the newly discovered land, a task he entrusted to Francisco Vázquez de Coronado on January 6, 1540, simultaneously appointing Hernando de Alarcón to travel by sea as a marine rear guard. Hernán Cortés, Nuño de Guzmán, Hernando de Soto, and Pedro de Alvarado also claimed the right to take on this conquest, adducing the contracts or appointments they had previously signed or received, either to explore the Mar del Sur or to colonize and govern a particular territory north of New Spain.[81] The legal process concerning these claims[82] ended with a royal charter issued on July 10, 1540, which proclaimed that neither Niza's excursion nor Vázquez de Coronado's ongoing expedition violated the jurisdiction formerly granted to any of the discordant captains.[83] Still, Viceroy Mendoza reached a compromise with Alvarado, too influential among the conquerors to be simply dismissed. They signed a contract on November 29 that conferred on Alvarado one-fifth of all the benefits resulting from the conquests achieved by Vázquez de Coronado up to that point, and half the benefits resulting from those that he might still achieve thereafter;[84] but Alvarado died in 1541 fighting against Cazcán rebels in the Mixtón War, so the agreement never came into effect.

Vázquez de Coronado's expedition, like Niza's excursion, is fairly well documented. Three general accounts by participant soldiers covering the whole expedition survive. Two of them, the narrative by Juan Jaramillo and the anonymous "Relación del suceso," are almost contemporary with the events, but the chronicle that Pedro de Castañeda Nájera wrote some twenty years later is the most extensive. Additionally we have several letters and short anonymous reports referring to particular events or periods of the enterprise.[85]

Vázquez de Coronado left Compostela late in February 1540, leading some three hundred soldiers of European origin and nearly one thousand Indian allies from Central Mexico, among them many Tlaxcalans—as the *Lienzo de Tlaxcala* shows[86]—and a group of Tlatelolco natives led by their own governor, Don

Alonso Cuauhnochtli, and his successor, Don Martín Cuauhtzin Tlacateccatl, both portrayed in plate 1 of the *Códice de Tlatelolco*.[87]

At Culiacán, Vázquez de Coronado parted with the bulk of the expedition, moving ahead on April 22 with a small mounted vanguard, including Friar Marcos de Niza, that reached Hawikuh (Zuñi) by July 7. This was the town where Estevan had been killed and which Niza had viewed from afar in 1539. The friar misheard the name as "Ahacus" from a Zuñi Indian he found living among the Pimas on his way to the Seven Cities. Frederick W. Hodge has proved that the friar's description of Cíbola corresponds to this pueblo, abandoned in 1670. Instead of calling it "Ahacus," however, Niza referred to it by the name Zuñis called themselves: *Shi-wi-nah* (Cíbola).[88]

In the meantime Hernando de Alarcón sailed north to the mouth of the Colorado River, and having lost track of his overland companions, followed its course until he finally decided to return, leaving a note should they ever reach the same place. When the infantry arrived in Hawikuh by November of 1540, Vázquez de Coronado had already sent Pedro Tovar to reconnoiter the Tusayán (Hopi) Pueblos of eastern Arizona and García López de Cárdenas to explore the Tizón River (Grand Canyon). He had also commissioned Hernando de Alvarado to travel east to the Rio Grande and beyond into the prairies, following an Indian from Cicuyé (Pecos) who offered his services as guide. Alvarado visited Acuco (Acoma), Taos, and Tiguex (today Bernalillo, in the central Rio Grande valley). During this excursion an Indian he nicknamed "The Turk" volunteered to take the Spaniards to Quivira, a riverside kingdom toward the northeast, rich in gold and extremely elegant. Following Alvarado's advice, the entire army moved to Tiguex for the winter toward the end of the month, but the soldiers' abuses provoked a widespread revolt that lasted until March 1541. Once in control of the situation and having burned a hundred "rebels" alive, Governor Vázquez de Coronado sent two captains to explore Quirix and led an expedition himself to Quivira. Between April and July the party wandered across the plains from eastern New Mexico to Oklahoma, and perhaps Kansas, guided by "The Turk," who said the Quivirans navigated a river "two leagues wide" in large canoes and had plenty of gold which they called *acochis*. At the place the guide identified as Quivira—a modest peasant settlement beside a moderate-sized river—no metal wealth appeared, so the Spaniards made the Indian confess to have purposefully led them astray and then garroted him.[89]

Janet Lecompte argues that this execution was the dreadful result of a misunderstanding, as "The Turk" may have been referring to the lower Mississippi River, the only one around that could be described as two leagues wide. After all, the Knight of Elvas, chronicler of the De Soto expedition to Florida that reached present-day Arkansas around the same period, described Qwapaw Indians crossing the Mississippi in large canoes with canopies. In addition, she contends, the word that the Wichita Indians living in that region had for metal was precisely *acochis* (ha:kwicis).[90]

Vázquez de Coronado returned to Tiguex in October 1541, and in April 1542, he was just as ready to abandon the province as most of the prospective settlers he ruled. By June of that year the expedition returned to Culiacán, leaving behind a Portuguese soldier, Andrés do Campo, and three missionaries, Juan de Padilla and two more whose names are not clear.[91] The missionaries were martyred at the hands of the Indians, but the soldier escaped and lived as a shaman before returning to New Spain five years later, walking from Quivira through the prairies and across the Sierra Madre Oriental until he arrived in Pánuco. A number of Indians from Zapotlán also remained among the Pueblo Indians.[92] Vázquez de Coronado continued to govern Nueva Galicia until September 1544. His residencia charged him with incompetence and dereliction of duty, but he was found not guilty and continued to serve as a minor public official until his death.[93]

For over a century historians and anthropologists have debated the routes that Cabeza de Vaca, Niza, and Vázquez de Coronado followed.[94] Since some of the kingdoms mentioned in their accounts, such as Corazones, Señora, and Totonteac, do not appear in seventeenth century reports of missionaries who traversed the area, many assume they lied about the size and complexity of aboriginal cultures. Daniel Reff believes that such mistrust may not be justified, as the archaeological record does indicate for the early years of those accounts the existence of complex sociopolitical structures and a larger population than observed in later times.[95] Sixteenth century Spaniards, Charles Gibson asserts, were quite conscious of settlement size distinctions for both legal and ideological reasons.[96] Therefore it is significant that Friar Marcos referred to *villas* or *pueblos* as opposed to *ranchos* or *aldeas*. Moreover, as Reff contends, the fact that he reported only three despoblados during his entire journey suggests that in 1539, northwestern Sonora and southern Arizona retained a sizeable population, possibly related to the Hohokam culture, which, if we trust Niza's descriptions, may have collapsed not in the first half of the fifteenth century as is generally believed, but much later.[97]

The polemic concerning the credibility of Niza's report centers on whether he really reached Pueblo Indian country. This question was already posed in his day, as he abandoned Vázquez de Coronado in August 1540 to escape the expeditionaries' rage at the sight of Cíbola. Hernán Cortés and Vázquez de Coronado raised bitter accusations against the friar, whose report they considered a fabrication.[98] In modern times, Bancroft, Bandelier, Horgan, Undreiner, and Reff have sustained the veracity of his *relación*[99] against such authors as Wagner, who considered the friar a victim of the overexcited imagination of his time;[100] Sauer, who thought the report was fabricated to block Cortés and other pretenders to the north,[101] or Hallenbeck, who adduced as proof of Niza's mendacity his incapacity to provide Vázquez de Coronado with clear distance indications.[102]

Whether Niza actually beheld Cíbola is not all that important for this book. What really matters is the strong influence that native stories concerning a province with seven luxurious and bountiful cities exerted over the Spaniards, be it Cíbola, or, as a decade earlier with Guzmán's Oxitipar informant, one of unrecorded name. In any case, Reff's contention that most doubts surrounding the *relación* reflect a misreading derived from erroneous presuppositions about aboriginal cultures and the sixteenth century Spaniards' capacity to observe seems correct.[103] Academic distrust of Niza's account also derives from a modern tendency to overlook the fact that Mexico City, the metropolis that Cortés saw and destroyed, did not recover its splendor until several decades later. David J. Weber, for example, regards Friar Marcos's claim that Cíbola was the best of the discoveries as "an extravagant recommendation from a man who knew firsthand the wealth of Mexico and Peru."[104] To think, as Weber did, that someone who saw the city in the 1530s and early 1540s for the first time had the same impression about it that Cortés's soldiers had in 1521 is an anachronism. As Bandelier remarked, the friar never saw Mexico-Tenochtitlan before it was destroyed, so when he spoke of Mexico he certainly referred to the colonial city, which in 1539 had a much smaller population than it did in 1521.[105] Likewise, as Reff contends, Niza did not follow the same trails as Cabeza de Vaca and Vázquez de Coronado did. Rather than following Estevan's lead, he relied on Indian guides and informants who probably took him along the same coastal route that frequent travelers to Cíbola also used, from Culiacán to Vacapa, whereas Vázquez de Coronado traveled inland, retracing Cabeza de Vaca's footsteps in Sinaloa and Sonora.[106] Therefore his inability to provide a precise orientation when he accompanied Vázquez de Coronado. Finally, the dazzling image of the Seven Cities that Niza produced is very much a transcription of his Indian informants' perception, as he was more restrained when describing what he himself saw. When he reported a pearl-rich island near Petatlán, for example, he clearly stated that he saw no pearls. All the grandiose descriptions of Cíbola he included after Vacapa came explicitly from reports by local natives and the envoys Estevan had sent back. The only elements Niza claimed to have seen are the turquoise ornaments and clothing made of cotton and hides that people wore in the many villages he came across after that point. Of the villages, he merely remarked on their large size, and in some cases, their practice of irrigation agriculture.[107] His own testimonial description comes at the end of the document and is very subdued: "I followed my way until I beheld Cíbola. It sits on a plain at the foot of a round hill. It has the beautiful look of a town, the best I have seen in these parts; houses are as the Indians said, made all of stone with their stories (*sobrados*) and flat roofs (*azuteas*), insofar I could appreciate from a nearby hill I stood on to see. Its population is larger than Mexico City's.... And telling the nearby Indian rulers I had as companions how good Cíbola seemed to me, they answered that it was the smallest of the Seven Cities, and that Tototonteac is much larger and better ... and has no end."[108] Niza did not want to enter the city, as he feared being killed like Estevan, so he decided to return immediately to Mexico City and spread the good news he had heard. It is precisely this confidence in the word of "the other" that matters here, since the construction of Nuevo México resulted largely from the Spanish acceptance of native views.

After Vázquez de Coronado returned from Cíbola, New Spain's northern frontier lived through a prolonged period of war that only ended around 1590. The Mixtón War, or Cazcán rebellion, contemporaneous with Vázquez de Coronado's adventure, was personally stifled by Viceroy Mendoza with the collaboration of numerous Indians from Central Mexico. The ensuing precarious peace did not last long. The opening of cart roads and the raiding for Indian slaves[109] that accompanied the discovery of silver mines in Xaltepec and Espíritu Santo (1543), Guanajuato (1544), Zacatecas (1546), and other places, provoked the fierce response of Indian groups such as the Zacatecos, Guachichiles, Guamares, Pames, and Tepehuanes.[110]

Like the Mixtón uprising, the Chichimeca War—an intermittent but ongoing struggle fought over forty years against these resisting tribes—induced the Spaniards to encourage a wide migration of Tlaxcalans, Mexicans, Tarascans, and other natives from the south to establish frontier peasant colonies aimed at enticing rebel Chichimecas into farming and obedience.[111] This was at once a peace effort and a means to secure laborers for the mines. Natives from Michoacán had lived in the city of Zacatecas since 1550, and by the beginning of the seventeenth century most mine workers in the city were Indians who spoke Náhuatl and Tarascan; many had fought on the Spanish side on the Chichimec frontier before settling down as day-laborers.[112] Cultural dislocation and readjustment in the hybrid communities that were thus constituted, as well as the expectations created among conquered groups eligible as buffer communities for the frontier, contributed to shape Nuevo México fantasies.

According to the municipal council records of Zacatecas, Juan de Tolosa discovered the first silver mines in the area on September 8, 1546. Three years later a massive flow of immigrants had turned Zacatecas into the second largest city of the viceroyalty; although it did not receive the title of *Ciudad* (City) until 1585,[113] it immediately became the principal headquarters for the organization of northward exploration which, for the following decades, targeted above all precious metal prospecting and exploitation. In 1554 Francisco de Ibarra set out from this city in pursuit of new silver veins, financed by his uncle Diego de Ibarra, one of Zacatecas's first settlers, who had quickly amassed a fortune in mining and cattle raising, as had others who would later figure in the conquest of Nuevo México.[114] In the following years Ibarra discovered the mines of Fresnillo, Sombrerete (also called Villa de Llerena since 1569), Chalchihuites, and San Martín, thereby starting a new colonization effort momentarily interrupted by a Zacateco-Guachichil rebellion in 1561.[115]

Documents concerning events after the rebels' defeat by Pedro de Ahumada are confusing regarding dates and sequence. Nevertheless, chronological precision is not as important here as the fact that, between 1561 and 1563, Francisco de Ibarra sought what he explicitly called "the ancient Mexicans' place of origin," which in those days was named Copala, according to the soldier-chronicler Baltasar de Obregón[116] and other documents discussed in chapter 6. As a result of this endeavor, Ibarra conquered a wide territory that he named Nueva Vizcaya, comprising the area he had tenuously settled since 1554 and all the unconquered lands beyond Nueva Galicia he might later subdue. Despite this goal, this and other related mid-century campaigns over the Zacatecas-Durango region—occupied by the Chalchihuites culture in preconquest times—are not usually connected to the emergence of Nuevo México in modern historiography. But soldiers in these campaigns spoke of another Mexico, and even a "new Mexico," which they defined as the land of Aztec origins. Some of their letters and testimonies associated this place of origin with lakes surrounded by villages or rancherías that they saw or heard about in the region. Moreover, the remnants of ancient farming civilizations located near the silver mines discovered in the 1550s and 1560s, such as La Quemada or Chalchihuites–Alta Vista, were apparently taken as evidence of the truth of Nahua migration stories and gave the final blow to European medieval imagery.

The importance of these mid-century campaigns for the reification of Nuevo México can be inferred on the basis of the following events. Ibarra wrote to the viceroy on June 6, 1562, that he had set out from San Martín with Friar Cintos (Jacinto de San Francisco)[117] and another monk to confirm repeated rumors about Copala, which they had been unable to verify due to pouring rains. The letter also informed the viceroy that the friars were staying near a certain valley they had discovered, "gathering the people . . . so they will continue to be at peace as they are now" and requested a hundred soldiers to complete the inspection because "we have news that the land is densely populated and [its residents are] dressed [in clothes] and it is rich in supplies, with adobe and stone houses, and its inhabitants are wholly settled."[118] Unfortunately, the letter records neither the date when this journey began nor the name of the valley.

Judging from Ibarra's 1574 *Memorial* and other reports, this could be the same expedition during which, accompanied by a group of Franciscan friars, he founded Nombre de Dios in the valley he named San Juan (May–June 1562), aimed at attracting the recently defeated Chichimecas to Christian life. An account in Náhuatl concerning the services of a group of Mexican and Tarascan

Indians in the founding of Nombre de Dios suggests the expeditions are one and the same. It asserts that Francisco de Vara (Ibarra) mandated the settlement process but left before it was accomplished, leaving behind three of the four friars involved—Gerónimo de Mendoza, Pedro de Espinareda, Diego de la Cadena, and Jacinto de San Francisco—to supervise the full establishment of the village.[119]

In response to this and other news, Viceroy Luis de Velasco appointed Ibarra governor and captain general for the exploration, conquest, and settlement of the land beyond the mines of San Martín and Avino. The main goal of this assignment, as the respective ordinance stipulated (July 24, 1562), was to bring under the Crown the large settlements where people "wore cotton clothing" that natives in the valley of San Juan had described.[120] In a letter dated May 1563, Velasco pinpointed the settlements as being in the thriving silver province of Copala.[121] It must be remembered that such was the name recorded in several testimonies as the place of origin of "the ancient culguas mexicanos," that is, the Aztecs. In compliance, Ibarra recruited a new group of volunteer soldiers in San Martín, including interpreters from the region who spoke the Náhuatl and Chichimeca languages, as well as soldiers who had been to Cíbola with Vázquez de Coronado. Toward early March 1563, after founding his soon-to-be capital, Durango, in the valley of Guadiana, he led a second expedition to Copala.[122] Once again Ibarra failed to find it, but he discovered the mines of Indehé, Santa Bárbara, and Coneto and then followed a female guide into the western mountains aiming to locate the large and populous town he had repeatedly missed. The village of Topia, or Topiamé, that he sighted near the end of April, had in his opinion the look of another Mexico,[123] so he brought his army from San Juan and took it over.

After the successful attack on Topia, Ibarra crossed the mountains and descended to the coastal plain, arriving at San Miguel de Culiacán early in 1564. His reports of 1574, Baltasar de Obregón's chronicle, and Antonio Ruiz's report on the conquest of Sonora and Sinaloa narrate this part of his endeavors.[124] Despite discrepancies among these accounts, it is clear that the governor headed north from Culiacán across the Mayo and Yaqui valleys, venturing into almost unexplored territory until reaching the ruins of the ancient city of Casas Grandes (Paquimé).[125] Either on departure or on his way back, he founded the village of San Juan Bautista de Cinaloa (June 1564), whence he would later reconquer the neighboring province of Chametla (1565).[126]

Francisco de Ibarra held the governorship of Nueva Vizcaya until his death, but none of the places he conquered matched his idea of what Nuevo México should actually look like, not even the province of Topia that he had once considered the most likely candidate. Other captains and missionaries took up his quest, as the slave-raiding and evangelizing incursions brought renewed reports of cities and people dressed in cotton beyond Santa Bárbara (modern Parral in Chihuahua), the northernmost Spanish enclave until 1581.

Cíbola Becomes Nuevo México

The comprehensive Ordinances for New Discovery and Settlement issued on July 13, 1573,[127] mark a fundamental change in the organization of territorial expansion. Conquest was to be replaced by pacification, which meant that grand military expeditions such as those of Cortés and Vázquez de Coronado were banned in favor of small-scale, peaceful settlement enterprises directed by missionaries, who should avoid the exercise of force except in self-defense. It was within this legal framework and through the missionizing zeal of a few friars that old Cíbola reappeared before Spanish eyes, now under the name of Nuevo México. Other royal charters similar in character had been issued previously, like that of December 30, 1549, prohibiting new conquest enterprises in the Indies.[128] Such a general ban was, of course, nothing more than wishful thinking, as New World colonists were not prepared to cancel their ambitions. In this sense the 1573 ordinance was much more realistic.

Between 1580 and 1590 four small expeditions, two organized by missionaries and two by lay adventurers, entered the region that later became Nuevo México, but none took permanent hold. In 1581, encouraged by Spanish residents of the northernmost mining centers in Nueva Vizcaya, the Franciscan friar Agustín Rodríguez recruited two fellow monks, Juan de Santa María and Francisco López, to evangelize the lands earlier visited by Francisco Vázquez de Coronado. Leaving Santa Bárbara in early June on a journey that lasted nearly a year, the adventurous friars brought an escort of nine soldiers headed by Francisco Sánchez de Chamuscado, and nineteen Indian guides, interpreters, and bearers.[129]

For a couple of months the expeditionaries journeyed north along the rivers Conchos and Grande (which they named Guadalquivir, today called Río Bravo in Mexico), being probably the first Spaniards to visit Acoma and Zuñi since 1542. According to Baltasar de Obregón and the *relación* by Hernando Gallego, beyond the Conchos River they heard of the miraculous healing performed by Cabeza de Vaca and the brutal acts of soldiers on previous expeditions. To counterbalance such memories they promised no harm would ensue from their visit and distributed crosses, instructing the natives to display them to every Spaniard they might come across in the future to avoid mistreatment. However, to gain Indian confidence was not as easy as Rodríguez imagined. In December 1581 (or January 1582) either Friar Francisco López or Juan de Santa María was killed at a place called Puaray in the Pecos River area. Most expedition members returned to New Spain at this point, and once in Santa Bárbara (April 15, 1582), reported that the surviving friars, who had preferred to stay behind, might be in danger.[130]

As a consequence, the Franciscan order prepared a small rescue mission headed by Antonio de Espejo.

This modest rescue party, organized from the city of Durango, lacked royal approval and official funding, though the governor of Nueva Vizcaya granted a late authorization after its departure that endorsed the permission initially given by the major of Cuatro Ciénegas, Juan de Ontiveros.[131] Four soldiers and two friars, Bernardino Beltrán and Pedro de Heredia, were all the men Espejo took along. They left from San Bartolomé (today Allende, in Chihuahua) in winter 1582, and having confirmed that the friars they had come to rescue had been killed, they headed west from Zuñi-Cíbola in search of a golden lake they never found.[132] Back in Santa Bárbara in September 1583, Espejo wrote a long report stating that he had discovered fifteen densely populated provinces, which all together he named Nueva Andalucía,[133] but other people continued to refer to the place as "el Nuevo México."[134] One of his companions, Diego Pérez de Luxán, also wrote an extensive report.[135]

Despite the little attention it has received compared with the widespread dissemination of Espejo's journey, the Friar Agustín Rodríguez incident is fundamental. Not only was it he who first applied the term "Nuevo México" to the land formerly called Cíbola, which the friar renamed San Felipe del Nuevo Mexico, but also his failed mission can be considered the immediate antecedent of Juan de Oñate's definitive conquest of Nuevo México.

In November 1582, before Espejo initiated his unauthorized *entrada*, Rodrigo del Río de Losa, lieutenant captain general of Nueva Galicia, requested of the king a reinforcement of at least three hundred soldiers to punish the murder of Rodríguez's comrade. The answer came as a royal charter, dated April 19, 1583, ordering the negotiation of a capitulación with a private individual who would be commissioned to assemble, at his own expense, a large and powerful army to subdue the province.[136] Although most petitions submitted to the viceregal and metropolitan authorities in the following years, seeking the commission, were rejected (those of Cristóbal Martín, Francisco Díaz de Vargas, Antonio de Espejo, Baltasar de Obregón, and Gaspar Castaño de Sosa), three contracts were indeed signed. Two never came into effect and the third is the one finally entrusting Juan de Oñate with the enterprise.[137]

The first of these never executed capitulaciones, granted to Juan Bautista de Lomas y Colmenares, was approved by Viceroy Villamanrique on March 11, 1589. The petitioner, a rich resident of the mines of Las Nieves, in Nueva Galicia, promised to assemble an army, absorbing the expense in full, receiving in exchange the governorship and general captaincy of Nuevo México for six generations, with a salary of eight thousand ducats, the title of count or marquis for himself and his offspring, and the right to fortify harbors in the Northern and

Southern seas.[138] Neither the king nor the Consejo de Indias ever confirmed this agreement. Therefore, Viceroy Villamanrique's successor, Luis de Velasco, signed a new contract in 1592 with Francisco de Urdiñola, a rich and powerful captain (later appointed governor of Nueva Vizcaya) who amassed a large estate dedicated to cattle raising in Nueva Vizcaya and had recently been in charge of organizing the transfer of four hundred Tlaxcalteca families to establish buffer settlements on the northern frontier (1591). This contract did not come into effect because before departing, Urdiñola was arrested on charges of poisoning his wife.[139]

Although no official expedition into Nuevo México took place until Oñate's, a couple of illegal attempts occurred in the years immediately preceding his departure. In July 1590 Cristóbal Martín and Gaspar Castaño de Sosa, lieutenant governor of Nuevo León, led 170 persons from Nueva Almadén (today Monclova, in Nuevo León), including women and children, to colonize the now famous province. Captain Juan Morlete and fifty soldiers were immediately sent after the would-be colonists, who withdrew in March 1591 in compliance with a detention order presented against Castaño de Sosa.[140] A couple of years later, Francisco Leyva Bonilla and Juan de Humaña,[141] earlier sent by the governor of Nueva Vizcaya to fight against Indian rebels on the frontier, carried out their own illegal incursion.[142] Despite the obscurity surrounding this entrada, it is known that a Pedro Cazorla was unsuccessfully sent after the insubordinates; also, that once they entered "unknown" territory, Humaña killed his comrade Leyva Bonilla.[143]

Around 1629 the Jesuit friar Gerónimo de Zárate Salmerón wrote that Oñate considered the remains of horses and iron objects he found in Quivira as sound evidence that Humaña was killed there. He also mentioned the only three survivors of this adventure: the Indian Jusepe, a Mulatto woman, and a Spaniard, Alonso Sánchez, who established himself in the region and by 1599 was enjoying the natives' respect.[144] Commenting on this text almost a century later, Friar Juan Armando Niel deplored its imprecision regarding the 1590–95 entradas, considering that the Indian Jusepe had served as a guide in the expeditions Oñate commanded after 1595 and was certainly alive in Zárate's day.[145]

Juan de Oñate's assignment to lead the conquest of Nuevo México was a difficult and much-interrupted process. Son of Cristóbal de Oñate, ex-governor of Nueva Galicia, Don Juan was married to a woman who was the daughter of Captain Juan de Tolosa, who had discovered the mines of Zacatecas; granddaughter of Hernán Cortés; and great-granddaughter of Moctezuma.[146] Oñate lived in Zacatecas, dedicated himself to mining and cattle raising, and was among the richest men in New Spain. It was no doubt because of his enormous fortune and kinship ties to such illustrious families that, as Simmons observes, Viceroy

Velasco encouraged him to apply for the post.[147] His appointment and departure, however, were much delayed due to the viceroy's succession and the late consideration of another petitioner.

Based on a few ordinances that authorized or banned Oñate's advance, most historians since Bancroft provide discordant accounts. Nevertheless the chronology can be surmised on the basis of Gaspar de Villagrá's *Historia de la Nueva México* (1610);[148] the minutes recording the act of possession of the territory, celebrated on April 30, 1598; the *Memorial de Nuevo México* that either Oñate himself or one of his officers compiled in 1602; a general evaluation of New Mexico's situation written in 1602 by Viceroy Gaspar de Zúñiga y Acevedo; another report, maybe also by the viceroy, covering the years 1597–99; and a *relación* that Oñate dictated to his secretary Juan Gutiérrez Bocanegra in 1601.[149]

According to the "Traslado de la posesión," the king signed a charter appointing Oñate governor and captain general of Nuevo México on June 21, 1595. Viceroy Velasco transmitted the order in August 24[150] and then summoned Oñate to court to sign the corresponding capitulaciones on September 21.[151] Meanwhile, the new viceroy, Zúñiga y Acevedo, had been appointed and had arrived at Veracruz on September 18. Before the succession ceremony took place in November, the officials discussed the issue by mail.[152] As a result, Zúñiga y Acevedo allowed Oñate to begin preparations for the journey, taking to Santa Bárbara the people he had recruited in Zacatecas. This occurred on October 21, but the new viceroy had to read the contract and confirm his approval, which did not happen until December 15.[153]

Oñate's original petition is lost but an American merchant, Josiah Gregg, saw it and wrote a summary in 1844.[154] Oñate was offering to recruit two hundred men at his own expense to serve in the dual role of soldiers and colonists, as well as to purchase the necessary food and clothing and take enough weapons, mining and blacksmith tools, medicine, seeds, plows, goods to trade with the Indians, and other items to meet the colonists' requirements. In exchange, he asked for the title of Adelantado, Governor, and General Captain, thirty leagues of land complete with vassals, a yearly salary of eight thousand ducats, and a mining tribute exemption. Viceroy Zúñiga y Acevedo approved the contract on December 15, 1595, but reduced Oñate's salary and tempered the legal powers and tribute privileges originally granted. He also ordered everything to be ready in Santa Bárbara by January 1596 rather than at the end of March.[155]

This deadline to finish up the recruitment campaign and preliminary preparations reveals the urgency the colonial authorities felt to secure a territory that—as the ever more frequent unauthorized entradas of the previous decade and numerous rejected petitions demonstrate—remained a potent lure for the colonizing ambitions of private adventurers. Because frontier people would not let go of the desire to appropriate this highly attractive region, it was imperative to incorporate them under an officially controlled plan, lest they organize their own autonomous enterprises and test the authority of the Crown and its viceregal representatives. In addition, the shattering of the Great Armada that Philip II had sent against Queen Elizabeth I in 1588 had left the northern frontier dangerously exposed,[156] because now there was nothing to block the establishment of other European colonies on the Atlantic coast of North America. This sense of defenselessness led to renewed fears that the English and French could settle the heart of the continent and threaten New Spain's mining districts and even Spanish trade with China and the Moluccas.[157] The same fears had led Cuba's governor, Pedro Menéndez de Avilés, between 1560 and 1573, to insist on the exploration of the north. Thus, if the defense policy had at first been centered on the sea and the fortification of Florida, the strategy now shifted toward achieving an effective inland colonization over the unknown area extending between Florida and California, which, according to Baltasar de Obregón, comprised the provinces of Cíbola, Paquimé, Quivira, and Nuevo México.[158]

Despite these imperial needs and even after Oñate accepted his assignment under the modified *capitulaciones* in Mexico City on December 16, 1595, starting on his way to Santa Bárbara in January 1596, he was again delayed. In February 1596, Viceroy Zúñiga y Acevedo reported on the state of Nuevo México's affairs to the king, hoping no doubt that his decisions would be simply acknowledged and his letters filed away. But the Consejo de Indias had made its own choice, granting the enterprise to another Spanish aspirant, Pedro Ponce de León. Therefore the king issued a royal charter (May 8, 1596) ordering Oñate to desist until the council could ponder both proposals and issue new instructions.[159] On June 6, 1596, the viceroy commissioned one Lope de Ulloa to visit Oñate in Zacatecas and determine whether he met the stipulated requirements. Oñate was notified in September of the order to stop preparations but was never told the real reason.[160] A series of complications ensuing from this *visita*—that need not be examined in detail here—delayed Oñate for almost another year, a period during which he nevertheless reached the valley of San Bartolomé, near Santa Bárbara. In the meantime, Ponce de León was turned down and it was decided that Oñate's army should be submitted to a second *visita*, which was conducted in the presence of the viceroy between December 1597 and January 1598 by Juan de Frías Salazar.[161]

It was January 26, 1598, when Viceroy Zúñiga y Acevedo issued his definitive approval and Oñate finally ventured with his company into *"tierra incognita."* They followed a new route, taking a more direct northward trajectory from the Conchos River than previous explorers had followed (map 6).[162] By April 20, the company reached the Rio Grande and ten days later, at the site of today's city of El Paso, Oñate celebrated the ceremony of possession that placed Nuevo México under the Spanish Crown.[163] Indians in the region took precautions: shortly after the ceremony a group of Athabascans came to the camp making the sign of the cross and saying *"manxo, manxo, micos, micos"* for *mansos* (tame) and *amigos* (friends).[164] They have been known ever since as Manso Indians. The anecdote indicates that local people had not forgotten the misfortune that ensued from the Spanish presence and were sufficiently familiar with Spanish language and culture to try a seemingly effective way to avert it.

At this point Oñate divided his company. On May 1, 1598, he led a small vanguard along the Rio Grande. Toward the end of the month, beyond a large despoblado, he came across a different village every day, some abandoned.[165] Horgan asserts that this group of Pueblos in the southern Rio Grande valley, where Vázquez de Coronado had also been, was the cluster of settlements near Vacapa that Friar Marcos de Niza had stopped to see on his hasty retreat back to Mexico.[166] Finally, on June 30 the group reached present-day Santo Domingo, where Oñate summoned the chiefs of seven Pueblos to have them swear obedience (July 7) and took as guides two Mexican Indians whom the ill-fated colonizer Castaño de Sosa had left behind in 1590. As soon as the bulk of the company, with the carts and cattle, caught up (July 27), the expedition moved north and established the capital of the province at a Tewa settlement named Okeh Oweenge (August 11). They named the new capital, on the east bank of the Rio Grande near its confluence with the Chama, San Juan de los Caballeros.[167] The great kingdom of Nuevo México, however, had vanished behind adobe houses and deserted lands, as neither precious metals nor a city like Tenochtitlan were ever found.

On August 20, 1598, forty-five soldiers were caught planning desertion. Oñate prepared to teach them a lesson in loyalty, a death sentence followed by a general amnesty next day.[168] The efficacy of this punishment depended on its being followed by wider exploration. Therefore, as autumn fell, Oñate sent Vicente de Saldívar east to the prairies in search of Quivira while he led a small party west in search of the Mar del Sur. The events that ensued are dramatic. Vicente de Saldívar returned to San Juan on November 8, having found nothing he considered worth pursuing. His brother Juan de Saldívar, in charge of the capital, then took thirty-one soldiers west to give Oñate the disappointing news of Quivira. Stopping in Acoma, the only Pueblo that had not yet pledged its allegiance, Juan de Saldívar requested supplies from the chief, Zutacapan, thereby causing a local uprising with terrible consequences.[169]

Ramón Gutiérrez attributes this violent eruption at Acoma Pueblo to divergent Indian and Spanish views regarding exchange of goods, because the small amounts of water, wood, tortillas, and maize that the Indians gave as gifts, with the attendant obligations of reciprocation, the Spaniards thought was surrendered as tribute and consequently expected to receive more. Thus when Juan de Saldívar took eighteen soldiers to the top of Acoma mesa on December 4 to collect the flour he had requested, Indian warriors attacked them as unwanted intruders after an all-too-confident Spaniard had stolen a pair of turkeys and raped a woman.[170] To avenge the death of ten soldiers, two servants, and Captain Juan de Saldívar, Oñate sent a punitive expedition on January 12, 1599. Acoma surrendered twelve days later, having lost 800 lives, including men, women, and children, as well as 580 prisoners. Not satisfied with this result, Oñate imposed a merciless sentence on the entire town: every man over twenty-five was condemned to serve twenty-five years of personal labor and have one foot mutilated, while every woman over twelve and every man between twelve and twenty-five was subjected to twenty years of personal labor.[171]

After the Acoma rebellion, Oñate moved his capital across the Rio Grande, from San Juan (Okeh Oweenge) to Yunge Oweenge (renamed San Gabriel)[172] and wrote a report to the viceroy, dated March 2, 1599.[173] His request for reinforcements was not fulfilled until the following year (December 1600), but the seventy-three soldiers finally sent were too few and too late. The next month, hoping perhaps to attract more official attention and resources, Oñate dispatched an embassy with an optimistic report, and between June and November of 1600 took one hundred men across the prairies in search of Quivira, completely ignorant of the intrigues of one of his messengers, Captain Gasco de Velasco. This captain challenged his lofty description of the land in a secret report accusing the governor and colonists of cruelty, theft, and abuse against docile Indians.[174]

The secret report was duly sent to the king, accompanied by a summary of Oñate's letters. Concomitantly, three colonists who had forsaken Nuevo México were interrogated by Judge Francisco de Valverde y Mercado. The responses were inconclusive, but apparently colonists in San Gabriel were so outraged by the meager rewards they had obtained that Lieutenant Diego de Peñalosa, who had stayed in charge of Nuevo México's government in Oñate's absence, could not stop their flight. The town was virtually deserted when the governor returned from Quivira, so he sent Vicente de Saldívar to Madrid in 1602 to request men, money, and supplies. The deserters' complaints, however, had already reached the court and Nuevo México was now a problem for the viceroy, the Audiencia, and the king, who pondered in secrecy the charges against its governor and considered how to depose him without having the entire colony disintegrate. Meanwhile Oñate explored the land west of San Gabriel between October 1604 and April 1605, reaching the Río de Buena Esperanza (today Colorado River) and following it down to the Gulf of California.[175] This was the last enterprise Oñate was allowed to undertake. The following year, the viceroy was instructed to discreetly summon him to Mexico and forbid new explorations.

The fate of the province was pondered until December 1608, when a report by Friars Lázaro Jiménez and Isidro Ordóñez asserting that seven hundred Puebloans had been converted convinced the Crown to keep a foothold in the colony, without any further expansion. Only a governor directly appointed by the king and fifty married soldiers for defense and peacekeeping purposes would remain. Oñate was replaced by Pedro de Peralta and put on trial, as usual. Afterward, the colony survived precariously for decades without new resources or colonists until a widespread revolt exploded in August 1680, drawing the participation of most local indigenous groups and forcing Governor Otermín and the few survivors to flee. Successive governors held office in exile at El Paso, in Nueva Vizcaya, and made several attempts to recover the territory that was finally reconquered in 1696 by Diego de Vargas Zapata.[176]

Part II

CHAPTER FOUR

The Medieval Hypothesis

A number of mythical and legendary themes helped Spanish conquerors make sense of the strange realities they faced in the New World. One among these constellations of topics has repeatedly caught the attention of modern observers in academic and nonacademic circles: a series of European fabled places and beings from the classical and medieval imagination, often regarded as the main inspiration for Spanish conquerors who ventured across unknown lands north of New Spain in the sixteenth and seventeenth centuries. But such European marvels, at least in the case of New Mexico—usually cited as the paramount example to illustrate this hypothesis—did not constitute a significant element in the collective imagination. As noted in previous chapters, the conceptual matrix structuring colonial penetration in the north was, rather, indigenous local knowledge and cosmology. Why this has not been clearly perceived deserves a few methodological considerations.

Documentary sources available for the study of preconquest and colonial Spanish America comprise a wide variety of manuscripts and printed items, as well as pictorial records elaborated for all sorts of reasons by Indian, mestizo, or Spanish authors. Historians frequently classify documents dealing with historical developments and cultural description in two major categories, according to whether the main issues they address are Indian- or Spanish-related topics. This binary and artificial criterion has defined the use of sources and has obscured transcultural processes such as the one analyzed in this book.

The first category comprises what may be defined as Spanish-focused sources; that is, accounts written by Spanish soldiers and settlers who wanted or were legally bound to report on conquest and exploration endeavors as well as their own performance. Some of these texts were intended for publication, but many were addressed to particular authorities rather than the public at large. Such is the case of testimony rendered before the Audiencias on occasion of the customary residencia trials or any other litigation over conflicts derived from expeditionary action. The same goes for routine *hojas de méritos y servicios,* itemizing what bureaucrats and soldiers considered themselves to have done "in the service of Your Majesty," as well as innumerable petitions to the viceregal and metropolitan authorities. Within this Spanish-focused category fall the reports of priests and missionaries to their superiors, as well as lists of individuals enrolled and resources invested in specific journeys, together with the instructions issued to the captains in charge. The group essentially comprises documents by Spaniards speaking about Spanish actions, failures, and achievements, and representing and emphasizing Spanish interests, rights, and privileges.

The other category comprises Indian-focused sources produced in the late preconquest period and during colonial times. This category includes pictorial records of indigenous forms of knowledge, historical accounts, and encyclopedic works by Indians or Spaniards compiled with the purpose of understanding or conveying the native past, beliefs, and practices. It also comprises personal memoirs and official reports partially or significantly devoted to ethnographic description, native accounts of Indian participation in conquest campaigns, and a wide variety of bureaucratic and legal items springing from the administration of Indian affairs and the settlement of disputes between Spaniards and Indians or among Indians themselves.

Certainly, a fair amount of the available materials cannot be classified into either of these categories. Others could belong to both, like most chronicles written by official historians appointed by the Consejo de Indias to register past and current developments in the colonies. Rather than suggesting a comprehensive classification scheme for all documents, definitive and valid for every specialist, my point is to remark that modern studies seldom combine these two types of evidence. Too often, source analysis reproduces a colonialist discourse that divides sixteenth- to eighteenth-century Spanish American actors into natives and intruders, Indians and Spaniards, conquered and conquerors, as if they were clearly opposed. Hence, Indian-focused sources are customarily used in combination with archaeological evidence to understand and depict native cultures in both the pre- and post-Columbian periods. In turn, to trace back and reconstruct the enterprise of conquest, its colonial achievements, structures, routines, and institutions, historians rely primarily on Spanish-focused sources.

It is true that the sources vary in their narrative strategies, forms of registry, and topical preferences according to their authors' purpose and cultural roots. In this sense it is pertinent to trace the social space and discursive arena wherein New World documentary production is inscribed. It is useful to know when sources are bound to the notions and styles characteristic of an indigenous tradition and when they follow Western paradigms, even when native and European traditions frequently converge in one and the same document.[1] It is also important to ponder the political and personal agendas that inform the sources one uses in research and to determine whether they come from Indian, mestizo, or Spanish authors. Nevertheless, this taxonomic procedure, valid for purposes of analyzing individual items or historiographic tendencies, turns problematic when applied as the ruling principle to define the relevant documentary groups for a research topic. Because there is no strict correlation between the ethnic origin of an individual and his or her personal interests, political loyalties, and beliefs, it often becomes a screen that obscures the hybrid character of the societies resulting from Spanish conquest, as well as the dialogical processes shaping them.

It is natural that scholars attempting to understand Amerindian cultures at the moment of European arrival, and their previous development, should turn their attention to those materials portraying indigenous societies, and so they have done, drawing a great deal of information from painted books elaborated by Indian scribes, treatises on native peoples written or compiled by missionaries, and the village- or ethnic-based histories and annals that Indian and mestizo authors composed in the interests of personal or communal betterment.[2] Traditions dealing with places of ancestral origin and migration stand out among the themes these sources address; these traditions are also treated in a number of Spanish-focused sources, which modern scholars writing on preconquest native societies seldom use.

Several Mesoamerican peoples claimed their ancestors were foreign to the lands they occupied, having left their primeval abode at the mandate of a patron god, to begin a long "pilgrimage" that would eventually lead them to a glorious future in a faraway country. Literature dealing with the symbolic meaning, or the cultural and political significance of this topic in the preconquest era is abundant, while its importance for the colonial enterprise has rarely been addressed, suffocated as it is under the weight accorded to marvels and monsters coming from Europe.[3]

No doubt European sources concerning the New World frequently mention Amazons, the Fountain of Youth, and the lost island of Antillia, but in continental North America such figures and places of medieval legend only come up in isolated instances, implying no organic relation between the different undertakings in which they appeared. Although often invoked in a number of contexts, these legendary destinations never achieved the quality of meaningful links between dreamed expectation and actual experience that would have made separate endeavors appear as one continuous enterprise to the actors involved. In contrast, the Aztec/Mexica migration story connected the Spanish journeys of conquest in one single process: a series of expeditions carried out in separate geographic areas that shared nothing except their northerly position in relation to the Valley of Mexico and culminated in the founding of Nuevo México. As will be seen in chapters 5 and 6, the starting and ending locations of the Aztec/Mexica migration story, as well as the main stops and events along the route, provided a programmatic basis for Spanish conquest that the universe of fabulous referents brought from Europe failed to supply.

The widespread assumption that Spanish conquerors designated and thus assimilated new American realities in terms of their own traditions, frequently acting on the basis of imaginary geographies from European fantastic lore, is exemplified by the following quotation from Lewis Hanke: "The wealth of ideas and legends developed with such luxuriance during the Middle Ages was transferred at once to America; this medieval influence was especially marked during the early years [when conquerors] sought for the Fountain of Youth or tried to locate—in the general region of Nebraska and Dakota—the Seven Enchanted Cities which were believed to have been established by seven Portuguese bishops who had fled there when the Arabs invaded the Iberian Peninsula."[4]

Other twentieth century historians who have devoted themselves to tracing European thinking across the Atlantic have elaborated on similar considerations. They have concluded that besides a crusading drive deeply seated in the Spanish society of that period and a crude ambition for precious metals, the most powerful stimulus behind conquest was the desire "to find confirmation for the existence of the marvelous" as it had been imagined in the Middle Ages.[5] The argument is particularly prominent in a number of studies specifically concerned with the role of popular culture—literary and otherwise—in molding the personal attitude of early Spanish conquerors and the way in which they perceived and portrayed America. Some of these works are global overviews drawing evidence from the whole continent;[6] others are monographic accounts focused on concrete journeys, particular areas or motifs generally regarded as the most spectacular instances of the compelling force of popular European chimeras. Most remarkable is that this alleged capacity of European myth to encode and condition conquering practice became commonplace in most academic approaches to the history of early colonial America, and as a result it continues to be cited—even when rarely discussed at length—to explain the conquerors' drive, and to a certain extent, the institutional support they received.

The past two decades have seen an increasing number of ethnohistorical studies that emphasize indigenous agency and pursue the dialectic between European and American cultures. Nevertheless, this theoretical position still has little bearing on scholars studying the Spanish conquest of the American Southwest who pay little attention to Indian-focused sources indirectly related to the region of their interest and therefore tend to overlook the complex cultural negotiation that resulted in the adoption of native views and cultures by the European intruders.

Modern scholars have singled out two thematic sources as constitutive of the mental baggage of sixteenth century conquistadors:[7] on the one hand, legends and fantastic stories resulting from the struggle against the Moors on the Iberian Peninsula; on the other, a mixture of references from fictional romances of chivalry and themes rehabilitated from the classical world. Fernando Ainsa suggested in 1992 that Europeans saw the discovery of America as the fulfillment of the prophecy contained in Seneca's tragedy *Medea*, which predicted that one day the ends of the earth would be overstepped, and thus, many fantastic places and beings described in classical and medieval literature were expected to exist in the New World.[8]

The Fountain of Youth that led Juan Ponce de León and Hernando de Soto to explore Florida between 1512 and 1539,[9] for instance, can be traced back to an episode narrated by Homer on how Medea used water from a spring to rejuvenate Aeson, father of the Argonaut Jason. The theme became popular in the fifteenth century through the writings of Sir John Mandeville, who claimed to have discovered the *Fons Juventutis* near a remote city he called Polombe.[10]

Similarly, references to Amazons are found in colonial chronicles and in documents associated with various journeys around the continent. Ancient Greeks reported that a tribe of warlike women called Amazons existed in Asia Minor. Rumors of such women persisted throughout the Middle Ages, always on the margins of the world known to the Europeans, in the writings of travelers like Mandeville, Marco Polo, and Pedro Tafur.[11] At the beginning of the sixteenth century the women were incorporated into a couple of popular chivalry tales, *Las sergas de Esplandián* and *Lisuarte de Grecia,* both of which provided the story after which the peninsula of Baja California was named.[12] The Amazons were successively absorbed into a long-standing set of European traditions from Columbus in the Caribbean (1492–94), through Hernán Cortés and Nuño de Guzmán in New Spain (1521–40), to Pedro de Valdivia in Chile (1539) and Francisco de Orellana in the heart of South America (1541). Finally, the island of Antillia, which gave its name to the Caribbean archipelago, appears on several fourteenth and early fifteenth century European maps. It seems to have developed from Plato's tales of Atlantis but was later fused with a legend according to which, around the year a.d. 734, when the Moors entered Spain, seven Portuguese bishops fled with their people and sailed to an island where each founded a city.[13]

Applied to the study of North America, the medieval hypothesis, as I call it, has resulted in a general disregard of the promise Spanish conquerors saw in Náhuatl origin myths for accomplishing their own particular ambitions. The problem is not simply that a primary source of pursuable illusions is left virtually unexplored. The excessive emphasis on medieval European imaginaries has also obscured the importance of indigenous politico-territorial interests—embedded in those Nahua traditions—for the development of the colonial enterprise at a regional level. It is true that the Amazons and the Fountain of Youth were sought, respectively, during the early exploration of California and Florida. It is also possible that, as Enrique de Gandía and Beatriz Pastor Bodmer propose, Spanish explorers who went after the Seven Cities of Cíbola that Friar Marcos de Niza described had in mind the cities supposedly founded by the Portuguese bishops.[14] Nevertheless, even if these motifs occasionally triggered expeditionary action, they did not provide a programmatic basis for colonial expansion north of Mexico because, no matter how much repeated, they were often restricted each to a single line of exploration, working at best as individual obsessions. They faded away under the influence of native traditions.

The same probably holds true for South America, at least for certain themes regularly circulated during the early conquest period. The quest for El Dorado, a golden civilization sought between 1529 and 1617 in the Colombian Amazonia and Guyana—first in the regions of Guatavitá and Cundinamarca, and then along the Amazon and Orinoco rivers—is a good example of the displacement of European fantasies by local indigenous referents. It is possible that the golden lake where Spaniards believed a local chieftain, El Dorado, covered his body every day with a film of gold dust which he washed off at night, derived from a 1527 secondhand report on power transfer rituals among Chibcha Indians from present-day Colombia, which disappeared before the end of the fifteenth century with the virtual extermination of its practitioners at the hands of Muysca Indians from Bogotá. During the ceremony preceding the investiture of each new cacique, the cargo of a huge balsa raft laden with gold and emeralds was jettisoned in the center of Lake Guatavitá to propitiate the spirits. Meanwhile, the gold-dusted cacique bathed in the lake's waters. Although it has been noted that the legend of El Dorado may be originally related to such topics as the Aurea Chersonesus (the Malay Peninsula, abundant in gold, of Ptolemy's *Geography*) and gold from Sudan,[15] it was the native story of El Dorado, the gilded man, that obsessed Europeans.[16] Similarly, the eventual relegation of reports of Amazon-like women to the South American jungles could well be related to the presence of comparable stories among the Kalina and Xikrin Indians from Surinam and central Brazil, whose traditions, according to various authors, also spoke of aggressive all-female tribes.[17]

Before discussing the European legend of the seven Portuguese bishops, unanimously and mistakenly considered the fundamental but concealed motivation behind the early exploration of present-day New Mexico, it is worth considering the Amazons. Their gradual disappearance from New Spain is an example of how the compelling power of European fantasies in America is more academic construction than historical fact.

New Spain and the Amazons

In 1510 Garci Rodríguez de Montalvo published in Seville *Las sergas de Esplandián* (The Deeds of Esplandián), the sequel to a popular Portuguese romance he had translated and published under the title of *Amadís de Gaula* (Amadís of Gaul) two years before.[18] The novel was a typical medieval story telling the adventures of the son of the great Amadís, both of them prototypical knights who devoted their lives to the defense of Christendom and all sorts of honorable causes. Chapters 157 to 178 take place on an island called California, populated by a tribe of Amazons ruled by Queen Calafia and celebrated for its abundance of gold and jewels. They narrate how the queen, allied with the King of Persia and other pagan princes to capture Constantinople, was defeated in personal combat by the superior skill of Amadís and the beauty of Esplandián, who had traveled to confront her in California in response to her defiance.[19] The popularity both novels achieved was so enormous that a number of subsequent romances continued the cycle through successive descendants of Amadís,[20] only one of which, *Lisuarte de Grecia* (1514), spoke of Queen Calafia again.

Columbus had reported on the existence of Amazons in the New World nearly twenty years before Montalvo wrote *Las sergas de Esplandián*. Both in Columbus's *Epistola de insulis nuper inventis* and in a letter addressed to the monarchs on February–March 1493 he mentioned the island of Mateunin (or Martinio),[21] supposedly populated only by women, who had male occupations.[22] Nevertheless, it was not through Columbus himself that the theme became so inextricably associated with mainland America, but through the hyperbolic manner in which Montalvo used the Admiral's exotic reports to frame his own book in the contemporary context, thus capitalizing—as Irving Leonard suggests—on the renewed interest the ancient legend had acquired: "Know ye," Montalvo wrote, "that on the right hand of the Indies there is an Island called California, very close to the earthly paradise, and inhabited by black women without a single man among them, for they live almost in the manner of Amazons[. . . .] Their weapons are all made of gold as well as the trappings of the wild beasts which they ride after taming, for there is no other metal on the whole island."[23]

If Columbus's reports on Amazon-like natives were thus picked up in Europe by Montalvo, and some years later, by Pedro Mártir de Anglería, the first historian of the New World,[24] they disappeared from the Admiral's own accounts after reaching the Gulf of Paria in Venezuela during his third voyage.[25] Perhaps this lapse was due to the unexpected appearance of unequivocal signs suggesting the proximity of an enormous landmass (South America), an event that challenged Columbus's Asiatic interpretation and made him consider the possibility that he was actually near the Terrestrial Paradise.

This is not the place to describe the process by which Columbus discarded his Asiatic theory. I simply note that once the identity of the lands he discovered was established as an entirely new world, and from the moment a permanent hold on the Caribbean islands was achieved at the turn of the century, Amazon sightings rebounded with the subsequent exploration of the mainland mass to the north, east, and south. However, contrary to the argument Leonard developed and which other authors have repeated ever since,[26] the importance of Amazons as beacons in the area that would later become New Spain was rather secondary. Furthermore, their actual existence was more controversial than these scholars make it appear.

The paradigmatic importance of chivalric literature for Spanish adventurers traveling to the New World is clearly attested to in New Spain by two well-known incidents. First, the oft-quoted declaration of Bernal Díaz del Castillo stating that upon their arrival conquerors thought the Valley of Mexico was "like the enchantments they tell of in the book of Amadís."[27] Second, the peculiar way that the peninsula of California derived its name from the story of Queen Calafia.

More than a blind belief in the marvels of Amadís, Díaz del Castillo's statement indicates that the cycle of chivalric fiction provided conquerors with conceptual tools for the assimilation of novelty, and, more important, that framing their descriptions with an exotic yet familiar imprint was an efficient means to transmit the sense of strangeness they experienced to other people who did not cross the ocean. As Greenblatt explains: "In the face of the undreamed, and consequently in a crisis of representation, Bernal Díaz turns to the language of medieval romance, with its dream images, its magical castles and temples, its rhetoric of amazement. . . . The absolutely other cannot be conveyed at all, cannot perhaps be even perceived, but the romance can at least gesture toward this other, marked with the signs of fantasy, unreality, enchantment."[28] The problem is, indeed, one of "representation." What the Amadís novelistic cycle provided was neither programmatic goals nor chimerical objectives, but metaphors. The same can be said about the reference to the fantastic in the naming of California, although in this case Montalvo's novel seems to have been more instrumental.

Hernán Cortés, in his fourth letter to the king (October 15, 1524), reported that in the province of Cihuatlán one of his captains, Gonzalo de Sandoval, received news from local caciques concerning a nearby island, rich in pearls and inhabited only by women. He described their behavior in the same terms as classical sources described that of the Amazons:

> And in the report that he made on those provinces he brought news about a very good harbor they found on that coast . . . and he also brought me a report from the lords of the province of Ceguatan, who are firmly convinced that there is an island nearby populated only by women, with not a single man, and that sometimes these women receive men from the mainland, giving them access, and those who become pregnant, if they give birth to girls they keep them, but if the babies are boys they send them away . . . I am also told that [the island] is very rich in pearls and gold: I shall work, when I get the opportunity, toward finding out the truth and will report at length about it.[29]

Shortly after his men reached the Pacific Ocean, during the conquest of Michoacán and Colima (1522–23) by Cristóbal de Olid and Gonzalo de Sandoval, to whom the previous report is owed,[30] Cortés prepared to explore the western coast by sea.[31] His main intention was to find suitable ports and routes for transpacific navigation and, concomitantly, to locate the mouth of the Strait of Anian allegedly leading to the Atlantic Ocean (its supposed "entrance" on the west coast was known as the Strait of the Bacallaos).[32] Despite his promise to the king, the female tribe of native reports seems of little importance to him, as he does not mention it again in any of his letters, even though he did explore the island "rich in pearls and gold," actually California.

Circumstances surrounding the discovery and naming of the Baja California peninsula have been the object of numerous studies. Edward Everett Hale proposed in 1862 that the source of the toponym was Montalvo's novel *Las sergas de Esplandián*, and the thesis has been reformulated thereafter with different emphases. Most authors maintain that conquerors who dreamed of Esplandián's and Amadís's adventures were misled to believe the island of Santa Cruz, as Cortés and his men called the peninsula from May 1536 on, was in fact the fantastic realm of Queen Calafia.[33] A few others, like Putnam and Priestley, or Portillo, argue that even though substantial evidence demonstrates conquerors named the peninsula after that legendary kingdom, there is no convincing basis for the thesis that they believed it to be such a place.[34]

Cortés obtained a royal permit to carry out his navigation program along the Pacific coast in June 1523. In 1525 he was even instructed to send some ships to the Moluccas (Spice Islands), but the crown soon opposed his maritime activities, as the expedition he had entrusted to the command of Álvaro de Saavedra failed to reach the Spice Islands. Four years later, however, after negotiating personally with the monarchs, Cortés signed a capitulación (October 1529) in which he agreed to search for the islands of the "Southern Sea." Between 1532 and 1539 he organized five expeditions. The second, led by Diego de Becerra and Hernando de Grijalva in 1533, confirmed the existence of a large, pearl-rich island—which later turned out to be a peninsula—near the coast of Cihuatlán. In 1535, excited by this discovery, Cortés led a third expedition, but the "island" turned out to be bare and almost deserted. Consequently, his projects to explore its shoreline dwindled out by the fifth expedition he organized, this time led by Francisco de Ulloa between 1539 and 1540.

It is impossible to determine the precise date when people began to call this landmass California. The report by Francisco Preciado on Ulloa's voyage already used the name as if it were customary,[35] but according to Portillo, this evidence is unreliable because the original document is lost and the only version known today is the Italian translation published by Ramusio in the 1550s.[36] Portillo believes that Preciado's Italian translator substituted "California" for the document's original designation of "Santa Cruz" in order to make clear a reference to a place that had already changed its name by the time he made the translation. Pedro de Palencia wrote the only other surviving testimonial account of Ulloa's expedition, but he consistently calls the peninsula Santa Cruz, not California. Thus, the first unequivocally documented use of the name for the peninsula corresponds to Juan Paez's 1542 report on the voyage of Juan Rodríguez Cabrillo, commissioned by Pedro de Alvarado, then governor of Guatemala.

The fact is that neither Cortés nor anyone in his service ever used the word "California," and apparently they did not use the term "Amazons" either. This suggests that even though the Spaniards eventually adopted the story of Esplandián as a means to identify the female-populated island, rich in pearls, of indigenous reports, they did not plan their westward seafaring adventures to search for Queen Calafia and her Amazons. On the contrary, they embraced the toponym only after they had dismissed the native report as a legend. Like Díaz del Castillo with the book of Amadís, they used the reference in a metaphorical sense because the island stood on the right hand of New Spain, just as fabled California stood "on the right hand of the Indies."

Women living without men appear in documents on the exploration and conquest of New Spain at a very early date. The report that Juan Díaz wrote on Juan de Grijalva's 1517 expedition along the shoreline north of Yucatan contains the first such reference to all-female societies.[37] Gonzalo Fernández de Oviedo's *Historia general y natural de las Indias*[38] contains an extensive summary of Diaz's report, which was first published in 1520; the complete Spanish versions existing today are translations from the 1520 Italian edition.[39] Amazons only appear once at the beginning of the text, when the army "found a tower on a tip of the land that is said to be inhabited by women who live without men." Immediately afterward comes the remark that "we believe they may be from the stock of the Amazons,"[40] but this seems to be an addition by the Italian translator of the original lost manuscript, because Oviedo, who follows Diaz's report closely in his summary, does not include a similar comment.

Three documents related to Hernán Cortés's performance must also be mentioned. First, the instructions he received from Governor Diego Velázquez before leaving Cuba (October 23, 1518), mostly devoted to establishing the military and administrative rules to be followed during the journey but also containing items that outline the expedition's main goals. The most important are (1) to look for Juan de Grijalva and Cristóbal de Olid, who had sailed to explore Yucatan earlier that year and had not yet returned; (2) to inquire about—and rescue if possible—six Spaniards from a lost vessel that, according to an Indian captive, Melchor, had been taken prisoner by local caciques; and (3) to gather general information and obtain samples of gold via barter exchange.[41] The brief and only reference to Amazons in the entire document is part of a passage of no more than ten lines. It requests the verification of various fantastic rumors spread by Melchor and another Yucatan Indian whom Cortés was taking along in his army: "[In every island you visit] you will try to get hold of an informant who will give you news about other islands and other places, as well as the nature and customs of their inhabitants; and also why it is said that there are people with large and wide ears, and others with dog-like faces, and you will also inquire where and in what direction are the Amazons, who dwell nearby according to the Indians that you are taking along."[42]

The second time Amazons are found in association with Hernán Cortés corresponds to the Indian reports concerning a women-only tribe that Captain Gonzalo de Sandoval (or someone in his service) gathered in the province of Cihuatlán. As noted above, Cortés included a brief account of the rumors in his fourth letter to the king, promising to gather as much information as he could about those women. Therefore, when he sent his nephew Francisco Cortés to explore that region more extensively, his instructions required him to ascertain the truth of such hearsay.[43] Among the documents produced in connection with Francisco Cortes's undertaking is a coat of arms that the Queen of Spain granted to a certain Jerónimo López (June 26, 1530) for feats performed "while searching for the Amazons in the said journey."[44] None of these documents, except perhaps Diego Velázquez' 1518 instructions, prove that Cortés, his superiors, or his subordinates were thinking of classical Amazons or Queen Calafia's cohorts. They only confirm that the explorers followed Native American reports that recall Amazon stories and that they sometimes used the term, perhaps metaphorically.

Cihuatlán and its stories of all-women tribes, disclosed to European invaders by the natives, continued to attract the attention of Spanish soldiers during Nuño de Guzmán's conquest of Nueva Galicia, a circumstance that scholars commonly use as evidence to prove that the belief in Amazons steered exploration in New Spain. Guzmán sent a report to the king from Omitlán on July 8, 1530, in which he asserted that once he reached the province of Astatlán [Aztatlán], he would "go in search of the Amazons, as I am told they are ten days away; some assert they inhabit the sea, others affirm they are located on an arm of the sea, and also contend they are rich and feared by the mainland inhabitants as if they were goddesses."[45] Various men in Guzmán's army confirm they also pursued this goal after having received similar reports in Astatlán.

The first anonymous *relación* on the conquest of Nueva Galicia, for instance, says that in Astatlán the army received plentiful news about the Amazons, who were called "Ciguatán" in the native language, as well as other news concerning many neighboring provinces rich in gold. According to this *relación*, many women from Ciguatán, who were very different from any seen before, were taken as prisoners. Later, says the report, they explained through interpreters that they had arrived by sea, and also that "in ancient times they kept the custom of having no husbands . . . but they received neighboring men, from time to time, for intercourse, and women who bore sons buried them alive while keeping their daughters to bring them up." However, the soldier also reports, they claimed to have ceased killing the boys in recent times.[46] In other examples, Gonzalo López declares that from Tepic he was sent "to search for the women,"[47] and Juan de

Sámano confirms that Guzmán's entire army went from Astatlán to the province of the Amazons, which he describes as a town "where plenty of women and very few men were found."[48]

Cihuatlán is a Náhuatl word that indeed means "place of women," but it is impossible to know exactly what the reference to a place of women signified in the native context. On the other hand, whether Amazons could actually be found in Cihuatlán was always a controversial issue among the Spaniards. Conquistador Pedro Carranza noted that although some soldiers believed Cihuatlán (Capuatan) was a women-only town, as many more women than men were found, this could not really be confirmed because the Spaniards did not have an interpreter.[49] Cristóbal Flores made a similar remark but denied categorically that those women were Amazons. If the army found so few men among them, he contended, it was because, at the time, they were preparing themselves to confront the Spaniards in war.[50] Gonzalo Fernández de Oviedo heard the story from Francisco de Arceo and observed that this was the same town of women that a captain in the service of Hernán Cortés—either Sandoval or Francisco Cortés—had found long before, which also bore the name Ciguatán. Then, hewing to the testimony of Gonzalo López, Oviedo declared that the place was a well-established town with good buildings and streets, where a great number of women, dressed in long, white chemises, were said to live on their own and to bring men in only a few months every year. Nevertheless, he concluded, "I later encountered Guzmán in Spain . . . and he said it is a great lie to say they are Amazons or live without men."[51]

From this review one might conclude that even if Amazon-like women and the rich island they supposedly inhabited were at some point suspected to exist in New Spain, the interest was short-lived and volatile. Furthermore, despite the naming of the peninsula of California after Montalvo's reworking of the classical theme, and notwithstanding the coat of arms granted on the basis of the supposed search for them, references to their existence faded away completely after Nuño de Guzmán. In fact, they were never posed as the main goal pursued by any given expedition. On the other hand, one must insist that, as in South America, it was a local indigenous belief—that of the Cihuatlán women—rather than European stories, that made conquerors so interested in the theme of an all-female tribe.

The Island of Antillia and Its Seven Bishops

A medieval legend tells of seven wondrous cities founded by Christian fugitives from the Moorish invasion of the Iberian peninsula. Many historians throughout the twentieth century considered the legend to have inspired Vázquez de Coronado's journey and subsequent ones into the area that later became Nuevo México.

In this view, Spanish explorers were spurred to engage in the enterprise because, among other things, they hoped to find these seven cities.

Long before Columbus arrived in America, several Europeans had tried to reach the unknown island named Antillia that figured in the cartography of the period and was sometimes identified as the place where the fleeing bishops had settled. Therefore it has been suggested that when the Caribbean islands, initially expected to include Antillia, proved to harbor no Christian peoples, conquerors were ready to seek the seven cities elsewhere, and after Cabeza de Vaca and Marcos de Niza spoke of wealthy cities to the north of New Spain, they were even prepared to accept that they might be located on the mainland, not necessarily on an island.[52]

Scholars often quote the following paragraph by Antonio de Herrera, official chronicler of the Indies, to support this theory of delusion on the part of the Spaniards:

> Ancient navigation charts depicted some islands amid the seas, in particular the island called Antillia, and they situated it little more than two hundred leagues west of the Canary Islands and the Azores. This island, the Portuguese thought to be the Island of the Seven Cities, so famous and longed for that it has led many people to rave, out of greed, and spend lots of money in vain. And the Portuguese, as they dream, say that this Island of the Seven Cities was populated by fellow countrymen, in the time when Spain was lost, during the reign of King Don Rodrigo; because fleeing from that [Muslim] persecution, seven Portuguese bishops embarked with many people and arrived on the said island, where each founded a town, and to prevent people from turning back they set the boats afire. [They also say] that in times of Infante Don Enrique de Portugal, a ship that had sailed from Portugal was caught in a storm and did not stop until reaching that island; and the islanders took people from the ship to the church to see if they were Christians and performed the Roman [Catholic] ceremonies; and when they learned they were, they begged them to stay and wait for their lord to return, but fearing to have their vessel burned and be retained, the sailors returned to Portugal very content . . . and after leaving that kingdom they never went back again.[53]

Judging from various documents, it seems unquestionable that during the earliest phase of exploration in America, several people on both sides of the Atlantic had in mind this legend, popularized in Castile by a chivalric novel titled *Crónica del Rey Don Rodrigo y la destrucción de España*.[54]

Friar Bartolomé de las Casas, one among several possible sources on whom Herrera based his passage, asserts that, according to Columbus, a Portuguese vessel arrived in 1460 at the island of Antillia and was met by Christian people.[55] The Admiral's son, Ferdinand Columbus, also mentions the story in his father's biography, *Historia del Almirante Cristóbal Colón*, while Francisco López de Gómara claims in his *Hispania victrix* (published 1553 in Zaragoza) that Columbus had tried to locate Antillia.[56] In fact it is López de Gómara's *Historia general de las Indias* (1552) that gives the clearest indication that in the years immediately succeeding the first contacts with the future New Spain, some people believed they were near the island of the Seven Bishops. He declares, despite his own skepticism, that certain soldiers considered some brass crosses Hernández de Cordoba had found in Yucatan as evidence that many Spaniards had been there "during the destruction of Spain by the Moors in the time of King Don Rodrigo."[57] It is possible therefore that Governor Velázquez was expecting to confirm the legend when he sent Hernán Cortés to follow the shoreline of Yucatan, as the twelfth item in his instructions requested that he find out the meaning indigenous people gave to the symbol of the cross: "Because on the said island of Santa Cruz, in many places and on top of certain tombs and burials crosses have been found, which are said to be highly revered, you will inquire the meaning of why they have them, and whether it is because they have heard of our Lord God before."[58]

In all truth, after Cortés established Spanish domination over the former Aztec empire, individuals exploring the north do not seem to have been particularly interested in the seven bishops. Nothing in Herrera's allusion to the money wasted because of this fantasy indicates that he was referring to the explorations by Vázquez de Coronado or any other conqueror in the north. The passage refers to maritime expeditions contemporaneous with, or prior to, Columbus. The same holds true for a paragraph by chronicler Gerónimo de Mendieta that John Phelan cites to support his assertion that Antillia was actively sought in the New World:

> I could rule with little help . . . a province of fifty thousand Indians organized and arranged in such good Christianity that it seemed as if the whole province were a monastery. And it was just like the island of Antillia of the Ancients . . . , which is located not far from Madeira. In our times it has been seen from afar, but it disappears upon approaching it. . . . They say that on this island there are seven cities with a bishop residing in each one and an archbishop in the principal city. The strange thing is that it seems to the author of the history of the Gothic kings (*Historia del Rey Don Rodrigo*) . . . that our Lord would be served by having this island discovered and placing it under the obedience and bosom of the Catholic Church. It would be equally appropriate to ask of our Lord that the Indians be organized and distributed in islands like those of Antillia; for they then would live virtuously and peacefully serving God, as in a terrestrial paradise.[59]

Fifteenth century efforts to locate the island of the Seven Cities are well documented. In a letter addressed to the monarchs dated July 25, 1498, the representative of Spain in London, Pedro de Ayala, reported that up to four ships seeking to find the islands of Brazil and the Seven Cities had set sail every year between 1491 and 1498, sponsored by the inhabitants of Bristol. We also know that Juan II, king of Portugal, granted several charters and licenses to private petitioners for the same purpose: In 1474 and 1475 Fernão Téllez received rights over any populated and cultivated land he might find while exploring the "so-called Isla de las Flores," previously discovered by Diego de Tieve, including that of the Seven Cities but excluding those in the seas of Guinea. The most famous expedition of this sort launched by the Portuguese king was to be led by Fernan Duolmo, under a license issued in 1485. It is not clear whether he actually made the journey, but documents containing details of its preparation testify that resources were indeed invested in the enterprise.[60] Finally, one year later the same monarch commissioned navigators Van Olmen and Juan Alfonso del Estreito to investigate whether the island of the Seven Cities was the same as that of Antillia.[61]

It has been said that medieval belief in the existence of wondrous islands in the middle of the ocean—not exclusive to Columbus, according to Luis Weckmann[62]—derived from the story of the lost continent of Atlantis that Plato registered around the year 360 b.c.[63] In his dialogues *Timaeus* and *Critias* the philosopher described Atlantis as the seat of an advanced civilization, ruled by descendants of Poseidon and a mortal woman. Having lived a simple and virtuous life for generations, they became deeply corrupted by greed and power. As punishment, the continent disappeared, swallowed up by the sea, leaving no trace except for an impassable barrier of mud and a number of unreachable islands. Such ideas about the ocean's imperviousness tumbled down as new geographical information was spawned from incipient extra-Mediterranean navigation in the late Middle Ages. Nevertheless, map makers recording the newly generated geographic knowledge still depicted reminders of the lost continent amid the sea.

The imaginary island bearing the name Antillia, probably related to the Atlantis legend, was first represented on the Pizzigani brothers' navigational chart (*portulano*) of 1367. In the fifteenth century it appeared again in another famous *portulano* by cartographer Zuane Pizzigano (1424), who was probably related to the Pizzigani brothers, and was later included in the maps of many cartographers: Bedario (or Bedrazio, 1434 or 1435), Andrea Bianco (1436), Fra Mauro (1460), Bartolomé Pareto (1475), Grazioso Benincasa (or Benacaza, 1463/76?); and Ortelius, Mercator, and Toscanelli (1484). After the discovery of America, Atlantis appeared on the *mappae mundi* by Jan Ruysch (1508) and on the globe by Schöner (1523).[64]

Cartographic representations of Antillia and the story of the seven bishops escaping by sea from the Moors fused into a single legend toward the end of the fifteenth century, its credibility enhanced by the alleged existence of fairly recent testimonial accounts. The oldest existing document containing a complete, explicit association of both legends is a globe made by Martin Behaim (also known as Martin Bohaemus), a member of the board constituted by the Portuguese king Juan II to develop the art of navigation. It was drafted in 1492 with information "taken very carefully," according to notes written on the globe itself, "from the books of Ptolemy, Pliny, Strabo and Marco Polo," the reports of Sir John Mandeville on certain countries that "Ptolemy was unaware of," and reports on the "most recent discoveries made by order of King Juan of Portugal in the year 1485."[65] Next to an island in the western extreme of the Atlantic, Behaim wrote an inscription that might be the primary source of the passage by Herrera quoted above: "In the year 734 after our Lord Jesus Christ was born, when all Spain was subjugated by the heathens that came from Africa, the said island Antillia called Septe Citade was populated by an Archbishop of Porto, in Portugal, and six other bishops, with a number of Christians, men and women, who had left, fleeing from Spain with their livestock and goods. In 1414 the ship that approached it most closely was a Spanish vessel."[66]

According to Gandía, we can trace this identification to the map of Benincasa, which records seven names next to the island of Antillia—Anna, Antioul, Anselli, Anseto, Ansolli, Ansoldi, and Cori—probably corresponding to the cities of the seven bishops.[67]

Historians have seen the quest for the "Seven Cities of Cíbola" as the tranference of expectations that the Spaniards had built around the theme of the seven bishops. Some even claim that a vague resemblance between this motif and the Nahua origin myth in Chicomoztoc (the Seven Caves) set off a powerful fantasy that repeatedly promoted expeditionary action. The problem is that, except for the numerical coincidence, no sound evidence is ever provided to support the argument.

The association between the cities of the seven Portuguese bishops and Antillia was such a widespread cultural theme in late medieval Europe that it was frequently articulated in texts, as the previous review clearly shows. If it had been as significant in northern New Spain as it was for early Atlantic navigation, or for the initial exploration of the Caribbean, comparable traces would be available in the textual sources, but they are not. Furthermore, the name Cíbola itself was never applied to the bishops' cities in any document concerning the European legend because it is entirely autochthonous—not just to America, but particularly to the Zuñi area in present-day New Mexico. As seen in chapter 3, Friar Marcos de Niza's 1539 report was the first document to contain the word "Cíbola," actually a mishearing of *Shi-wi-nah,* a Zuñi Indian self-designation in their own language. Therefore, the hypothesis about this particular phenomenon of delusion—the search for Antillia and the seven cities of the bishops—supposedly involved in the quest for Nuevo México is merely the result of academic speculation and cannot be upheld in the face of the evidence.

The argument, formulated in 1929 by Enrique de Gandía and uncritically repeated thereafter to sustain the assertion that Spanish conceptualizing strategies subsumed all things American into ready-made images brought from Europe, appeared in a book titled *Historia crítica de los mitos de la conquista americana*. The volume traced the legendary themes most repeated in colonial chronicles and in other contemporary accounts concerning the New World to an ultimate European source from classical antiquity. His argument was based on the premise that medieval Europeans accorded particular authority to Greek and Latin wise men whose cosmographic ideas codified the Orientalist obsessions prevalent at the time America was discovered.

Gandía also noted the influence of Native American beliefs and proposed three inspirations capable of inducing the legend of the Seven Cities of Cíbola: first, the legend of the seven bishops from Portugal; second, the Nahua myth of origin in Chicomoztoc (the Seven Caves); and third, the appearance of the Pueblo villages seen from afar by Marcos de Niza.[68] He believed that because Chicomoztoc was located, according to native stories, in the same direction where the seven cities that Niza reported also stood, the Spaniards were soon convinced that the Seven Caves of Nahua ancestors and the cities of the Portuguese bishops were the same place. That native Chicomoztoc and Niza's Cíbola were frequently taken to be the same place is attested to by evidence discussed in previous and following chapters of this book, yet just how the cities of the Portuguese bishops come into this equation remains totally undocumented.

To support the first point of his argument, Gandía quotes the passage by Herrera discussed above, the sea expeditions launched by the inhabitants of Bristol and the Portuguese crown in the fifteenth century, and some of the maps depicting Antillia or the island of the Seven Cities, both prior to Columbus's first voyage and after. For his second and third points Gandía quotes Gerónimo de Mendieta's assertion that Niza's journey was aimed at verifying rumors concerning a populous land of well-dressed people living in multistory houses,[69] and an incident from Vázquez de Coronado's subsequent expedition told by López de Gómara. According to the latter author, at the village of Tiguex the expeditionaries heard of the country of Quivira, ruled by a king called Tatarrat, bearded, white-haired, and wealthy, who prayed at prescribed hours and worshipped a golden cross and the image of a woman.

Gómara's fragment does testify to the fact that Spanish conquerors believed there were Christians living beyond Cíbola. However, none of the reports written throughout or shortly after the expedition (or the late but detailed chronicle by Castañeda Nájera) mentions King Tatarrat or the worship of a cross or woman, although they all mention the high expectations that news of the rich country of Quivira stirred.[70] The only document by a participant that suggests the Spaniards expected to find Christians in the area is Captain Juan Jaramillo's 1542 "Relación," stating that when the army approached Harache and Quibira,

Vázquez de Coronado wrote a letter "to the governor," whom "we thought to be a Christian from the armies lost in Florida, because the Indian [guiding us] had described the nature of his government and civility (*policía*) in such a way that made us entertain that belief."[71]

One cannot dismiss entirely the possibility that Gómara based his statement on testimony, oral or written, containing news about Tatarrat, but the incident Gandía interpreted in his particular way clearly had a different meaning for the Spanish actors involved. Rather than thinking they were near the cities founded by the Portuguese bishops, Vázquez de Coronado and his men were certain—attending to Jaramillo's comment—that the country their Indian informant described, rich in gold and silver and ruled by a refined and powerful governor,[72] had already been discovered by Spaniards who might have survived one of the disastrous attempts to conquer Florida that preceded their journey, namely that of Juan Ponce de León in 1521, Lucas Vázquez de Ayllón in 1526, and Pánfilo de Narváez in 1528. What Jaramillo's testimony indicates is that in the eyes of the Spanish soldiers, Tatarrat's lifestyle was Christian. They concluded he was a surviving conqueror who had managed to integrate into native society and become a local ruler, instead of attempting a return to the Spanish world. After all, a similar incident had occurred in Yucatan. Gonzalo Guerrero survived a shipwreck in 1511 and was a slave among the Mayas, but in 1519 he rejected Cortés's offer to be rescued because he had married a daughter of the lord of Chactemal (modern Chetumal), from whom he begot three children, and he served as a sort of war advisor to his father-in-law.[73]

Gandía was not the first to suggest an association between Cíbola and the seven bishops. Other historians preceded him, such as Adolph F. Bandelier, E. G. Bourne, Frederick W. Hodge and Theodore H. Lewis, and Herbert E. Bolton,[74] yet his dubious contribution was to furnish the argument with a more detailed, though misleading, follow-up of the sources. He linked the legend of the seven bishops with late medieval navigation and early American exploration, and, more important, asserted that the seven bishops were sought primarily in New Mexico because the Indian myth of Chicomoztoc worked as a confirmation of the conquerors' own mental baggage, to which Marcos de Niza's description of Cíbola was later added.[75]

Shortly after Gandía published his book, Robert Ricard developed the thesis further in two articles aimed at demonstrating that the medieval legend found its way into the conquerors' imagery through the black slave whom Niza took along as guide.[76] He argued that Estevanico, being a Moor from the Arab city of Azamor that was occupied by the Portuguese from 1513 to 1542, was acquainted with the legend, though he was not the only possible vehicle, since Portuguese influences in New Spain are well documented. Again, Ricard's argument rests on the commonsense assumption that all places referred to as "Seven Cities" must be the same, necessarily deriving from Old World obsessions, but he provides no evidence that somebody ever linked the seven cities north of New Spain with the Portuguese bishops. On his part, a couple of decades ago Fernando Ainsa added another possible European legendary source for the conquerors' fable-driven aspirations. He established a connection between the Seven Cities of Cíbola and the City of the Caesars mentioned in the legend of Prester John, who supposedly founded a Christian enclave beyond the barrier of Islam.[77]

The list of modern authors sustaining that the northwestward colonial penetration, and more particularly, the conquest of New Mexico, was carried out by gold-thirsty Spaniards who seized upon the old medieval myth of the seven cities is long.[78] A close analysis of their sources reveals that they ultimately rest on Gandía, directly or indirectly, or earlier scholars who laid the foundation for the history of the American Southwest (Bandelier, Bolton, Hodge), with some additions such as Niza's report and a few other sixteenth century documents that do not explicitly mention the Portuguese legend, let alone its association with Chicomoztoc.

The uncritical repetition of this "modern myth," to borrow an expression from Matthew Restall's recent *Seven Myths of the Spanish Conquest*,[79] deserves a thorough revision not merely as an erudite exercise. It is important because of its unwillingness to recognize that Spaniards could take native knowledge and historical discourse seriously. Even authors who consider the possibility that Spanish explorers relied on indigenous myths in conceptualizing the unknown territory limit themselves to suggesting that "mythical" Chicomoztoc worked as a confirmation of the European fables through which the explorers had already formulated their image of the land. This is an interpretive premise that results in equivocal research methodologies of self-reassurance, which obscures the importance that native discourse held for the colonial enterprise.

CHAPTER FIVE

From the North We Came Walking

Traditions of Ancestral Origin among Nahuas

Many Mesoamerican peoples in the late preconquest period articulated their foundation narratives around the theme of foreign ancestry and primordial migration. This was not merely a coincidence. As shown in chapter 2, archaeological evidence and the fragmentary distribution of the multiple languages spoken in the area at the time of Spanish invasion—more than eighty, belonging to more than fifteen language families[1]—indicate that migration was integral to the sociopolitical dynamics of Mesoamerica in the Post-Classic Horizon (a.d. 900/1000–1519).

Historians, archaeologists, and anthropologists have long debated the status that such migration narratives, as contained in Indian-focused sources, should be accorded.[2] Their historical validity has been doubted, not only because they are suggestively similar and include a number of episodes involving supernatural intervention, but also because places recorded as origin lands and first stops along the route are seldom identifiable in actual geography. These stops frequently occupy different positions in the stories of different groups, who are nevertheless depicted as partially sharing a migration route and even starting the journey together.

Glottochronological research based on languages documented early in the sixteenth century corroborates that successive waves of immigrants—primarily Náhuatl but perhaps also Pame, Otomí, or Mazahua speakers—flowed into the heartland of Mesoamerica between the eighth and fourteenth centuries, conquering and displacing other groups already established in the highland valleys of Central Mexico.[3] As a consequence, multiple, competing polities with reduced dimensions emerged, quickly developing regional networks of alliance and domination that had repercussions in the Mixteca, the Maya area, and western Mesoamerica.[4] In this context of increasing conflict over territorial control and regional hegemony, ancestral migration became the common idiom of historical representation throughout Mesoamerica. This idiom, López Austin and López Luján suggest, was part of an ideological system serving to legitimize what they call the "Zuyuano" political order. Zuyuano governance represented a novel solution to an old problem already faced by powerful polities such as Teotihuacan: the need to achieve control over multiple microcommunities of different languages and geographic origins without seriously interfering with their internal, lineage-based organization. The goal was to make economic extraction more efficient at the least possible expense.[5] This overarching political order theoretically could explain why many peoples considered their sixteenth century home a gift from a patron god and portrayed their forebears as roaming across the wilderness under the guidance of specific patron deities in a journey that lasted several generations.[6]

At the local level, Zuyuano governance entailed regional integration, under the globalizing authority of complex hegemonic organisms, of a variable number of virtually autonomous city-states, each retaining its traditional rule but fulfilling, as a subordinate entity, a particular politico-economic function. According to López Austin, the changing relations, internal cohesion, and territorial claims of these polities found ideological expression in the highly normative structure of most migration stories. This type of origin story "amounts to the collective birth of a group, its journey to the promised land, and the founding miracle that validates its right to possess" the territory it inhabits at any given time.[7]

Nearly every group in the Zuyuano universe represented the departure from its land of origin as a supernatural covenant celebrated with a specific god who launched an exclusivist history, culminating miles away and generations later with the miraculous apparition of an emblematic sign predefined by the commanding divinity. This god also gave the group concerned not only lands but also particular forms of livelihood, a specific expertise, and the appropriate tools to satisfy its needs. The *Relación de Michoacán* (circa 1540), for example, describes how the migrant Uacúsechas recognized in Lake Pátzcuaro the site that the god Curicaueri had reserved for them (*Tzacapu-hamúcutin-pátquaro*).[8] Similarly, most sources dealing with Aztec history depict the moment when Chief Cuauhtlequetzqui came across a sign previously revealed by the god Huitzilopochtli to indicate the place where, having changed their name to Mexicas at an early stage in their migration, the Aztecs would accomplish their glorious destiny (Mexico-Tenochtitlan).[9]

If the end point of any given migration was construed in terms so particularistic as to deserve the label of a "promised land," the point of departure was frequently conceived as the common birthplace of various groups, bearing in fact an equivalent name in the traditions of peoples who spoke unrelated languages. The Chicomoztoc of Náhuatl sources is called Vucub Zíván in Maya sources.[10] Literally, the expressions mean "Seven Caves" (*chicome* = 7 + *oztotl* = cave) and "Seven Gorges" (Vucub Zíván) and find glyphic correspondence in a number of well-known pictograms from Central Mexico that represent a kind of multiple womb, suggesting the first arrival of the migrants in the world all together.[11] Outstanding examples of Chicomoztoc renderings appear in the *Mapa de Cuauhtinchan no. 2, Historia Tolteca-Chichimeca, Codex Mexicanus, Codex Azcatitlan,* and *Selden Roll* (plates 1–3, figs. 1–2).[12]

According to López Austin and López Luján, this attribution to a common place of origin may be interpreted as a symbolic acknowledgment of existing networks of intergroup relations, because the list of seven groups issuing from Chicomoztoc is different in each particular tradition and frequently mirrors the state of regional politics at the time. From this perspective, the human diversity that characterized regional webs of economic interdependence, systemic war, and political subordination was ideologically neutralized with the concept of the essential unity of humans in the world order at the time of creation. At the same time, the notion of a separate, deity-inspired migration leading to a promised land legitimized the right of the group concerned in any given narrative to possess a specific territory, justifying the internal authority and external domination of its ruling elite.[13] Migration histories throughout Mesoamerica represented a way to discuss the respective positions different groups occupied within the regional political structure, and they were therefore constantly reformulated as political conflicts and realignments took place.[14]

Whether and to what extent ancestral migration stories convey empirical information about the past, or whether one should take them as primarily symbolic, is a complex issue beyond the purposes of this book. But given that several colonial accounts by Spanish authors emphasize the place where the ancient Mexicans came from as the principal goal that conquerors pursued north of Mexico City, outstanding themes from Aztec/Mexica historical discourse should be examined. Furthermore, Central Mexican Indians participated throughout the sixteenth century in northbound expeditions of conquest that traced the ancient routes of Mesoamerican settlers beyond the frontiers of agriculture and back (reviewed in chapter 2). Their participation indicates that ancestral origin and migration narratives, though fulfilling ideological functions, also contained historical memory. Without attempting an accurate reconstruction of actual migrations, nor a full discussion of the symbolic meanings of migration narratives, this chapter explores how their pre-Hispanic political functionality and historical content intersect with Indian involvement in the colonial expansion into Aridamerica and Oasisamerica.

Not surprisingly, Nahua migration traditions took on renewed ideological pertinence as the Spanish colonization of the north progressed. For several centuries before Europeans arrived, Nahuas had been numerically dominant in Central Mexico, their major settlements concentrated in the valleys of Mexico, Toluca, and Puebla-Tlaxcala, as well as in the *tierra caliente* of present-day Morelos. By the time of the conquest, they had attained a hegemonic position in this region, consequently assuming important roles in the colonial regime as they became fundamental Spanish allies, contributing valuable information and warrior troops for the subjugation of other native peoples.[15] The Spaniards' ready adoption of Náhuatl as a lingua franca when they realized the importance of promoting a non-Castilian language for regular cross-ethnic dealings is indicative of the wide scope of Nahua influence.[16] According to calculations based on sixteenth century *Relaciones geográficas,* over 90 percent of Central Mexico's population spoke Náhuatl as a mother tongue or second language at the time of the conquest, and several groups in regions beyond Mexica control, such as Jalisco and Nayarit, were also partially bilingual. Therefore, a 1570 royal charter declared Náhuatl the official language "for general use among the Indians," and further decrees favoring its learning and teaching followed until 1592.[17] As H. R. Harvey remarked, this policy of linguistic acculturation, reinforced by resettling native Central Mexicans in remote localities away from the circuit of regular Spanish activity, only intensified a process already well under way before the European invasion.[18]

Although a common ethnicity is frequently attributed to Nahua groups on the grounds of their linguistic and cultural uniformity, they by no means considered themselves a unit. Like other Mesoamerican peoples, they were organized in relatively small, lineage-based polities that Spanish sources refer to interchangeably under the label of "nations" (*naciones*), "peoples" (*gentes, pueblos*), "tribes" (*tribus*), or "lineages" (*linajes*). These collective polities (*calpolli* or *altepetl* in Náhuatl documents) had no "assertive consciousness of unity" as a group,[19] but maintained a clear sense of distinctiveness, rooted in historical memories of specific migrations.[20] The fact that indigenous authors continued to write profusely on the topic of ancestral migrations, even at the beginning of the seventeenth century, when the Spanish advance reached its northernmost limit, is symptomatic: far from disappearing, old rivalries, loyalties, and alliances persisted in the colonial regime, as indigenous communities turned to their parochial identities to negotiate advantageous positions in the new power structure.

Archaeological evidence and documentary sources concur that the Valley of Mexico was divided among forty to fifty polities of varying size and complexity when the Spaniards arrived. The polities were founded between a.d. 1100 and 1350 and later absorbed into regional state systems headed by hegemonic altepetl.[21] A similar situation existed in the valley of Puebla-Tlaxcala, despite peculiarities concerning internal political organization. The definition of collective identity and group affiliation among central highland Nahuas at the time will be further discussed below along with ethnicity and political structures, for Indian participation in the quest for Nuevo México followed the lines of preconquest group divisions. For now, suffice it to note that all migration narratives relevant to that quest expressed the interests of different communities in a well-established arena of preconquest regional politics.

Native Sources

Native accounts of ancestral history have come to us in three distinct types of documents: (1) pictorial manuscripts, usually called *mapas, lienzos,* or *códices,* depending on their formal characteristics, produced by specialized Indian scribes before or after the Spanish conquest; (2) chronicles, histories, and general surveys written in Náhuatl or Spanish in alphabetic script, sometimes combined in bilingual texts; (3) hybrid documents that unite alphabetic and pictorial elements.

The practice of recording history in Mesoamerica goes back to the fourth or fifth century b.c., but most of the extant examples were physically produced in the colonial period.[22] Only fifteen of the approximately five hundred pictorial manuscripts known at present are of indisputable preconquest elaboration, all made outside the Mexica heartland.[23] However, many colonial records reflect local knowledge current before the Europeans arrived. Some are copies or glosses of pre-Hispanic prototypes that were later lost or destroyed; others seem to be accurate transcriptions of the recitations accompanying traditional "public readings" of pictorial records.[24] Yet outside of a few early colonial pieces that preserve indigenous stylistic conventions mostly untouched, they all combine Western and Indian traditions, their composition involving the collaboration of native informants, Spanish missionaries, and European, mestizo, and Indian wise men or administrators.

The episodes in the Aztec/Mexica migration that crop up most frequently are compiled in the last section of this chapter. They can be taken as the "base tradition" that sixteenth century Spanish conquerors built on to construe the unknown lands to the north as the cradle of ancient Mexican civilization. It is admittedly difficult to determine which particular narratives the Spaniards had access to; they seldom quoted specific documents, it being likely that most migration stories became known to soldiers and settlers by word of mouth. Nonetheless, there is enough evidence that some Spanish captains did see and read pictorial and alphabetic narratives concerning Central Mexican Nahua history. Furthermore, the oral versions they heard must have been similar to those contained in the codices and chronicles known today, as indicated by the frequent though inexact congruence between certain episodes quoted in their reports and the corresponding passages repeated in several Indian-focused sources.

The narrative reconstruction of Aztec/Mexica ancestral origin and migration offered in this chapter is compiled from primary sources specifically devoted to the Mexica past, as well as from some other groups who claimed a common origin in Chicomoztoc.[25] The sample also includes documents concerning groups that did not claim to have migrated with the Aztecs but still considered Chicomoztoc their own primordial place of origin. Such is the case of Oaxacan groups from the Coixtlahuaca Valley. Because the multiple versions of the story told in these documents contain individual variations, my reconstruction brings together episodes that may appear in some accounts while being omitted in others.

Modern studies on Mesoamerican pictorial writing often make a twofold distinction between "profane paintings" devoted to mundane issues and "religious or sacred paintings" dealing with the cosmic order, calendars, rituals, and deities. This approach is completely alien to native culture and reproduces the Christian perspective introduced in the sixteenth century by Spanish missionaries who, in order to understand local knowledge and cosmologies, forced new structural principles on continuing indigenous pictoglyphic recording traditions and the alphabetic writing that Indians later adopted.[26]

Sixteenth century Nahuas apparently classified their painted records according to their combination of topic and function: *tonalámatl* (record of the 260-day ritual cycle), *xíhuitl* or *ilhuiámatl* (feast distribution according to the 365-day calendar), *teoamoxtli* (book of the gods), *tlacamecayoámatl* (lineage record), *tlalámatl* (land record), *temicámatl* (book of dreams), and *xiuhámatl* or *xiuhtlapohualli* (year-count book or annals of events).[27] These may represent specific preconquest book genera but their names come from Spanish, or late sixteenth-century indigenous texts; therefore, they may also signal the reclassifying process of written discourse addressed above. In any case, many codices traditionally categorized as "ritual" or "sacred" also recorded specific information about geography, politics, and history, just as historical accounts and territorial depictions seen as "profane" from the Western perspective were frequently structured according to a ritualized image of the cosmic order.

Codices consulted for the discussion that follows are of the *xiuhtlapohualli* kind; that is, linear accounts of events displayed along the axis provided by the secular calendar cycle of fifty-two years. Elizabeth Hill Boone distinguishes between items in these accounts that follow a *res gestae* (deeds done) narrative modality and the prototypical year-count annals. The narrative modality is focused on important events and their participants, while the year-count annals are organized around a continuous flow of individually represented years in which only significant events are correspondingly represented. Both types contrast with space-oriented representations of history and cosmogonic *teoamoxtli*, which dictate an entirely different "reading" order.[28]

Ten pictorial manuscripts dealing extensively with Aztec/Mexica history exist today. Only eight contain full accounts of the migration period in the form of year-count annals. The best-known is *Códice Boturini,* a screenfold of native paper that recounts the migration from Aztlan to Colhuacan. The document was formerly considered to be of preconquest elaboration but is now regarded as early colonial.[29] It follows the classical *xiuhámatl* pattern of a continuous stream of individually represented years, with a line of footprints indicating movement in space as well as reading direction. However, according to Donald Robertson, the way historical events are portrayed at specified locations, between lengthy blocks of year-sign groupings (fig. 3), reveals the post-conquest editing of a pre-Columbian prototype. The original format would have been closer to screenfolds such as the *Codex Mexicanus* and *Tira de Tepechpan*, which, while later, preserve the linear format of the year-sign axis (plates 3–4).[30]

The extensive historical section of *Codex Mexicanus* (numbered as plates 18–87 in the facsimile edition by Menguin, 1952) portrays the complete Aztec/Mexica migration and goes on to record more than seventy years of Spanish colonial history. Other sections cover nonhistorical indigenous and Christian subjects. Although painted by several artists at widely scattered times, a single scribe apparently drew the annals up to 1574.[31] In contrast, *Tira de Tepechpan*—painted around 1596 according to Carrera Stampa—is a *xiuhámatl* exclusively devoted to historical events.[32] An interesting example of how Mexica-Tenochca history was regionally an important point of reference, the document—covering the period 1298–1590—shows the history of the town of Tepechpan synchronically represented above a row of year-signs, with the corresponding period of Mexica history below the row.

Codex Aubin, also known as *Códice de 1576*, is painted on European paper bound like a book and combines pictorial records with Náhuatl alphabetic texts. Like *Codex Mexicanus*, it is diverse in content and authorship but is far more influenced by European models; though it preserves the classical year-sign axis, large units of uneventful time are presented as blocks of individual years (plate 5) similar to those appearing in *Códice Boturini*. Painted between 1576 and 1608,[33] it contains a lengthy *xiuhámatl* covering the migration and post-foundation history of Tenochtitlan to 1591, with two additions, 1595–96 and 1597–1608. Very similar in format and content is a late seventeenth-century manuscript known as *Histoire mexicaine depuis 1221 jusqu'en 1594*. Depicting the journey from Aztlan to Tenochtitlan, and ending in 1573, this is a copy of an older prototype lost today.[34] Except for the year-signs and a few episodes painted in the traditional manner, most of its information comes in the form of Náhuatl texts. *Codex Azcatitlan*, another *xiuhámatl* heavily acculturated in style, is also painted on European paper and bound like a book but has no alphabetic text except for a few glosses. Despite its European shape and pictorial style it has a completely indigenous structure, as it consists of an uninterrupted year-count that follows the Mexicas from Aztlan to Tenochtitlan and then continues until the first decade of Spanish domination (fig. 4). Carrera Stampa dated it at around 1530, but later studies affirm that it was made in the last third of the sixteenth century.[35]

The two remaining pictorial year-count annals concerning the Aztec/Mexica migration are contained in *Codex Telleriano-Remensis*, painted in Mexico between 1549 and 1563,[36] and *Codex Vaticano Ríos*, presumably painted in Italy between 1566 and 1589.³⁷ Sections on ritual calendars and religious ceremonies precede the annals in both documents, which emphasize the history of Mexico-Tenochtitlan during the migration period. For a long time, scholars considered the *Codex Vaticano Ríos* a copy of *Telleriano-Remensis* due to their similarities. In 1941 Eric S. Thompson argued that both could have derived from a common original lost today, which Robert Barlow called *Codex Huitzilopochtli*,³⁸ but the current consensus maintains that *Codex Vaticano Ríos* is indeed a copy by Friar Pedro de los Ríos of *Codex Telleriano*, itself a synthesis of several prototypes all done before 1549.

Two Mexica pictorial documents remain to be mentioned. Neither follows the year-count pattern. One is the *Codex Mendoza*, painted between 1541 and 1550 by order of Viceroy Mendoza.³⁹ It records the conquests of the three polities whose alliance constituted the Aztec empire, containing also the annals of Mexico-Tenochtitlan up to the rule of Moctezuma II, an index of tribute paid by subject peoples, and conventional depictions of the daily life of an individual from birth to old age. The other document is *Mapa Sigüenza*, a cartographic history of the Aztec/Mexica migration painted in a single panel, most probably in the sixteenth century.⁴⁰

Two closely related pictorial manuscripts from the valley of Puebla not devoted to the Mexica past are nevertheless relevant because they also attribute a Chichimeca origin to the peoples they portray.⁴¹ The *Historia Tolteca-Chichimeca*, year-count annals with extensive Náhuatl texts dated around 1533, begins with the populating of Tula and ends twenty-six years after the Spanish conquest. According to H. B. Nicholson, its drawings were probably copied from pre-Hispanic documents, while the texts represent faithful transcriptions of the corresponding oral recitations.⁴² The *Mapa de Cuauhtinchan no. 2*, devoted to the migration of the Totomihuaques from Chicomoztoc to Cholula and Cuauhtinchan, was painted sometime between 1533 and 1563 and is part of a wider group of Cuauhtinchan maps.⁴³ Finally, the *Selden Roll*, a native paper strip painted in the early colonial period, also traces a Chichimeca migration from Chicomoztoc to the Coixtlahuaca Valley in western Oaxaca.⁴⁴

Events portrayed in these manuscripts are also narrated in a number of textual sources in Latin script. Some are first-generation alphabetic versions of preconquest codices; others are later derivations written according to European narrative conventions.

First in relevance are five documents known as the "*Crónica X* group" after the name that Robert Barlow (1945) coined for the hypothetical single manuscript that he suggested was behind them all.⁴⁵ Their content is so closely related that the connections between them have undergone profuse debate, it having been suggested that one can identify *Crónica X* as a wide oral tradition rather than a single lost prototype.⁴⁶ The so-called Tovar manuscript—not consulted here—and "Treatise I" of Friar Diego Durán's *Historia de las Indias de Nueva España e islas de la tierra firme* (1579-81) seem to derive from the same original Náhuatl text. Most scholars believe that the piece by Durán is an expanded adaptation of the Tovar manuscript, which is deemed a straightforward translation of a Náhuatl prototype by the Jesuit Juan de Tovar. The other documents in the group are the *Crónica mexicana* by Hernando Alvarado Tezozómoc (1598), an original Spanish text substantially similar to that of Durán; the manuscript known as *Códice Ramírez* (circa 1581-90), also attributed to Juan de Tovar and regarded as based on Durán; and book 7 of José de Acosta's *Historia natural y moral de las Indias* (1590), which includes large fragments apparently taken from *Códice Ramírez*.[47]

Also important is the work by four indigenous and mestizo authors, all Christians educated in Spanish institutions. Hernando Alvarado Tezozómoc, who traced his descent to the ruling lineage of Mexico-Tenochtitlan, wrote the above-mentioned *Crónica mexicana* and another book in Náhuatl regarding the same events: *Crónica mexicáyotl* (1600-10). Together with the *Crónica X* group, the *Crónica mexicáyotl* is viewed as the "official" Mexica version of Aztec history.[48] Working also at the turn of the sixteenth century, Fernando de Alva Ixtlilxóchitl was descended from the last ruler of Tetzcoco and could also trace his lineage back to Cuitláhuac, one of the last Aztec emperors. He wrote a number of short *Relaciones históricas* (circa 1608-25) and a lengthy *Historia de la nación chichimeca* (circa 1616) in Spanish, all basically dealing with the populating of Tetzcoco by immigrant Acolhua-Chichimeca groups.[49]

Domingo Francisco de San Antón Muñón Chimalpahin Cuauhtlehuanitzin, related to the family that ruled Chalco Amaquemecan in 1519,[50] wrote a series of annals, the number and extension of which have not yet been determined.[51] Only some of his eight *Relaciones* and his *Memorial breve acerca de la fundación de la ciudad de Culhuacan* were employed for this book. The chronology of their elaboration is obscure, but the *Relaciones* apparently date from 1620-29, while the *Memorial* (1631) was the result of a 1620 commission by the Indian governor of Amaquemecan to write an official history of the altepetl.[52] The eight *Relaciones* recount the migrations and wars of every group that had a political presence in the province of Chalco Amaquemecan from the mid-twelfth century, including the Mexicas, whose migration is contained primarily in the *Tercera relación*. The *Memorial*, though revolving around the populating and dynastic succession of Culhuacan, also concentrates on Mexica history.[53]

Cristóbal del Castillo, atypical among sixteenth-century indigenous historians due to his modest origins,[54] wrote a couple of precolonial and conquest history books in Náhuatl. Substantial parts of them were lost in the nineteenth century. His *Historia de la venida de los mexicanos y de otros pueblos*, written between 1597 and 1600, indicates that he was not a Mexica because he sometimes counters the canonical traditions of this group, which he portrays as illegitimate and demonic.[55] Most likely a mestizo born in the Valley of Mexico in the 1520s or 1530s, he was probably educated in a Franciscan institution, as he wrote in the Latin alphabet and used the Náhuatl terms these missionaries had coined to refer to the Christian God and pre-Hispanic deities.[56]

Particularly important are several brief, anonymous narratives that reflect local indigenous knowledge virtually unchanged. The earliest, published in 1939 under the title *Unos anales históricos de la nación mexicana*, follows the Aztec/Mexicas from Aztlan-Chicomoztoc-Quinehuayan to the founding of Tenochtitlan and continues with the history of Tlatelolco through the Spanish conquest. It pertains to a collection of five interdependent accounts in Náhuatl known as a group as *Anales de Tlatelolco*, which are contained in two very similar manuscripts. According to Rafael Tena, these can be dated, respectively, at circa 1560 and circa 1620, but their content was probably taken from notes compiled a few years after the Spanish conquest by an Indian eyewitness who also knew ancient history.[57]

Also from the Culhua Mexica tradition are three documents published in 1891 by Joaquín García Icazbalceta. *Historia de los mexicanos por sus pinturas*, written around 1547, registers the Aztec/Mexica migration and other remarkable events up to the time of Nuño de Guzmán's expedition to Nueva Galicia.[58] It has been attributed to Friar Andrés de Olmos, who was commissioned in 1533 by the Audiencia president to compile a book on ancient Mexican culture which has never been found. Therefore, scholars believe that *Historia de los mexicanos por sus pinturas* is either a summary of a lost book titled *Tratado de antigüedades mexicanas*, which Olmos reconstituted from memory several years after having sent all his manuscripts to Spain,[59] or a summary of his work by someone else.[60] The other two documents, very similar to each other in content, are *Origen de los mexicanos* and *Relación de la genealogía y linaje de los señores que han señoreado esta tierra de la Nueva España, después que se acuerdan haber gentes en estas partes*. Written between 1530 and 1532 by Franciscan friars at the request of Bishop Juan de Zumárraga, they were intended to back up the land retribution request that Juan Cano made to the Crown in favor of his wife Isabel Moctezuma, daughter of Moctezuma II. Both trace Mexico-Tenochtitlan's ruling lineage to its Culhua roots, recording the successive migrations that crowded the central highlands since the Toltec period. They are acknowledged to be based on preconquest pictorial documents owned by Isabel's family that are lost today.[61]

Three additional anonymous narratives remain to be mentioned. *Histoire du Mechique* is a French translation of a now-lost Spanish document.[62] Edouard de Jonghe, its first publisher, thought it was part of *Historia de los mexicanos por sus pinturas*, but Garibay argued that Olmos, the reputed author of *Historia de los mexicanos por sus pinturas*, never saw Quivira and Culiacán, places the document describes with some detail. Therefore he attributed its content to Marcos de Niza, whose notes another friar would have later put together with other notes on mythology by a different author, most probably Olmos.[63] In any case, the original text must be posterior to 1542, when Vázquez de Coronado first visited Quivira. Finally, the *Anales de Cuauhtitlán* (1570), considered by Carlos Martínez Marín as the first indigenous history of the Valley of Mexico as a whole,[64] and *Leyenda de los soles* (1558), are part of the manuscript known as *Códice Chimalpopoca*, originally written in Náhuatl and translated into Spanish by Faustino Galicia Chimalpopoca in the nineteenth century.[65]

Several well-known sixteenth century treatises by Franciscan missionaries discuss the same history in substantial detail. The most important are Bernardino de Sahagún's *Historia general de las cosas de Nueva España* (the Spanish section of *Códice Florentino*, compiled between 1558 and 1577); Gerónimo de Mendieta's *Historia eclesiástica indiana*, finished in 1597 and extensively copied by Juan de Torquemada in his *Veinte y un libros rituales y monarquía indiana* (1615);[66] and the two major surviving works by Toribio de Benavente Motolinía: *Memoriales* and *Historia de los indios de la Nueva España*, written between 1527 and 1565.[67]

Calpolli, Altepetl, Tlatocáyotl: Three Intersecting Arenas of Nahua Corporate Identity

Modern literature on ancient Mesoamerica, in its attempt to make sense of polyvalent forms of indigenous group identity, uses the concept of "ethnicity" inconsistently. This confusion of meaning is partly because the sources, fragmentary and mutually contradictory, do not allow for an accurate reconstruction of autochthonous principles of human classification. Further, they result from negotiation between the incommensurate taxonomies of colonizers and colonized, as well as the need to render indigenous concepts intelligible to contemporary Spanish readers.

The inconsistency also reflects the intrinsically ambiguous character of the concept itself. Most often, scholars invoke ethnicity to distinguish between human groups with different geographic origins and languages. They also use the concept to indicate a shared cultural matrix in smaller communities of same-language speakers and to typify social relations established through ties of consanguinity. Underlying these perspectives is a definition of ethnicity—based on blood, language, and culture—that anthropologists like Edmund Leach (1954) and Frederick Barth (1969) criticized for its inadequacy to explain "the complex relationships existing between cultural expression, speech, and social and political organization."[68] In the past few decades Mesoamerica specialists have applied a more current approach, influenced by recent debates centered on self-adscription that emphasize the presumption of common descent over actual consanguinity,[69] but interpretive difficulties persist.

The Zuyuano model briefly discussed above, the most complete approach so far to politics and ethnic identity in Mesoamerica, suggests that two complementary yet conflicting systems of group affiliation and political dominance coexisted in the area for a long period, intersecting with each other in ways still not fully understood. One, based on kinship, privileged consanguinity as the main criterion for group membership and promoted lineage-based forms of authority. The other, based on territory, created a sense of community and political loyalty among people who shared a place of residence. The model considers social relations based on affinity of language and descent as "ethnic," while reserving the category "political" to distinguish forms of social solidarity and collective identity deriving from residential vicinity and territorial domination.[70] Nevertheless, the intricacies of Nahua corporate identity are better understood in terms of indigenous terminologies and with no recourse to the concept of "ethnicity" and its derivates.

Indigenous group identity in Mesoamerica was remarkably fluid. Individuals acknowledged ties with various units of divergent dimensions, thus configuring patterns of social solidarity and political allegiance that tended to bolster factionalism and resulted in constant segmentation and reaggregation. López Austin described the situation clearly in stating that personal loyalties and feelings of attachment in the area operated according to a hierarchy of groups and subgroups that encompassed each other in a pyramidal structure where the major unit was the large linguistic group (for example, Nahua, Otomí, Matlatzinca) and the minor unit was the family.[71] This explains why sixteenth century documents frequently use various names—according to language, tribal chief, origin, or place of residence—to address the same human group (for example, Azteca = Mexica = Tenochca) but also subsume, in certain cases, various culturally and linguistically unrelated peoples under the same label.[72] The term "Chichimeca," which many Nahuas applied to their own ancestors, for example, also designated contemporary groups of hunter-gatherers, fishers, and part-time farmers living in the northern regions they called Teotlalpan, whom they regarded as barbaric in opposition to the archetypal Toltec civilization, to which they also traced significant ancestral connections.

To understand how Central Mexican self-ascribed identity and historical memory interlock with Spanish-Nahua collaboration in the conquest of the north, the native universe of mutually intersecting groups in sixteenth century Mesoamerica is worth addressing. The basic political unit in Central Mexico was the *altepetl*, literally meaning "water (*atl*) and hill (*tepetl*)," or "the water(s), the hill(s)" from the metaphorical expression *in atl, in tepetl*, bringing together the essential elements for a stable social life.[73] Beyond this etymological analysis, no adequate translation exists for the term, as no equivalent institution is found in the Western world. Nevertheless, scholars frequently compare it with the Mediterranean city-state of Greek antiquity because it was a sociopolitical entity defined by a deep sense of distinctiveness unto oneself, control over a certain territory, and an autonomous government—headed by a dynastic ruler or *tlatoani* (plural *tlatoque*)—to which a variable number of constituent segments paid tribute and owed obedience.[74]

Visually, the altepetl appeared as a compact urban complex containing public buildings, surrounded by a variably dense network of residential compounds and hamlets.[75] Deceived by its appearance, the Spaniards came to conceive of the altepetl in terms of their own institution back at home, the municipality. The municipality was the minor unit of political organization at the local level; composed of a *cabecera*, or capital, ruling a set of *sujetos*, or subject hamlets. Unlike Spanish municipalities, however, each altepetl was "a sovereign or potentially sovereign entity," though frequently inscribed within wider political configurations as a result of the aggregation of various independent altepetl via confederation and conquest, or from internal fissioning due to excessive growth or political schisms. Furthermore, *sujetos* of a Spanish municipality were hierarchically related to the cabecera, pinnacle of a centrally organized institution, whereas the minor, self-contained communities constitutive of the altepetl were related to one another symmetrically.[76] Modern academic literature typically refers to these constituent microcommunities in an altepetl as *calpullis* (Hispanicized plural form of *calpolli*). Yet in Náhuatl sources, subunits of an altepetl are preferably designated by other terms—most commonly *tlaxilacalli*—while *calpolli* often refers to the original sibling groups that issued from Chicomoztoc, or their constituent segments.

Like the altepetl, a calpulli was virtually autonomous and self-sufficient, and it generally coincided with a residential ward. Its members—usually of the same linguistic group and geographic origin—were clearly linked by ties of reciprocity and solidarity, the worship of a common tutelary god (*calpulteotl*), and the collective ownership of the plots they worked and lived on.[77] Each calpulli had its own internally elected sub-rulership and held particular religious ceremonies in its own temples. Since documentary sources do not provide sufficient information about the role of kinship and residential vicinity as mechanisms for recruitment and boundary definition, the internal articulation of the calpulli has been the subject of intense controversy. Interpretations range between two extreme positions. One considers the calpulli as, above all, a group of kin-related families with strong endogamic tendencies, though not necessarily prescriptive marriage rules.[78] The other is skeptical about the importance of consanguinity and emphasizes the political, territorial, and administrative aspects of the calpulli.[79]

As constituent parts of the altepetl, calpullis collectively faced such obligations as the payment of tribute, corvée labor service, and participation in general cults and external wars, systematically contributing to these wider state affairs through mechanisms of fixed task rotation. This mode of organization, Lockhart observes, "can be termed cellular or modular as opposed to hierarchical" since it followed an associative, not a centralized, pattern of authority, replicated above the level of individual altepetl into a succession of increasingly complex political entities of which the so-called Aztec empire is the supreme example.[80]

Indeed, most late preconquest polities in Central Mexico were conglomerations of various altepetl, some sovereign and some subordinated, loosely held together in politically unstable entities, internally shaken by perennial rebellions and succession disputes and externally engaged in continuous wars and alliance negotiations. They fought and conquered other, similar polities, but territorial occupation rarely occurred as long as the defeated party recognized the overlordship of the victorious opponent—duly paying the tribute or providing the services imposed.

This picture resonates with the "galactic polity" model that Stanley Tambiah developed for late nineteenth-century ruler-realm relations in traditional Southeast Asian kingdoms. He defined their interaction as "large fields of coexisting galaxies" constantly forming factional coalitions and continually shifting boundaries.[81] The Nahua notion of rulership, like "the *imperium* of the . . . universal king" in Burma and Thailand as described by Tambiah, was graduated according to particular ranks of power. The Náhuatl word *tlatocáyotl*, which denoted both government and realm at various levels of politico-territorial organization, derived from the term *tlatoani* ("he who speaks-commands-governs")—the dynastic ruler of the altepetl. Preceded by the particle *huey*, as in *huey tlatocáyotl*, it referred to hegemonic polities ruling over several individual altepetl that recognized a dominant tlatoani as the superior authority but kept their local governments for internal affairs.[82] In practical terms, this meant that commoners had to pay tribute and give personal or military service to both their own tlatoani and that of the dominant altepetl in the tlatocáyotl. Also, local commercial routes and facilities in subordinate altepetl became integrated to the overall market system of the whole.

At the time of the conquest, eight huey tlatocáyotl existed in the Valley of Mexico, each presided over by the most powerful of its constitutive altepetl and named after it. Interestingly, the eight coincide with the social units most frequently listed in the sources as migrant groups from Chicomoztoc: Tenochtitlan (Mexica), Tlacopan (Tepaneca), Tetzcoco (Acolhua) Xochimilco (Xochimilca), Cuitláhuac (Cuitlahuaca), Culhuacan (Culhua), Chalco (Chalca), and Mixquic (Mixquica).[83]

Correspondences between the "galactic polity" model and the Amerindian order are not simple coincidence. Like nineteenth century Southeast Asia, preconquest Mesoamerica was populated overwhelmingly by peasants. Even urban dwellers often lived on agriculture, but regular surplus production and distribution were never assured. In both Southeast Asia and Mesoamerica topographic and environmental conditions were suitable for subsistence forms of production but inappropriate for the efficient transportation and storage of excess produce. Under these conditions, surplus accumulation depended on the capacity to control the labor of masses of people, which resulted in internecine confrontation among polities of nearly every size and a system of domination that combined full local autonomy with the imposition of economic obligations, enforced primarily through the threat of war and an overarching cosmology periodically enacted in elaborate rituals. As in Tambiah's examples,[84] the power of a Central Mexican ruler or *huey tlatoani* resided in his capacity to "extract goods and services" from the commoners and mobilize them for the construction and maintenance of irrigation systems and roads, and for the performance of state and religious ceremonies.[85] Not surprisingly, the similarity between the political economies of traditional Asian and Native American societies was the basis for much academic literature on the Inca and Aztec states produced after Karl Wittfogel published *Oriental Despotism* in 1957.[86]

The Spaniards mostly called the altepetl "pueblo," as translated in Friar Alonso de Molina's Náhuatl-Castilian dictionary (1555) and Sahagún's *Códice Florentino*.[87] This Castilian word for town or people—applicable to settlements of any size—conveys the sense of a conglomerate of people tied together through feelings of common identity. Therefore, as James Lockhart contends, it described the altepetl better than "the standard terminology" that Spaniards used to designate their own urban entities in both Europe and the New World: *ciudad* (city) for the highest rank, *villa* (town) for the second, and *aldea* (village) for smaller dependencies.[88] Nonetheless, Spanish understanding of indigenous community belonging and group allegiance was only superficial, which is manifest in the terminology they used to describe native sociopolitical arrangements.

Sixteenth century Spanish authors assumed that one's mother tongue was an important marker of corporate identity in Central Mexico, though aware that language groups seldom constituted integrated political units. They also realized that greater importance was accorded to the individual's adscription to the small-scale communities they called "nations" or "lineages." Although principles articulating these units were unclear to them, in their attempt to establish the ultimate origin of native peoples and explain their cultural diversity, Spaniards could sense how important the common historical experience of migration was for indigenous identity. José de Acosta wrote, in his *Historia natural y moral de las Indias*:

> The ancient and first residents of the province we call Nueva España were very barbarous and rustic men who lived solely on hunting, and this is why they were called Chichimecas. . . . Since they neither harvest nor plant the soil, they left the best and most productive land vacant, and this was then occupied by foreign *nations* whom, because they are politically organized, they

call Nahuatlaca [Náhuatl speakers], meaning people that speak clearly and make themselves understood.... These second Nahuatlaca settlers came from another, very remote land to the north, where a kingdom that has been called Nuevo México was recently discovered. Two provinces lie in that country, one is named Aztlan, meaning Place of Herons, the other Teuculhuacan, meaning Land of Those Having Divine Grandfathers. In these provinces [of New Spain], the Nahuatlaca have their houses and fields and gods, rites, and ceremonies in good order and civility. They are divided in seven *lineages* or *nations* . . . and they say that from seven caves they came to populate this land of Mexico.[89]

Friar Diego de Durán's history contains similar passages, though it places emphasis on the fact that the Nahuas did not leave their longtime home in the Seven Caves all at once:

The news I have of their origin and beginnings . . . only starts from those Seven Caves they inhabited for a long time, which they abandoned in order to come and seek this land; some first, others later, and still others much later.[90] Those who came from the said caves were the six *kinds of people*: the Xochimilca, the Chalca, the Tepaneca, the Culhua, and the Tlahuica and Tlaxcalteca. However, it is worth noting that not all of them came together, nor all in the same year, but some first and the others later. . . , while the Mexica remained behind according to divine will, they say.[91]

Similar remarks appear in the atypical version of Nahua origin that Bernardino de Sahagún included in the last paragraph, chapter 29, book 10 of his *Códice Florentino*, devoted to describing "all the generations that have come to populate this land." The paragraph—bearing the subtitle "About the Mexicans" (*De los mexicanos*)—records a joint migration of several groups, including the Tolteca, the Chichimeca, and other non-Náhuatl speakers. It asserts that having arrived by sea at Pánuco, they populated the central highlands and then dispersed, traveling north separately until reaching Chicomoztoc. Then, after an unspecified period, the Nahuas departed again, heading south to reestablish the settlements they had once abandoned in the valleys of Mexico and Puebla-Tlaxcala, but since the Mexica, unlike the Tepaneca, Acolhua, Chalca, Huexotzinca, and Tlaxcalteca, had traveled beyond Chicomoztoc, they were the last to return. In this account, as in Durán's, Chicomoztoc is not a place of ultimate origin. Nonetheless both authors depict all Nahuas as living there at a certain time before parting, divided into different groups who traveled separately to the south.[92]

Setting aside, for now, the explicit association Acosta draws between Aztlan-Teuculhuacan-Chicomoztoc and the newly discovered Nuevo México, as well as the fact that Sahagún's portrayal of Nahua migrations from Chicomoztoc as a return to Central Mexico resembles two early documents by Franciscan friars,[93] these passages reflect two important issues concerning a native collective sense of belonging that must be noted. First, Nahuas derived the segmentary character of their identity from the argument that their ancestors arrived in the basin of Mexico at different times, settling on separate tracts of land to establish separate politico-territorial entities. Second, wider supra-community allegiances can be recognized in the variation, from source to source, in the list of original sibling groups issuing from Chicomoztoc, numbering six, seven, eight, or even more "lineages." Occasionally, mother tongue appears to define this higher level of corporate identity, as in Acosta's treatment of the seven Nahuatlaca "lineages or nations," but non-Náhuatl speakers are sometimes included in the list as well. According to Toribio de Benavente Motolinía, for example, all the inhabitants of New Spain came from Chicomoztoc, where each of six sons (Xelhua, Tenuch, Ulmecatl, Xicalancatl, Mixtecatl, and Otomitl) begotten by the ruler became the leader of a group that each guided in search of a place to settle.[94] While some of these groups represent wider linguistic wholes, like the Mixtecas or the Otomí, others, like the Tenochca, represent a particular group of a larger linguistic family.

The terms that Spanish writers used to designate indigenous sociopolitical units reveal a significant misconception of how people, land, and rulership were related in Nahua societies. It is my contention that they projected a distinction, seemingly absent in native understanding, between human groups as such (*gentes, naciones, tribus, linajes*) and the polities they organized (*pueblos, señoríos*). At the same time, they failed to detect the contrast between *migrant* and *settled* collectivities implied in native categories, thereby conflating categories that Indians conceived of as separate. Náhuatl documents have no expression equivalent to such terms as *gentes, naciones, tribus, or linajes*, collective nouns that Spanish writers applied to every human group irrespective of territory. Rather, native writers consistently call settled communities *altepetl*, whereas migrant collectivities, detached from any particular land, are always referred to as *calpolli* or one of its derivatives.

Consider the following examples from Alvarado Tezozómoc's *Crónica mexicáyotl*, a history of how the great "*altepetl* ciudad Mexico Tenochtitlan" originated and became, in due course, lord and master "of each and every *altepetl* located anywhere in this recently constituted New Spain."[95] Throughout the chronicle, the word *altepetl* is used to designate Tenochtitlan, Aztlan-Chicomoztoc, and various other entities,[96] always implying "an organization of people holding sway over a given territory;"[97] that is, urban centers and the polities they embodied, which the Spaniards called *pueblo, ciudad,* or *señorío* (place ruled by a noble lineage). In contrast, the author employs the term *calpolli* (or its derivatives like *chiconcalpoltin*)[98] whenever he refers to migrant corporate entities.[99] However, instead of the six, seven, or eight groups represented in other sources as coming from Chicomoztoc, the "seven *calpoltin*" he mentions are subgroups (perhaps clans) of the Mexicas who became established in Tenochtitlan and Tlatelolco.[100] It is notable that Tezozómoc uses no general, all-encompassing term to designate the Mexicas as one among other similar human aggregates.

To summarize, while the territorial and administrative aspects of what the Indians called *altepetl* are represented in Spanish sources by the words "*pueblo*," "*ciudad*," or "*señorío*," what we would call its ethnic aspect is represented by the words "*nación*" or "*linaje*," but such a distinction did not exist in native understanding. At least one additional Náhuatl document, *Histoire mexicaine*, confirms that from an indigenous perspective the distinction that mattered was migrant versus settled condition. Although the document never employs the term *altepetl*, consistently addressing established polities simply by their specific names, it always refers to migrant groups as *calpolli*—be they Mexica constituent subunits or other groups also departed from Chicomoztoc.[101] The lack of a concept conveying the sense of human groups, understood as abstract conglomerations of people, in native terminology discloses the radical parochialism of indigenous identity, which is also manifest in the hesitant application of the term *nación* by the anonymous, probably Spanish, author of the *Relación de la genealogía* (circa 1530–32): "In this New Spain live three sorts of people, I do not know whether to call them nations, as they call Spaniards, French, or Castilian; though it seems I should, attending to the manner in which they began to populate [the land]."[102]

From Aztlan to Tenochtitlan

The Aztec/Mexica migration from Aztlan to Tenochtitlan took place between the twelfth and fourteenth centuries. According to indigenous sources, it began in the year 1 Tecpatl, which corresponds to the Christian year 1168 or possibly 1116.[103] Both correlations appear in the documents. Glosses accompanying the corresponding glyph in plate III of *Codex Azcatitlan* and plate 18 of *Codex Mexicanus*, for instance, deem it 1168, but Chimalpahin offers three different correlates: 1064, 1116, and 1168.[104] The same sources date the founding of Mexico-Tenochtitlan in the year 2 Calli, either 1325 or 1345 according to most scholars, despite discrepancies among colonial sources.[105] How they lived in Aztlan, their original homeland, why they left, and what they did before arriving in the Valley of Mexico differ in almost every account. The schematic summary below makes no attempt at establishing the complete story or validating any particular version but picks up significant episodes and discusses modern interpretations when appropriate for the overall argument of this book.

Aztlan was an urban settlement, seat of a stratified society, like any altepetl in the Valley of Mexico. Its location within a lake or at least almost completely surrounded by water resembled that of Tenochtitlan. Most written sources portray

Aztlan as an island,[106] although *Codex Mexicanus* represents the nearby water in the form of a river (plate 6) and Chimalpahin's *Memorial* speaks of an arm of the sea.[107] Pictorial images of Aztlan in documents like the *Mapa Sigüenza* and codices *Azcatitlan, Aubin,* and *Boturini* (plates 7–9, fig. 5) are strikingly similar to Mexico-Tenochtitlan in the *Codex Mendoza, Codex Aubin,* and *Histoire mexicaine* (plates 10–11, fig. 6). Like many written sources, these also contain details on the political system prevalent in both places: temples existed in Aztlan as well as in Tenochtitlan, indicating a somewhat institutionalized religion, and the inhabitants, who lived on agriculture, fishing, and gathering lake produce, were governed by a dynastic ruler.[108]

None of the etymologies that the chronicles and codices provide for the name *Aztlan*—associated with herons,[109] reeds,[110] or the white flower called *aztaxochitl*[111]—is a strict phonetic derivation accordant with the rules of Náhuatl word composition, but as Duverger remarks, they all denote whiteness and correspond to a marshy environment, two elements also characteristic of Tenochtitlan.[112] As to its geographic location, the sources are vague and contradictory. Like José de Acosta in the quotation above, Alvarado Tezozómoc and *Códice Ramírez* assert that Aztlan lay in the recently discovered province of Nuevo México,[113] but Alva Ixtlilxóchitl places it toward the west beyond Xalisco, Durán near Florida, and *Histoire du Mechique* "beyond the mountain of Tholman that Florida natives call Quivira."[114] The last three sources, however, all produced shortly after or around the time that a conquest enterprise took place in the region, hint at the overall direction of Cíbola/Nuevo México.

Interpretations concerning Aztlan's elusive location and its similarity to Mexico-Tenochtitlan range between two opposite poles. One position considers that migration narratives do not describe historical events but are essentially symbolic constructs, linked to cosmology or the necessities of power legitimacy. Eduard Seler, for instance, saw Aztlan as "a mythical hypostasis" of Mexico-Tenochtitlan and the full story as a symbolic chart of the cosmos referring to cardinal directions rather than real places,[115] and Michel Graulich argued the story symbolizes the conflict between foreignness (hunter-gatherer newcomers) and autochthony (local fisher-agriculturists).[116]

The other position holds that migration narratives do spell out real facts, though clothed in mythical images, and therefore it is possible to reconstruct on the map the route that migrants may have followed. The most generally accepted hypotheses are by Wigberto Jiménez Moreno, who suggested Aztlan stood in the lake of Mexcaltitlán in present-day Nayarit;[117] and Kirchhoff, who proposed it lay close to present-day San Isidro Culiacán, in southwest Guanajuato.[118] Miguel Acosta Saignes attributed discrepancies in the sources to the actual existence of two travel routes followed by different groups who met and merged in Tollan,[119] whereas Jiménez Moreno, Kirchhoff, and Martínez Marín believed a single migration route was much likelier and attributed the Aztlan-Tenochtitlan similarities to the Mexica preference for lake environments.[120]

The Aztecs began their march alongside other calpoltin, guided by four chiefs and a woman who carried the "magic bundle" containing the relics and spirit of the tribal god. The reasons most frequently quoted as prompting their departure are four: (1) dynastic or religious conflicts between two brothers,[121] (2) the collective desire to conquer new territories,[122] (3) to escape the tyranny of an overlord,[123] and (4) the command of the god Huitzilopochtli—directly, in his bird form, or indirectly, through a priest.[124] Other names registered for the tribal god are Mexi, Tetzauhtéotl, Tetzáhuitl, and Tlacatecólotl (a Náhuatl word that missionaries coined for the devil). In some accounts, Mexi and Huitzilopochtli are also the names of the Aztec leader, who was deified after death in Coatepec and thenceforward identified with the patron god.

Only a few of the multiple places where the Aztec/Mexicas settled for periods of variable length are relevant here. Two places, Colhuacan (also Teocolhuacan) and Chicomoztoc (also Quinehuayan), are often indistinguishable from each other and occasionally, even from Aztlan. Colhuacan, regularly the first stop en route, appears as the place of origin of an additional set of groups, usually eight, who temporarily joined the migrant Aztecs (plate 12). Chicomoztoc is singled out in textual sources as a sacred site where the migrant collective groups performed propitiatory rituals before they could actually get on the road. The two locations sometimes appear as different names for the same place of common origin, but most frequently they are represented as contiguous, successively visited spots. Written and pictorial sources alike remark on the subordinate position that the eight calpoltin from Colhuacan/Chicomoztoc assumed during their ephemeral alliance with the Aztecs, having begged acceptance as travel companions and recognized Huitzilopochtli as a superior deity. The list varies in different accounts but is identical—or very similar—in nearly half the sources reviewed, usually including the principal altepetl of the Valley of Mexico but sometimes covering whole cultures from all over Mesoamerica except the Maya area, such as the Mixtecs, the Otomí, and the Tarascans (Michuaque).

From Colhuacan the Aztecs and their new companions marched together until reaching a large standing tree; under its shade the Aztecs built a small altar for Tetzáhuitl Huitzilopochtli. This episode and the events that follow it are enigmatic. They involve the breaking of the tree (fig. 7), preceded or followed by Huitzilopochtli's mandate that the Aztecs abandon the eight calpoltin.[125] An apparition amid the desert of certain characters referred to as demons or *mimixcoa* in written sources immediately follows, and they are sacrificed or enslaved by the Aztecs (fig. 8), whereupon the group adopts a new name in response to Huitzilopochtli's desires: Mexica or Mexitin.[126] López Austin has pointed out the fundamental resemblance between the broken tree episode and the rupture of the tree of Tamoanchan, which, according to other myths, stands at the center of the cosmos, connecting the human world and the divine realm. This incident, added to the Aztecs' sudden separation from their newfound companions and their acquisition of a new name, suggests the renewal of the exclusive bond they had with their patron god.[127] As chapter 6 will show, the Spaniards well understood the message these episodes encoded, recognizing them as the supernatural endowment of the political order that prevailed in Central Mexico when Cortés arrived.

Subsequent episodes reveal other schisms that lead to the successive abandonment of small, misbehaving factions of the group. One incident occurred in Mechoacan, or Lake Pátzcuaro, and another in Malinalco, where due to her sorcery, Malinalxoch, Huitzilopochtli's sister, was left behind while sleeping. Much later her son Cópil would trace the Mexicas' steps to Chapultepec and plot a regional war to avenge their deceit. A third, more dramatic schism is depicted next to Coatepec hill, where, according to Durán, Alvarado Tezozómoc, and Torquemada, the Mexicas built a dam that turned the place into a garden of abundance, so sweet and blissful that Coyolxauhqui and her followers asked Huitzilopochtli to end the migration. Furious, the deified leader slaughtered the impatient dissidents instead.[128] The episode is omitted in several sources such as *Anales de Tlatelolco* and *Origen de los mexicanos,* which mention Coatepec simply as a stopping-place where nothing remarkable happened.[129] Others, such as *Codex Azcatitlan* (plate 13) and *Historia de los mexicanos por sus pinturas,*[130] instead of a mundane event, present it as the miraculous birth of the god Huitzilopochtli, born in armor from the womb of Coatlicue to slay his sister, Coyolxauhqui, and his innumerable brothers, who were planning to kill his still-pregnant mother. This version is substantially the same as the cosmogonic myth of Huitzilopochtli, included as an independent narrative—unrelated to the Aztec migration—in the section that Sahagún's chronicle devoted to native mythology.[131]

Though usually appearing as just another site on the journey, unmarked by any particular event, the next important stop after Coatepec is Tula (Tollan). Its inclusion in the migration itinerary, however unremarked, is nevertheless significant since it was widely acknowledged as the cradle of civilization. Most Post-Classic polities of Central Mexico saw ostensible Toltec ancestry as a conspicuous source of legitimacy conferring hegemonic power. Flourishing between the years a.d. 950 and 1150, Tula and the Toltecs represent one of the most problematic issues that Mesoamerican specialists confront; partly because textual descriptions seem gross exaggerations when compared with the archaeological site of Tula Xicocotitlan, the only one of several places bearing the name that could match the demographic characterizations, cultural descriptions, and date of collapse recorded in ethnohistorical sources for the Toltec state. The

Relación de la genealogía asserts that Tula was "the first city ever to exist in these regions,"[132] whereas Sahagún described the Toltecs as a virtuous and knowledgeable people living in a realm of agricultural abundance and refined urbanism[133] who knew all the mechanical arts, invented the calendar and script, astronomy and divination.[134] These remarks would seem to apply to Teotihuacan better than to Tula Xicocotitlan, but Teotihuacan's collapse and abandonment predate the Mexica migration by several centuries.

Archaeological evidence shows that small groups of farmers, seemingly encompassed within the economic macrosystem of Teotihuacan, inhabited the area where Tula Xicocotitlan was later established, which experienced an abrupt population increase followed by a period of steady growth toward the beginning of the eighth century. Along with the sudden appearance in Tula of a type of ceramics formerly limited to local elites of southeast Guanajuato, Zacatecas, and Jalisco, this growth indicates a massive arrival of migrants that coincides with the global contraction of northern Mesoamerican frontiers (discussed in chapter 2). The process may correspond to what the *Relación de la genealogía* pictures as the arrival of a large group of "Culhuas" coming from "Teoculhuacan," led by a certain character called Topilci (Topiltzin Quetzalcóatl or just Quetzalcóatl),[135] who established himself first in Tulancingo and then in Tula.[136] The civil and ceremonial complexes that make up archaeological Tula were built only during the period that followed (a.d. 800–950), also marked by the proliferation of a type of ceramics characteristic of Teotihuacan. Therefore, scholars consider that Tula's population must have comprised two main stocks: the Culhua or Tolteca-Chichimeca, who various sources trace back to Teoculhuacan-Chicomoztoc (that is, immigrants from Guanajuato-Zacatecas-Jalisco), and the Nonoalca, probably a Náhuatl speaking branch of Teotihuacan descent also mentioned in the sources.[137]

Ethnohistorical records are often contradictory regarding the collapse of the Toltec state. Yet they all portray internal factionalism frequently leading to the exile of the ruler/priest Topiltzin Quetzalcóatl, and eventually, the complete abandonment of Tula, nearly deserted early in the thirteenth century, according to archaeological evidence.[138] Scholars agree that Tula's fall eased the flow of successive waves of Chichimeca immigrants—of whom the Mexica were the last—into the basin of Mexico and surrounding valleys. They also agree that the Toltec diaspora took a significant group of Tolteca-Chichimecas to the valley of Puebla,[139] whereas a smaller group, probably comprising the ruling lineage, eventually became established in Culhuacan.[140] Sources like *Relación de la genealogía*, *Origen de los mexicanos*, *Anales de Cuauhtitlán*, and Alva Ixtlilxóchitl identify the Culhua with the Toltecs and their lineage with that of Topiltzin Quetzalcóatl.[141] The apparently contradictory use of the label Tolteca-Chichimeca for some groups of Tula founders, who were not uncultured but did come from the north, derives from the polysemic character of the term Chichimeca, applied by the Spaniards to all "rustic," uncivilized peoples whatsoever, but serving in preconquest times to identify peoples with a common geographic origin in the north.[142]

The Valley of Mexico was already dense with towns and hamlets when the Mexicas arrived, some founded by the eight calpoltin whom they had left at the site of the broken tree. Hence they initially came to participate as just another subordinate entity in a regional network of interdependent but competing altepetl with well-established mechanisms for legitimation of power. Only one altepetl, Culhuacan, was unequivocally a Toltec successor, since it maintained dynastic continuity with its founding Tula refugees. Chichimeca invaders established the other altepetl later on. Of these, the group led by Xólotl was particularly prominent, as the dynasty he initiated in Tenayuca and Tetzcoco eventually ruled the entire eastern sector of the valley. The Tepanecas founded Azcapotzalco; the Otomí, Xaltocan; the Acolhuas, who settled down in Coatlinchan, intermarried with Xólotl's descendants and became part of the tlatocáyotl of Tetzcoco; the Totolimpanecas founded Chalco, and the Xochimilcas, Xochimilco. Other Chichimeca groups such as the Totomihuaques, the Tlaxcaltecas, and the Huexotzincas peopled the adjacent valleys to the south.[143]

By the time the Mexicas arrived, the lake basin of Mexico was dominated by a confederation, sometimes described as constituting a Triple Alliance (*Excan Tlatoloyan* in Náhuatl) where Tepaneca, Acolhua, and Toltec peoples were represented respectively by the allied cities of Azcapotzalco, Coatlinchan, and Culhuacan.[144] This system of regional politics was current at least since the time of Toltec supremacy, when a confederation of three tlatocáyotl (Tollan-Otompan-Culhuacan) constituted the Toltec empire. The system was replicated after Tula's collapse by a new confederation (Xaltocan-Tenayuca-Culhuacan) that was later replaced by the Triple Alliance that the Mexicas encountered in the valley (Azcapotzalco-Coatlinchan-Culhuacan), in turn substituted by the one they themselves led (Tlacopan-Tetzcoco-Mexico).[145]

It is noteworthy that the Mexica circuit after Tula includes stops in important altepetl in all three allied tlatocáyotl. They lived for a long period in one altepetl, Chapultepec, as vassals of Azcapotzalco until a regional war forced them to request asylum from the tlatoani of Culhuacan, who allowed them to settle the barren and desolate quarter of Tizaapan and serve him as vassals.

Sources from the Mexica tradition use the period at Tizaapan to establish the Mexicas as a cunning and courageous lot, capable of enduring the most difficult situations thanks to the protection of Huitzilopochtli. As late intruders whose customs often collided with local cultural canons, the Mexicas aroused suspicion among most of the valley's inhabitants, a situation their enemy Cópil had capitalized on to orchestrate the war that had expelled them from Chapultepec.

According to Durán and Alvarado Tezozómoc, when the Culhua tlatoani granted them Tizaapan, he thought they would perish, bitten by poisonous snakes that swarmed the place, but making the most of adversity, the Mexica ate the serpents.[146] There is no need to review in detail how Culhua-Mexica relations evolved into the confrontation that put an end to the stay in Tizaapan. Suffice it to say that neither the excessive tribute obligations nor the disadvantageous conditions under which they served as mercenary troops had the shattering effect that Culhua nobility expected. On the contrary, the military prowess the Mexicas displayed in the war against Xochimilco startled the Culhua tlatoani. His policy thereafter changed to promote Culhua-Mexica intermarriage and give women of his own lineage in marriage to high-ranking Mexica men. Nevertheless, a sacrifice the Mexicas performed to consecrate the temple of Huitzilopochtli enraged the Culhua ruler and forced them to flee once more, taking shelter among the reeds and rushes before discovering their promised land.[147]

The founding of Mexico-Tenochtitlan, one of the most complex episodes of the migration story, occurred after Huitzilopochtli miraculously delivered his revelation in a tiny islet near the western shore of Lake Tetzcoco: an eagle devouring a serpent and perched on a prickly pear cactus tree that grew from the heart of Cópil, whom the Mexicas had killed in ritual sacrifice on discovering his plot in Chapultepec. The portents marked the Mexicas' final destination: the site where Cópil's heart, thrown into the middle of the lake, had hit the ground. Finally they could establish their own altepetl, which they named Tenochtitlan (Near the Prickly Pear Cactus).[148] The scene is depicted in folio 2 recto of *Codex Mendoza* (plate 11), showing a large rectangle within a blue border of stylized water divided by two intersecting diagonal stripes that create the four sectors into which the city was divided. At the center stands a glyphic sign representing an eagle, a cactus, and a stone. The glyph is also carved on a preconquest stone monument known as the Teocalli de la Guerra Sagrada (plate 14).[149] Framing the page in the *Codex Mendoza* is a continuous count of fifty-one years that begins in the upper left-hand corner with the year 2 Calli and continues counterclockwise until ending at 13 Acatl; that is, from the apparition of the miraculous sign to the final year of the reign of Tenoch, the Mexica ruler since their stay in Culhuacan.[150] In the lower register we see two Mexica conquests achieved in this period.[151] Other pictorial representations of Tenochtitlan's founding include *Tira de Tepechpan* (plate 4), *Codex Aubin* (plate 10), *Codex Azcatitlan* (fig. 4), and *Histoire mexicaine* (fig. 6).

Despised by local people as a conflictive band of intruders, the Mexica were initially forced to accept the condition of subjects of Azcapotzalco, given the location of their altepetl in Tepaneca territory. Moreover, after their tlatoani died in the Chapultepec war, they had no dynastic ruler, an essential condition for political autonomy. To achieve an effective presence in local politics, the Mexicas needed to link their own dynasty to that of a hegemonic altepetl; that is, the dominant of the three major confederate huey tlatocáyotl constituting the Triple Alliance—the Excan Tlatoloyan—which represented the larger population stocks in the region: Tepaneca, Acolhua-Chichimeca, and Culhua-Tolteca. The Mexica-Tenochcas[152] decided to base their ruling lineage in Culhuacan, due to its legitimizing connotations as the descent line most closely linked to Toltec ancestry.[153] Later on they also secured Tepaneca blood by marrying their second ruler, Huitzilíhuitl, to the daughter of Tezozómoc, tlatoani of Azcapotzalco.[154]

As subordinate rulers, the first few Mexica-Tenochca tlatoque had very limited power, but participation in their overlord's imperial wars gave them land and the right to receive tribute. After the 1418 Tepaneca conquest of Tetzcoco, for example, Azcapotzalco's tlatoani distributed part of the conquered territory among subordinate allies, granting Huexutla to Tlatelolco and the city of Tetzcoco itself to Tenochtitlan.[155] Thus, by the fifteenth century, the Mexicas had developed such mighty force and strong alliances that in 1426, capitalizing on Tepaneca succession conflicts, they engineered a widespread revolt resulting in the defeat of Azcapotzalco (1433), for which the collaboration of Tetzcoco and Tlacopan was fundamental. After this victory a new Triple Alliance perfectly fitting the Excan Tlatoloyan tradition was formalized, its members positioned as the successors of the formerly dominant confederation. Mexico-Tenochtitlan replaced Culhuacan, and its ruler took the title of *culhuatecuhtli* (lord of the Culhuas), whereas the rulers of Tetzcoco and Tlacopan, respectively substituting for Coatlinchan and Azcapotzalco, took the corresponding titles of *chichimecatecuhtli* (lord of the Chichimecas) and *tepanecatecuhtli* (lord of the Tepanecas). Nominally all three tlatocáyotl were equal, but the Mexicas were in fact the dominant partner.[156]

This Triple Alliance, the so-called Aztec empire, soon extended its domination beyond the limits reached by all previous powers in Mesoamerica. Nevertheless, a few highly resistant polities, entrapped within its territory, remained independent states until Spanish contact: Tlaxcala and Huexotzinco in the Puebla-Tlaxcala region, Tototepec del Norte and Meztitlán to the northeast, and Yopitzinco, Tototepec del Sur, and Teotitlan in the south.[157] These ancient rivalries also shed light on the significance their collaboration in the Spanish search for Nuevo México could have had for the Mexicas, Tlaxcaltecas, and Huexotzincas, whose well-documented participation in several sixteenth-century conquest expeditions will be further discussed in chapter 6.

Image Plates

Plate 1. Chicomoztoc, *Mapa de Cuauhtinchan no. 2* (detail). Reproduced with permission from CONACULTA-INAH-MEX.

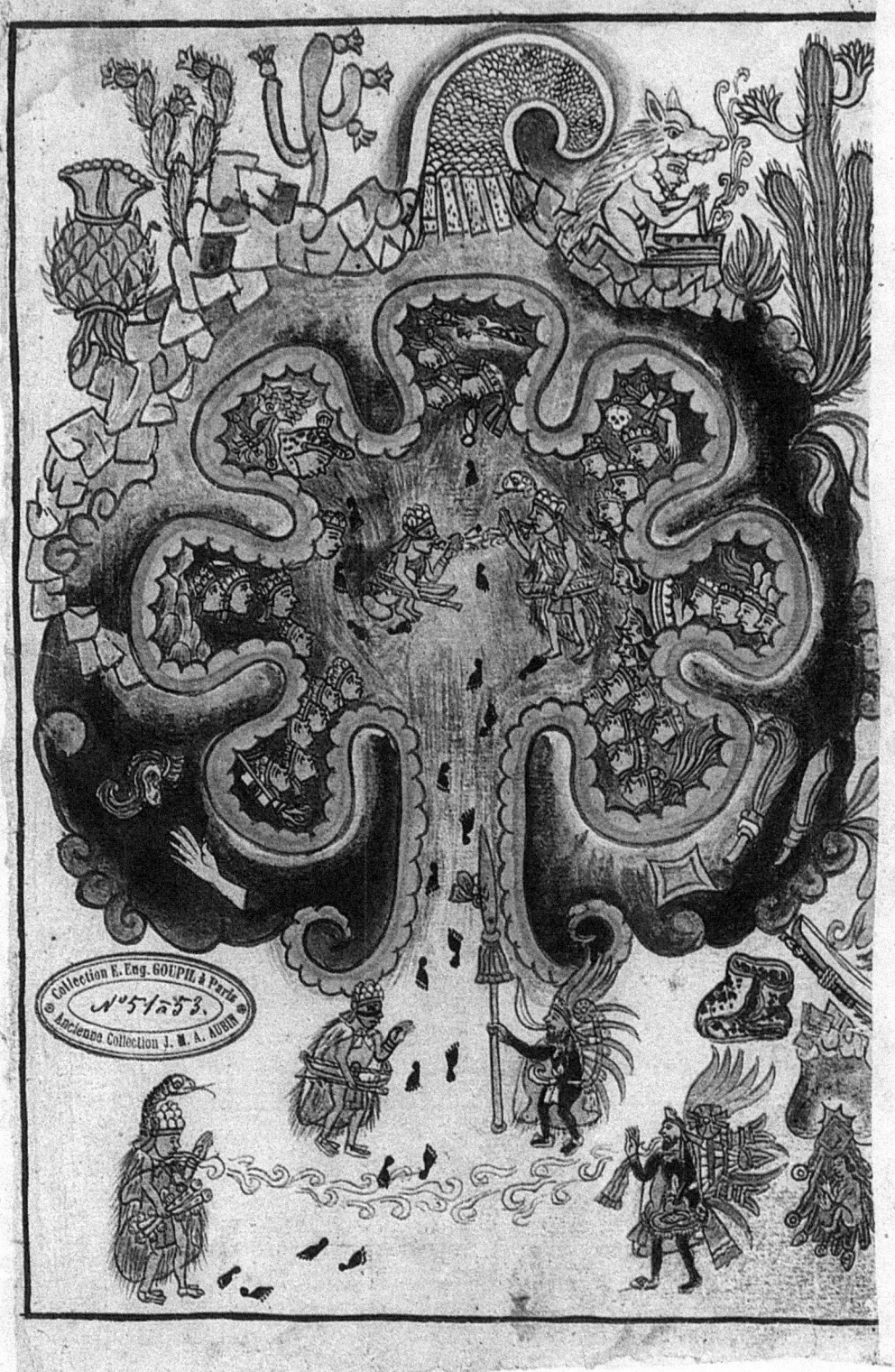

Plate 3. (*Above*) Chicomoztoc, *Codex Mexicanus*, plate 22. Reproduced with permission from Bibliothèque Nationale de France.

Plate 2. (*Opposite*) Chicomoztoc, *Historia Tolteca-Chichimeca*, f. 16r. Reproduced with permission from Bibliothèque Nationale de France.

Plate 4. Foundation of Mexico-Tenochtitlan, *Tira de Tepechpan*, plate 5. The lower register shows the founding of Tenochtitlan in the year 4 Tochtli (1366). The upper register shows the death of Icxicuahtli, Chichimeca ruler of Tepechpan, and the enthronement of his successor in the year 13 Tochtli (1362). Reproduced with permission from Bibliothèque Nationale de France.

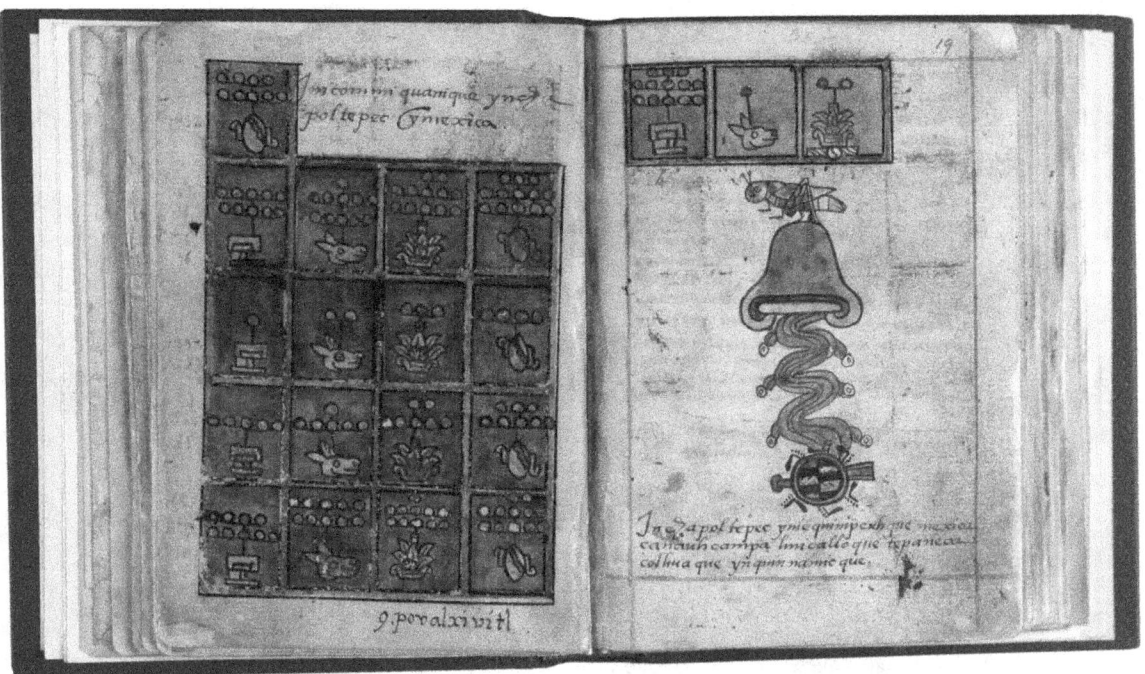

Plate 5. Year-sign grouping, *Codex Aubin*, f. 18v–19r. The scene corresponds to the Mexica stay in Chapultepec. Reproduced with permission. © Trustees of the British Museum.

Plate 6. Aztlan, *Codex Mexicanus*, plate 18. Reproduced with permission from Bibliothèque Nationale de France.

Plate 7. Aztlan, *Mapa Sigüenza* (detail). Reproduced with permission from CONACULTA-INAH-MEX.

Plate 8. Aztlan, *Codex Azcatitlan*, plates I–II. Reproduced with permission from Bibliothèque Nationale de France.

Plate 9. Aztlan, *Codex Aubin*, f. 3r. Reproduced with permission. © Trustees of the British Museum.

Plate 10. Foundation of Mexico-Tenochtitlan, *Codex Aubin*, f. 25v. Reproduced with permission. © Trustees of the British Museum.

Plate 11. (*Opposite*) Foundation of Mexico-Tenochtitlan, *Codex Mendoza*, f. 2r. Reproduced with permission from Bodleian Library, Oxford University.

Plate 12. Colhuacan, *Codex Azcatitlan*, plate III. Reproduced with permission from Bibliothèque Nationale de France.

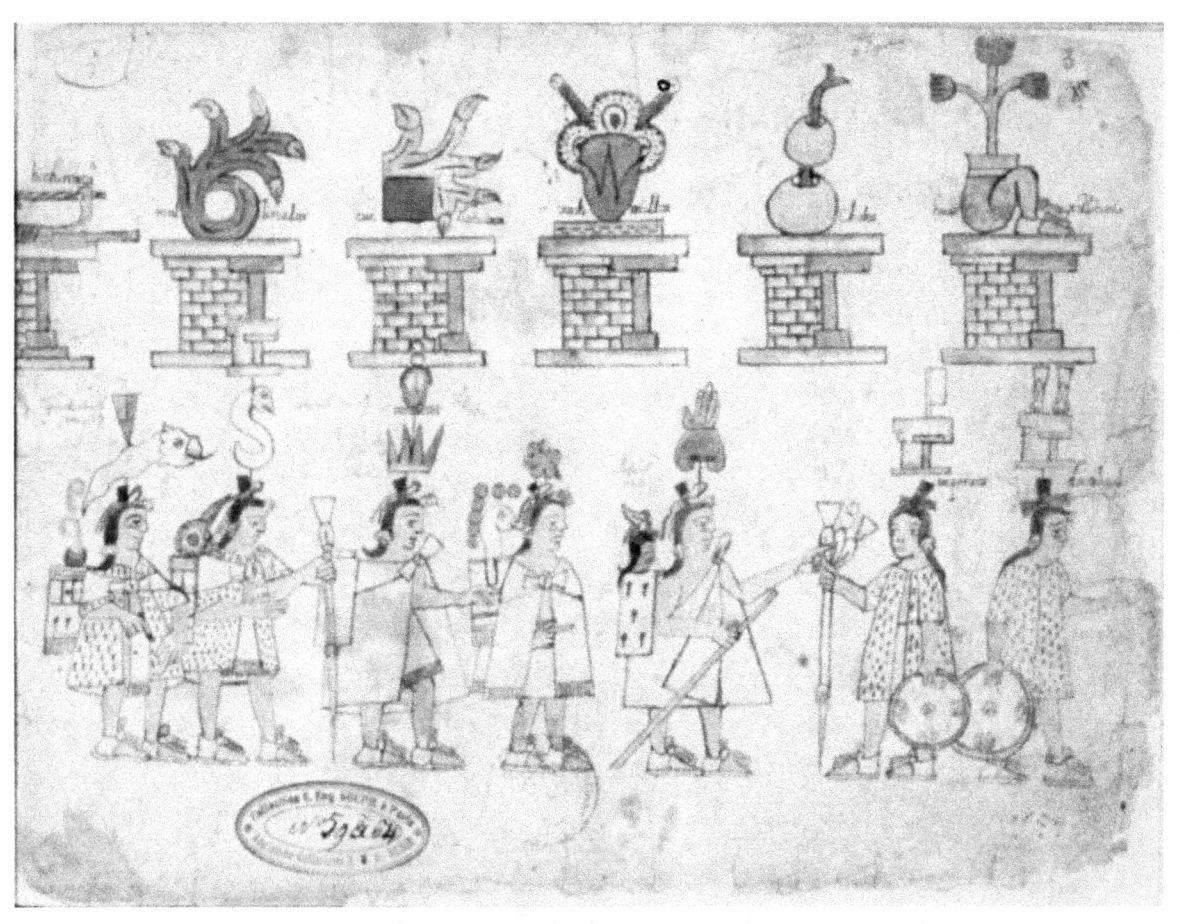

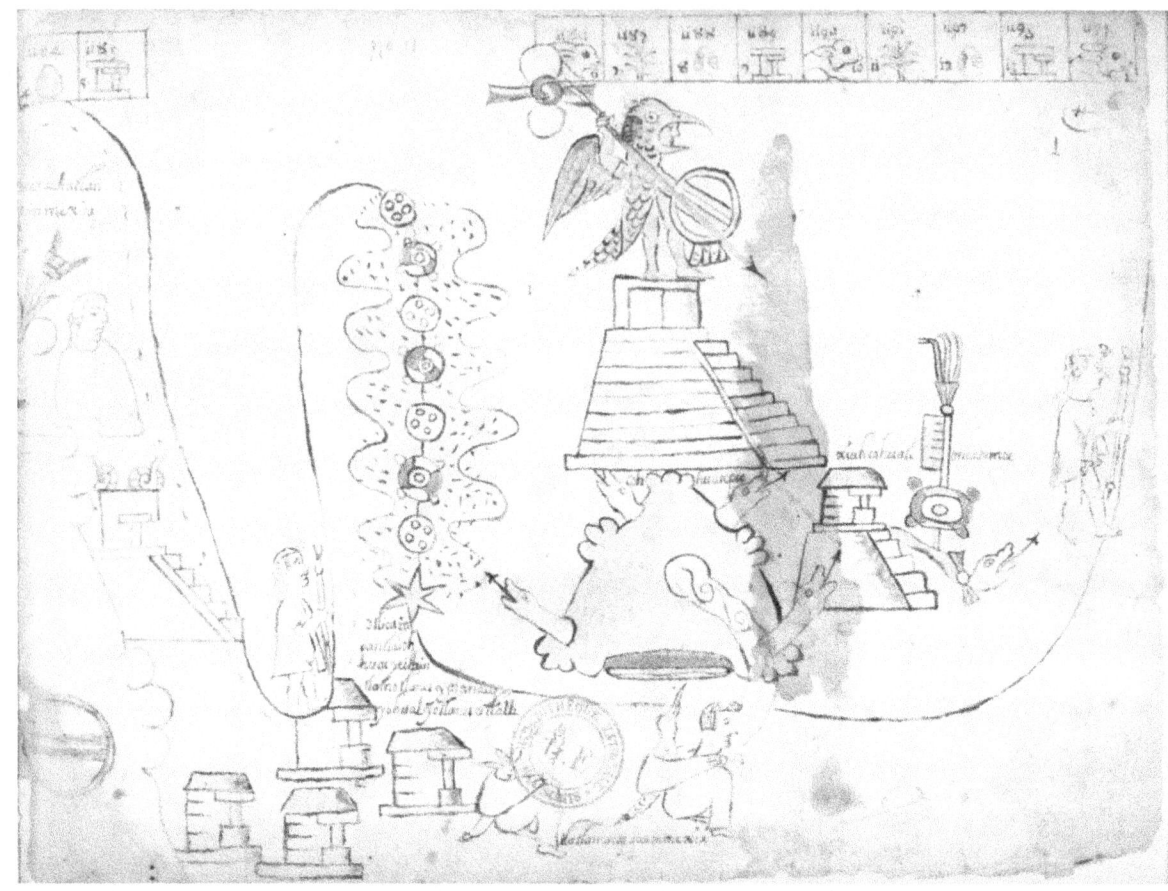

Plate 13. Coatepec, *Codex Azcatitlan*, plate VI. Reproduced with permission from Bibliothèque Nationale de France.

Plate 14. (*Opposite*) Teocalli de la Guerra Sagrada. Engraved monolithic monument, Museo Nacional de Antropología e Historia, Mexico. The figure represents the sign that marked the founding of Tenochtitlan, which became the toponym glyph for Mexico-Tenochtitlan. Reproduced with permission from CONACULTA-INAH-MEX.

Plate 15. *Códice de Tlatelolco*, plate I. Tlatelolca troops that Francisco Vázquez de Coronado took to the conquest of Cíbola, and Tlatelolca warriors under the command of Viceroy Antonio de Mendoza in the Mixtón War. Reproduced with permission from CONACULTA-INAH-MEX.

Plate 16. (*Following pages*) Terra Antipodv̌ Regis Castele, chart XII of an atlas by Fernão Vaz Dourado (*Portulanatlas Alte Welt und Terra Nova*), 1580. Reproduced with permission from the Bayerische Staatsbibliothek.

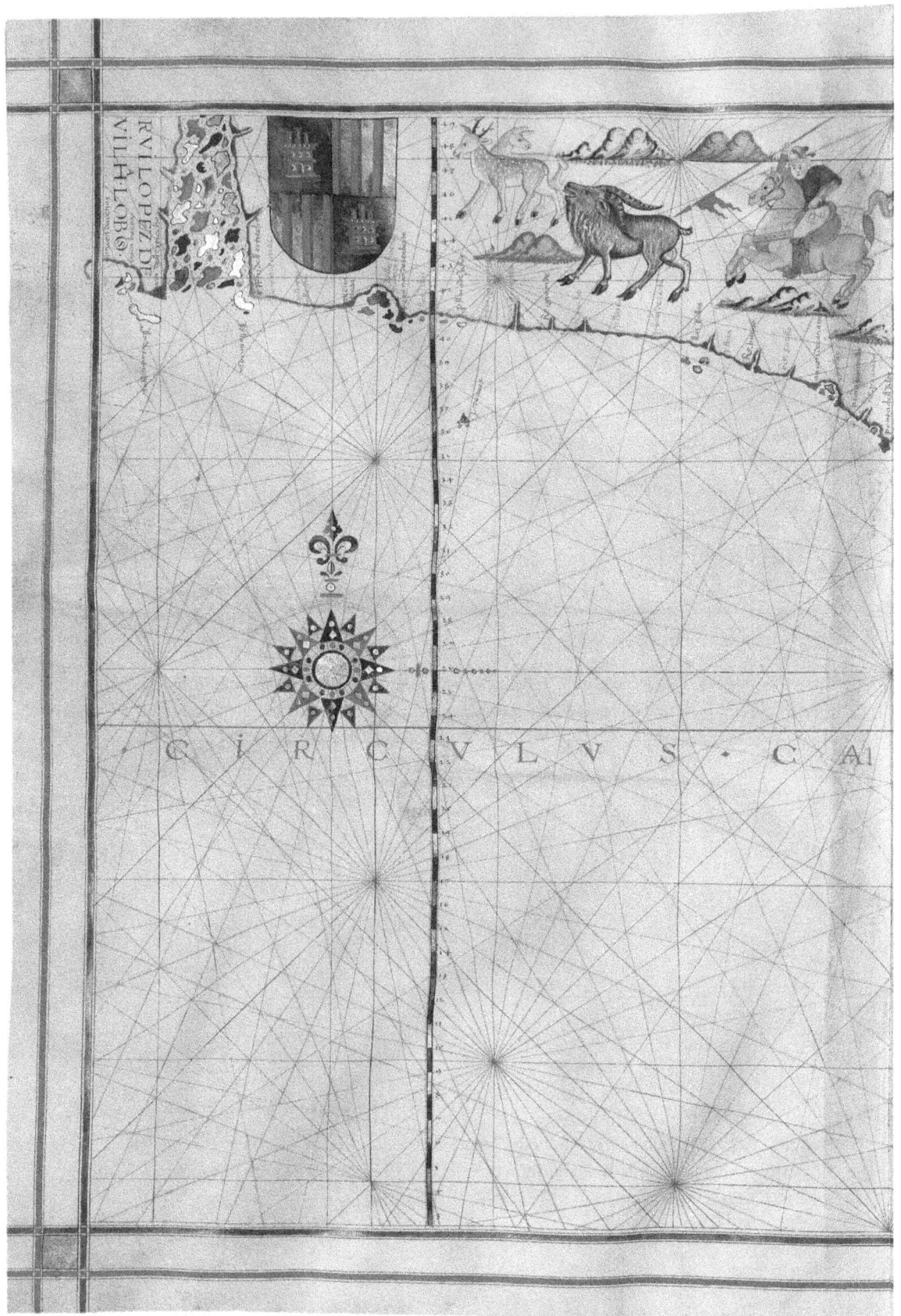

Maps

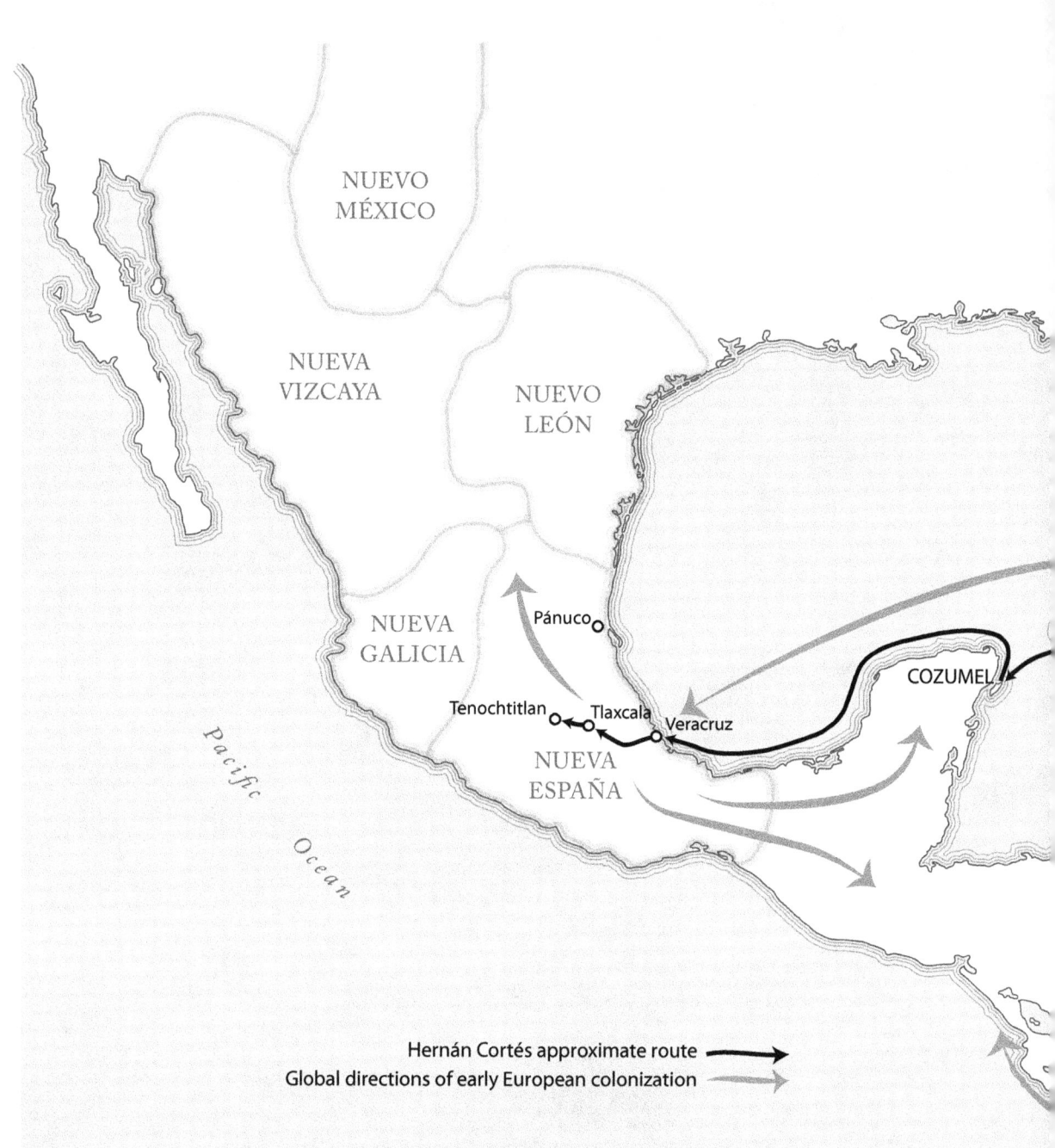

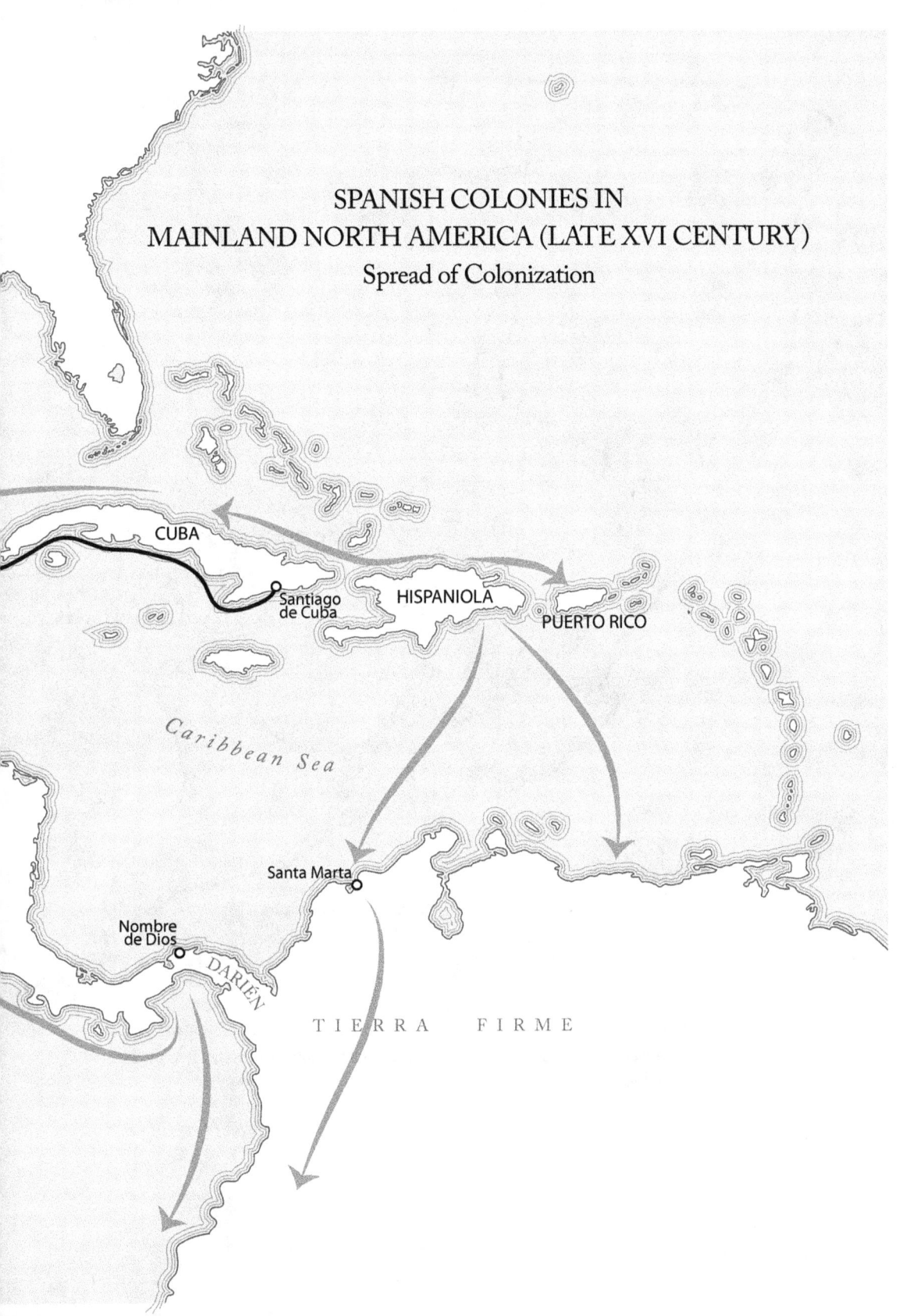

Map 1. Spanish colonies in mainland North America. *Based on a map by Armando Égido.*

Map 2. Mesoamerica, Aridamerica, and Oasisamerica. This map also shows the span of two relevant archaeological cultures in North America: the Chalchihuites and Aztatlán cultures. *Based on a map by Armando Égido.*

Map 3. Central, western, and northern Mexico. *Based on a map by Armando Égido.*

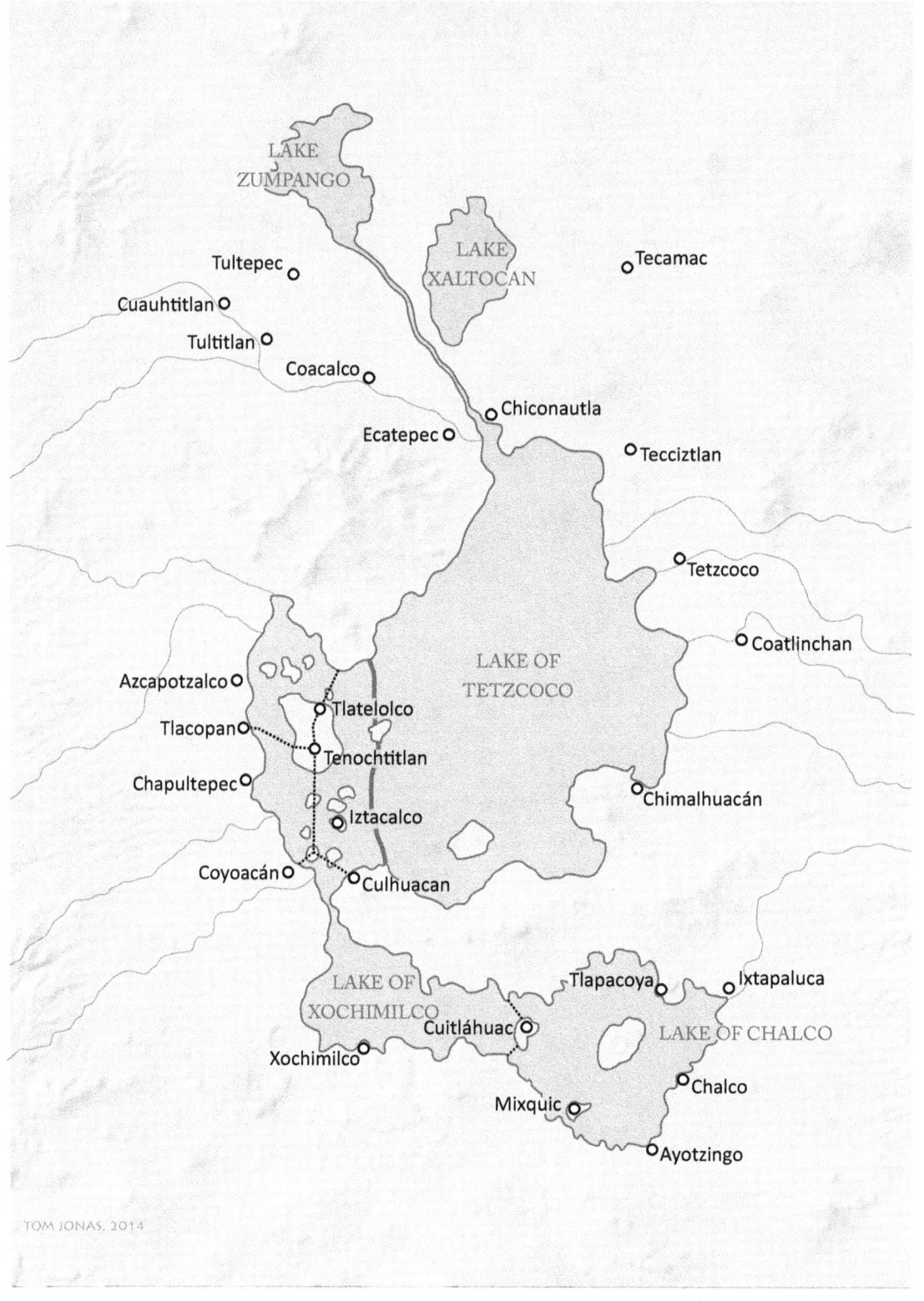

Map 4. Lake basin of Mexico in 1519. *Based on a map by Armando Égido.*

Map 5. (*Opposite*) Map of Mexico-Tenochtitlan attributed to Hernán Cortés. Nuremberg 1524. Reproduced with permission from the Getty Research Institute.

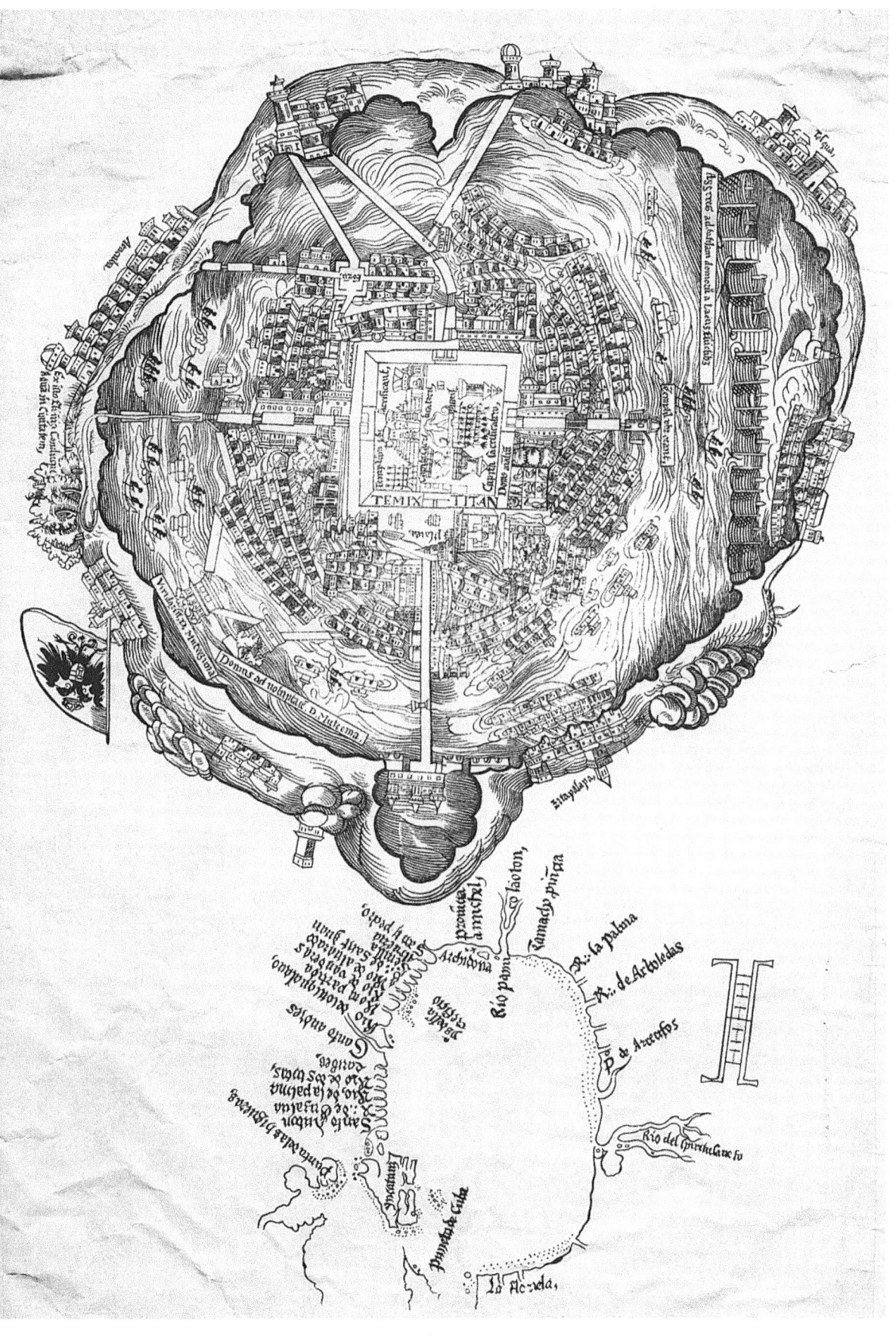

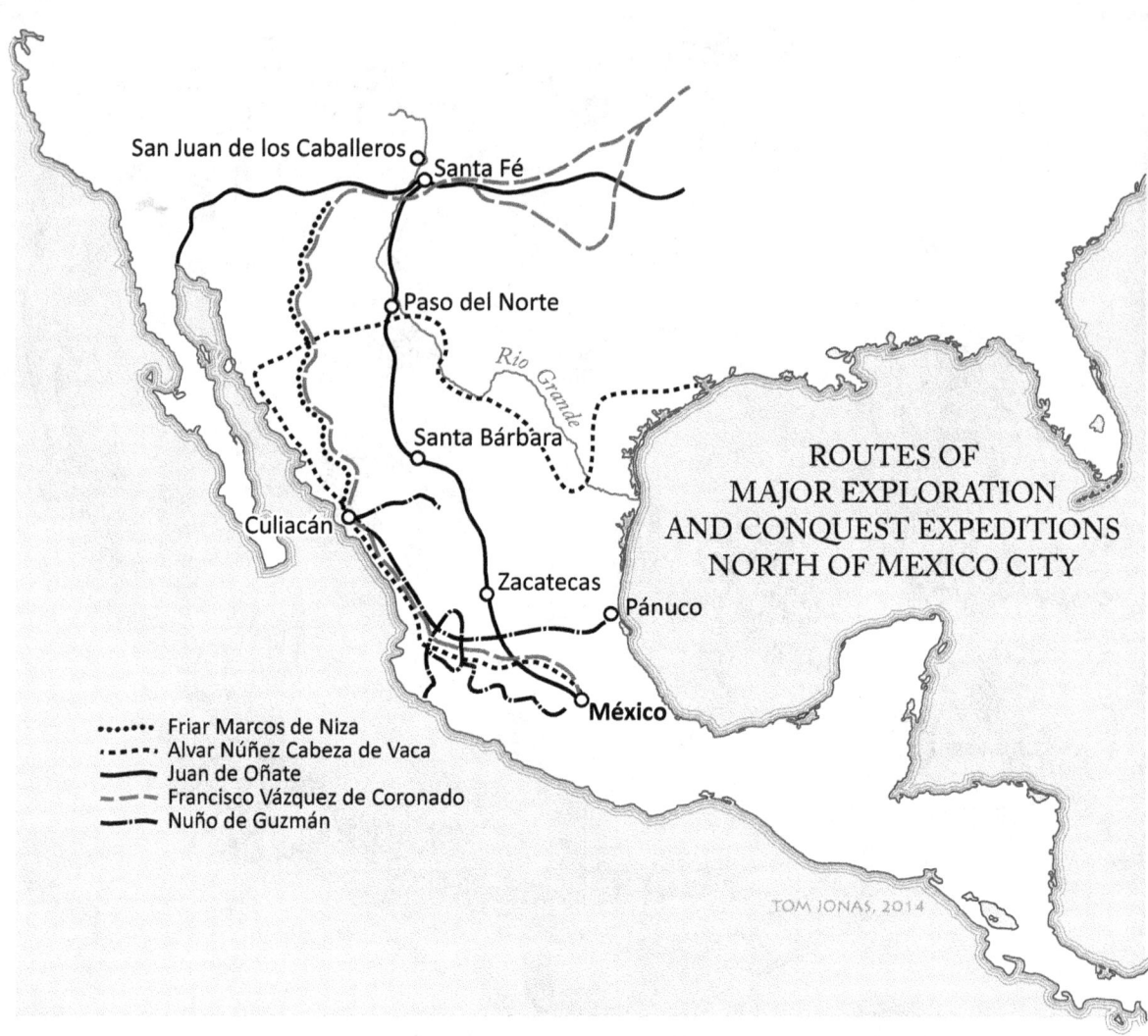

Map 6. Sixteenth century exploration and conquest expeditions north of Mexico City. The routes shown include Alvar Núñez Cabeza de Vaca, Nuño de Guzmán, Friar Marcos de Niza, Francisco Vázquez de Coronado, and Juan de Oñate. *Based on a map by Armando Égido.*

Figure 1. Chicomoztoc, *Codex Azcatitlan*, plate IV. Chicomoztoc is represented as a hill with an animal head resembling that of a bear. It is a European-influenced distortion of the indigenous glyph for cave (*oztotl*) consisting of a monster opening its mouth. The caves, which could be mistaken for the animal's feet, appear in the lower part of the hill. Reproduced with permission from Bibliothèque Nationale de France.

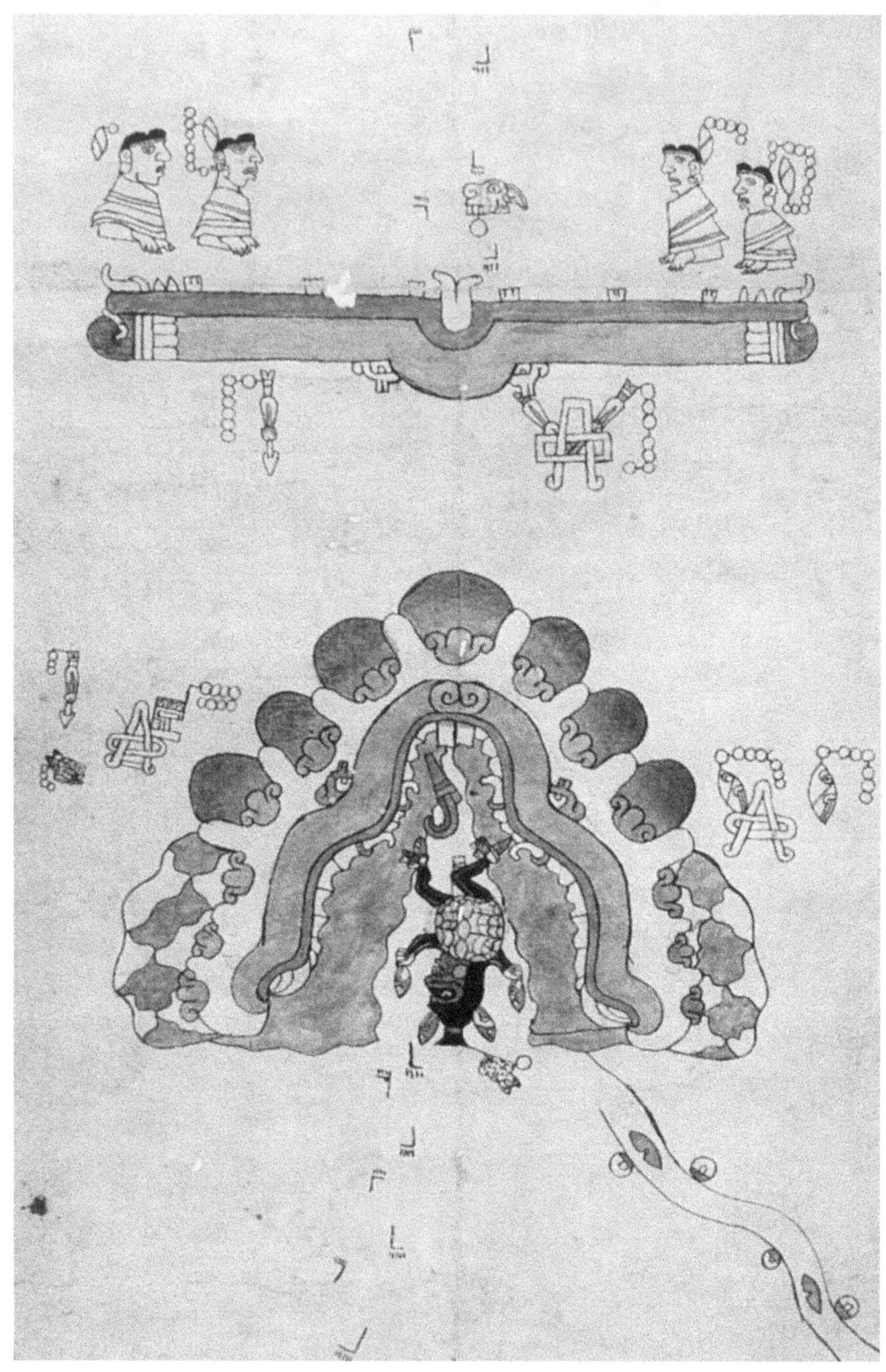

Figure 2. Chicomoztoc, *Selden Roll*, plate 2. Reproduced with permission from the Bodleian Library, Oxford University.

Figure 3. Chapultepec, *Códice Boturini*, plate XIX. The scene beside the group of year-signs represents the Mexica defeat in the war that expelled them from Chapultepec. Reproduced with permission from CONACULTA-INAH-MEX.

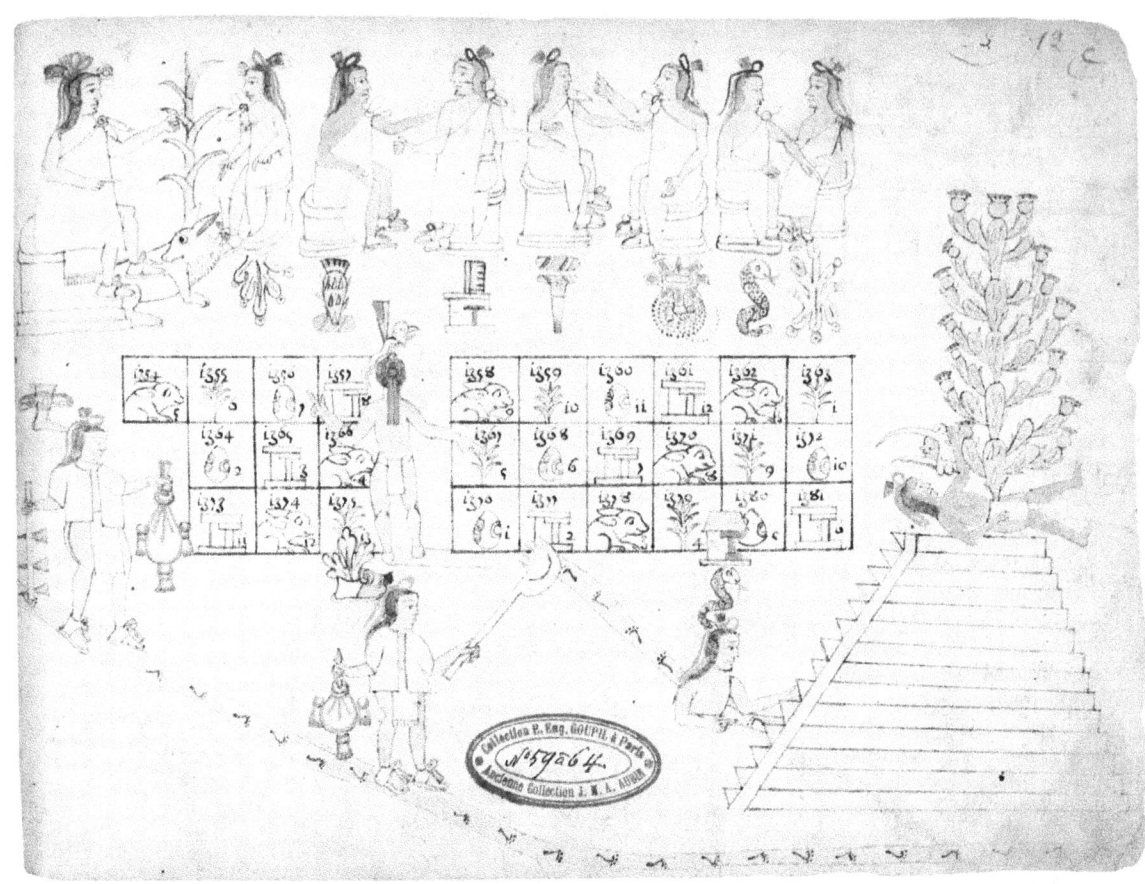

Figure 4. Foundation of Mexico-Tenochtitlan, *Codex Azcatitlan,* plate XII. At the center of the page is a year-sign grouping. The foundation scene appears at the far right of the plate. It is atypical as it represents the cactus growing from a sacrificed individual, presumably Cópil, on top of a pyramid. Reproduced with permission from Bibliothèque Nationale de France.

Figure 5. Aztlan, *Códice Boturini*, plate I. Reproduced with permission from CONACULTA-INAH-MEX.

Figure 6. Foundation of Mexico-Tenochtitlan, *Histoire mexicaine depuis 1221 jusqu'en 1549*, fol. 8r. Reproduced with permission from Bibliothèque Nationale de France.

Figure 7. Breaking of the tree, *Códice Boturini*, plate III. Reproduced with permission from CONACULTA-INAH-MEX.

Figure 8. Sacrifice of the demons or *mimixcoa*, *Códice Boturini*, plate IV. Reproduced with permission from CONACULTA-INAH-MEX.

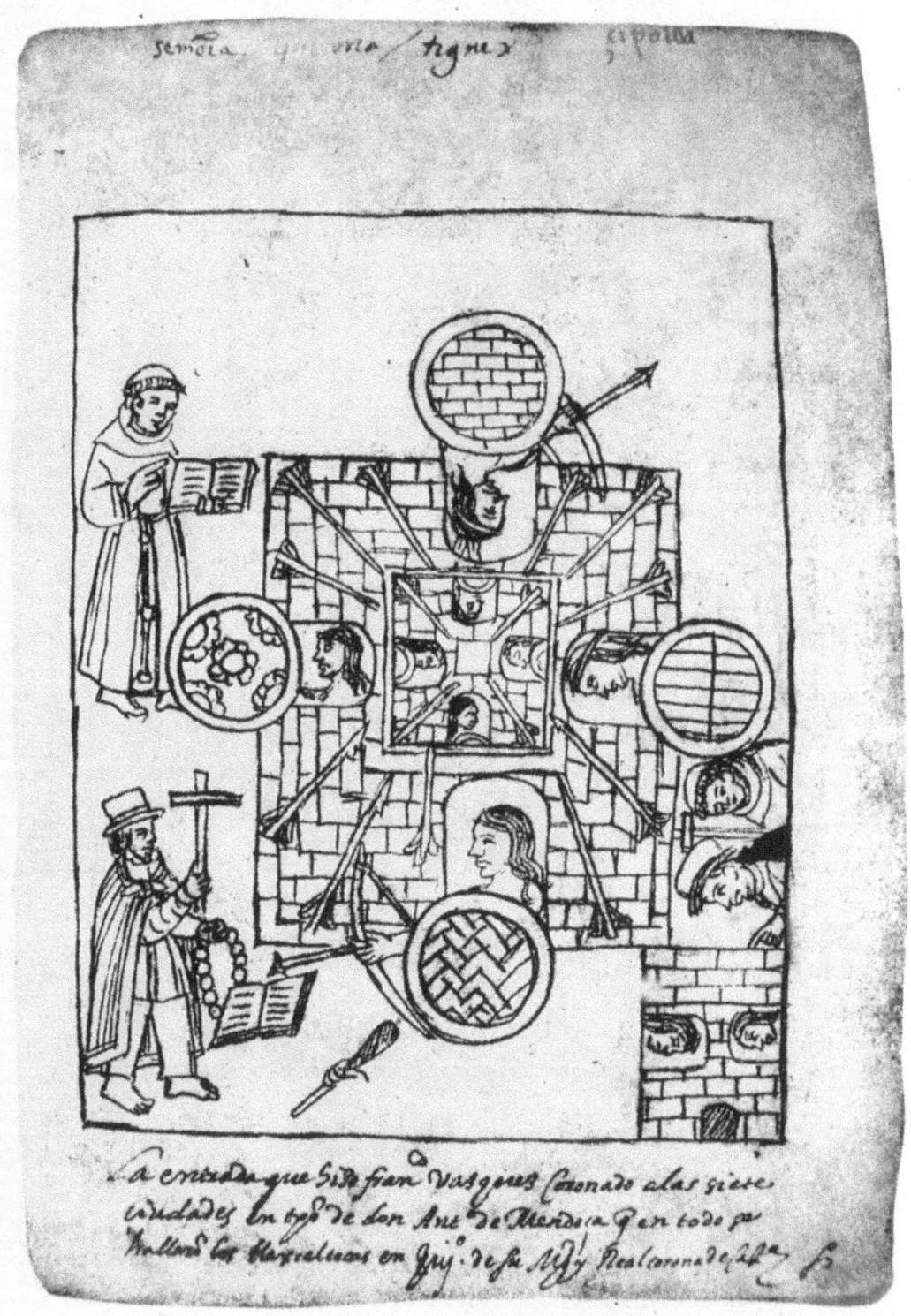

Figure 9. Cipolla (Cíbola/Zuñi), *Tlaxcala Codex*, in Diego Muñoz Camargo, *Descripción de la ciudad y provincia de Tlaxcala*, f. 317. The city of Cíbola is shown with seven gates (four in the large building of the central square and three in the small building in the lower right-hand corner) reminiscent of the seven caves of Chicomoztoc. Reproduced with permission from CONACULTA-INAH-MEX.

CHAPTER SIX

Your Past Is Our Future

Documenting a Cross-Cultural Loan

> *Ye shall utterly destroy all the places, wherein the nations which ye shall possess served their gods, upon the high mountains, and upon the hills, and under every green tree: and ye shall overthrow their altars, and break their pillars, and burn their groves with fire; and ye shall hew down the graven images of their gods, and destroy the names of them out of that place.*
>
>   Deuteronomy 12:2–3

The paradox that Spanish conquerors experienced when confronting urban life in Mesoamerica, and the ambivalent attitude they assumed toward indigenous culture after witnessing the strange yet familiar marvels of Mexico-Tenochtitlan, inscribe their sixteenth century expansion over present-day Mexico and the southwestern United States. As elsewhere in the New World, the conquerors behaved as if programmatically guided by Yahweh's prescription in Deuteronomy, laying waste to Indian settlements with spectacular thoroughness. They demolished the people's altars, destroyed their buildings, and burned the images of their gods—a suppressive performance that indigenous and early Spanish records of colonial history dramatically depict[1] and that modern literature on sixteenth century colonial discourse has taken as the hallmark of the European conceptualization of Amerindian otherness in general. Nonetheless, and without denying that the profound asymmetries and violence of colonialism had important repercussions at the level of representation, the "quest for Nuevo México" shows that in Mesoamerica, indigenous views were neither completely neglected nor entirely suppressed. On the contrary, they became part of the conquerors' cognitive repertoire, molding their expectations and informing their interpretation of the landscape and people they subsequently came across.

Despite twentieth century claims that the power of representation exercised by European conquerors as a cognitive strategy for domination was so entrenched in their own cultural categories that their understandings remained unaffected by indigenous ideas, several Spanish colonial sources remark that the original

Mexican homeland described in native pictorial records was the main target of various expeditions organized in New Spain. Some authors even declare to have seen vestiges of Aztec wanderings dating back to their ancient migration.

Besides the explicit assertions that Aztlan was in Nuevo México by José de Acosta (1590), by Alvarado Tezozómoc (1598), and in *Códice Ramírez* (ca. 1581–90),[2] the clearest testimonies linking Nuevo México to Nahua origin stories are contained in a couple of texts written by soldiers who participated in the expeditions led by Francisco de Ibarra to Nueva Vizcaya and by Juan de Oñate to Nuevo México. One is Baltasar de Obregón's *Historia de los descubrimientos antiguos y modernos de la Nueva España* (1584), which contains lengthy accounts of the main expeditions carried out between 1562 and 1582 in the present-day states of Sinaloa, Sonora, Durango, Chihuahua, New Mexico, and Arizona. The other is the epic poem by Gaspar de Villagrá, *Historia de la Nueva México* (1610), the most complete account of Oñate's 1595–98 expedition of conquest. Though focused on Francisco de Ibarra's performance in Nueva Vizcaya, the chronicle by Obregón links together a series of expeditions posterior to the subjugation of Mexico-Tenochtitlan for the first time: Friar Agustín Rodríguez's (1581) and Antonio de Espejo's (1582–83) entradas "in the land of Cibola" appear as the culmination of the same historical process initiated, according to Obregón, by Hernán Cortés and continued by Cabeza de Vaca (1528–36), Niza (1539), and Vázquez de Coronado (1540–42). More than two decades later, Villagrá also traced the antecedents of the enterprise in which he took part, that is, Oñate's 1598 conquest expedition, back to Hernán Cortés.

Neither Obregón nor Villagrá used the names Aztlan, Colhuacan, or Chicomoztoc. However, both mentioned the Mexicas' primeval abode, their migration, and the indigenous codices recording the story. Obregón, for instance, wrote that Hernán Cortés and Viceroy Antonio de Mendoza intended to "discover the origin, root, stock, and advent of the ancient Culgua Mexica, seriously suspecting numerous Indians, towns, and riches" existed there "to be placed under the mantle of our holy Catholic faith."[3] Twenty-five years later, Villagrá claimed that along the way from Mexico to Nuevo México, vestiges of ruined buildings and broken ceramics stood as witnesses to the migration of the ancient Mexicans.[4]

Statements of this kind are not only present in this type of reflective texts, composed several years after the narrated events as general overviews that supplement personal recollections with information from other sources, or in chronicles by historians who took no part in the feats they narrate. They also appear in all sorts of petitions, legal claims, or testimonial accounts submitted to the viceroyal or metropolitan authorities in connection with ongoing or projected journeys. A review of such material shows that the legitimacy of colonial penetration in the north was anchored, to a large extent, to the image of the Nahuas' primeval abode, and it was both represented and experienced as a backward reconstruction in time and space of the route followed by the forefathers of the Aztecs and other Nahuas, the procedure being an "*un*-walking" of the ancestral way, a "*de*-migration." The fact that indigenous historical discourse came to shape Spanish colonial objectives, prompting the projection of the name Nuevo México onto the north, is clearly spelled out in the following paragraph by Obregón: "The first and foremost reason why [the Spaniards] aspired to the discovery and journey to the provinces of Cíbola and Mexican place of origin was that the marquis [Cortés] found the chronicles, hieroglyphs, and paintings among the paraphernalia, furniture, and treasure of the powerful king Moctezuma, which revealed the origin, stock, and advent into these kingdoms of the Culguas and ancient Mexicans."[5]

Previous chapters discussed the importance commonly attributed to European legendary themes that the Spanish conquistadors, bewildered by the scene they found in Central Mexico, presumably projected onto the geographic and social space they colonized in North America. The Portuguese legend about seven fugitive bishops escaping the Moorish invasion of the Iberian Peninsula, I argued, did not inform Vázquez de Coronado's expedition or any other subsequent journey into the area that later became New Mexico. The "medieval hypothesis," resting on the assumption that Spanish conquistadors acted on the basis of imaginary geographies that tainted their vision with well-known European chimeras, pertains to a historiographic tradition that reduces the ideal worlds of conquerors to the notion of "the marvelous," a distinctive element of popular culture in medieval Europe. Fully developed by Enrique de Gandía in 1929, the thesis became current in the 1940s, when authors like Irving Leonard and Ida Rodríguez Prampolini reinterpreted the early history of the Spanish expansionist career, emphasizing that European fantastic imagery shaped the New World enterprise as much as the Crown's imperial project, the spirit of crusade, and the ambition for gold and spices.[6]

At the time, this was an important contribution, but excessive emphasis on the preestablished mental baggage of Europeans resulted in a general disregard for the role that native traditions played in forging the sixteenth century image of the New World. In the study of northern New Spain, in particular, this emphasis diluted the importance of native Mesoamerican historical discourse—and indigenous politico-territorial interests—in shaping the colonizing process. Greek and Roman legendary beings and places were certainly sought in the Americas, but, as shown in chapter 4, they evaporated in the continental territory to the north once Cortés subjugated the so-called Aztec empire. On what basis do historians sustain the idea that the compelling force of such imaginings survived the colonization of Central Mexico? The sources suggest that after facing the complex, hierarchical societies of Mesoamerica, the Spaniards renovated their conceptual tools to meet the challenges that the land offered, which means they constructed *with* their Indian subjects a transcultural object of desire.

New Mexico's early history is one of alternating hope and disenchantment. As conquest progressed beyond the mining districts of Nueva Vizcaya, the settlers' dreams of rapid enrichment and social enhancement vanished, for neither spectacular wealth nor great urban centers came into view north of Santa Bárbara (modern Parral, Chihuahua). Yet lay and religious adventurers gave complete credence to rumors promising findings similar to those in the Valley of Mexico. Scholars mystified at such discordance between expectation and "empirical reality" cannot explain why the Spaniards were so reluctant to abandon the hope that the north concealed a world of incredible wealth and urban refinement. Certainly the old Aztec capital resembled nothing Europeans had seen before, but the supposition that this made them blind to local historical knowledge and credulous of the legends they had grown up with disregards the intersubjective dimensions of practice. Wild dreams of wealth and power provoked by the overwhelming encounter with Mexico-Tenochtitlan could only develop into feasible projects with the firm support of solid evidence, and it was Nahua traditions of ancestral origin, indigenous reports concerning extant locations, and personal experience that served as such. Thus, it was not a feverish imagination lost in the pursuit of chimeras, but the formulation of an empirical reality that propelled the Spaniards northward.

The circa 1530–32 testimonies on Isabel Moctezuma's ancestry titled *Origen de los mexicanos* and *Relación de la genealogía* testify to the early Spanish awareness of ancient migrations and the urban origin of Náhuatl-speaking Culhuas. Both documents record an original migration from Central Mexico to a place called "Culhuacán" or "Teuculhuacán," where an urban civilization had developed before the migrants went back to establish Tula, and much later, resettle the Valley of México.[7] Both documents ponder the veracity of the pictorial documents and indigenous oral traditions telling the story, but *Origen de los mexicanos* is more explicit about the fact that conquerors believed them to be true: "Where this land [of Culhacán] is, [the Indians] cannot tell. Spaniards say there is one, and it exists, but until now no other land has been discovered that is better than this we are in, so we cannot assert it is as people say, that supposedly six cities exist there, and one is just like this one here [Mexico]."[8]

It shall be remembered from chapter 3 that various *relaciones* on the conquest of Nueva Galicia by soldiers in Nuño de Guzmán's army affirmed they knew about the "seven cities" before initially leaving Mexico, so it is clear that the Spaniards had Nahua historical discourse in mind from an early date. By the mid-sixteenth century, New Spain's imaginary geography comprised an allegedly rich, densely populated country defined in the sources as the ancient Mexicans' place of origin. The province of Nuevo México was established in the course of the search for this imaginary place. As shown below, several sixteenth and some early seventeenth century sources using the term "Nuevo México" actually meant the starting point of the Aztec/Mexica migration as described in Nahua traditions. This represents the culmination of a process of semantic duplication that began in 1521 with the naming of New Spain.

Spaniards Attest to the Truth of Aztec/Mexica Migration Stories

Conquerors were able to plan their exploits on the basis of indigenous historical narratives because they fulfilled two basic requirements to qualify as true and authoritative knowledge. For one thing, they were chronologically structured as annals (that is, records of events in yearly sequence), a well-reputed format for preserving historical knowledge in Europe, too. For another, although orally transmitted, they were contained in pictorial codices that conquerors readily identified as books.[9] Indians had no alphabetic writing, but they drew characters (*caracteres*) that Spaniards praised as hieroglyphic texts, not simple drawings. Thus, the authoritative status of writing in Christian culture made of these traditions legitimate knowledge, as is clear from Obregón's quotation above on the "chronicles, hieroglyphs, and paintings" Cortés found in Moctezuma's palace and from the following passage by Villagrá:

> From these new regions it is notorious
> Publicly known and famous
> That those most ancient Mexicans descended,
> Who to the famous City of México
> They gave their name to be
> Forever and eternally remembered
> ....
> The truth of which is proved and verified
> By those very ancient paintings
> And hieroglyphic means they use
> To negotiate, speak and understand each other[10]
>   Canto 1

Another element conforming to Iberian conventions that had a legitimizing effect was the fact that multiple testimonies—oral and documentary—told the same story. This fitted well with the criteria for authenticity and credibility current in the Spanish legal and political practice of the time, which established the veracity of any given statement through the accumulation of testimonies. Therefore, since many informants from different localities told the same story in a similar way, certainty over its trustworthiness became stronger as new versions came to light.

As seen in chapter 5, Nahua migration narratives shared a general structure that fulfilled political legitimizing functions in preconquest times. Most accounts start from a place in the underworld, the "Seven Caves" (Chicomoztoc), combined in the Aztec/Mexica story with another location surrounded by water: Aztlan. Sometimes Chicomoztoc, rather than a starting point, is categorized as a sanctuary visited early on to receive divine protection. The migrants, invariably instructed by a tutelary god who offers a glorious destiny, set out on a long pilgrimage after crossing an arm of the sea, a lake, or a stream, and their journey continues until finding a sign, previously revealed by the god, which indicates the end point or Promised Land. In the Mexica tradition, the god Huitzilopochtli is the commanding divinity and the waters crossed are those of the lake wherein the island city of Aztlan stood.

Let us start then by analyzing in detail the passages corresponding to the Aztec/Mexica migration in Villagrá's *Historia de la Nueva México*.[11] A late-arriving soldier in Oñate's army (around 1597), he published this epic poem in 1610, when the province was running the risk of being officially abandoned. In the first part of the work, Villagrá argues, as did Baltasar de Obregón decades before about Francisco de Ibarra's exploits, that long before heading in its direction, Spaniards knew of the land of Mexican origins. Villagrá calls it Nueva México instead of Cíbola because this was the name of the now-conquered province with the Pueblo villages as its central core. In contrast to Obregón, however, the poet-soldier expands on the migration and relates some of its episodes to things he saw along the journey.

After stating the geographic position of this territory, which he contributed to conquering, Villagrá declares that it is publicly known to be the original homeland of the ancient Mexicans. Then he narrates Nahua migration traditions, arguing that they lend truth to its reputation, also confirmed by other tales heard by soldiers on the frontier of New Spain. Natives in those regions, he declares, repeated unanimously that far to the north the land concealed a "rough, hollow cave" (*la cóncava caverna desabrida*), from which "two most spirited brothers of royal lineage" (*dos briossisimos hermanos / de altos y nobles reyes descendientes*) had departed long before, each guiding a large group of people and spurred by the desire to extend the scope of their empire. Not far from where they set out, however, they saw an apparition. A well-known demon euphemistically termed *aquel maldito* (that accursed one) suddenly rose before them, disguised as an old, horrible woman, to deliver the devil's instructions. On her head this grisly woman carried an enormous piece of pure iron in the shape of a turtle shell, and after declaring that she approved of the brothers' ambition of power and glory, she commanded one to return and tend to their father, old and sick, while instructing the other to follow the destiny of his noble fate and continue down the road to found Mexico-Tenochtitlan. I quote the words that Villagrá attributes to the demon, which correspond, though distortedly, to the mandate of Huitzilopochtli that prompted the Aztec/Mexica migration:

> And to prevent that most of his estates
> Like fugitive comet that goes away
> Remain due to his end and sorrowful death
> Without a natural lord for their protection
> It is necessary that one of you return
> And the other shall pursue his noble fate
> Prosperous destiny and settle down
> . . . .
> Where on a hard and solid crag
> By clear water entirely surrounded
> You will see a prickly pear tree standing
> And on its thick and wide leaves perching
> An enormous eagle, beautiful, misshapen
> Fiercely feeding on
> A big snake that in its claws
> You will observe is twisted, tightly grasped
> For there he wants to be established
> The high and generous metropolis
> Of the almighty state
> That he expressedly commands
> To be baptized Mexico-Tenochtitlan
> And with this memorable insignia
> You will later raise after new battles
> And future glories your coat of arms.[12]
>   Canto 2

These passages contain the central elements of the Aztec/Mexica migration as recounted in Nahua tradition: the place of origin, Chicomoztoc, represented by "the rough, hollow cave"; the departure at the request of a god, Huitzilopochtli (here the disguised demon); and the emblematic sign of the eagle devouring a serpent as indicative of the arrival into the Promised Land (the Valley of Mexico). Furthermore, they also contain, in a somewhat distorted form, the tree-breaking episode that marked the first schism of the Nahua migrant group in *Códice Boturini* and other related sources; that is, the moment when following Huitzilopochtli's mandate, the Aztecs parted with the other Nahua groups (the eight calpoltin) and changed their name to Mexicas.[13] Villagrá expresses this episode first with the demon's instructions ordering one brother to return home, thereby enabling the other to proceed; and second with the piece of iron shaped like a turtle shell that the demon uses to indicate, marking the soil as if it were a map, the way in which the migrants had to settle the territory once they reached the Promised Land:

> And because greed, clumsy vice
> Of mean acquisition frequently causes
> Great disagreement and conflict,
> To avoid confrontation and dissent
> I shall better mark the boundaries
> Limits and milestones of the lands
> That each of you for your own government
> Should recognize without pretending
> To any other domain, neither more nor less
> Than what herein will be marked off.
> And raising up her heels
> Firmly standing on her toes
> She lifted her thin yet powerful arms,
> And then propelled her monstrous cargo [the load of iron],
> As if it were a fierce thunderbolt
> That with great terror and astonishment amazes
> ....
> Thus with sudden roar and noise
> She released the mighty load
> And as it hit the solid ground
> That was left quaking, totally shaken
> It broke itself to pieces that sprinkled all around
> ....
> In this same manner, plan, and mode
> The mighty land they divided.[14]
>   Canto 2

Villagrá does not reveal the sources on which he based this account. Most probably he used orally transmitted information, though he could have seen some of the versions recorded on the topic by missionaries in the second half of the sixteenth century. It is difficult to know whether he saw any of the indigenous pictorial documents that he characterized as "very ancient paintings" and "hieroglyphic means." However, his oral sources were certainly well-informed. Though written later, two of the four versions of the Aztec/Mexica migration contained in Chimalpahin's *Memorial breve* and *Octava relación* exhibit significant coincidences with Villagrá's story:

> This is how Tetzauhtéotl [the devil] came guiding the *mexitin* whom he had taken away: they were settled and had their city in Aztlan Chicomóztoc, where the Azteca Chicomoztocas ruled, and their *huey tlatohuani* was named

Moteuczoma and ruled over the Aztecs and other peoples at once. This *huey tlatohuani* Moteuczoma had two sons; and when he was about to die he passed on to them his lordship. The elder, whose name is unknown, became *tlatohuani* of the Cuextecas and other peoples; the younger was called Chalchiuhtlatónac and became *tlatohuani* of the Mexicas. Once Chalchiuhtlatónac became *tlatohuani* of the Mexicas his elder brother hated him and said in anger: this cannot be, only one must be *tlatohuani*, of the Mexicas [too]; I will rule over the Mexicas as a whole like my father did.[15]

According to this version, the Mexicas then left Aztlan, after having repeatedly crossed an arm of the sea to deposit oblations in Chicomoztoc for the devil, Tetzauhtéotl Yaotequihua, until at last the priest Huitziltzin announced they had finally succeeded in leaving Aztlan. At this point they were close to the coast, so they settled down and lived on fishing. But the narrative is interrupted at this point, giving way to the start of another, different version of departure:

Herein begins the other tale, here is painted the initial journey of the ancient Mexicans: when these Mexica-Azteca-Teochichimecas left the place called Aztlan, they departed from amid the waters divided in seven *tlaxilacaltin* or *calpules*. That is how they went in their canoes to make penitence and offerings of *oyamel* branches in Chicomoztoc, [so called] because there is a rocky cave with seven openings. . . . And when it was time to leave . . . for three days at dawn a bird named *huitzitzilcuicuítzcatl* was calling, and also for three nights the bird was calling the Mexitin saying: let us go, the time has come, the night is clearing, it is dawn. . . . This he cried out for three days to the guardian of the god and priest named Huitziltzin . . . because it was the devil Tetzauhtéotl Yaotequihua who spoke, also appearing before him in human form; and prior to their departure he gave Huitziltzin six divine or diabolic commandments, ordering him to comply.[16]

Certainly Villagrá's version is far from identical. To begin with, Villagrá omits the dynastic dispute incident, transforming it into one among several instructions the devil delivered when the group split up. Nevertheless, like Chimalpahin, he mentions a great lord ruling Aztlan who, close to death, left to each of his two sons the government of a sector of the people he ruled. On the other hand, both authors attribute the departure to a diabolic mandate. The elements in Villagrá's poem that evoke Chimalpahin's chronicles are tenuous but unequivocal: the cave, the two brothers who are leaders, the schism, the devil appearing in human form and his mandates. Further research is required to determine why an old, horrible woman substitutes in the poet-soldier's text for the singing or crying bird, which appears not only in Chimalpahin but other Nahua sources. Most probably Villagrá blended misunderstood fragments, maybe even pictorial representations, from this and other cosmogonic stories, as it seems he did in describing as "a fierce thunderbolt" the propelled piece of iron this devil-woman threw to inscribe her land demarcation commandment.

Plate VI of *Codex Azcatitlan* shows Huitzilopochtli atop a pyramid on the hill of Coatepec holding a shield and ready to throw his spear (plate 13). The scene corresponds to a dramatic schism between the migrant Mexicas, reviewed in chapter 5, when a number of dissidents who wanted to end the migration prematurely were slain by their deified leader.[17] Durán, Alvarado Tezozómoc, Torquemada,[18] and *Historia de los mexicanos por sus pinturas* also narrate the episode, but the latter describes it in the same terms as Sahagún narrates the cosmogonic myth where the god Huitzilopochtli, born in armor, slays Coyolxauhqui and his innumerable brothers, using a fire-serpent called *xiuhcoatl* by way of a spear.[19] The myth is concerned with the birth of the sun, but Villagrá could have interpreted the fire-serpent as lightning, and he could even have seen a pictorial representation similar to the one in *Codex Azcatitlan* where the fire-serpent, instead of a spear shape, had a rather serpentine shape.

Despite its multiple distortions, Villagrás's narrative reflects a wealth of local historical knowledge that circulated among the Spaniards, who shared with one another the information they heard, read, and absorbed. As a captain in Juan de Oñate's army, Villagrá had access to firsthand information on the Indian civilization the conquest had destroyed. For instance, Oñate's father, Cristóbal, had arrived in New Spain in 1524, participated in the conquest of Nueva Galicia under Nuño de Guzmán, and later became governor of Nueva Galicia.[20] Other captains under Juan de Oñate in the conquest of Nuevo México also had direct kinship ties to original conquerors and settlers. As for the events concerning the colonizing process before Oñate's expedition, it is quite possible that Villagrá obtained most information from oral sources as well. He frequently mentions that his assertions are based on eyewitness accounts when speaking of things he did not personally see. Besides, we know that many of his fellow soldiers had participated in earlier expeditions. He may also have been familiar with the reports by Núñez Cabeza de Vaca (1542) and the passages on the conquest of Nueva Vizcaya, Cíbola, and Nuevo México contained in early printed chronicles such as Baltasar de Obregón's.

The most remarkable aspect of the first cantos in Villagrá's poem, however, is not the degree of detail with which they reconstruct past events he may have known of from hearsay or through other texts. Rather, it is Villagrá's remarks as an eyewitness (*como testigo de vista*) that are most revealing; particularly the empirical evidence he provides to confirm the Aztec/Mexica migration story, as well as the way in which he connects Nahua myths, his own experience, and the reports concerning the Seven Cities that Spanish soldiers constantly heard from Indian informants.

To begin with, Villagrá asserts that just as the obelisk—"that memorable needle"—stands in the ruins of Classical Rome, "the big [iron] milestone that remained right where it was planted" (*el gran mojón que allí quedó plantado*) stood as a monument on the way to Nuevo México. Therefore, he continues, every soldier in Oñate's army could see the portent and realize in complete amazement that it proved the Mexica story. Moreover, to convince the reader, he argues that he could see the metal was as pure and fine as *Copella* silver, and no iron vein that could explain its provenance existed in the vicinity.[21] Second, he mentions the ruins of a large city—most probably La Quemada—and the abundant ceramic shards that the army constantly came across:

> That it is from this new territory where
> The refined Mexicans first departed is indicated
> By the large, destroyed city
> Everyone can see in Nueva Galicia
> With its massive buildings turned to ruins,
> Which the natives of the land
> Assert was erected and founded
> By those New Mexicans who left
> The land we now are searching for
> ....
> Plus, beyond this place the cautious soldiers
> Everywhere they walked discovered
> Spread out far and wide
> Obvious traces, tracks, and signals
> Of the truth we now investigate
> For across all those deserted lands
> We always found, without intending
> Lots of fine and poor ceramics
> Sometimes gathered in large piles
> Sometimes spread around, dispersed.[22]
>   Canto 2

It could be argued, of course, that his was a post-factum interpretation, elaborated after the province was established and at a time when the colonial and metropolitan authorities were questioning the benefit of keeping it as a colony, thereby making it necessary to find justifications for its maintenance. In addition, it is clear from other documents that, in publishing his poem, Villagrá sought to back up his request to be appointed governor of a mining region, as at the time of its writing he was negotiating in Spain the corresponding royal charter.[23] Both circumstances suggest it could be strategically beneficial to present Nuevo México as the Aztec ancestral homeland and to show that many other conquerors since Cabeza de Vaca and Cortés himself had tried to find the place. Still, the usage of the Aztec original abode as a lure to magnify New Mexico's worth proves that Aztlan was a widespread, long-held object of desire, and also that Spaniards took native historical traditions as valid knowledge. Earlier documents (letters, reports, and petitions) deriving from the 1580s expeditions to the Pueblo area and other enterprises not necessarily planned to explore that region also refer to Nuevo México in such terms that an association with the original Aztec homeland, when not explicit, is inescapable.

The first pertinent document to bring forth is the one Gordon Brotherston and Ana Gallegos call the *Tlaxcala Codex*;[24] that is, the final section (folios 236–317) of Diego Muñoz Camargo's *Historia de Tlaxcala*.[25] It is a sixteenth century pictorial manuscript that consists of a series of 156 scenes primarily depicting the battles Tlaxcalan Indians fought against other native peoples as part of the obligations deriving from their alliance with Cortés and other European captains. The *Tlaxcala Codex* is no doubt related to the document known as *Lienzo de Tlaxcala*, painted around 1550, as it contains almost the same scenes in the same order and with the same Náhuatl glosses.[26] However, it expands on the lienzo to include the conquests of Guatemala, Oriente, Nicaragua, and Oaxaca, as well as Vázquez de Coronado's expedition to Cíbola (Cipolla in the codex glosses). This latter scene occupies the last folio and shows an enclosed town with seven entrances or gates (fig. 9)[27] that resonate with the seven Chicomoztoc caves.[28] Brotherston thinks the document "reflects the ancient history as if repeated archetypally in sixteenth-century events."[29]

The *Tlaxcala Codex* was painted by indigenous scribes, which indicates that while Spaniards alone conceptualized Mexico as a Nueva España, the toponymic projection of Mexico onto the northwest was the product of the collaborative construction of Spaniards and Nahua Indians, involved at least since the 1540s in the common enterprise of subduing the Chichimeca territory. This native interest in the land beyond a preconquest and colonial cultural frontier is clearly stated not only in the *Tlaxcala Codex* but also in another pair of indigenous documents that, in addressing the attempted conquest of Cíbola and the Mixtón War, are far from portraying Nahua troops as merely having an "auxiliary" role in Spanish conquests.

The first plate of the *Códice de Tlatelolco*, painted in the second half of the sixteenth century, shows the participation of Tlatelolca warriors in Vázquez de Coronado's expedition to Cíbola (1540–42), as well as the armies under Viceroy Mendoza fighting in the Mixtón War (1541–42) (plate 15). It is remarkable that while small characters on horseback at the bottom of the page represent the Spanish troops with their captains (including the viceroy himself), large Indian warriors on foot represent the leading caciques of the Indian companies, indicating that for the scribe, both expeditions were, rather, an indigenous enterprise with the auxiliary aid of Spaniards.³⁰ A similar attitude of pride is manifest in the account that Francisco Acauzitli, cacique of Tlalmanalco, wrote about the performance of his people—whom he personally commanded—in the Mixtón War.³¹

Many Central Mexican Nahuas and other Mesoamerican Indians went along in the expeditions of conquest heading north after the Mixtón rebels were subdued. As explained in chapter 3, a group of Tarascan and Mexican warriors and settlers collaborated with Francisco de Ibarra and founded the village of Nombre de Dios. It is not impossible that Indian collectivities such as this contributed to convincing the Spanish captains that the search for the ancestral Nahua homeland was a feasible enterprise. Obregón asserts in his chronicle that Francisco de Ibarra's uncle, Diego, was determined to "discover the Nuevo México, which in those days was called Copala" and which many people thought to be the place of origin of the "ancient Culguas Mexicanos."³² The 1563 *Relación de lo que descubrió Diego de Ibarra en la provincia de Copala, llamada Topiamé*,³³ and the *Relación de las cosas de la gobernación de la Nueva Vizcaya e informaciones referentes al servicio de Francisco de Ibarra*³⁴ provide the corresponding firsthand testimonies, both discussed in chapter 3. We must add here, however, that according to both documents Francisco de Ibarra, searching for Copala, was led by local guides into an area called Topia or Topiamé where a multitude of Indians lived in flat-roofed, white houses, and they dressed like Mexicans and played certain wooden drums (*teponaztles*) also like the Mexicans did. Therefore, Francisco thought the place, which he saw from a prudent distance, was another Mexico. Further, the report by a soldier contained in the 1563 *Relación de lo que descubrió Diego de Ibarra* asserts that Francisco sometimes claimed to have discovered Nueva Vizcaya and Nuevo México ("que la Nueva Vizcaya había descubierto y el Nuevo México").

Although Francisco and Diego de Ibarra did not use the term Aztlan, they did say of certain places that they could well be a "New Mexico" and also stated openly the desire to find the Mexican ancestral homeland. And it is precisely to this period that the first documented uses of the term "Nuevo México" as a place name belong. The earliest is a report by Friar Jacinto de San Francisco (1561). Quoted below is the relevant passage:

> Hoping to witness in my time another conversion process like that which took place in this land, *I set out from this city* [Mexico] in the company of two other friars, more than two years ago, *in the search for Nuevo México, the existence of which is known since we arrived in [New Spain], although it has not yet been verified*, . . . and we came to a point one hundred and fifty leagues from this city, where there are many different people. . . . This [exploration] I would undertake willingly . . . in order to contribute . . . to opening the way to Santa Elena and to the new land where Francisco Vázquez de Coronado went, and

many leagues beyond, so that . . . the truth of Nuevo México could be finally established.[35]

Note that the friar here does not refer to the region later identified as Nuevo México. The term, in the text, is indeed the name of a place but not a known place. Nuevo México appears in his discourse as an elusive, hidden objective, the existence of which the Spaniards struggled to verify; a place, in short, that conquerors and missionaries dreamed about on the basis of Indian tales. An interesting document dated a few years later represents the first moment when the mythical goal was reified; that is, a chart recording the act of taking possession of the "Lake of Nuevo México," which was discovered on November 8, 1568, by a certain Francisco Cano, lieutenant major of the mines of Mazapil: "Having set out to discover mines of gold and silver and other metals, today, the aforementioned date, he arrived with sixteen soldiers at a large lake, which he, the said Lieutenant, with the soldiers' approval, named the Nuevo México; around this lake there were many *rancherías* and numerous Indians, who are Chichimeca fishers and seem to be of the stock of the Florida Indians; . . . and the smoke of many fires of many peoples can be seen all around, and [the said Lieutenant] asked me, the Royal Notary, to render testimony that . . . he took possession [of the land]."[36]

Wigberto Jiménez Moreno and Sergio Ortega affirm this lake was the Laguna Grande de Coahuila, also known as Ciénega de Patos, in the heart of the Comarca Lagunera (Lake District) where the city of Torreón stands today. Extending over a portion of present-day Coahuila and Durango, the district is constituted by a series of basins separated by low ridges that form a large bolson enclosed by mountains. To a certain extent the landscape in that region does resemble the shallow lake basin of Mexico, reason for which in 1554 someone else believed he had already discovered Lake Copala in nearby Guatiampé.[37]

A Mirror Image: Mexico-Tenochtitlan and Nuevo México-Cíbola-Copala

The similarity between Aztlan and Mexico-Tenochtitlan has been the subject of intense academic debate, and not just in the nineteenth and twentieth centuries. Just as modern scholars have done, Spaniards noted from the beginning the obvious resemblance that indigenous painted books and oral traditions attributed to the starting and ending points of the Aztec/Mexica migration. None of the pictographs on this topic that Cortés and his men saw in the early contact years seems to have survived. Nonetheless, the representation of Aztlan in *Mapa Sigüenza* (plate 7) mirrors that of Mexico-Tenochtitlan's founding in *Codex Aubin* (plate 10) and *Histoire mexicaine* (fig. 6), though the bird announcing the arrival into the Promised Land that the *Mapa Sigüenza* depicts, probably Huitzilopochtli, is substituted by an eagle devouring a serpent in *Codex Aubin* and an eagle in *Histoire mexicaine*. On the other hand, the emblem representing the foundational miracle engraved on the preconquest stone monument known as Teocalli de la Guerra Sagrada (plate 13) confirms the symbolic resemblance, even if instead of a serpent, the eagle on this piece holds the symbol of sacred war (*atl tlachinolli*) in its beak.

Somehow, narratives on the Aztec/Mexica migration, as contained in standard preconquest and contact period versions, invited verification. In preconquest times, Moctezuma I (1439–69) sent a group of wise men to follow his ancestors' pilgrimage route back to their land of origin, but they could not follow the traces beyond Tula, so they appealed to magic.[38] Modern interpretations of migration narratives aim to unravel the symbolism of this resemblance or to reconstruct the migratory path in order to locate Aztlan. For some scholars, like Paul Kirchhoff, this would amount to solving "the problem of the degree of credence that Mexican indigenous traditions in general can be accorded."[39] Curiously, in his attempt to overcome the difficulties that Moctezuma's envoys had solved through magic, Kirchhoff engaged in a sort of "*de*-migration" structurally similar to the one that sixteenth century conquerors also carried out. Like them, he matched the localities mentioned in ethnohistorical sources with present-day localities by comparing the landmarks described in the chronicles and codices with those observable on the ground. This verifying strategy depends on assuming, when using sources from a culture different from one's own, that the cognitive relation one establishes to the world as a means for building knowledge is essentially similar to the cognitive structure that articulates the alien discourse about the world one wants to obtain knowledge from, which entails, of course, identification. As seen in chapter 1, it was precisely this cognitive operation that opened the space for transcultural negotiation that made the Spaniards believe there was a second indigenous metropolis where they could repeat their exploits.

For the Spaniards, Nuevo México *was* Aztlan, even if they did not spell it out by using both terms together. A coastline map published in a 1580 atlas by the Portuguese cartographer Fernão Vaz Dourado corroborates that this was already a widespread assumption among Europeans in the period preceding Oñate's conquest of the Pueblo Indian country, even beyond the confines of the Spanish empire (plate 16).[40] The chart, intended as an instrument for navigation, shows in a central position the Pacific coast of North America, including Baja California. Although few geographic elements are represented within the land mass, the few mountains, drawn completely at random, are accompanied by two highly revealing elements on the right side of the chart: a pair of large, blue, neuron-like motifs clearly representing two lakes interconnected by a narrow line (apparently a stream or path). The motifs evoke the map of Tenochtitlan attributed to Hernán Cortés (map 5), the image of Chicomoztoc in *Mapa de Cuauhtinchan no. 2*, and *Historia Tolteca-Chichimeca* (plates 1–2), and to a lesser degree, that of Aztlan as it appears in prototypical codices such as *Azcatitlan* and *Boturini* (plate 8, fig. 5).

We know at least that the lower lake on the chart represents Mexico-Tenochtitlan, as it is surrounded by the legend "Fernão Cortes a tomovporar Matecvma," and it crosscuts another, horizontal legend: "Tenostitan Civitas Mexico." The second, smaller, upper lake has no identifying caption but I contend it is Nuevo México. The large legend beside it seems to make reference to the whole territory represented in the chart rather than the lake alone: "Terra Antipodv̆ Regis Castele inveta: a Xp̄oforo Colv̆bo: ian vĕsi" (Antipodal Land to the Kingdom of Castile, discovered by Christopher Columbus, thus far explored).[41] A little down to the left from this northern lake is an even smaller body of water, also connected to the lake of Mexico below and identified with a vertical legend: "Bimini Regio," name of the Fountain of Youth sought in Florida by Juan Ponce de León many decades before. This chart is very similar to chart 16 of a circa 1576 atlas also attributed to Dourado that shows the northern lake larger than that of Mexico and has the legend "Bimini Regio" just below it in a horizontal, not vertical, position.[42] This earlier chart lacks the small spring that in the 1580 version seems to represent Bimini. Instead it has the drawing of a tree from which a coat of arms is suspended, the same coat of arms that appears to the left of the lake identified as Mexico-Tenochtitlan in the 1580 chart.

The slight differences between these two charts by Dourado are revealing. In the earlier 1576 chart the northern lake represents Bimini, as the horizontal legend below it clearly indicates. Four years later, however, in 1580, people were preparing to search for a northern lake district, conceived of long before as the place where the ancient Mexicans came from, and they spoke of it profusely. Therefore, it seems that the cartographer decided to add to his new chart a small spring to represent Bimini and leave the northern lake unmarked to represent the original home of the ancient Mexicans.

Tenochtitlan mirrors Aztlan in that both are surrounded by water, and Nuevo México as represented in the 1580 map—a lake situated exactly to the north of the lake where Mexico-Tenochtitlan once stood—does the same. Let us not forget that in 1568 Francisco Cano claimed to have discovered the "Lake of Nuevo México" somewhere around the mining district of Mazapil in present-day Zacatecas,[43] located north of the basin of Mexico but south of the region where it appears in Dourado's map, which roughly coincides with the actual position of New Mexico. Furthermore, other explorers of the same period—and after—who identified Nuevo México with other geographic locations also refer to a densely populated lake district, and some even reproduce additional elements typically pointed out by modern scholars as characterizing the mirroring of Aztlan in Tenochtitlan in native traditions.

For example, Friar Pedro de Espinareda, a Franciscan missionary in the mines of San Martín, Nueva Vizcaya, who collaborated with Francisco de Ibarra and was, with Jacinto de San Francisco, among the founders of the village of Nombre de Dios,[44] wrote in a letter dated January 20, 1567:

> I affirm that . . . about nine years ago, *traveling over the land of Pánuco—the coast of the Northern Sea*—with other missionaries during the above-mentioned enterprise, I learned from Pánuco natives that further inland, approximately one hundred and fifty leagues toward the north, there was *a great lake surrounded by large settlements which had plenty of gold*, although I rather believed it was copper, *and I understood the place was called the white Mexico*, and certain Spaniards wanted to go and see, but they got lost on the way. . . . And after I came to this land of San Martín, a fellow missionary named *Friar Cindos [Jacinto de San Francisco] heard the same news* from these people and I also say that *the Viceroy sent Captain Francisco de Ibarra to Copala, which I understand is precisely that place*, but following his own ideas and dismissing ours he went toward the Southern Sea to Sinaloa. . . . Thus I think it would be a great service to God and the King to discover this land [the lake area, also known as Copala] because two things then could be done; one, to convert those souls, and the other, to open the way for these mines so the Spaniards here could find relief and join efforts with Melendiz's conquest [of Florida] to prevent the French or any other rivals from finding their way into [the region].[45]

In light of Obregón's assertion, twenty years later, that Copala was Nuevo México's former name,[46] Espinareda's contention that the lake he was eager to discover was called "the white Mexico" is illuminating. It resonates with the fact that both Aztlan and Tenochtitlan were associated with whiteness in Nahua tradition. Aztlan's etymology suggests this indirectly, as the objects designated by the words probably constituting its linguistic root are all white (herons, reeds, the flower aztaxochitl).[47] As for Tenochtitlan, Friar Diego de Durán describes the founding miracle as follows: "The first thing they saw was an all-white sabine tree, very beautiful, at the foot of which flowed the spring. Secondly they saw that every willow surrounding the spring was white, without a single green leaf. Every reed in that place was white, and every bulrush around. From the water then began to pop out frogs, all white, and fish, all white, and among them some water snakes, white and spectacular. Priests and elders, remembering what their god had said, began to cry in joy and to show extreme displays of pleasure and happiness, saying: now, at last, we have found the place we were promised and may see the solace and peace of this tired Mexican people."[48]

After 1539 and until approximately 1600, northern New Spain's imaginary geography comprised a number of places with non-fixed positions that moved around in spatial discourse and cartographic representations. Initially all the vast unknown territory beyond the frontier of New Spain, between Florida and California, was divided into three zones: Quivira to the northeast in the Great Plains; Cíbola to the north on the banks of the Rio Grande (known today as Rio Bravo in Latin America), and Copala to the northwest, somewhere on the Colorado River above the Gulf of California. From the 1560s on, different sections of this overall area were known as Nuevo México, although little by little the region associated with this name became more defined as toponyms construed upon indigenous references were assigned to specific locations. Thus, while Baltasar de Obregón claimed that Copala was the former name of Nuevo México, by the time Oñate conducted his conquering enterprise, Quivira and Copala both fell outside the boundaries of the province of Nuevo México, which had become clearly identified with Cíbola, that is, Pueblo Indian country. This ambiguity is significant, particularly the confusion between Copala and Nuevo México. It indicates that ancestral Nahua migration stories somehow informed Spanish representations of the land long before Villagrá said so explicitly in verse. Some reports since Francisco de Ibarra's time put Copala (a lake densely surrounded by cities, frequently considered the Mexica ancestral homeland) north of California. May we affirm that Spaniards in this case interpreted the Gulf of California as the stream of water that the migrant Aztec/Mexicas crossed in the initial stage of their journey?

From the 1580s on, explicit connections between Nuevo México, the ancestral Aztec homeland, and a still-hidden, thoroughly urbanized lake district multiplied. The chronicle by Baltasar de Obregón and the "*Relación breve y berdadera del descubrimiento del Nuevo Mexico, que descubrimos nueve compañeros que salimos de Santa Barbora, en companía de tres religiosos de la orden de señor Sant Francisco*,"[49] which reports on Friar Agustín Rodríguez's 1581 journey to the Conchos River, are clear examples of this kind of mixture.

According to this latter document, the party set out from Santa Bárbara, Chihuahua, on July 5, 1581. After walking thirty-one days across a territory inhabited by naked Chichimecas (*jente desnuda chichimeca*), and then nineteen days more without seeing any people at all, the expeditionaries met an Indian who said that one day farther they would find abundant maize and people dressed in colors, like the Spaniards; and he did not lie: "On August 21, we discovered a town that had forty-five houses, two and three stories high . . . and later on we discovered five more villages. . . . And two days later came a cacique . . . from whom we learned that farther ahead there was a great number of towns."[50]

In all, the party "discovered" sixty-one towns, the houses of which stood close together along well-delineated streets and often clustered around plazas. According to the report, Friar Bernardino Beltrán, a monk who shortly after entered the region with Captain Antonio de Espejo, "was told about a large lake nearby, surrounded with many settlements of many people who navigate in canoes ornamented with large, brass-colored globes on the prow."[51] Obregón wrote of Rodríguez and Chamuscado's expedition that more and more frequently as their march progressed, they came across clothed people who reported on others beyond who lived in large houses and "spoke the Mexican language." The party also saw willow granaries (*trojes*) throughout the region, "mimicking those of Mexicans." Finally, when they learned that further ahead the Indians were bellicose, the friars "had no doubt they were related to the ancient Culhua-Mexicas" (*no dudaron ser estos de la misma población de los antiguos culguas mexicanos*).[52]

Traditional historiography frequently explains the meaning of the term Nuevo México as stemming from the fact that Spaniards, overwhelmed by the sight of Mexico-Tenochtitlan, engaged in a vigorous search for another, similar place. But to postulate the existence of a Nuevo México entailed more than imagining a replica of the preconquest Aztec capital. The peculiarity of the toponym rests on the fact that it is the only sixteenth century example where the adjective "new" precedes an indigenous place-name, yet in the popular usage of the time, the designation "México" was not limited to Mexico City. Very frequently it alluded to the region Hernán Cortés initially conquered, where Náhuatl, a language Spaniards usually called *lengua mexicana*, was spoken by people from different polities (altepetl) who, as seen in chapter 5, held distinctive, exclusive identities, though acknowledging a common northern origin. Therefore, a simple transference based on the expectations aroused by Mexico-Tenochtitlan is no sufficient explanation for the toponymic projection.

Sixteenth century exploration of northwest New Spain was characterized by the massive participation of Náhuatl speakers from the basin of Mexico and the Puebla-Tlaxcala valley. The chronicles written in that language by indigenous authors, who attached great importance to native participation, speak about *Yancuic Mexico*.[53] The word *yancuic*, regularly translated as "new" (*nuevo*), has ambiguous connotations. In Náhuatl it means "the new" as in "the most recent" but also "the original," "the primeval."[54] Thus, *Yancuic México* may also be translated as "the first, the original México"; that is, Aztlan. This was precisely the way many Spanish conquerors, at least since the 1560s, understood the expression, even when in their own language the word *nuevo* meant something very different: "another," in the sense of "a second thing of the same kind," the "recently created" (*recién hecho*), and the "never seen before."[55]

A first, inescapable conclusion resulting from evidence thus far reviewed is that beyond the lust for power and glory, the Spanish will to retrace the ancestral Mexica migration responded also to their deepest Christian convictions. For the Judeo-Christian West, origin signifies innocence. If Mexicans represented for Spaniards the conceptual challenge of a civilization as worthy as the European but perverted by demonic, bloody sacrifice and idolatry, perhaps the return to the Mexicans' origin would mean retracing the path of the fall. Perhaps Aztlan/Nuevo México seemed to Spaniards the same Indian civilization they so admired in Mexico but without the devil, for was it not Satan, in the figure of Huitzilopochtli, who ordered the Aztecs to abandon the lake paradise they lived in, commanding even a name change and bloody rituals for his own delight?

Now, if colonial expansion north of New Spain represented for many Spaniards the promise of recuperating Aztec greatness in its pristine state, for many Central Mexican Indians from non-Mexica altepetl it represented, among other things, the opportunity to recover, at least partially, the original autonomy they had lost with the imposition of Mexica domination over the altepetl their forefathers had founded. Thus, the political significance of ancestral migration stories was renewed through colonial engagement.

Before the Spanish conquest, migration narratives represented a way to negotiate the respective positions that different groups occupied in the regional political structure, helping to justify territorial occupation and political authority, within and among individual altepetl linked in a dominant-subordinate relation.[56] After the conquest these stories continued to be the common idiom of regional power legitimacy but now they also became the arena for the negotiation of collective rights and privileges vis-à-vis the Spanish overlordship.

Nahua preconquest origin stories clearly acquired renewed relevance for natives themselves as the penetration into the north advanced. At least half the Indian-focused sources containing accounts of ancestral migrations from a northern place of origin were elaborated between 1540 and 1600, precisely the period when the subjugation of Nueva Galicia, Nueva Vizcaya, Sonora, and Nuevo México was achieved thanks to the massive participation of Central Mexican natives. Moreover, the narratives specifically dealing with the Aztec/Mexica migration written in European script by Indian authors such as Alvarado Tezozómoc (1598, 1600-10) or Chimalpahin (1620-29, 1631) are contemporaneous with Nuevo México's definitive conquest and establishment as a colonial province. Their authors came from altepetl that were members of the three hegemonic tlatocayotl constituting the confederation we know as the Aztec empire, or from rival societies that remained independent like Tlaxcala (Diego Muñoz Camargo). Not by pure chance does the list of native allies engaged in the overall enterprise of "Spanish" northward expansion include the names of groups depicted in such traditions as having a common origin in Chicomoztoc. These groups kept their internal cohesion and a fair degree of autonomy when integrated into these collaborative expeditions, as is documented for the Tarascan and Mexican founders of Nombre de Dios in Nueva Vizcaya, or the Tlaxcalan sixteenth-century multiple collaboration recorded by Diego Muñoz Camargo and many other documents, the *Lienzo de Tlaxcala* and the *Tlaxcala Codex* among them.

As in pre-Hispanic times, migration narratives served to define and defend the legitimacy of the polities they pertained to, and to support their politico-territorial claims, but now they were also implicated in vindicatory schemes that were projected into the future as well as played out in the past. Conquering the Mexica place of origin as allies of the Spaniards could mean for non-Mexica altepetl a triumphal return to the land whence they came as well. For the Mexicas, it could have been a way to reassert the hegemony that Spaniards had recently sequestered. Recruitment strategies for Indian allies have only recently begun to be studied, and they are a complicated topic that could make a book itself. For the argument here it is enough to remark that for the most part, Indians did not enlist in conquering armies or colonizing parties as individuals but as corporations, and they were usually headed by their own governors or caciques as captains.[57]

Scholars attempting to understand the nature and significance of such traditions seldom look at Spanish-focused sources associated with the exploration and conquest of New Spain's northern provinces; thereby missing the light these can shed on the cultural and ideological meanings Indian communities attached to their voluntary collaboration in the colonial enterprise.

The perils of ignoring these sources are clear in examining the controversial interpretations offered for the famous passage by Sahagún's Mexica informants on the populating of New Spain (contained in chapter 29, book 10 of his *Historia general*). Mexico's first inhabitants are said to have come by sea from a land called Panutla guided by their god. First they arrived in Tamoanchan, to the south, where the numen granted them lands, but after an indeterminate period, he left, taking along the wise men and books and promising to return. The narrative goes on to tell how the original group split into various subunits, all of which left Tamoanchan and dispersed. Some went to Teotihuacan and then continued on, divided in groups of different languages, until reaching the northern deserts of Chicomoztoc, where they became hunter-gatherers. Eventually they returned, each at a different time, to the southern provinces they had once abandoned.

According to Alfredo López Austin, one must read the following statement between the lines: "We, the Mexicans, are part of the original people who came to this land following God's will. He gave us this land to profit but warned us that he would return. We are neither complete newcomers nor Chichimecas and have the same right to this land as those who did not go to Chicomoztoc, or who went and came back before we did." Before the Spanish conquest, López Austin explains, the Mexicas based their territorial claims on "rights of conquest," but as the argument became moot once the Spaniards conquered them, the notion of "divine gift" became more important, even if names of particular indigenous deities had to be omitted, as these were all considered demons by the Spaniards. Hence the use of such abstract forms to address the divinity as *Totecuyo*

(Our Lord), a term used in pre-Hispanic times for any god whatsoever; *Tloque Nahuaque* (Owner of what is near and what is beside); or *Yohualli Ehécatl* (Night and Wind, that is, the invisible and untouchable). The passage, therefore, is a secularized history, a strategic adaptation of the traditional story for European consumption, aimed at preserving local knowledge and discourse but rendered credible for Christian readers.[58]

Although this interpretation may be partially correct, inasmuch as it explains the pre-Hispanic ideological functions fulfilled by the symbolic content of this discourse, the reluctance to accord a factual basis to native historical accounts is reductionist. Marie-Areti Hers has proposed a different interpretation for the same passage, which, as it happens, resonates also with similar fragments of Alva Ixtlilxóchitl's *Historia de la nación chichimeca*,[59] the anonymous *Relación de la genealogía*, and *Origen de los mexicanos*.[60] All three also explain the Mexica arrival in the Valley of Mexico as a homecoming. As Hers demonstrated, this is a synthetic account of the enlargement and shrinking of Mesoamerica between the second and twelfth centuries of the Christian era documented by archaeological research reviewed in chapter 2.[61] Spanish-focused sources discussed in this book show how exploration and conquest followed ancient cultural corridors because it was frequently native knowledge that dictated routes and goals. Indigenous historical traditions do have a factual basis as well as a symbolic dimension, which is why Spaniards took them seriously.

Cross-cultural interactions between Indians and Spaniards are far more complex than usually acknowledged. In the sixteenth century quest for Nuevo México, the opposition "Spanish conqueror versus conquered Indian" does little justice to a negotiation process where native historical memory, preserved in oral traditions and pictoglyphic documents, appealed to European intellect and also undergirded the actions of Indian subjects as allied warriors and frontier settlers. The methodological conclusion of this book, therefore, is that in analyzing the colonial situation in Hispanic North America, one must extend inquiry beyond indigenous-Spanish relations to focus on how the presence of alien Spaniards affected native interethnic relations as well. In other words, one must cease reproducing the traditional binary classification that divides sixteenth to eighteenth century actors in Spanish America into the opposed categories of natives and intruders, conquered and conquerors, Indians and Spaniards.

Juan de Oñate's dismissal as governor of Nuevo México in 1610 marks the end of the story this book is concerned with. During his explorations, the imagined kingdom of Nuevo México became a reality only to lose ground among Spanish aspirations. Nevertheless, the great 1680 Pueblo Revolt deserves some comment because it represents, among other things, a local development of the idea of Aztlan-Chicomoztoc-Nuevo México. The revolt, led by a Tewa Indian called Popé who had been a presidio prisoner,[62] was a typical millenarian movement of the kind Peter Worsley described for Melanesia and the Pacific.[63] That is, a movement of resistance to colonial rule articulated around the prophetic declarations of a charismatic leader proclaiming the end of one age and the dawn of another, characterized by the reversal of current conditions of inequality and involving the inversion of the prevalent order. Millenarian movements of this kind differ from those of the European Middle Ages that Norman Cohn studied in their direct link to colonialism.[64] As a response to foreign imposition they seek to reestablish the order prevailing prior to external intervention and frequently represent that return as an inversion of the sociopolitical structure. Thus it is not the kingdom of God described in the Apocalypse that they pursue, but rather a utopian order of abundance and freedom generally expected to be brought by the ancestors who will make themselves present in a material, objectified form.

The behavior and ritualized practice of Pueblo rebels, like the rhetoric their leader displayed, was formally similar to those characteristic of such Melanesian movements. This is clear from a letter by an eyewitness describing an incident at the town of Santa Ana, where Popé prepared a large table with the food and things the Spaniards used, and then, taking the seat of honor, he ordered chalices to be brought for a toast.[65] Moreover, through his preaching, Popé convinced his followers that he was the lieutenant of Moctezuma and that as such he periodically received the visit of three spirits, who came from the underworld through the lake of Copalla to give instructions and provide their superhuman support. Many Spaniards and Pueblo Indians in the seventeenth century considered this lake to be the place of origin of Náhuatl-speaking Indians.[66]

Like the charismatic leaders that Worsley studied, Popé announced the overthrow of the existing society and the reinstatement of the traditional order, though this time, united as one people, the Indians would live in a doubly bountiful kingdom. Once the Spaniards decided to flee after a series of exceedingly violent attacks that could be described, in Taussig's terms, as mimicry of the violence that the colonists themselves had displayed one hundred years before, Popé was elected chief of an Indian confederation.[67] Traditional dances suppressed by the missionaries were reinstated, Catholic marriages were invalidated and the use of Christian names prohibited, and, most important, it was agreed that only local crops like maize, cotton, beans, and squash should be grown in the future.[68] The history of this rebellion and the brief period of local utopian independence that ensued stand as witness to the hybrid Hispanic/Nahua notions about Nuevo México as the original abode of the ancient Mexicans, beliefs so powerful that they figure among the imagery at play in native resistance movements among Oasisamerican peoples.

Conclusion

A little more than thirty years ago, in one of a classic collection of essays titled *First Images of America: The Impact of the New World on the Old*, John Elliott argued that preconceptions deriving from the Judeo-Christian and classical traditions guided European perceptions of the New World, functioning as a sieve for the selective contemplation of novelty and thus obscuring the repercussions of New World realities on European cultural configurations. Nevertheless, he contended, both traditions were diverse and contradictory enough to allow for the incorporation of new impressions, which became less and less dependent on established European cosmology as personal experience proved more authoritative than authority itself.[1]

Toward the end of the twentieth century, many writers on the conquest of the Americas turned their attention to cultural representation, but their explorations of European cognitive responses to alterity and how these responses were expressed in colonial discourse took an almost opposite direction. The analysis of what Stuart B. Schwartz called "implicit ethnographies," that is, understandings of self and other, not necessarily codified, that permeate the way in which people meeting across cultures think about and act when encountering the "other," then became a major concern among historians.[2] This perspective, closer to the kind of postcolonial critique developed by Edward Said (1978) and Homi Bhabha (1994), neglects the fact that, as Elliott observed, new expressions in the Old World–New World contact period became less and less dependent on established European cosmology. Instead it emphasizes how, in facing the external world, Europeans refashioned their self-identity through the construction of an essentialist discourse that solidified the contrast between ruler and ruled in such a way that the righteousness of colonialist practice became naturalized. This is what Bhabha terms "colonial discourse," defining it as a construct that represents the colonized as a population of degenerate types who are in need of an externally imposed structure of administration and instruction.[3]

Stephen Greenblatt, who exemplifies colonial discourse analysis, maintained that early representations of the New World and its inhabitants, rather than reflecting "knowledge of the other," were devices to "act upon the other" that resulted from imagination, not from reasoning or empirical observation.[4] This tendency to see European representations of America as a language for domination based on preestablished notions of the exotic also characterizes authors like Bernard McGrane, who argued that Renaissance cosmography measured America against the Christian myth of the fall, paradoxically robbing indigenous culture of its non-European distinctiveness while recognizing the human essence of Indians as non-Christian, but nevertheless, potential Christians.[5] Peter Mason, too, studied the European imagery of the exotic projected onto the New World and affirmed that European observers' inability "to go beyond their own familiar frames of reference" was a function of the destruction and political domination they exercised.[6] The transfer of classical and medieval themes to America had been studied as early as the 1930s, but not in relation to colonialism and domination.

A different interpretation from that of colonial discourse was offered in 1982 by Tzvetan Todorov, who contended that Europeans could in fact understand the American "other" because Europeans had developed writing, a powerful technology for the mastery of signs, which Native Americans lacked. The cultural difference regarding the capacity for rapid adaptation to the unforeseen that writing allowed, he argued, explains the apparently inexplicable Spanish success in subduing complex and populous societies like the Aztecs. However, he did not even consider the possibility that Spanish understanding of the Aztec world could translate into cultural exchange or cultural appropriation on the part of colonizers.

This book has attempted to show that viewing the Euro-American encounter in terms of discrete, opposing totalities that emerged from this confrontation as victors and vanquished is a simplifying perspective that often loses sight of the specificities of local negotiations, sectorial realignments, and small-scale processes of resignification. The picture of European imperviousness drawn in the 1920s and 1930s by authors who developed the medieval hypothesis reviewed in chapter 4 resembles late twentieth-century characterizations of the conquest of America written from the perspective of colonial discourse analysis. The deaf monologue they depict, in the sense that native beliefs and knowledge appear as nearly devoid of influential weight upon colonizers and as subject to a process of thorough erasure, is equally reductionist. Although authors practicing this kind of analysis contributed indeed to revealing the ideological mechanisms of colonial domination, they frequently overlooked the epistemological ruptures that might have occurred in the process of subduing the other. Such ruptures not only opened alternative possibilities of historical development but also help explain why Amerindian peoples succeeded in resisting their absolute assimilation into the West.

The principal concern of this book—like that of authors engaged in postcolonial criticism—lies in the assessment of New World encounters from the perspective of the European experience of cultural dislocation. However, it harks back to Elliott and distances itself from the "overall European civilization perspective" and the binary divide of conquered versus conqueror to address a particular intersubjective space: the social field constituted by a concrete set of Europeans who arrived in America to stay and the Indian groups they interacted with, a social field viewed as a new emergent sociocultural reality in its own right. As John and Jean Comaroff made clear in their study of missionaries and colonialism in nineteenth century Africa, "colonial societies rarely consisted . . . of two discrete worlds, each whole unto itself, caught up together in the interdependencies of a Hegelian master-slave relationship." Rather, they "were increasingly integrated totalities."[7] Hence the importance of studying the "localized cultural forms" that emerged in "European worlds abroad."[8]

Nuevo México came into being as the transcultural formulation of an "imaginary world," incorporated toward the mid-sixteenth century into the conquerors' hypothetical map of mainland North America among the unknown territories to be "discovered." Before it existed as a colonial province with concrete territorial boundaries, it was a disembodied object of colonial desire. Its construction and reification involved the convergence of two parallel historical processes. On the one hand there was the gradual accumulation of eyewitness and secondhand reports concerning a distant province north of New Spain where cotton-clad people, allegedly exploiting rich deposits of precious stones and metals, inhabited large and refined cities. On the other hand there was the Spanish conviction that they could locate, and should appropriate, the place where Mexican ancestors ultimately came from according to Nahua origin and migration traditions.

For Spanish conquerors, and probably their Nahua Indian allies also, Nuevo México (*Yancuic Mexico* in Náhuatl) was the original Mexico, Aztlan-Chicomoztoc, traces of which they sought in several regions until deciding it corresponded to Pueblo Indian country. Thus, more than European medieval imagery, traditionally regarded as the topical horizon framing the Spanish colonial enterprise, Amerindian historical discourse was, in this region at least, far more important, because it soon became the common idiom of geographic representation. Likewise, the memory of Aztlan became the arena for the negotiation of rights and privileges among different parties involved in conquest endeavors.

Like the extensive adaptations that characterized the Hispanic style of municipal government set up in Central Mexico, thoroughly studied by James Lockhart; in the quest for Nuevo México, far from spelling the end of indigenous culture, the colonial order established a complex mixture of native and Hispanic elements. This process of cultural and institutional salvage, which apparently did not occur in the Caribbean, was possible in Central Mexico because conquerors recognized conspicuous affinities between this region and their own motherland. Such recognition is inscribed in the coinage of the toponym Nueva España and the later construct of Nuevo México.

The term "Nueva España" has traditionally been interpreted as a sign of colonial appropriation, or as the expression of perceived geographic affinities between Mesoamerica and the Iberian Peninsula. If evaluated only through testimonies relating to the period when the toponym was devised, both interpretations seem self-evident. However, chapter 1 demonstrated that compared with other, previously chosen place names such as Hispaniola, which connotes, unequivocally, a possessor-possessed relation, it reveals a conceptual relation of homology between Spain and its American replica. It also proved that the most significant similarities in the operation of considering Mesoamerica another, "New," Spain pertain to the sphere of social life and politics. Unlike Caribbean "savages," New Spain's native inhabitants had palaces, roadways, and marketplaces. They also had an organized religion—albeit in the perverted form of idolatry—and most important, a system of domination seemingly parallel to the political order of Old Spain in that it subordinated local to regional sovereignties. These in turn were subordinated to the central power in a successive hierarchical scale that culminated with the great tlatoani of Tenochtitlan. It is no coincidence then that in New Spain, conquerors translated *tlatoani* as *señor,* thus placing the rulers of subordinate indigenous states on the same level as European princes, dukes, and counts, while in the Caribbean they had been content to use the Taíno word *cacique* or the Spanish terms *rey, régulo,* or *reyezuelo* to designate any individual who exercised authority, without further describing the nature of such authority.

In this sense Carmen Bernand and Serge Gruzinski are right to suppose that after the encounter with Mesoamerica, Spaniards distinguished two types of societies and made an explicit connection between the presence of religion—which they qualified by characterizing objects of worship as "idols"—and the existence of a political order resembling the one their own society had inherited from Roman times.[9] The distinction is clear in sources discussed in chapter 1. The Spanish exclusive use of the indigenous word *zeme* to designate objects invested with supernatural attributes in the Caribbean correlates with the almost complete absence of social and political description in the chronicles written in that phase of conquest. Contrastingly, most accounts concerning the exploration and conquest of Mesoamerica, which replace the word *zeme* with "idol" and introduce such terms as "vassal," "lord," and "law," contain reasonably detailed passages on the native political and social order. Conquerors clearly perceived *zemes* as the ritual counterpart of a lawless, disjointed society, whereas they took idols to be a sign of civilization, in the Roman-derived sense of civic oriented community life.

The colonists' application of European categories such as "idolatry" or "priest" are frequently seen as evidence of their inability to bridge incommensurability.

The selective recourse to their own terminology, however, demonstrates that they did relate conceptually to the social realities they confronted, even if partly misrepresenting them. Hence the importance of reading New Spain's documents alongside earlier evidence from the Caribbean, where a deep sense of alienation had not only resulted in descriptive reticence but also prompted the ready adoption of native vocabulary to designate things and institutions unheard of before.

As noted in chapter 1, the Spanish relation to *zemes* must be compared to the Portuguese reaction to the "fetish" as described by Pietz; that is, a venerated object essentially different from every object of worship familiar to Europeans before they witnessed West African forms of handling the supernatural. Unlike Christian images and pagan idols—iconic representations of divine beings—the artifacts that Portuguese observers called "fetishes" were supernaturally powerful objects in themselves, and this is precisely what Spaniards took *zemes* to be. Yet, whereas in the period and region that Pietz discussed, the category of "fetish" came to replace that of "idol" as the embodiment of the non-Christianity other, in sixteenth-century Hispanic America, *zemes* as concepts defining ritually powerful objects displaced idols only temporarily. This, I contend, was because after experiencing profound incomprehensibility in the Caribbean, Europeans witnessed an unexpectedly readable alterity in Central Mexico. This apparent transparency in the native order had major epistemological consequences, as it opened a space for cognitive negotiation that made communication across cultures possible. Because conquerors could label the strange world they now confronted with the same categories they applied to their own society and material artifacts (books, temples, idols, vassals, markets, and so on), they conceived indigenous and European representations of the past as analogous forms of knowledge. Conquerors therefore granted credibility to Nahua migration stories and set out to follow the footsteps of the kingdom that the ancient Mexicans had allegedly abandoned centuries before.

The authoritative status accorded to the particular expression of indigenous discourse that Spaniards interpreted as historical knowledge shows that although European contact with Amerindian reality was mediated, as Greenblatt contended, by culturally constituted representations from Christian cosmology and a heterogeneous collection of archetypes of Oriental and ancient alterity,[10] such imported symbolic structures receded in the process of engagement. Certainly self-projection pervaded the early phases of any given nation's colonial enterprise in America, and at the level of personal experience, many individuals' confrontation with the exotic when they first arrived. Furthermore, the Spanish goal of subjecting New World people and territories to political control, economic exaction, and cultural and religious conversion surely entailed an assault on indigenous institutions, beliefs, and habits. However, in the particular case of New Spain, Mexica society, shattered by the Spaniards on the political front, went on to take center stage in the collective imagination of the colonial world. Often it supplanted Europe as the referent against which other indigenous societies were defined, while the partly symbolic history of its remote origins provided the colonists—be they Spaniards or "Indian friends"—with a prospective horizon, also serving as a chart for decoding the landscape.

But indigenous interests and understandings not only worked their way through a modified Spanish consciousness; they also maintained social consistency through Indian agency itself. Indian allies were not simply forced to take part in conquest expeditions. They participated because such enterprises allowed for the possible fulfillment of their own agendas, not defined exclusively, and perhaps not even primarily, in relation to European domination but with regard to pre-Hispanic political alignments, as shown in chapters 5 and 6. This is a complex issue only slightly touched on in this book, which deserves detailed research. Let us simply remember that groups providing warriors to those northbound expeditions in which the idea of Nuevo México evolved participated in the political network of allied, subordinate, or perpetual-enemy altepetl in Central Mexican Nahua hegemonic structures, and they also appeared as principal actors in Nahua narratives of ancestral origin and migration.

An analysis of the quest for Nuevo México reveals that standard historiography has placed too little emphasis on the intersubjective character of cross-cultural representational engagement. How, then, can colonial intersubjectivity in the field of discourse and representation be addressed, and why is it important at all? If the claim of many postcolonial critics that every discourse on alterity is more a form of self-projection than a reliable description of the other is correct,[11] how can an understanding of the process whereby two or more contacting cultures intermesh be achieved?

Comaroff and Comaroff observed that even when historical dynamics that characterize the opposition between colonizers and colonized have produced discursive objectifications that represent both fields as distinguished by irreducible contrasts, neither side was ever an "undifferentiated sociological or political reality."[12] To emphasize intersubjectivity, therefore, would require breaking through dual oppositional representations and recognizing, at the concrete level of local developments, that each of the contacting "social fields" in colonial encounters is constituted by various agents with often divergent interests. Moreover, even the response of one single individual to the confronted other is frequently unstable and ambivalent, varying according to particular circumstances or specific aspects of the other's culture, behavior, and practice.

Once the heterogeneity of colonizers and colonized is acknowledged, and the polyvalence of their discourse recognized, their interaction appears as entanglement rather than simple oppositional confrontation, because the outlook and interests of certain social groups on each side may be closer to those of certain groups in the opposite field than to those of competing sectors in their own field. As Jovita Baber recently noted, "native people consciously and strategically negotiated their interests within the empire and, in so doing, contributed to an imperial system that emerged as a fluid convergence of negotiated interests."[13] Thus, beneath the grand level of imperial-project enforcement and behind the curtain of preset representational systems, cross-cultural interaction is a complex process of realignment and conceptual redefinition that involves, like the sixteenth century quest for Nuevo México, an uneven mixture of imposition, resistance, collaboration, borrowing, revivalism, and misunderstanding. This circumstance allows the researcher access to the process of entanglement by contrasting the vast array of visual and discursive representations of self and other that actors involved in any given encounter produce, and then examining their interaction. In addition, addressing intersubjectivity involves acknowledging the instability of every sign and cultural product. Ideas, technologies, and institutions seldom stay identical to themselves when entering a process of cross-cultural engagement.

Nahua traditions of ancestral origin and migration remained a fundamental point of reference in the colonial world but had different meanings for different social actors. Among Central Mexican natives, origin myths continued to cement self-identity, sometimes slightly modified to prove autochthony, as in the texts by Sahagún's Mexica informants, Alva Ixtlilxóchitl, or the anonymous authors of *Relación de la genealogía* and *Origen de los mexicanos* concerning the populating of New Spain.[14] Most important, as suggested in chapters 5 and 6, for several Nahua groups these traditions prompted a collective urge to recover the land of ancestral origin, and with it, the autonomy of primordial times that was lost with the consolidation of Mexica hegemony. Spanish settlers and colonial authorities, of course, invested the theme with yet further meanings. Still, these divergent interpretations—and the practice they undergirded—paved the way for the Spanish conquest of northwest New Spain and were later on locally appropriated and resignified, as in Popé's call for insurrection in the 1680 Pueblo Indian rebellion. Furthermore, in the postcolonial worlds that resulted from Spanish conquest and the imperial growth of the United States, the Aztec migration and Nahua original homeland are still socially and politically relevant, even if their significance is far removed from original meanings. In Mexico they have long served the official ideology through which the state promotes national identity and establishes its political legitimacy, claiming the Mexica arrival in Central Mexico as its own foundational origin, but the myth has been lately reappropriated by subaltern sectors of Mexican society who contest the social and cultural project enforced by the state. Likewise, Chicano cultural resistance in the southwestern United States has adopted Aztlan as its main symbol of identity to fight against Anglo-American marginalizing racism via urging a return to indigenous roots and denouncing the imposition of Western modernity and its attendant social and ecological "disasters."[15]

Two basic models for the assessment of cross-cultural interaction between European and non-European societies current in contemporary scholarship were outlined in the introduction to this book. Whether focused on the European experience of the other, as the "medievalist" and "Western systems of alterity" perspectives are; or the response of imperialized others to European intrusion, as in the many works on native acculturation and resistance produced all over the globe; these models do not allow a proper appreciation of the cultural intricacy that characterizes colonial societies.

"European worlds abroad," as Comaroff and Comaroff contend, have never been refractory micro-Europes, successfully—or unsuccessfully—imposing alienation onto native subjects,[16] nor were they simple admixtures resulting from the juxtaposition of culturally constituted material and immaterial items. They have always been intersubjective spaces of contamination. This is where Bhabha's notion of "hybridity" proves an adequate analytic instrument, as it conveys a lot more than the combination of culturally specific practices, objects, and ideas. The concept remarks on the opening up of "a contingent, borderline experience . . . *in-between* colonizer and colonized" that entails "deformation and displacement" of the discriminatory principles upon which domination rests.[17] This surely occurred when the Spaniards recognized Mesoamerican institutions as constitutive of a political order similar to their own, consequently submitting their own judgment to the authority of indigenous historical knowledge, though still retaining a generally derogatory attitude toward Indian culture and individuals.

The concepts of "transculturation" and "colonial semiosis" also help to assess the process of hybridization that unsettles, according to Bhabha, the representational modalities characterizing colonial discourse. Addressing the dialogic dimension of cultural creativity, both concepts challenge the assumption that hierarchical relations must necessarily take the form of a monologue that would reduce the possibilities of colonized peoples to overt, violent resistance or to perform as the passive recipients of Western inscription. Colonial semiosis, as defined by Walter Mignolo, encompasses the whole variety of semiotic interactions taking place in colonial situations, including colonial discourse.[18] The concept emphasizes multidirectionality, thereby suggesting that cross-cultural, albeit asymmetric, encounters give rise to the multivocal agency of innumerable individuals who are at once objects and subjects, never fully autonomous, never fully conscious of their role in the agendas of the multiple others they engage with, as Talal Asad has also observed.[19] Likewise, Fernando Ortiz's concept of transculturation forces a non-centric approach to the process of cultural transition embodied in colonial societies born from the permanent relocation of people. Transculturation is not about colony-metropole relations but about the economic, institutional, aesthetic, epistemological, linguistic, ethical, and sexual repercussions of social and geographic displacement. It cannot be spelled out in terms of the opposition between colonialist intruders and imperialized natives because the local field it concerns, like the intruding one, is heterogeneous as regards both culture and power. Not all foreign groups transplanted to colonial Cuba, the instance to which the term transculturation originally referred, shared in the hegemonic position nor were they members of the same cultural matrix. Alongside Iberian conquerors and settlers, colonization brought considerable numbers of Africans to the island from the Atlantic regions of that continent including Senegal, Guinea, the Congo, Angola, and Mozambique. Sporadic waves or continuous flows of immigrants also brought people as culturally diverse as Amerindians from the mainland, Anglo-Saxons, and even Asians from Macao or Canton.[20] By the same token, indigenous peoples were far from constituting a unified social field. Congruent with Ortiz, the findings of this book indicate that the history of early colonial New Spain ought to incorporate subaltern and postcolonial perspectives, but with a critical reformulation of "representation" as a strategy of domination that considers dialogic interaction a possibility.

The sixteenth century quest for Nuevo México was clearly a result of transculturation: a process in which colonial semiosis, as manifest in the manifold resignification and mutual contamination of Aztec ancestral history and Christian sacred history, played a central role. In this sense the quest can also be categorized as a "way of worldmaking," a concept Nelson Goodman coined to indicate that the order of any given representation of the world we perceive, its objects and relations, are not found but fabricated in a refashioning process that turns old worlds into new through different interpretive operations.[21] Although Goodman's worlds are neither specific depictions of particular places nor historical narratives of any kind, but rather the overall intellectual systems through which our scholarly perception of sociocultural reality is organized (functionalism, structuralism, and so on), his argument can be extended to define those collective processes of imagination that, like the quest for Nuevo México, lead to the translation, through interpretation, of one pre-extant world (the original abode of Nahua traditions of ancestral origin) into another (a politico-territorial entity to be searched and colonized).

Notes

Introduction

1. Peter Mason, "Imaginary Worlds, Counterfact and Artifact," in E. Magaña and P. Mason, eds., *Myth and the Imaginary in the New World* (Amsterdam: Centrum voor Studie en Documentatie van Latijns-Amerika, 1986), 43, 53–60; *Deconstructing America: Representations of the Other* (London: Routledge, 1990), 15–27; and "Continental Incontinence: Horror Vacui and the Colonial Supplement," in R. Corbey and J. Leerssen, eds., *Alterity, Identity, Image: Slaves and Others in Society and Scholarship* (Amsterdam and Atlanta: Rodopi, 1991), 151–90. I make a critical appropriation of this concept. Mason essentially developed it to reflect on the role of the classical and medieval inherited cultural background of European conquerors in understanding and shaping colonial America, whereas I apply it to the role that Native American culture had in shaping European imagination and its attendant colonizing practice.

2. The concept of "worldmaking" is taken from Nelson Goodman, *Ways of Worldmaking* (Ann Arbor, Mich.: Harvester Press, 1978).

3. "Mexica" and "Aztec" designate the same people in most modern literature and popular culture. The usage is, however, incorrect. The group of people who founded and inhabited Mexico-Tenochtitlan, leading the so-called Aztec empire until the Spanish conquest, were called Mexicas. Azteca was the name of the Mexica ancestors in their original homeland and during the first stage of their migration. In many colonial documents the term Mexican is applied to all Náhuatl speakers from the central highlands, including the Mexica.

4. The term "reify" is used in the sense of thinking of, or treating something abstract as if it were a real and tangible object. Reified conceptions do not always become objectified as material objects, but in the particular case studied here, this did occur.

5. Howard F. Cline, "Ethnohistorical Regions of Middle America," in H. F. Cline, ed., *Handbook of Middle American Indians*, vol. 12, *Guide to Ethnohistorical Sources*, pt. 1 (Austin: University of Texas Press, 1971), 170, 173.

6. Bernard S. Cohn, *An Anthropologist among the Historians, and Other Essays* (Oxford: Oxford University Press, 1990), 42, 46–47.

7. Santa Arias and Mariselle Meléndez, "Space and the Rhetorics of Power," in S. Arias and M. Meléndez, eds., *Mapping Colonial Spanish America: Places and Commonplaces of Identity, Culture, and Experience* (Lewisburg, Pa.: Bucknell University, 2002), 14–16.

8. For example, Jacques Le Goff, "Les mentalités: une histoire ambigue," in J. Le Goff and P. Nora, eds., *Faire de l'histoire* (Paris: Gallimard, 1974), 3:76–94; Carlo Ginzburg, *The Cheese and the Worms: The Cosmos of a Sixteenth-Century Miller*, translated by J. A.

Tedeschi and M. Tedeschi (Baltimore, Md.: Johns Hopkins University Press, 1980); and Robert Darnton, *The Great Cat Massacre and Other Episodes in French Cultural History* (New York: Vintage, 1985).

9. In fact, Edward B. Tylor, Lewis H. Morgan, Emile Durkheim, Marcel Mauss, and other founding thinkers of anthropology were concerned with the historical process, comparing modernity with past and contemporary non-modern cultures and establishing historical sequences of social and cultural development. Kinship theory itself, the most emblematically anthropological specialty, originated from the consideration of the history of Roman law, while the historically based work of sociologists like Max Weber, particularly his 1930 book on the Protestant ethic and the rise of capitalism, have been highly influential in anthropological scholarship. Nevertheless, toward the beginning of the twentieth century, anthropology's self-identity came to be abundantly reinstated by establishing a sharp border with other disciplines, history among them. Mary Douglas, foreword to M. Mauss, *The Gift: The Form and Reason for Exchange in Archaic Societies*, translated by W. D. Halls (New York: W. W. Norton, 1990), vii–x. See also Jerry D. Moore, *Visions of Culture: An Introduction to Anthropological Theories and Theorists* (Walnut Creek, Calif.: Altamira Press, 1997), 17–39.

10. The last decades of the twentieth century saw renewed interest in political history, albeit from novel, anthropologically informed perspectives. For example, Reynaldo C. Ileto, *Pasyon and Revolution: Popular Movements in the Philippines, 1840–1910* (Quezon City, Philippines: Ateneo of Manila University Press, 1979); Benedict Anderson, *Imagined Communities: Reflections on the Origin and Spread of Nationalism* (London: Verso, 1983); Jean Comaroff, *Body of Power, Spirit of Resistance: The Culture and History of a South African People* (Chicago: University of Chicago Press, 1985).

11. B. Cohn, *Anthropologist*, 39–40, 64–66; Roger Chartier, *El mundo como representación: historia cultural, entre práctica y representación*, translated by C. Ferrari (Barcelona: Gedisa, 1995), 23–27.

12. Clifford Geertz, *The Interpretation of Cultures: Selected Essays* (London: Fontana, 1973), 9.

13. Darnton, *Great Cat Massacre*, 3.

14. The post-functionalist anthropologists I refer to are concerned with the link between colonialism, anthropology, representation, and artifact appropriation. For example: Talal Asad, introduction in T. Asad, ed., *Anthropology and the Colonial Encounter* (London: Ithaca, 1973), 9–19; and *Genealogies of Religion: Discipline and Reasons of Power in Christianity and Islam* (Baltimore, Md.: Johns Hopkins University Press, 1993); Nicholas Dirks, "Introduction: Colonialism and Culture," in N. Dirks, ed., *Colonialism and Culture* (Ann Arbor: University of Michigan Press, 1992), 1–25; Nicholas Thomas, *Entangled Objects: Exchange, Material Culture, and Colonialism in the Pacific* (Cambridge, Mass.: Harvard University Press, 1991); and *Colonialism's Culture: Anthropology, Travel, and Government* (Cambridge, U.K.: Polity Press, 1994); Michael Taussig, *Mimesis and Alterity: A Particular History of the Senses* (London: Routledge, 1993).

15. Eric R. Wolf, *Europe and the People without History* (Berkeley: University of California Press, 1982).

16. Following Nigel Rapport and Joanna Overing, I take cognition to be "the knowledge which people employ so as to make sense of the world, and the ways in which that knowledge is acquired, stored and retrieved." *Social and Cultural Anthropology: The Key Concepts* (London and New York: Routledge, 2000), 50.

17. I have discussed these issues elsewhere: Danna Levin Rojo, "The Road to Aztlan Ends in New Mexico," in V. M. Fields and V. Zamudio-Taylor, eds., *The Road to Aztlan: The Art of a Mythic Homeland* (Los Angeles, Calif.: Los Angeles County Museum of Art, 2001), 248–61; "Nuevos nombres viejos lugares: España y México reproducidos como topónimos en el Nuevo Mundo," *Secuencia* 57 (September–December 2003), 7–36; and "La búsqueda del Nuevo México: un proceso de-migratorio en la América española del siglo XVI," in C. Bonfiglioli, A. Gutiérrez, and M. A. Olavarría, eds., *Las vías del noroeste I: una macrorregión indígena americana* (Mexico: Instituto de Investigaciones Antropológicas, Universidad Nacional Autónoma de México, 2006), 133–68. To my knowledge there is no other study touching on this topic, even though Carroll L. Riley has recently noted that the concept of Aztlan powerfully affected the Spaniards, leading them to launch at least one major expedition to search for it between 1539 and 1542. Carroll L. Riley, *Becoming Aztlan: Mesoamerican Influence in the Greater Southwest, A.D. 1200–1500* (Salt Lake City: University of Utah Press, 2005), 5–6.

18. Marie-Areti Hers, "Los chichimecas: ¿Nómadas o sedentarios?" in A. Fábregas Puig, M. A. Nájera Espinoza, and C. Esteva Fabregat, eds., *Continuidad y fragmentación de la Gran Chichimeca* (Mexico: Seminario Permanente de Estudios de la Gran Chichimeca, 2008), 33–59; and "La Sierra Tepehuana: imágenes y discordancias sobre su pasado prehispánico," in C. Cramaussel and S. Ortelli, eds., *La Sierra Tepehuana: asentamientos y movimientos de población* (Zamora, Michoacán: El Colegio de Michoacán, Universidad Juárez del Estado de Durango, 2006), 17–44; María Teresa Cabrero García, *El hombre y sus instrumentos en la cultura bolaños* (Mexico: Universidad Nacional Autónoma de México, 2005); Patricia Carot, "Cronología de la ocupación en Loma Alta, Zacapu, Michoacán, o los antecedentes de la cultura purépecha," in *Antropología e interdisciplina, homenaje a Pedro Carrasco: XXIII Mesa Redonda de la Sociedad de Antropología* (Mexico: Sociedad Mexicana de Antropología, Universidad Nacional Autónoma de México, 1998), 2:46–63; and *Le site de Loma Alta, lac de Zacapu, Michoacan, Mexique* (Oxford, U.K.: Archaeopress, 2001); Patricia Carot and Marie-Areti Hers, "La gesta de los toltecas chichimecas y de los purépechas en las tierras de los antiguos pueblo ancestrales," in C. Bonfiglioli, A. Gutiérrez, and M. A. Olavarría, eds., *Las vías del noroeste I*, 47–82; Patricia Plunket and Gabriela Uruñuela, "Social and Cultural Consequences of a Late Holocene Eruption of Popocatepetl in Central Mexico," *Quaternary International* 51 (July 2006), 19–28; Beatriz Braniff, ed., *La Gran Chichimeca: el lugar de las rocas secas* (Mexico: Consejo Nacional para la Cultura y las Artes, 2001). New interdisciplinary approaches to preconquest and colonial history of the territory comprising Mexico's north and the U.S. Southwest that share the spirit of this book are contained in Carlo Bonfiglioli, Arturo Gutiérrez, Marie-Areti Hers, and María Eugenia Olavarría, eds., *Las vías del noroeste II: propuestas para una perspectiva sistémica e interdisciplinaria* (Mexico: Instituto de Investigaciones Antropológicas, Universidad Nacional Autónoma de México, 2008).

19. Several authors discussed at length in chapter 4 propose this identification. For example Enrique de Gandía, *Historia crítica de los mitos de la conquista americana* (Madrid: Sociedad General Española de Librería, 1929); Warren Beck, *New Mexico: A History of Four Centuries* (Norman: University of Oklahoma Press, 1969); David J. Weber, *Myth and the History of the Hispanic Southwest* (Albuquerque: University of New Mexico Press, 1987); Luis Weckmann, "The Middle Ages in the Conquest of America," *Speculum* 26, no. 1 (1951): 130–41; Beatriz Pastor Bodmer, *The Armature of Conquest:*

Spanish Accounts of the Discovery of America, 1492-1589 (Stanford, Calif.: Stanford University Press, 1992).

20. Hubert H. Bancroft, *The Works of Hubert Howe Bancroft*, vol. 17, *History of Arizona and New Mexico, 1530-1888* (San Francisco: History Company, 1889); Herbert E. Bolton, *Spanish Exploration in the Southwest, 1542-1706* (New York: Charles Scribner's Sons, 1916).

21. Raymond Corbey and Joseph Leerssen, "Studying Alterity: Backgrounds and Perspectives," in R. Corbey and J. Leerssen, eds., *Alterity, Identity, Image: Slaves and Others in Society and Scholarship* (Amsterdam and Atlanta: Rodopi, 1991), xx; Rapport and Overing, *Social and Cultural Anthropology*, 9.

22. Edward W. Said, *Orientalism: Western Conceptions of the Orient* [1978] (London: Penguin, 1995); Anthony Pagden, *The Fall of Natural Man: The American Indian and the Origins of Comparative Ethnology* (Cambridge: Cambridge University Press, 1982); Peter Hulme, *Colonial Encounters: Europe and the Native Caribbean, 1492-1797* (New York: Methuen, 1986); Bernard McGrane, *Beyond Anthropology: Society and the Other* (New York: Columbia University Press, 1989); Mason, *Deconstructing America*; Machiel Karskens, "Alterity as Defect: On the Logic of the Mechanism of Exclusion," in R. Corbey and J. Leerssen, eds., *Alterity, Identity, Image*, 75-90.

23. Emmanuel Levinas, *Totality and Infinity: An Essay on Metaphysics* (Pittsburgh, Pa.: Duquesne University Press, 1969), 40-42, 215-36; *Time and the Other* (Pittsburgh, Pa.: Duquesne University Press, 1987), 67-90; Michel Foucault, *Historia de la locura en la época clásica* [1st French ed. 1964], 2 vols., translated by J. J. Utrilla (Mexico: Fondo de Cultura Económica, 1976); Alan Sheridan, *Michel Foucault: The Will to Truth* (London: Tavistock, 1980).

24. Karskens, "Alterity as Defect," 78-83; Mason, *Deconstructing America*, 169-78; Fernando Ainsa, *De la Edad de Oro a El Dorado: génesis del discurso utópico americano* (Mexico: Fondo de Cultura Económica, 1992), 70-71.

25. Johannes Fabian, *Time and the Other: How Anthropology Makes Its Object* (New York: Columbia University Press, 1983); McGrane, *Beyond Anthropology*, 7-42; Stephen Greenblatt, *Marvelous Possessions: The Wonder of the New World* (Chicago: University of Chicago Press, 1991), 16-23, 30-37, 43-52.

26. Pagden, *Fall of Natural Man*, 117-18; Mason, *Deconstructing America*, 52-53; and "Continental Incontinence," 151-90; Hulme, *Colonial Encounters*.

27. Mason, *Deconstructing America*, chap. 2.

28. Mason, *Deconstructing America*, 164.

29. Edmundo O'Gorman, *La invención de América: investigación acerca de la estructura histórica del Nuevo Mundo y del sentido de su devenir* [1958] (Mexico: Fondo de Cultura Económica, Secretaría de Educación Pública, 1984); Serge Gruzinski, *La colonización de lo imaginario: sociedades indígenas y occidentalización en el México español, siglos XVI-XVIII* [1st French ed. 1988], translated by J. Ferreiro (Mexico: Fondo de Cultura Económica, 1991).

30. McGrane, *Beyond Anthropology*, 132-33; Ainsa, *De la Edad de Oro*, 67-71; Roger Bartra, *El salvaje en el espejo* (Mexico: Universidad Nacional Autónoma de México, 1992), 13; José Rabasa, *Inventing America: Spanish Historiography and the Formation of Eurocentrism* (Norman: University of Oklahoma Press, 1993), 3-19; Eduardo Subirats, *El continente vacío: la conquista del Nuevo Mundo y la conciencia moderna* (Mexico: Siglo XXI, 1994); David Abulafia, *The Discovery of Mankind: Atlantic Encounters in the Age of Columbus* (New Haven, Conn.: Yale University Press, 2008).

31. N. Thomas, *Colonialism's Culture*, 36.

32. Homi K. Bhabha, *The Location of Culture* (London: Routledge, 1994), 38, 85–92, 207–209.

33. John L. Comaroff, "Images of Empire: Contests of Conscience," in F. Cooper and A. L. Stoler, eds., *Tensions of Empire: Colonial Cultures in a Bourgeois World* (Berkeley and Los Angeles: University of California Press, 1997), 163–97; Ann Laura Stoler, "Rethinking Colonial Categories: European Communities and the Boundaries of Rule," *Comparative Studies in Society and History* 13, no. 1 (1989), 134–61. See also Frederick Cooper and Ann Laura Stoler, "Between Metropole and Colony: Rethinking a Research Agenda," in F. Cooper and A. L. Stoler, eds. *Tensions of Empire*, 1–56; and Vicente L. Rafael, *Contracting Colonialism: Translation and Christian Conversion in Tagalog Society under Early Spanish Rule* (Durham, N.C.: Duke University Press, 1993).

34. Susan M. Deeds, *Defiance and Deference in Mexico's Colonial North: Indians under Spanish Rule in Nueva Vizcaya* (Austin: University of Texas Press, 2003); Stephanie Wood, *Transcending Conquest: Nahua Views of Spanish Colonial Mexico* (Norman: University of Oklahoma Press, 2003); Cynthia Radding, *Landscapes of Power and Identity: Comparative Histories in the Sonoran Desert and the Forests of Amazonia from Colony to Republic* (Durham, N.C.: Duke University Press, 2005); Ethelia Ruiz Medrano, *Mexico's Indigenous Communities: Their Lands and Histories, 1500 to 2010*, translated by R. Davidson (Niwot: University Press of Colorado, 2010); Ida Altman, *The War for Mexico's West: Indians and Spaniards in New Galicia, 1524–1550* (Albuquerque: University of New Mexico Press, 2010).

35. James Lockhart, *The Nahuas after the Conquest: A Social and Cultural History of the Indians of Central Mexico, Sixteenth through Eighteenth Centuries* (Stanford, Calif.: Stanford University Press, 1992); and *Of Things of the Indies: Essays Old and New in Early Latin American History* (Stanford, Calif.: Stanford University Press, 1999); James F. Brooks, *Captives and Cousins: Slavery, Kinship, and Community in the Southwest Borderlands* (Chapel Hill: University of North Carolina Press, 2002).

36. For example, Edmundo O'Gorman, "La falacia histórica de Miguel León Portilla sobre el encuentro del Viejo y del Nuevo Mundo," *Quinto Centenario* 12 (1987): 17–31; Carlos Aznárez and Néstor Norma, eds., *500 años después: ¿descubrimiento o genocidio?* (Madrid: Nuer, 1992); Juan Antonio Estrada, *¿Quinto centenario de qué?* (Santander: Sal Terrae, 1992); Roger Izada, ed., *¿500 años de qué?* (Lima, Peru: Universidad Nacional Mayor de San Marcos, 1992).

37. B. Cohn, *Anthropologist*, 44.

38. Robert Redfield, Ralph Linton, and Melville J. Herskovitz, "Memorandum for the Study of Acculturation," *American Anthropologist* 38 (1936): 149–52; Ralph Linton, ed., *Acculturation in Seven American Indian Tribes* (New York: Appleton-Century, 1940); Ruth Benedict, "Two Patterns of Indian Acculturation," *American Anthropologist*, n.s., 45 (April–June 1943): 207–12; Ralph L. Beals, "Notes on Acculturation," in S. Tax, ed., *Heritage of Conquest: The Ethnology of Middle America* (Glencoe, Ill.: Free Press, 1952), 225–32; Edward H. Spicer, *Cycles of Conquest: The Impact of Spain, Mexico, and the United States on the Indians of the Southwest, 1533–1960* [1962] (Tucson: University of Arizona Press, 1981), 567–80; Gonzalo Aguirre Beltrán, *El proceso de aculturación en México* (Mexico: Universidad Iberoamericana, 1970); Nathan Wachtel, "La aculturación," in J. Le Goff and P. Nora, eds., *Hacer la historia*, translated by J. Cabanes (Barcelona: Laia, 1978), 1:135–55; Peter Stern, "Marginals and Acculturation in Frontier Society," in R. H.

Jackson, ed., *New Views of Borderlands History* (Albuquerque: University of New Mexico Press, 1998), 157–91.

39. Gruzinski, *La colonización de lo imaginario*.

40. See Wachtel, "La aculturación," 136, 142–46; Benedict, "Two Patterns of Indian Acculturation," 207; Linton, ed., *Acculturation in Seven American Indian Tribes*; Spicer, *Cycles of Conquest*, 569–76.

41. Fernando Ortiz, *Cuban Counterpoint: Tobacco and Sugar* [1940], translated by H. de Onís, introduction by B. Malinowski, with a new introduction by F. Coronil (Durham, N.C.: Duke University Press, 1995), 102–103.

42. Fernando Coronil, introduction to Ortiz, *Cuban Counterpoint*, xv.

43. For example, Ruiz Medrano, *Mexico's Indigenous Communities*; Jovita Baber, "Empire, Indians, and the Negotiation for the Status of City in Tlaxcala, 1521–1550," in E. Ruiz Medrano and S. Kellogg, eds., *Negotiation within Domination: New Spain's Indian Pueblos Confront the Spanish State* (Boulder: University Press of Colorado, 2010), 19–44; Laura Matthew and Michel R. Oudijk, eds., *Indian Conquistadors: Indigenous Allies in the Conquest of Mesoamerica* (Norman: University of Oklahoma Press, 2007).

44. See Mikhail Bakhtin, *The Dialogic Imagination: Four Essays*, edited by M. Holquist, translated by C. Emerson and M. Holquist (Austin: University of Texas Press, 1981).

45. Walter D. Mignolo, "Signs and Their Transmission: The Question of the Book in the New World," in E. H. Boone and W. D. Mignolo, eds., *Writing without Words: Alternative Literacies in Mesoamerica and the Andes* (Durham, N.C.: Duke University Press, 1994), 220–70; "The Movable Center: Geographical Discourses and Territoriality during the Expansion of the Spanish Empire," in F. J. Cevallos-Candau et al., eds., *Coded Encounters: Writing, Gender, and Ethnicity in Colonial Latin America* (Amherst: University of Massachusetts Press, 1994), 15–45; and *The Darker Side of the Renaissance: Literacy, Territoriality, and Colonization* (Ann Arbor: University of Michigan Press, 1995); Bhabha, *Location*, 85–92, 207–209; Taussig, *Mimesis and Alterity*, 199.

46. For example, David J. Weber, *The Spanish Frontier in North America* (New Haven, Conn.: Yale University Press, 1992); Robert H. Jackson, ed., *New Views of Borderlands History* (Albuquerque: University of New Mexico Press, 1998); Brooks, *Captives and Cousins*; Deeds, *Defiance and Deference*; Jesús Frank de la Teja and Ross Frank, *Choice, Persuasion, and Coercion: Social Control on Spain's North American Frontiers* (Albuquerque: University of New Mexico Press, 2005).

Chapter 1. The Semantics of Place Names

1. For interesting discussions about the inscription of political projects in the names of Latin American nations, see José Carlos Chiaramonte, Carlos Marichal, and Aimer Granados, eds., *Crear la nación: los nombres de los países de América Latina* (Buenos Aires: Editorial Sudamericana, 2008).

2. The term "civilization," in its modern sense as the ideal order of human society accomplished through the exercise of rationality, was coined in France in the 1750s to designate the superior stage on a unitary and universal scale of progress that only a few societies—the French among them—had achieved. The term seems to have come into English around 1772 and probably entered Spanish in the same period. Yet, similar notions about the ideal conditions of social life and the existence of an overall scale of human perfection, in which Christians occupied the pinnacle, began to develop among

Western Europeans in the Age of Discovery, given the exposure to deeply contrasting indigenous ways of life in the Americas. See Charles H. Long, "Primitive Religion," in C. J. Adams, ed., *A Reader's Guide to the Great Religions* (New York: Free Press, 1977), 5; Marshall Sahlins, *How "Natives" Think: About Captain Cook, for Example* (Chicago: University of Chicago Press, 1995), 10–11. Documents of the early colonial period do not speak of more-civilized or less-civilized peoples; they speak of peoples with greater or lesser rational capacity, who have or lack government institutions, organized religious cults, and *policía,* a term deriving from the Greek word for the minimum political unit: the city-state, or *poleis*. The term "civilization" is used in this sense throughout this book, as the expression of a political order incarnating the ideal condition of social life.

3. For example, Mason, *Deconstructing America*; and "Continental Incontinence"; McGrane, *Beyond Anthropology*; Greenblatt, *Marvelous Possessions*. These authors use examples from the conquest of America to develop arguments on cultural imperialism, based on the notion of "alterity as defect." The main point in such theorizing is that Western self-identity rests on a bipolar system of categorization, which confronts "self" and "other" through a series of contrastive distinctions along a positive–negative axis. According to this view, America was defined in conformity with previously established notions of alterity and therefore underwent a process of inferiorization and consequent deprivation of speech.

4. Corbey and Leerssen, "Studying Alterity," viii.

5. Foucault, *Historia de la locura en la época clásica*, 1:462–529; Sheridan, *Michel Foucault*, 37–40.

6. Ruiz Medrano, *Mexico's Indigenous Communities*, 12, 30–48.

7. Mignolo, "Movable Center," 16, and *Darker Side of the Renaissance*, 336. Mignolo's intention in coining the term "colonial semiosis," which encompasses that of colonial discourse, was to redraw the limits of a field of study that up to that point included mostly alphabetic texts written by colonizers or in the languages of colonizers. Mignolo broadens this field of study to include a wider spectrum of semiotic interactions in Amerindian languages and nonalphabetic scripts. His own work emphasizes the written aspect of colonial semiosis. Here I use the concept to describe a wider set of semiotic interactions: those occurring at the level of certain categories irrespective of their placement within any specific text. The notion of colonial semiosis as defined in the Mignolo quote provides a sophisticated analytic tool that will aid in a better understanding of cultural hybridization, more than concepts such as acculturation or cultural synthesis.

8. Sherburne F. Cook and Woodrow W. Borah, *Essays in Population History* (Berkeley and Los Angeles: University of California Press, 1971), 1:80–82. Despite the criticism their estimates have undergone, they are still the most widely accepted for Central Mexico. Ross Hassig, *Trade, Tribute, and Transportation: The Sixteenth Century Political Economy of the Valley of Mexico* (Norman: University of Oklahoma Press, 1985), 155–59, provides an interesting analysis of the regional distribution of population decline in this area. He attributes the disparity in mortality between the coastal lowlands—which suffered a more precipitous drop in population—and the highland plateau to regional settlement patterns, as well as the kind of diseases Europeans introduced. Declines in population for early northwest New Spain, an area corresponding roughly to present-day Colima, Sinaloa, and Sonora, are also very dramatic: native population was reduced from 820,000 individuals in 1519 to 310,000 in 1600. See Peter Gerhard, *The North Frontier of New Spain* (Princeton, N.J.: Princeton University Press, 1982), 24. The best

demographic study for the northern portion of New Spain, besides Gerhard, is Carl Sauer, *Aboriginal Population of Northwestern Mexico* (Berkeley: University of California Press, 1935).

9. John H. Elliott, "The Spanish Conquest and the Settlement of America," in L. Bethell, ed., *The Cambridge History of Latin America* (Cambridge: Cambridge University Press, 1984), 1:171–72; Charles Gibson, "Indian Societies under Spanish Rule," in Bethell, ed., *Cambridge History of Latin America*, 1:384–85.

10. John H. Elliott, "Spain and America in the Sixteenth and Seventeenth Centuries," in Bethell, ed., *Cambridge History of Latin America*, 1:289.

11. The administrative system of the Spanish empire overseas remained rather flexible due to difficulties in long distance control. See John H. Parry, *The Spanish Seaborne Empire* (London: Hutchinson, 1967); and Elliott, "Spain and America."

12. This and all further translations of Spanish colonial chronicles and documents are mine unless otherwise indicated. "Poder que otorga Hernán Cortés a Juan Ochoa de Lejalde," Tepeaca, August 6, 1520, in José Luis Martínez, ed., *Documentos cortesianos* (Mexico: Universidad Nacional Autónoma de México, Fondo de Cultura Económica, 1990), 1:115.

13. The "Carta del Cabildo" (July 10, 1519) was a letter of report signed by the officials Cortés had appointed in Veracruz to legalize his conquest. He sent the letter to the king via two emissaries, the *procuradores* Francisco de Montejo and Alonso Hernández Portocarrero. Although Cortés himself did not sign it, the letter is usually considered a substitute for his "Primera carta de relación," which either never existed or has been lost. The letter is contained in Hernán Cortés, *Cartas de relación* (Mexico: Porrúa, 1994), 7–27.

14. Juan de Torquemada, *Monarquía indiana: de los veinte y un libros rituales y monarquía indiana, con el origen y guerras de los indios occidentales, de sus poblazones, descubrimiento, conquista, conversión y otras cosas maravillosas de la mesma tierra* [1615] (Mexico: Universidad Nacional Autónoma de México, 1975), 2:23.

15. Juan Díaz, "Itinerario de la armada del Rey Católico a la isla de Yucatán, en la India, en el año 1518, en la que fue por Comandante y Capitán General Juan de Grijalva," in Germán Vázquez, ed., *La conquista de Tenochtitlan*, by Juan Díaz, Andrés de Tapia, Bernardino Vázquez de Tapia, and Francisco de Aguilar (Madrid: Historia 16, 1988), 37–57. The original manuscript, written in 1519 and first published in Venice in 1520 in Latin and Italian, was lost in the colonial period. We only know the text through the Italian version used in Venice, of which all subsequent Spanish editions are translations. See Joaquín García Icazbalceta, ed., *Colección de documentos para la historia de México* (Mexico: Librería de J. M. Andrade, 1858), 1:xiii–xvi.

16. Martínez, *Documentos cortesianos*, 1:60–61.

17. Emphasis mine in the phrase "*y en otras muchas cosas que le equiparan a ella.*" Cortés, *Cartas*, 96.

18. Also known as Peter Martyr d'Anghiera. His original Italian name was Pietro Martire d'Anghiera. Mignolo, *Darker Side*, 171.

19. Pedro Mártir de Anglería, "Epístola 665, A los Marqueses," March 14, 1520. The term "civilized" comes from the Spanish translation here quoted: Pedro Mártir de Anglería, *Cartas sobre el Nuevo Mundo*, translated by J. Bauzano, introduction by R. Alba (Madrid: Polifemo, 1990), 106. The word in the original Latin text is most probably a derivation of the term *civitas* signifying the existence of a "body politic" in the classical

sense, essentially characterized by non-kin-based forms of political authority, law, and urbanism. By "Coloacana," Mártir certainly meant Culúa, or Colúa, (Colhuacan), the name of a Nahua community in the Valley of Mexico that the Aztecs had adopted as an epithet or supplement to their own name. The Spaniards who had explored the coast of the Gulf of Mexico in 1517 and 1518 had repeatedly heard the name used by natives for Mexico, core of the Aztec empire. "Olloa" (Ulúa) was an island off the coastal village of Veracruz, where Cortés founded the first municipality in New Spain, and "Cozumela" the island where he first landed, off the coast of Yucatan.

20. Hernández Portocarrero and Montejo had left Veracruz on July 26, 1519. José Luis Martínez, *Hernán Cortés* (Mexico: Universidad Nacional Autónoma de México, Fondo de Cultura Económica, 1990), 178.

21. Cortés, "Segunda carta-relación al Emperador," *Cartas*, 66.

22. An Italian translation of Mártir de Anglería's first *Decade* was published in 1504, although the original Latin text was not printed until 1511 (Seville) and again in 1516, together with the other *Decades,* in a volume titled *Deccas Occeana* (Alcalá de Henares, Spain). In 1530 a new Latin edition appeared as *De Orbe Novo Decades.* See José Juan Arrom's introduction to Ramón Pané, *Relación acerca de las antigüedades de los indios* [ca. 1498], edited by J. J. Arrom (Mexico: Siglo XXI, 1974), 11. The Spanish edition I use in this book is Pedro Mártir de Anglería, *Décadas del Nuevo Mundo por Pedro Mártir de Anglería, primer cronista de Indias*, preliminary study and appendices by E. O'Gorman, translation by A. Millares Carlo (Mexico: José Porrúa e Hijos, 1964–65).

23. Quoted by José Juan Arrom in a footnote to his edition of Hernán Pérez de Oliva, *Historia de la invención de las Indias* [1525–28], edited by J. J. Arrom (Mexico: Siglo XXI, 1991), 46.

24. Pérez de Oliva, *Historia de la invención*, 46.

25. Quoted from Margarita Zamora's English version of the original text, in Stephen Greenblatt, ed., *New World Encounters* (Berkeley and Los Angeles: University of California Press, 1993), 3–4, 5.

26. William Pietz, "The Problem of the Fetish, I," *Res: Anthropology and Aesthetics* 9 (Spring 1985): 7; and "The Problem of the Fetish, II," *Res: Anthropology and Aesthetics* 13 (Spring 1987).

27. Carmen Bernand and Serge Gruzinski, *Historia del Nuevo Mundo*, vol. 2, *Los mestizajes, 1550–1640*, translated by M. A. Neira Bigorra (Mexico: Fondo de Cultura Económica, 1999), 190–91.

28. Pané, *Relación acerca de las antigüedades*, 34.

29. Ibid., 42.

30. Pérez de Oliva, *Historia de la invención*, 47.

31. The expression "edificios de cal y canto" appears repeatedly in official and personal letters and legal testimony of the time. The presence of masonry buildings was among the first things the "Carta del Cabildo" noted (Cortés, *Cartas*, 8, 21). Francisco de Aguilar, who participated in the assault on Mexico-Tenochtitlan, also remarked upon this fact ("Relación breve de la conquista de la Nueva España" [ca. 1570], in Vázquez, *Juan Díaz*, 161–206). An early letter by Alonso Zuazo, dated in Cuba, November 14, 1521, did the same (in García Icazbalceta, *Colección de documentos*, 1:358–67). Based on information gathered by Grijalva, the governor of Cuba decided to send Hernán Cortés to explore the mainland; Zuazo held a judiciary post on the island at the time and was among the most enthusiastic supporters of the enterprise. Later on he was sent to New Spain and

occupied the governorship temporarily when Cortés was absent in Honduras (García Icazbalceta, *Colección de documentos*, 1:xvii). The same remark about stone and mortar buildings is conspicuous in Mártir de Anglería's account concerning Hernández de Córdoba's 1517 expedition, the first to sight Yucatan; see Henry R. Wagner, *The Discovery of Yucatan by Francisco Hernández de Córdoba: A Translation of the Original Texts* (Berkeley, Calif.: Cortes Society, 1942), 33.

32. Cortés, *Cartas*, 41, 62–63; Conquistador anónimo, *Relación de la Nueva España*, edited by J. Bustamante (Madrid: Polifemo, 1986), 147; Bernal Díaz del Castillo, *Historia verdadera de la conquista de la Nueva España* [ca. 1555], edited by C. Sáenz de Santa María (Madrid: Instituto Gonzalo Fernández de Oviedo, Consejo Superior de Educación Científica, 1982), 192.

33. "Towers" was how Spaniards described pyramids, which they also called "mezquitas." The worship of idols in mosques is one of the most-repeated themes in sixteenth century sources concerning New Spain; see, for example, the fragments of early chronicles on the first arrivals at Yucatan in 1517, contained in Wagner, *Discovery of Yucatan*. See also the first and second letters by Cortés.

34. Carmen Bernand and Serge Gruzinski, *De la idolatría: una arqueología de las ciencias religiosas*, translated by D. Sánchez (Mexico: Fondo de Cultura Económica, 1992), 14–17, 29–30, 40–56, 68–69, 190–91; Serge Gruzinski, *La guerra de las imágenes: de Cristóbal Colón a Blade Runner (1492–2019)*, translation by J. J. Utrilla (Mexico: Fondo de Cultura Económica, 1994), 20–21.

35. Emphasis mine. Cortés, *Cartas*, 20.

36. See, for example, the letters by Mártir de Anglería, *Cartas*, and the fourth of his *Décadas del Nuevo Mundo*. See also Cortés, "Segunda carta-relación al Emperador," *Cartas*, 31–96; Díaz, "Itinerario de la Armada"; Aguilar, "*Relación breve*"; and the two "Relaciones" by Andrés de Tapia and Bernardino Vázquez de Tapia, in Vázquez, ed., *La conquista de Tenochtitlan*, 40, 57, 79, 86, 93, 97, 140, 141, 142, 165, 171, 173, 174. The only account among these to call Moctezuma "emperador," however, is the one by Aguilar, written around 1570. Therefore, one has to be cautious concerning the use of this particular term, which may have been adopted retrospectively for the Mexica *tlatoani* toward the late sixteenth century as a rhetorical means to make of Cortés's adventure a more impressive achievement. Still, it is notable that an eyewitness, in recasting the events, chose precisely the word "emperador" and not just "príncipe" or "rey." This shows that the first conquerors of New Spain were clear about the character of Moctezuma's position as an overlord.

37. Robert Haskett, *Indigenous Rulers: An Ethnohistory of Town Government in Colonial Cuernavaca* (Albuquerque: University of New Mexico Press, 1991), 133.

38. For the origin and indigenous meaning of the word "cacique," see Manuel Alvar, *Americanismos en la historia de Bernal Díaz del Castillo* (Madrid: Consejo Superior de Investigaciones Científicas, Revista de Filología Española, 1970), 55–56; and Haskett, *Indigenous Rulers*, 133–37.

39. Díaz del Castillo, *Historia verdadera*, 115.

40. Ibid., 177.

41. Haskett, *Indigenous Rulers*, 133–37.

42. Cortés, *Cartas*, 22.

43. Ibid., 41.

44. Ibid.

45. Cortés, *Cartas*, 45–46.

46. Ibid., 66.

47. I use "entitlement" as in Kenneth Burke, that is, to remark on the capacity of symbolic action to confer particular identities to persons, things, and situations. "What are the signs of what? (A theory of entitlement)," in *Language as Symbolic Action: Essays of Life, Literature, and Method* (Berkeley: University of California Press, 1966), 359–79.

48. Lockhart, *Nahuas*, 445; and "Double Mistaken Identity. Some Nahua Concepts in Postconquest Guise," in *Of Things of the Indies*, 98–119. Hugh Thomas has also pointed out the similarities between sixteenth-century Spain and preconquest societies in Central Mexico in *The Real Discovery of America: Mexico, November 8, 1519* (New York: Moyer Bell, 1992), 19–28; and *The Conquest of Mexico* (London: Pimlico, 1993), xi–xiv.

49. Quoted by Wagner, *Discovery of Yucatan*, 33, 42. Thomas, *Real Discovery*, 91, provides other derivations for the word "Yucatán," such as *ciuthan*, "they say so."

50. The Philippine islands were named after King Philip II, Cape Mendocino after Viceroy Antonio de Mendoza, Juana after the king's son Juan, Fernandina after King Ferdinand the Catholic.

51. Álvaro del Portillo y Diez de Sollano, *Descubrimientos y exploraciones en las costas de California* (Madrid: Escuela de Estudios Hispanoamericanos de Sevilla, 1947) discusses the dynamics of place-naming with a different perspective from the one herein adopted.

52. See J. N. Hillgarth, *The Spanish Kingdoms, 1250–1516*, vol. 2, *1410–1516* (Oxford: Clarendon Press, 1978).

53. Columbus wrote to the Pope in 1502: "This island is Tharsis, Cethia, Ofir and Ophaz and Cipango, and we have called it Española." Quoted in Ainsa, *De la edad de oro*, 119.

54. Peter Hulme elaborates on the possible meanings and implications of the toponym Hispaniola, arguing that besides a literal way to take possession by naming, this was a form of assimilating the foreign through domestication and, in consequence, a device to familiarize the menacing exotic. "Tales of Distinction: European Ethnography and the Caribbean," in S. B. Schwartz, ed., *Implicit Understandings: Observing, Reporting and Reflecting on the Encounters between Europeans and Other Peoples in the Early Modern Era* (Cambridge: Cambridge University Press, 1994), 166–67.

55. The definition of "espanto" provided by the Spanish Royal Academy (1732) is "terror, amazement, a state of emotional disturbance and consternation, something that causes disquiet and alters the senses. . . . Also meaning wonder and awe, not out of fear but due to the realization and consideration of some novelty." Real Academia Española, *Diccionario de autoridades* [1732] (Madrid: Gredos, 1984), my translation.

56. Aguilar, *Relación breve*, in Vázquez, ed., *La conquista de Tenochtitlan*, 176. It seems that Captains Pedro de Alvarado and Bernardino Vázquez de Tapia, who were sent to have a look at Tenochtitlan around the same time but only got as far as Tetzcoco, did not reach a point where they could attain a panoramic view of the whole valley. See Vázquez de Tapia, "Relación de méritos y servicios," in Vázquez, ed., *La conquista de Tenochtitlan*, 139–41.

57. Mártir de Anglería, "Epístola 717: A los Marqueses" (March 7, 1521), *Cartas*, 109.

58. Eduardo Noguera, "Sitios de ocupación en la periferia de Tenochtitlan y su significado histórico-arqueológico," *Anales de Antropología* 11 (1974): 66–67.

59. Hassig, *Trade, Tribute, and Transportation*, 41–45, provides a detailed description of the Valley of Mexico including its size and topography, the hydrological conditions in and around the lakes, and the development of *chinampa* agriculture. Frances Berdan,

The Aztecs (New York: Chelsea House, 1989), 29–32, also describes the valley in detail. For an evaluation of the sociopolitical implications of chinampa agriculture, see Elizabeth M. Brumfiel, "Agricultural Development and Class Stratification in the Southern Valley of Mexico," in H. R. Harvey, ed., *Land and Politics in the Valley of Mexico: A Two Thousand Year Perspective* (Albuquerque: University of New Mexico Press, 1991), 43–62; and Jeffrey R. Parsons, "Political Implications of Prehispanic Chinampa Agriculture in the Valley of Mexico," in Harvey, ed., *Land and Politics in the Valley of Mexico*, 17–42.

60. Quoted in Noguera, "Sitios de ocupación," 56.

61. Ibid., 57.

62. The most important archaeological recoveries of Mexico-Tenochtitlan were done in the 1970s and 1980s during the subway construction and in two major excavation projects held at the Great Temples of Tlatelolco and Tenochtitlan.

63. Conquistador anónimo, *Relación*, 141.

64. José Luis de Rojas, *México Tenochtitlan: economía y sociedad en el siglo XVI* (Mexico: El Colegio de Michoacán, Fondo de Cultura Económica, 1986), 43; Noguera, "Sitios de ocupación," 67.

65. The second letter of Cortés, almost contemporary with the events, is the earliest account we have of the Spaniards' arrival at Tenochtitlan. The other documents referred to are also eyewitness accounts, though written from memory some years later. The *Relación* of the Conquistador anónimo, first published in 1556 by Giovanni Batista Ramusio in an Italian translation, was written between 1531 and 1556; the chronicle by Díaz del Castillo dates from about 1555, Tapia's "Relación" from 1539, and Aguilar's "Relación breve" from about 1570 (the last two, published in Vázquez, ed., *La conquista de Tenochtitlan*, are cited above).

66. Díaz del Castillo, *Historia verdadera*, 192.

67. Aguilar, "Relación breve," in Vázquez, ed., *La conquista de Tenochtitlan*, 180. See also Andrés de Tapia's comments on Moctezuma's meals and palaces (in Vázquez, ed., *La conquista de Tenochtitlan*, 105–106), and the descriptions of Tenochtitlan by Cortés, *Cartas*, 66–68, and the Conquistador anónimo, *Relación*, 141–53.

68. Conquistador anónimo, *Relación*, 147.

69. Ibid., 141.

70. Thomas, *Real Discovery*, 612.

71. Rojas, *México Tenochtitlan*, 65.

72. Thomas, *Conquest of Mexico*, 609–14, provides an excellent summary of twentieth-century demographic debates concerning New Spain, and the Valley of Mexico in particular. Compare the figures quoted from Rojas with the contemporary population of Greater London, that is, London with Westminster and suburban environs—about 50 to 60 thousand inhabitants in the 1520s—and Paris—about 200 thousand inhabitants at the end of the sixteenth century; see Penelope Corfield, "Urban Development in England and Wales in the XVI and XVII Centuries," in J. Barry, ed., *The Tudor and Stuart Town: A Reader in English Urban History, 1530–1668* (London: Longman, 1990), 39; and Leonardo Benevolo, *The European City*, translated by C. Ipsen (Oxford, U.K.: Blackwell, 1993), 140.

73. Hassig, *Trade, Tribute, and Transportation*, 92–103.

74. Letter by Alonso Zuazo, November 14, 1521, in García Icazbalceta, *Colección de documentos*, 1:366.

75. Hassig, *Trade, Tribute, and Transportation*, 93.

76. *Codex Mendoza* lists the tribute collected from four hundred towns between 1516 and 1518. See Frances F. Berdan and Patricia R. Anawalt, eds., *The Essential Codex Mendoza* (Berkeley and Los Angeles: University of California Press, 1997).

77. Juan Díaz, "Itinerario de la armada," in Vázquez, ed., *La conquista de Tenochtitlan*, 57.

78. Hulme, *Colonial Encounters*, 20.

79. Pastor Bodmer, *Armature*, 12–13.

80. Fragments of colonial chronicles concerning this expedition of Hernández de Córdoba to Yucatan are found in Wagner, *Discovery of Yucatan*. See also Mártir de Anglería's fourth *Decade* of *De Orbe Novo*; Gonzalo Fernández de Oviedo, *Historia general y natural de las Indias*; and Francisco López de Gómara, *Historia de las Indias*.

81. Moctezuma may have been informed of the presence of strangers when the ships of Hernández de Córdoba were sighted. He certainly was when Grijalva came, for he sent messengers to receive the Spanish captain near San Juan de Ulúa. By this time the Spaniards had already heard of the rich and powerful country of "Culúa," Mexico. Martínez, *Hernán Cortés*, 120–22.

82. Martínez, *Hernán Cortés*, 121, 157, 161–62.

83. Gandía, *Historia crítica*; O'Gorman, *La invención*; Lewis Hanke, *Aristotle and the American Indians: A Study in Race Prejudice in the Modern World* (Bloomington: Indiana University Press, 1959); Weckmann, "Middle Ages"; and Weckmann, *La herencia medieval de México* (Mexico: El Colegio de México, 1984); Pastor Bodmer, *Armature*; McGrane, *Beyond Anthropology*; Mason, *Deconstructing America*; Hulme, *Colonial Encounters*, 20–36.

84. Martínez, *Hernán Cortés*, 129; Díaz del Castillo, *Historia verdadera*, 7–29.

85. The term "Chichimeca" is complex and ambiguous. It will be discussed in chapter 2, but here it is used in the most common Spanish sense as a generic term for all part-time farmers and hunter-gatherers living in the arid environment of what is now northern Mexico. Recent studies have shown that the sedentary agriculturist versus nomadic hunter-gatherer dichotomy, formerly used to distinguish Mesoamerican populations from those living north of New Spain, is an equivocal simplification. See Marie-Areti Hers et al., eds., *Nómadas y sedentarios en el Norte de México: homenaje a Beatriz Braniff* (Mexico: Universidad Nacional Autónoma de México, Instituto de Investigaciones Estéticas, 2000). Nevertheless, native societies in the north that did not subsist on the practice of year-round agriculture presented a major obstacle to Spanish conquest and colonization.

86. None of the written testimonies Cabeza de Vaca and other shipwreck survivors produced mentions the province of seven cities, but letters by Viceroy Antonio de Mendoza and the chronicler Gonzalo Fernández de Oviedo suggest they had mentioned hearing the rumor among the natives they came across. Further details on the Cabeza de Vaca expedition and the attendant reports and chronicles follow in chapter 3.

87. Marcos de Niza, "Relación del descubrimiento de las siete ciudades," September 2, 1539, in Carmen de Mora, *Las siete ciudades de Cíbola: textos y testimonios sobre la expedición de Vázquez de Coronado* (Seville: Alfar, 1992), 158.

88. Baltasar de Obregón stated that Nombre de Dios, in Nueva Vizcaya, was established to "pacify robbing caribs" who roamed in the mountains nearby. He also noted that Topia and environs were "populated by many thieving caribs." *Historia de los descubrimientos antiguos y modernos de la Nueva España* [1584] (Mexico: Secretaría de

Educación Pública, 1924), 49, 52. The introduction to a seventeenth-century map collection portraying the Pacific coast of New Spain says that beyond Compostela the land "is inhabited by infinite numbers of bellicose *caribe* Indians." The document is titled "Mapas de las costas de la Nueva España en el Mar del Sur desde la última población de españoles en ellas, ques la ciudad de Compostela, en adelante" (Biblioteca Nacional, Madrid, ms. 2957, p. I).

Chapter 2. Mexican, Chichimeca, and Pueblo Indians

1. Geographic descriptions in this and the following paragraphs are based on Abram J. Jaffe, *The First Immigrants from Asia: A Population History of the North American Indians* (New York: Plenum, 1992); Robert M. Carmack, Janine Gasco, and Gary H. Gossen, *The Legacy of Mesoamerica: History and Culture of a Native American Civilization* (Upper Saddle River, N.J.: Prentice Hall, 1996), 9–14, 18–19; J. Charles Kelley, "Mesoamerica and the Southwestern United States," in G. F. Ekholm and G. R. Willey, eds., *Handbook of Middle American Indians*, vol. 4, *Archaeological Frontiers and External Connections* (Austin: University of Texas Press, 1966), 95; Thomas D. Hall, *Social Change in the Southwest, 1530–1880* (Lawrence: University Press of Kansas, 1989), 35–36; Richard B. Woodbury, "Prehistory: Introduction," in W. C. Sturtevant, ed., *Handbook of North American Indians*, vol. 9, *The Southwest* (Washington, D.C.: Smithsonian Institution, 1979), 25; Michael E. Bonine, *Atlas of Mexico* (Austin: Bureau of Business Research, University of Texas, 1970), 7; and Gerhard, *North Frontier*, 3.

2. Paul Kirchhoff, "Los recolectores cazadores del norte de México," in *El norte de México y el sur de Estados Unidos: tercera reunión de la mesa redonda sobre problemas antropológicos de México y Centro América* (Mexico: Sociedad Mexicana de Antropología, 1943), 133–44; "Mesoamérica: sus límites geográficos, composición étnica y caracteres culturales," *Acta Americana* 1, no. 1 (1943): 92–107; and "Gatherers and Farmers in the Greater Southwest: A Problem in Classification," *American Anthropologist* 56, no. 4 (1954): 529–60. Mexican archaeologists and anthropologists using Kirchhoff's model include Eduardo Matos Moctezuma, "Mesoamérica," in L. Manzanilla and L. López Luján, eds., *Historia antigua de México*, vol. 1, *El México antiguo, sus áreas culturales, los orígenes y el horizonte preclásico* (Mexico: Instituto Nacional de Antropología e Historia, Universidad Nacional Autónoma de México, Porrúa, 1994), 49–73; Jesús Nárez, "Aridamérica y Oasisamérica," in Manzanilla and López Luján, eds., *Historia antigua de México*, 1:75–111; Arturo Guevara, "Oasisamérica en el posclásico: la zona de Chihuahua," in L. Manzanilla and L. López Luján, eds., *Historia antigua de México*, vol. 3, *El horizonte posclásico y algunos aspectos intelectuales de las culturas mesoamericanas* (Mexico: Instituto Nacional de Antropología e Historia, Universidad Nacional Autónoma de México, Porrúa, 1995), 329–54; Alfredo López Austin and Leonardo López Luján, *El pasado indígena* (Mexico: Fondo de Cultura Económica, El Colegio de México, 1996).

3. Luis Pericot y García, *América indígena*, vol. 1, *El hombre americano y los pueblos de América* (Barcelona: Salvat, 1961), 165–66.

4. Susan Deeds, *Defiance and Deference*; and "Indigenous Rebellions on the Mexican Mission Frontier: From First-Generation to Later Colonial Responses," in D. J. Guy and T. E. Sheridan, eds., *Contested Ground: Comparative Frontiers on the Northern and Southern Edges of the Spanish Empire* (Tucson: University of Arizona Press, 1998), 32–51; Cynthia Radding, "The Colonial Pact and Changing Ethnic Frontiers in Highland Sonora,

1740–1840," in Guy and Sheridan, eds., *Contested Ground*, 53–57; Cecilia Sheridan, "Social Control and Native Territoriality in Northeastern New Spain," in Teja and Frank, eds., *Choice, Persuasion, and Coercion*, 121–48; Stern, "Marginals and Acculturation," 157–88.

5. Deeds, *Defiance and Deference*, 40–41.

6. My example of colonial classification of native peoples in the African and Indian contexts comes from Cooper and Stoler, "Between Metropole and Colony," 4; Nicholas Dirks, "The Original Caste: Power, History and Hierarchy in South Asia," *Contributions to Indian Sociology* 23, no. 1 (January 1989): 61, 71–72; Terence Ranger, "The Invention of Tradition in Colonial Africa," in E. Hobsbawm and T. Ranger, eds., *The Invention of Tradition* (Cambridge: Cambridge University Press, 1983), 247–54; Martin Chanock, *Law, Custom, and Social Order: The Colonial Experience in Malawi and Zambia* (Cambridge: Cambridge University Press, 1985), 20–21, 219–39; Cohn, *Anthropologist*, 238–47.

7. Marie-Areti Hers and María de los Dolores Soto, "La obra de Beatriz Braniff y el desarrollo de la arqueología del norte de México," in Hers et al., eds., *Nómadas y sedentarios*, 42.

8. Examples of dehumanizing labels from other places are discussed by Michael Taussig, "Culture of Terror, Space of Death: Roger Casement's Putumayo Report and the Explanation of Torture," *Comparative Studies in Society and History* 26 (1984): 467–97, and Pamela Scully, "Rape, Race, and Colonial Culture: The Sexual Politics of Identity in the Nineteenth Century Cape Colony, South Africa," *American Historical Review* 100 (1995): 335–59.

9. For example, Frederick Cooper and Ann Laura Stoler, introduction to "Tensions of Empire: Colonial Control and Visions of Rule," special issue of *American Ethnologist* 16 (1989): 609–21; John L. Comaroff and Jean Comaroff, *Of Revelation and Revolution*, vol. 1, *Christianity, Colonialism, and Consciousness in South Africa* (Chicago: University of Chicago Press, 1991); and *Of Revelation and Revolution*, vol. 2, *The Dialectics of Modernity on a South African Frontier* (Chicago: University of Chicago Press, 1997); Stoler, "Rethinking Colonial Categories"; Thomas, *Colonialism's Culture*.

10. Cooper and Stoler, "Between Metropole and Colony," 1.

11. Ileto, *Pasyon and Revolution*; Rafael, *Contracting Colonialism*; and Jean Comaroff, *Body of Power*, examine how Christianity was made local in the Philippines and South Africa, turning into a form of resistance against the colonial institutions of church and state. On the other hand, John L. Comaroff, "Images of Empire," discusses the undermining effects that missionizing had on the legitimacy of the system of indirect rule that British administrators negotiated in South Africa.

12. Kirchhoff, "Gatherers and Farmers," 550.

13. Clark Wissler, *The American Indian: An Introduction to the Anthropology of the New World* [1917] (Gloucester, Mass.: Peter Smith, 1938), xix–xxi, 217–18. Other central works that outlined the concept and attendant methodology are Alfred L. Kroeber, *Anthropology: Race, Language, Culture, Psychology, Pre-History* [1923] (New York: Harcourt, Brace 1948); and *Cultural and Natural Areas of Native North America* (Berkeley: University of California Press, 1939); Walter Krickeberg, *Etnología de América*, translated by P. Hendrich (Mexico: Fondo de Cultura Económica, 1946); Kirchhoff, "Los recolectores," 133–44; "Mesoamérica," 92–107; and "Gatherers and Farmers," 529–60.

14. For a well-balanced summary of early classifications of Native American peoples, see Pericot y García, *América indígena*, 161–66.

15. One of the most comprehensive taxonomies of Amerindian languages registered more than 2,000 at the time of European arrival: Daniel G. Brinton, *The American Race: A Linguistic Classification and Ethnographical Description of the Native Tribes of North and South America* (New York: N. D. C. Hodges, 1891).

16. Kirchhoff, "Gatherers and Farmers," 531.

17. Brinton, *American Race*.

18. Kroeber, *Cultural and Natural Areas*, 1–2.

19. See, for instance, Hers et al., eds., *Nómadas y sedentarios*; Braniff, *La Gran Chichimeca*; Carlo Bonfiglioli, Arturo Gutiérrez, and María Eugenia Olavarría, eds., *Las vías del noroeste*, vol. 1, *Una macrorregión indígena americana* (Mexico: Universidad Nacional Autónoma de México, 2006).

20. For this general characterization of Mesoamerica and the more detailed description that follows, a wide variety of literature is available. Most information herein included is now common knowledge; therefore, specific references are often omitted. The overview relies essentially on the following sources: Robert C. West and John Augelli, *Middle America: Its Lands and Peoples* (Englewood Cliffs, N.J.: Prentice Hall, 1976); Sonia Lombardo and Enrique Nalda, eds., *Temas mesoamericanos* (Mexico: Instituto Nacional de Antropología e Historia, 1996); Pedro Armillas, "Condiciones ambientales y movimientos de pueblos en la frontera septentrional de Mesoamérica," in Seminario de Estudios Americanistas and the Seminario de Antropología Americana, eds., *Homenaje a Fernando Márquez Miranda* (Madrid: Universidades de Madrid y Sevilla, 1964), 62–82; Pedro Armillas, "Northern Mesoamerica," in J. D. Jennings and E. Norbeck, eds., *Prehistoric Man in the New World* (Chicago: University of Chicago Press, 1964), 291–329; Ignacio Bernal, "Formación y desarrollo de Mesoamérica," in D. Cosío Villegas, ed., *Historia general de México* (Mexico: El Colegio de México, 1977), 1:12–164; Pedro Carrasco, "The Peoples of Central Mexico and their Historical Traditions," in G. F. Ekholm and I. Bernal, eds., *Handbook of Middle American Indians*, vol. 11, *Archaeology of Northern Mesoamerica*, pt. 2 (Austin: University of Texas Press, 1971), 459–73, and "Social Organization of Ancient Mexico," in Ekholm and Bernal, eds., *Handbook of Middle American Indians*, vol. 10, *Archaeology of Northern Mesoamerica*, pt. 1 (Austin: University of Texas Press, 1971), 349–75; Anne Chapman, "Mesoamérica ¿Estructura o historia?" in A. Guzmán and L. Martínez O., eds., *La validez teórica del concepto de Mesoamérica* (Mexico: Instituto Nacional de Antropología e Historia, Sociedad Mexicana de Antropología, 1990), 21–29; Kirchhoff, "Mesoamérica"; López Austin and López Luján, *El pasado*.

21. Alfredo López Austin, *Los mitos del tlacuache: caminos de la mitología mesoamericana* (Mexico: Alianza Editorial, 1990); Carmack, Gasco, and Gossen, *Legacy*.

22. All three are usually grown in the same plot. Maize stalks support the climbing bean vines, which enrich the soil with nitrogen, while the soil beneath is protected against erosion by the creeping foliage of squash. This cultivation technique is still applied in many Mexican locations. West and Augelli, *Middle America*, 229.

23. This is not to say Andean cultures were less developed; they simply found other means to satisfy their needs. Although the Inca system of recording data by means of knotted strings (*khipu* or *quipu*) was sophisticated and may have registered more than merely quantitative knowledge, it has a different logic from that of writing, as shown by Marcia Ascher and Robert Ascher, *Code of Quipu: A Study in Media, Mathematics, and Culture* (Ann Arbor: University of Michigan Press, 1981), and Tom Cummins, "Representation in the Sixteenth Century and the Colonial Image of the Inca," in Boone and

Mignolo, eds., *Writing without Words*, 188–219. For a brief but suggestive discussion on markets in the preconquest Andes, see John V. Murra, "Did Tribute and Markets Prevail in the Andes before the European Invasion?" in B. Larson and O. Harris, eds., *Ethnicity, Markets, and Migration in the Andes: At the Crossroads of History and Anthropology* (Durham, N.C.: Duke University Press, 1995), 57–72. For a classic and more extended discussion of this topic see Karl Polanyi, "The Economy as Instituted Process," in K. Polanyi, C. Arensberg, and H. Pearson, eds., *Trade and Markets in the Early Empires* (Glencoe, Ill.: Free Press, 1957), 243–70.

24. Kirchhoff, "Mesoamérica," 99–102.

25. Alfredo López Austin, "La religión, la magia y la cosmovisión," in Manzanilla and López Luján, eds., *Historia antigua de México*, 3:447–50.

26. Matos Moctezuma, "El proceso de desarrollo en Mesoamérica," *Boletín de Antropología Americana* 5 (1982): 117–31; and "Mesoamérica," 56–57.

27. Julio C. Olivé Negrete, "Estado, formación socioeconómica y periodificación de Mesoamérica," in J. Monjarás Ruiz, E. Pérez Rocha, and R. Brambila, eds., *Mesoamérica y el centro de México* (Mexico: Instituto Nacional de Antropología e Historia, 1985), 81–114; Joseph Whitecotton and Richard Piles, "New World Precolumbian World Systems," in Frances Joan Mathien and Randall McGuire, eds., *Ripples in the Chichimeca Sea* (Carbondale: Southern Illinois University Press, 1986), 183–204; Carmack, Gasco, and Gossen, *Legacy*.

28. Jaime Litvak King, "En torno al problema de la definición de Mesoamérica," *Anales de Antropología* 12 (1975): 171–95; Alfredo López Austin, "El fundamento mágico religioso del poder," *Estudios de Cultura Náhuatl* 12 (1976): 199–200; and *Los mitos del tlacuache*, 28–29; López Austin and López Luján, *El pasado*, 62–63; Chapman, "Mesoamérica," 28–29.

29. Carmen Lorenzo, "La circulación," in Manzanilla and López Luján, eds., *Historia antigua de México*, 3:355–81; Frances Berdan, "Economic Dimensions of Precious Metals, Stones, and Feathers: The Aztec State Society," *Estudios de Cultura Náhuatl* 22 (1992): 291–323; and "La organización del tributo en el imperio azteca," *Estudios de Cultura Náhuatl* 12 (1976): 187–91.

30. The internal division of Mesoamerica is also much debated. Here I follow López Austin and López Luján, *El pasado*, 75.

31. Bonine, *Atlas*, 54–55; Carmack, Gasco, and Gossen, *Legacy*, 83–84.

32. Christine Niederberger, *Páleopaysages et archeologie pré-urbaine du bassin de Mexico* (Mexico: Centro de Estudios Mexicanos y Centroamericanos, 1987).

33. Kent V. Flannery, *Guilá Naquitz: Archaic Foraging and Early Agriculture in Oaxaca, Mexico* (New York: Academic Press, 1986).

34. Theories about the development of full-time maize-based agriculture vary widely. For general assessments see Flannery, "The Origins of Agriculture," *Annual Review of Anthropology* 2 (October 1973): 271–310; and John E. Staller, Robert H. Tykot, and Bruce F. Benz, *Histories of Maize: Multidisciplinary Approaches of Prehistory, Linguistics, Biogeography, Domestication, and Evolution of Maize* (Burlington, Calif.: Elsevier, Academic Press, 2006).

35. López Austin and López Luján, *El pasado*, 26; Bruce D. Smith, "Reassessing Coxcatlan Cave and the Early History of Domesticated Plants in Mesoamerica," *Proceedings of the National Academy of Sciences of the United States of America* 102, no. 27 (2005): 9438–39.

36. The morphological characteristics of wild teosinte cobs make the grain inaccessible to harvesting. Therefore it was probably not consumed as a grain, but before fully mature, as a vegetable. See following note for sources of this information.

37. Bruce D. Smith, *The Emergence of Agriculture* (New York: Scientific American Library, 1995), 150–60; Bruce F. Benz, "Maize in the Americas," in Staller, Tykot, and Benz, *Histories of Maize*, 13–18; Hugh H. Iltis, "Origin of Polystichy in Maize," in Staller, Tykot, and Benz, *Histories of Maize*, 23, 25–29.

38. Puerto Marquez, in Guerrero; Tlacuachero, in Chiapas; and Palo Hueco, in Veracruz. Carmack, Gasco, and Gossen, *Legacy*, 47–48.

39. López Austin and López Luján, *El pasado*, 99–164.

40. Alfredo López Austin, "El texto sahaguntino sobre los mexicas," *Anales de Antropología* 22 (1985): 320–25; and *Los mitos del tlacuache*, 29.

41. A detailed discussion of Nahua preconquest identities is provided in chapter 6.

42. Armillas, "Condiciones ambientales," 62–63.

43. Braniff, *La Gran Chichimeca*, 33–34, 84; Nárez, "Aridamérica," 75.

44. Guevara, "Oasisamérica," 329–31; Kirchhoff, "Gatherers and Farmers," 531, 533; Hall, *Social Change*, 41; Beatriz Braniff Cornejo, "La frontera septentrional de Mesoamérica," in Manzanilla and López Luján, eds., *Historia antigua de México*, 1:125; Linda S. Cordell, *Archaeology of the Southwest*, 2nd ed. (San Diego, Calif.: Academic Press, 1997), 124–26; Wirt H. Wills, "Patterns of Prehistoric Food Production in West-Central New Mexico," *Journal of Anthropological Research* 45, no. 3 (1989): 139–40.

45. William L. Merrill asserts that maize arrived in the southwestern United States no later than 2100 b.c.; "The Diffusion of Maize to the Southwestern United States and its Impact," *Proceedings of the National Academy of Sciences of the United States of America* 106, no. 50 (2009): 21019–26.

46. Marie-Areti Hers believes this incongruity between the proven antiquity of agriculture in northern Mexico and the American Southwest results from the lack of evidence, due to the scarcity of archaeological research conducted south of the international border. It may not reflect historical reality (personal communication).

47. Gerhard, *North Frontier*, 3–4; Beatriz Braniff Cornejo, "Sistemas agrícolas prehispánicos en la Gran Chichimeca," in Hers et al., eds., *Nómadas y sedentarios*, 130–31.

48. Enrique Nalda, "La frontera norte de Mesoamérica," in Lombardo and Nalda, eds., *Temas mesoamericanos*, 256.

49. Braniff, "La frontera," 120; Braniff, *La Gran Chichimeca*, 9–11; López Austin and López Luján, *El pasado*, 125–26.

50. Kirchhoff, "Los recolectores"; and "Mesoamérica"; Armillas, "Condiciones ambientales"; "Northern Mesoamerica"; and "The Arid Frontier of Mexican Civilization," *Transactions of the New York Academy of Sciences*, ser. 2, vol. 31, no. 6 (1969): 697–704.

51. J. Charles Kelley, "Archaeology of the Northern Frontier: Zacatecas and Durango," in Ekholm and Bernal, eds., *Handbook of Middle American Indians*, vol. 11, *Archaeology of Northern Mesoamerica*, pt. 2 (Austin: University of Texas Press, 1971), 768–801; "Speculations on the Culture History of Northwestern Mesoamerica," in B. Bell, ed., *The Archaeology of West Mexico* (Ajijic, Jalisco: West Mexican Society for Advanced Study, 1974), 19–39; and "Mesoamerican Colonization of Zacatecas-Durango: The Loma–San Gabriel and Chalchihuites Cultures," in M. T. Cabrero, J. Litvak King, and P. Jiménez Betts, eds., *Homenaje al Dr. John Charles Kelley (1913–1997)* (Mexico: Universidad Nacional Autónoma de México, 2002), 83–98; Carrasco, "Social Organization," 459;

Marie-Areti Hers, *Los toltecas en tierras chichimecas* (Mexico: Universidad Nacional Autónoma de México,1989), 13, 38–39; Braniff, "La frontera," 117–20; Charles Di Peso, "Prehistory: Southern Periphery," in Sturtevant, ed., *Handbook of North American Indians*, vol. 9, *Southwest*, 152–54.

52. Braniff, *La Gran Chichimeca*, 83–94.

53. Mesoamerican immigrants who occupied the central and western portions of Marginal Mesoamerica probably came from western Mesoamerica and, perhaps, the central valleys of Mexico and Puebla-Tlaxcala, but the colonization occurred at different paces in different areas. See López Austin and López Luján, *El pasado*, 126–31; Braniff, *La Gran Chichimeca*, 83, 113, 120; Carot and Hers, "La gesta," 56. Several authors have seen the presence of circular architecture (*guachimontones*) and burial chambers (*tumbas de tiro*) in the Mezquitic-Bolaños area of southwest Zacatecas as evidence of the penetration of influences, and perhaps migrants, from the Mesoamerican west. María Teresa Cabrero, "Algunas referencias al área del río Bolaños (Zacatecas y Jalisco) en los documentos del siglo XVI y XVII," *Anales de Antropología* 23 (1986): 108; Phil C. Weigand, "Architectural Principles Illustrated in Archaeology: A Case Study from Western Mesoamerica," in B. Dahlgren and M. D. Soto de Arechavaleta, eds., *Arqueología del norte y del occidente de México: homenaje al Dr. J. Charles Kelley* (Mexico: Universidad Nacional Autónoma de México, 1995), 159–60; Ricardo Jaramillo Luque, "Consideraciones sobre la arqueología del valle de Valparaíso, Zacatecas, Occidente y Norte de México," in Dahlgren and Soto de Arechavaleta, eds., *Arqueología*, 173–76; Peter Jiménez Betts, "Algunas observaciones sobre la dinámica cultural de la arqueología de Zacatecas," in Dahlgren and Soto de Arechavaleta, eds., *Arqueología*, 38–39. More recently, other authors have emphasized the appearance and wide distribution in Zacatecas, northern Jalisco, and Durango of Chupícuaro-Morales and Loma Alta ceramics and iconography originally from Guanajuato and Michoacán. On this basis they propose two main phases of Mesoamerican colonization in the area where the Chalchihuites culture evolved, the first starting approximately with the Christian era and the second around a.d. 550/600. They also mark a third period of Mesoamerican expansion on the Pacific Coast from about a.d. 850/900, when most farmers elsewhere in Marginal Mesoamerica were moving back to the south. These studies have contributed to document and explain the ties and similarities that Kelley ("Mesoamerica and the Southwestern United States," 100–104) had noticed between the Chupícuaro culture of the late Pre-Classic and early Classic Michoacán-Guanajuato border, the Pre-Classic cultures of the Valley of Mexico, the Chalchihuites culture of Classic Zacatecas-Durango, and the Anasazi (ancestral Pueblo) of New Mexico and Arizona. Braniff, *La Gran Chichimeca*, 94–109, 113–54; Carot and Hers, "La gesta," 51–62, 73.

54. Emil W. Haury, "The Problem of Contacts between the Southwestern United States and Mexico," *Southwestern Journal of Anthropology* 1, no. 1 (1945): 55–74; Kelley, "Mesoamerica and the Southwestern United States," 95–97, 100–102; Woodbury, "Prehistory: Introduction," 26; Hers, *Los toltecas*, 48–51; Braniff, "La frontera," 116–17; Carot and Hers, "La gesta."

55. Hers, *Los toltecas*, 39–52; López Austin and López Luján, *El pasado*, 128–131; Braniff, *La Gran Chichimeca*, 113–16. Other authors, including Charles Kelley, restrict the Chalchihuites culture to a smaller area, from what archaeologists identify as the Malpaso-La Quemada cultural complex in northern Jalisco and Zacatecas, to the Chalchihuites–Loma San Gabriel complex in Durango.

56. Kelley, "Settlement Patterns in North-Central Mexico," in G. R. Willey, ed., *Prehistoric Settlement Patterns in the New World* (New York: Wenner-Gren Foundation for Anthropological Research, 1956), 128–32; "Mesoamerica and the Southwestern United States," 99; and "Speculations on the Culture History"; Jaramillo Luque, "Consideraciones sobre la arqueología," 173–76. For early archaeological theories on Chalchihuites culture sites, see José Humberto Medina and Baudelina L. García Uranga, eds., *A 100 años de su descubrimiento: Alta Vista*. (Mexico: Consejo Nacional para la Cultura y las Artes, Instituto Nacional de Antropología e Historia, 2010), 45–87.

57. Merrill, "The Diffusion of Maize"; Lisa W. Huckell, "Ancient Maize in the American Southwest: What Does It Look Like and What Can It Tell Us," in Staller, Tykot, and Benz, *Histories of Maize*, 97–98, 104–106.

58. Hers, *Los toltecas*, 24–29.

59. Braniff, *La Gran Chichimeca*, 139–48; and "Las salas de las columnas en La Quemada," in Dahlgren and Soto de Arechavaleta, eds., *Arqueología*, 93–113; Jiménez Betts, "Algunas observaciones," 58–60.

60. Armillas, "Condiciones ambientales," 67–76; and "Northern Mesoamerica."

61. Hers, *Los toltecas*, 29–31, 35–36, 42–43.

62. Cabrero, "Algunas referencias," 108–109.

63. Braniff, *La Gran Chichimeca*, 148–54.

64. La Quemada is the only possible place Torquemada could have meant, since no other major archaeological site fitting his description exists in or around the area. Noguera, *La Quemada: Chalchihuites* (Mexico: Instituto Nacional de Antropología e Historia), 21–23.

65. Torquemada, *Monarquía indiana*, 1:117–18.

66. Antonio Tello, "Fragmentos de una historia de la Nueva Galicia, escrita hacia 1650," in J. García Icazbalceta, ed., *Colección de documentos para la historia de México* (Mexico: Porrúa, 1973), 24–30; Francisco Javier Clavijero, *Historia antigua de México*, 1781, edited by M. Cuevas (Mexico: Porrúa, 1964), xvii, 68.

67. Hers, *Los toltecas*, 14–15.

68. Ibid., 39–52, 106–18; and Hers, "Las salas," 106–109.

69. E.g., Alfred L. Kroeber, *Native Culture of the Southwest* (Berkeley: University of California Press, 1928); and *Cultural and Natural Areas*, 142, 150–53; Spicer, *Cycles of Conquest*; Bertha P. Dutton, *American Indians of the Southwest* (Albuquerque: University of New Mexico Press, 1983); Paul E. Minnis and Charles L. Redman, *Perspectives on Southwestern Prehistory* (Boulder: Westview Press, 1990); Linda S. Cordell and Bruce D. Smith, "Indigenous Farmers," in B. G. Trigger and W. E. Washburn, eds., *The Cambridge History of the Native Peoples of the Americas*, vol. 1, *North America*, pt. 1 (Cambridge: Cambridge University Press, 1996), 201–34. The *Handbook of North American Indians*, vol. 9, includes an article by Di Peso, "Prehistory: Southern Periphery," 152–61, on the southern periphery of the "Southwest" that covers Mexican areas down to Zacatecas, Guanajuato, and San Luis Potosí. In the same volume, however, the articles by Alfonso Ortiz, "Introduction," and Woodbury, "Prehistory: Introduction," 22–30, are much less inclusive.

70. Nárez, "Aridamérica," 77–81, 92–93; López Austin and López Luján, *El pasado*, 19–54.

71. For the Arid/Oasisamerica model see the definitions Kirchhoff provided in his seminal articles of 1943 and 1954, as well as recent literature that uses the terminology. Few authors elaborate on the model as such; therefore I may be adding meanings

to which particular authors do not subscribe. From the Mexican school I also rely on Leopoldo Martínez Caraza, *El norte bárbaro de México* (Mexico: Panorama Editorial, 1983); Arturo Guevara, *Apuntes para la arqueología de Chihuahua* (Mexico: Centro Regional de Chihuahua del Instituto Nacional de Antropología e Historia, 1985); and "Oasisamérica." Most authors using this model restrict their research to Mexican territory, where archetypal Oasisamerican societies had disappeared long before written records were made of them; therefore they only include prehistoric developments that left archaeological traces—usually stopping around a.d. 1500. Because the scope of this book goes beyond the international border, North American authors who look ahead into the historical period must be considered, even if they speak of "the Southwest." Authors such as Braniff, who reject both taxonomies, are also used: Braniff, "Arqueología del norte de México," in I. Bernal, ed., *Los pueblos y señoríos teocráticos*, pt. 1 (Mexico: Secretaría de Educación Pública, Instituto Nacional de Antropología e Historia, 1975), 217–78; and "El Formativo en el Norte de México," in M. Carmona Macías, ed., *El preclásico o formativo: avances y perspectivas: seminario de arqueología "Dr. Román Piña Chan"* (Mexico: Museo Nacional de Antropología, Instituto Nacional de Antropología e Historia, 1989), 443–60.

72. The policy of isolating Indians on government reservations that gave rise to much early ethnographic research had as its main purpose ensuring that Anglo-American expansion could proceed unimpaired.

73. Otis T. Mason, "Environment," in F. W. Hodge, ed., *Handbook of American Indians North of Mexico* (Washington, D.C.: Bureau of American Ethnology, 1907), 427–30; Pliny E. Goddard, quoted by Kirchhoff, "Gatherers and Farmers," 535.

74. Unlike other regions in the United States, where Indians were annihilated or forcibly removed, native societies in the Southwest had persisted in situ relatively untouched since precolonial times. Consequently the area offered privileged conditions for the research of native culture. Keith H. Basso, "History of Ethnological Research," in Sturtevant, ed., *Handbook of North American Indians*, vol. 9, *Southwest*, 14.

75. Frank H. Cushing, John Wesley Powell, Adolph F. Bandelier, Jesse W. Fewkes, Cosmos Mindeleff, and Alfred V. Kidder, who set the foundation for the modern study of Pueblo peoples, embraced this restricted notion of the Southwest. See Albert Schroeder, "History of Archaeological Research," in Sturtevant, ed., *Handbook of North American Indians*, vol. 9, *Southwest*, 5–13.

76. Mercedes Junquera, introduction in G. de Villagrá, *Historia de la Nueva México* [1610] (Madrid: Historia 16, 1989), 10, asserts there were between seventy and eighty inhabited towns in the Southwest at the moment of European intrusion, but David J. Weber, *Spanish Frontier in North America*, 18; and Fred Eggan, "Pueblos: Introduction," in Sturtevant, ed., *Handbook of North American Indians*, vol. 9, *Southwest*, 230, say there were ninety or more. Documentary sources of the period provide different figures: Pedro de Castañeda Nájera, "Relación de la jornada de Cíbola" [1560–65], in Mora, *Las siete ciudades*, 123–24, said the provinces that Vázquez de Coronado and his army visited (1540–42) had sixty-six towns, but the itemized list he provided included seventy-one. The anonymous 1541 "Relación postrera de Sibola," in Mora, *Las siete ciudades*, 177–78, mentions twenty-four towns, which the anonymous author visited during the same expedition. He makes no general statement on total numbers. Two witnesses from Agustín Rodríguez and Francisco Sánchez Chamuscado's 1581 expedition reported that the party saw sixty-one "pueblos" housing about 130,000 inhabitants (Felipe de Escalante and Hernando Barrando, "Relación breve y berdadera del descubrimiento del Nuevo

México," October 1583, Archivo General de Indias, Seville, Spain [hereinafter AGI], Patronato 22, R. 4, 01149–50), published in *Cartas de Indias* (Madrid: Ministerio de Fomento / Atlas, 1974), 1:230–33. Obregón, *Historia de los descubrimientos*, 281, repeats this information but asserts that it only refers to towns along the Rio Grande, excluding those Vázquez de Coronado, Francisco de Ibarra, and Antonio de Espejo visited to the west, north, and south. At the end of his book, Obregón lists the provinces that Espejo visited in 1582, counting a total of seventy-eight "towns" (Obregón, *Historia de los descubrimientos*, 303–304). Although Pueblo demography in the preconquest period is difficult to establish, Ann M. Palkovich, "Historic Population of the Eastern Pueblos, 1540–1910," *Journal of Anthropological Research* 41, no. 4 (1985): 408, asserts that the figure of 60,000 individuals Oñate provided in 1598 is consistent with archaeologically based studies of the human carrying capacity of the region.

77. Evidence of interlocking networks of economic relationships, usually interpreted as trade, includes the wide distribution of marine shells in southwestern archaeological sites, the extensive salt trade that Spanish settlers took over, and the distribution of certain types of ceramics in New Mexico, Arizona, and northern Chihuahua for the period of about a.d. 800–1600. See Woodbury, "Prehistory: Introduction," 25; Linda S. Cordell, "Prehistory: Eastern Anasazi," in Sturtevant, ed., *Handbook of North American Indians*, vol. 9, *Southwest*, 146; Cordell and Smith, "Indigenous Farmers," 202. Regular commercial routes along well-established trails have been identified, some extending beyond the limits of the Pueblo region into Mesoamerica. Thomas J. Ferguson and E. Richard Hart, *A Zuni Atlas* (Norman: University of Oklahoma Press, 1990), 53–55.

78. Castañeda Nájera, "Relación de la jornada," 119–20.

79. Ibid., 118–19; Diego Pérez de Luxán, "Account of the Antonio de Espejo Expedition into New Mexico, 1582," in G. P. Hammond and A. Rey, *The Rediscovery of New Mexico, 1580–1594: The Explorations of Chamuscado, Espejo, Castaño de Sosa, Morlete, and Leyva de Bonilla and Humaña* (Albuquerque: University of New Mexico Press, 1966), 153–212.

80. Eggan, "Pueblos: Introduction," 224, 227; Dutton, *American Indians*, 18, 32–34.

81. Dutton, *American Indians*, 14–16; Pericot y García, *América indígena*, 666–69; Hall, *Social Change*, 37–39; Weber, *Spanish Frontier*, 18–19; Cordell and Smith, "Indigenous Farmers," 202–203.

82. It is not clear when the Athabascan groups began to migrate south, but by the sixteenth century they were already in Colorado and northern New Mexico, divided into seven tribes. According to Lamar and Truett, the Mezcalero and Navaho tribes were the first to arrive, around the mid-fifteenth century, while the tribes later kown as Eastern Apaches (Chiricahua, Jicarilla, Kiowa, and Lipan) arrived by 1700. Most continued to be specialized hunter-gatherers well into the colonial era, but the Navahos quickly adopted agriculture and a Puebloan-style semi-sedentary residence pattern. Chronicles of early Spanish expeditions in the area (1540–42) make little reference to nomadic hunter-gatherers of Athabascan semblance, but by the 1580s reports frequently mention Apaches, sometimes also called Querechos. See Paul S. Martin, George I. Quimby, and Donald Collier, *Indians before Columbus: Twenty Thousand Years of North American History Revealed by Archaeology* (Chicago: University of Chicago Press, 1947), 157–58; Lamar and Truett, "The Greater Southwest and California from the Beginning of European Settlement to the 1880s," in Trigger and Washburn, eds., *The Cambridge History of the Native Peoples of the Americas*, vol. 1, *North America*, pt. 2 (Cambridge: Cambridge

University Press, 1997), 63–64, 73; Dutton, *American Indians*, 63–66, 105–20. Other band societies, Ute and Comanche, entered the region from the north in the seventeenth century and are therefore beyond the scope of this book.

83. Cynthia Radding, *Wandering Peoples: Colonialism, Ethnic Spaces, and Ecological Frontiers in Northwestern Mexico, 1700–1850* (Durham, N.C.: Duke University Press, 1997), 28–29. Nárez, "Aridamérica," 105–109, provides different dates (a.d. 1060–1340) for the flourishing of Paquimé culture as a whole.

84. Wissler, "American Indian," 241; Kroeber, *Cultural and Natural Areas*, 32–33, 152–55.

85. Ralph L. Beals, "Northern Mexico and the Southwest," quoted in Kirchhoff, "Gatherers and Farmers," 536, 537–39, 542.

86. Examples of recent studies challenging the validity of the concept of "culture area" are Bonfiglioli and others, eds., *Las vías del noroeste I*; and *Las vías del noroeste II*; Hers et al., *Nómadas y sedentarios*.

87. Kirchhoff, "Gatherers and Farmers," 543, 546; Guevara, "Oasisamérica," 329–31.

88. Nárez, "Aridamérica," 92.

89. Braniff, "Arqueología del norte," 218–20; Nárez, "Aridamérica," 80.

90. Ramón A. Gutiérrez, *When Jesus Came, the Corn Mothers Went Away: Marriage, Sexuality, and Power in New Mexico, 1500–1846* (Stanford, Calif.: Stanford University Press, 1991), xxi–xxiii, 14, 24–25; Hall, *Social Change*, 39–40; Nárez, "Aridamérica," 92, 94, 97, 98, 102–107; Guevara, "Oasisamérica," 334–35; Peter M. Whiteley, "Unpacking Hopi Clans: Another Vintage Model Out of Africa?" *Journal of Anthropological Research* 41, no. 4 (1985): 364–67.

91. Gutiérrez, *When Jesus Came*, xxii–xxv, 12–16.

92. Armillas, "Condiciones ambientales," 63–64; Kirchhoff, "Los recolectores."

93. López Austin and López Luján, *El pasado*, 28–37.

94. West and Augelli, *Middle America*, 241. Confusion might arise because agriculture and sedentism have also been posited as key attributes of Mesoamerica. The division that sets Oasisamerica apart rests on social organization, as it completely lacked social classes and state institutions, typical of Mesoamerica.

95. Carlos Martínez Marín, "La cultura de los mexicas durante la migración: nuevas ideas," in M. León Portilla, ed., *De Teotihuacán a los aztecas: antología de fuentes e interpretaciones históricas* (Mexico: Universidad Nacional Autónoma de México, 1971), 250–52; Víctor M. Castillo Farreras, *Estructura económica de la sociedad mexica, según las fuentes documentales* (Mexico: Universidad Nacional Autónoma de México, 1972), 33; Luis Reyes García and Lina Odena Güemes, "La zona del altiplano central en el posclásico: la etapa chichimeca," in Manzanilla and López Luján, eds., *Historia antigua de México*, 3:243.

96. Hers, "Los chichimecas," 33–37.

97. Quoted in Adrián Blázquez and Thomas Calvo, *Guadalajara y el Nuevo Mundo: Nuño Beltrán de Guzmán, semblanza de un conquistador* (Guadalajara, Spain: Institución Provincial de Cultura Marqués de Santillana, 1992), 205n. *Teul* is a mishearing of the Náhuatl word *teotl*, meaning god or divinity. As a prefix in the word *Teochichimeca* (wrongly transliterated as *Teuchichimeca* or *Teules Chichimecas* by most Spaniards) it meant "authentic" or "divine."

98. "Petición de Melchor de Alava para Descubrir Quivira," 1574 (AGI, Indiferente General, 1384).

99. "Ynstrucción que por Mandado de SM Hizo el Virrey Martín de Enriquez para el Conde de Coruña, su Sucesor," September 25, 1580, Biblioteca Nacional de España, Madrid, Spain (hereinafter BNE), Varios papeles tocantes a Yndias, signatura 8553, f. 29).

100. Harold E. Driver and Wilhelmine Driver, *Ethnography and Acculturation of the Chichimeca Jonaz of Northeast Mexico* (Bloomington: Indiana University Press, 1963), 4–5; Hall, *Social Change*, 63–65; Reyes García and Güemes, "La zona del altiplano," 227. For the importance of Indian allies, see Philip Wayne Powell, *La Guerra chichimeca*, translated by Juan José Utrilla (Mexico: Fondo de Cultura Económica, 1977).

101. Toribio de Benavente Motolinía, *Historia de los indios de la Nueva España* [1565], critical study by E. O'Gorman (Mexico: Porrúa, 1969), 2–3. A similar passage is contained in Motolinía, *Memoriales: libro de oro, MS JGI 31* [1541], edited by N. J. Dyer (Mexico: El Colegio de México, 1996), 122–23.

102. The *Códice Florentino* is an encyclopedic compilation of indigenous history, beliefs, and customs made in close collaboration with native Náhuatl speakers. The Spanish portion of this bilingual document, taken from a sixteenth century copy found in the convent of Tolosa, Spain, was published under the title *Historia general de las cosas de Nueva España* in the early nineteenth century. Although the origin of the manuscript is unclear, nearly every modern edition derives from it. The complete Spanish text written by Sahagún in the codex itself was not published until 1989 as Bernardino de Sahagún, *Historia general de las cosas de Nueva España: Primera versión íntegra del texto castellano del manuscrito conocido como Códice Florentino* [1558–77], introduction and paleography by A. López Austin and J. García Quintana (Mexico: Consejo Nacional para la Cultura y las Artes, Alianza Editorial, 1989), 2, 650–76.

103. Demetrio Sodi, "Consideraciones sobre el origen de la Toltecáyotl," *Estudios de Cultura Náhuatl* 3 (1962): 55; Xavier Noguez, "La zona del altiplano central en el posclásico: la etapa tolteca," in Manzanilla and López Luján, eds., *Historia antigua de México*, 3:197–98; Reyes García and Güemes, "La zona del altiplano," 226–27.

104. Driver and Driver, *Ethnography and Acculturation*, 4–5; Pedro Carrasco, "La sociedad mexicana antes de la conquista," In D. Cosío Villegas, ed., *Historia general de México* (Mexico: El Colegio de México, 1977), 1:173; Lina Odena Güemes, "La composición étnica en el posclásico y la cuestión chichimeca," in F. Sodi Miranda, ed., *Mesoamérica y el norte de México, siglos IX–XII* (Mexico: Instituto Nacional de Antropología e Historia, 1990), 2:241–44; Carot and Hers, "La gesta."

105. The Olmecas and the Nonoalcas, although generally not considered Chichimecas, are portrayed as people with origins in Chicomoztoc in some sources like the *Codex Vaticano Ríos* (f. 66v) and *Codex Telleriano* (f. 25r).

106. Later indigenous sources apply the term *teuchichimeca* to the Aztecs or Mexicas, who were not considered "authentic Chichimeca." E.g., Fernando Alvarado Tezozómoc, *Crónica mexicáyotl* [ca. 1600–10], introduction and translation from Náhuatl by A. León (Mexico: Universidad Nacional Autónoma de México, 1992), 3; and Domingo Chimalpahin, *Las ocho relaciones y el memorial de Colhuacan*, 2 vols. [ca. 1620–31], paleography and translation from Náhuatl by R. Tena (Mexico: Consejo Nacional para la Cultura y las Artes, 1998). This poses a problem of interpretation I will not discuss, but the answer may be sought in the type of reelaboration that Indian historical discourse underwent in the colonial situation, studied in detail by Alfredo López Austin, "El texto sahaguntino"; and *Tamoanchan y Tlalocan* (Mexico: Fondo de Cultura Económica, 1994), 46–71.

107. Depicted in several mid-sixteenth century pictorial documents, such as *Codex Xólotl*, and the *Tlotzin* and *Quinatzin* maps. Written histories discussed in chapter 5 also mention this group.

108. Wigberto Jiménez Moreno, "Tribus e idiomas del norte de México," in *El norte de México y el sur de Estados Unidos: tercera Reunión de la Mesa Redonda sobre problemas antropológicos de México y Centro América* (Mexico: Sociedad Mexicana de Antropología, 1943), 121–33; and "La colonización y evangelización de Guanajuato en el siglo XVI," *Cuadernos Americanos* 1, no. 3 (1944): 6; Pedro Carrasco, *Los otomíes: cultura e historia prehispánicas de los pueblos de habla otomiana* [1950] (Mexico: Universidad Nacional Autónoma de México, 1976), 244.

109. Braniff, *La Gran Chichimeca*, 34; Carot and Hers, "La gesta," 71.

110. Miguel León Portilla, "El proceso de aculturación de los chichimecas de Xólotl," *Estudios de Cultura Náhuatl* 7 (1967): 59–86; Carrasco, "Social Organization," 465.

111. My interpretation of Otonchichimeca, Nahuachichimeca, and Cuextecachichimeca as ethnologic categories that acknowledged the relative influence of other languages on Chichimeca groups, and of Tamime and Teochichimeca as categories indicating places of long-term historical origin and lifestyle, differs from Reyes García and Odena Güemes, "La zona del altiplano," 226, who take Sahagún's passage to refer to an overarching Chichimeca language taxonomy divided into three types: Tamime (Huasteco speakers), Otomí (Otomí speakers) and Teochichimeca (Náhuatl speakers).

112. Phil C. Weigand, "La prehistoria del estado de Zacatecas: Una interpretación," *Anuario de Historia* 1 (1978): 212.

113. Nuño de Guzmán, "Letter to the king," Omitlán, July 8, 1530, in Blázquez and Calvo, *Guadalajara*, 205.

114. Eugene B. Sego, *Aliados y adversarios: los colonos tlaxcaltecas en la frontera septentrional de Nueva España* (San Luis Potosí: El Colegio de San Luis, 1998); Jesús Gómez Serrano, "El exterminio de los chichimecas en el norte de la Nueva Galicia y los criterios de repoblación indígena," in Fábregas Puig et al., eds., *Continuidad y fragmentación*, 185–94; Ida Altman, *The War for Mexico's West: Indians and Spaniards in New Galicia, 1524–1550* (Albuquerque: University of New Mexico Press, 2010); Michel R. Oudijk and Matthew Restall, "Mesoamerican Conquistadors in the Sixteenth Century," in Matthew and Oudijk, eds., *Indian Conquistadors*, 28–54; Bret Blosser, "By the Force of Their Lives and the Spilling of Blood: Flechero Service and Political Leverage on a Nueva Galicia Frontier," Matthew and Oudijk, eds., *Indian Conquistadors*, 289–304.

Chapter 3. The Exploration and Conquest of Nuevo México

1. E.g., Bancroft, *Works*; Frederick W. Hodge and Theodore H. Lewis, *Spanish Explorers in the Southern United States, 1528–1543* (New York: Scribner, 1907); Herbert E. Bolton, *Spanish Exploration in the Southwest*; and *The Spanish Borderlands: A Chronicle of Old Florida and the Southwest* (New Haven, Conn.: Yale University Press, 1921); Beck, *New Mexico*; Donald Cutter, *España en Nuevo México* (Madrid: Mapfre, 1992); David J. Weber, *New Spain's Far Northern Frontier: Essays on Spain in the American West, 1540–1821* (Albuquerque: University of New Mexico Press, 1979); and *Spanish Frontier*; George Hammond and Agapito Rey, *Narratives of the Coronado Expedition, 1540–1542* (Albuquerque: University of New Mexico Press, 1940); *Don Juan de Oñate, Colonizer of New Mexico 1595–1628* (Albuquerque: University of New Mexico Press, 1953); and *Rediscovery of New Mexico*.

2. Niza recorded Cíbola as the name of the only Pueblo he visited; "Relación," 150.

3. Ibid.

4. "Carta de Juan de Zumárraga a su sobrino," Mexico, August 23, 1539, in Joaquín García Icazbalceta, *Colección de documentos para la historia de México* (Mexico: Librería de J. M. Andrade, 1889), 2:281–83. In February 1540, responding to a petition by Vázquez de Coronado, Viceroy Mendoza compiled a testimonial report on the people enlisted for the expedition. Both the petition and testimonies indicate how controversial the sheer number of soldiers recruited was, as some people thought their departure might cause a notable depopulation of the already settled portion of New Spain. Published under the heading "Información del virrey de Nueva España Don Antonio de Mendoza de la gente que va a poblar la Nueva Galicia," in *Colección de documentos inéditos relativos al descubrimiento, conquista y organización de las posesiones españolas en América y Oceanía* [hereinafter *CDIAO*] (Madrid: Imprenta de José María Pérez, 1870), 14:373–84.

5. Obregón, *Historia de los descubrimientos*, 39–41.

6. The few exceptions include Jack D. Forbes, *Apache, Navaho, and Spaniard* (Norman: University of Oklahoma Press, 1960), 42–43.

7. Beck, *New Mexico*, 49–50; Lamar and Truett, "Greater Southwest," 68.

8. Radding, *Wandering Peoples*, 11; Peter Gerhard, *A Guide to the Historical Geography of New Spain* (Cambridge: Cambridge University Press, 1972), 5, 8; and *North Frontier*, 8–10.

9. "Interrogatorio general presentado por Hernando Cortés para el examen de los testigos de su descargo," in Martínez, *Documentos cortesianos*, 2:221–91.

10. "Algunas declaraciones de Andrés de Tapia," in Martínez, *Documentos cortesianos*, 2:351. Tapia visited the province of Tuxpa on the Gulf Coast of Mexico. See also the answers by Martín Vázquez on the small parties Cortés sent accompanied by Moctezuma's messengers, in Martínez, *Documentos cortesianos*, 2:337.

11. Cortés, *Cartas*, 66; and Díaz del Castillo, *Historia verdadera*, 186, describe Moctezuma's tribute records, a pictographic codex today known as the *Matrícula de tributos*.

12. Cortés, *Cartas*, 56–57.

13. Martínez, *Hernán Cortés*, 262.

14. Ibid., 662–63, 351–56.

15. René Acuña, *Relaciones geográficas del siglo XVI*, vol. 9, *Michoacán* (Mexico: Universidad Nacional Autónoma de México, 1987); Cortés, *Cartas*, 176; J. Benedict Warren, *La conquista de Michoacán, 1521–1530*, translated by A. García Alcaraz (Morelia, Michoacán: Fimax Publicistas, 1979), 34. About the mines in Michoacán, see Sylvie Lecoin, "Intercambios, movimientos de población y trabajo en la diócesis de Michoacán en el siglo XVI: un aspecto de las relaciones geográficas de 1580," in T. Calvo and G. López, eds., *Movimientos de población en el occidente de México* (Zamora, Michoacán: El Colegio de Michoacán, Centro de Estudios Mexicanos y Centroamericanos, 1988), 130.

16. It is not clear from the sources which captain was responsible for the first assault on Colima, Villafuerte or Olid himself. Carl O. Sauer, *Colima of New Spain in the XVI Century* (Berkeley: University of California Press, 1948), 11–17; and Warren, *Conquista de Michoacán*, 73–75, consider Villafuerte a much likelier candidate.

17. Martínez, *Hernán Cortés*, 356–57.

18. María del Carmen Velázquez, *Establecimiento y pérdida del septentrión de Nueva España* (Mexico: El Colegio de México, 1974), 28, 31.

19. Heads of expeditions attempting to subdue Florida: Juan Ponce de León (1512–13 and 1521), Diego de Miruelo (1516), Francisco Hernández de Córdoba (1517), Lucas Vázquez de Ayllón, judge of the Audiencia of Santo Domingo (1526), Hernando de Soto

(1539), and Tristán Luna y Arellano (1559–61). See Bernard and Gruzinski, *Historia del Nuevo Mundo*, 1:337, 341–44; Gerhard, *North Frontier*, 5.

20. The exclusive rights the Pope granted to Spain and Portugal over the colonization of America gave rise to a long-lasting conflict between the French and Spanish monarchies. Because the Treaty of Cateau-Cambrésis, which put an end to the 1552–59 war, included no explicit articles on the New World, competition over who was to settle Florida continued. After Tristán Luna y Arellano failed to colonize Punta de Santa Elena (1559–61), the French took the lead and began building a fort in 1562. By 1564 a group of Huguenots established a colony in the peninsula, but Pedro Menéndez de Avilés, then governor of Cuba and Florida, destroyed it the following year. Despite the temporary withdrawal of the French and the establishment of a Spanish garrison, the conflict persisted until the following century. Velázquez, *Establecimiento y pérdida*, 29–34.

21. Martínez, *Hernán Cortés*, 365–68; Gerhard, *North Frontier*, 5, 10; Fausto Marín Tamayo, *Nuño de Guzmán* (Mexico: Siglo XXI, 1992), 26–27.

22. Gerhard, *North Frontier*, 26–27; Elliott, "Spanish Conquest," 165–66.

23. Woodrow Borah, *El siglo de la depresión en Nueva España* (Mexico: Secretaría de Educación Pública, 1975), 55.

24. According to Sauer, *Colima*, 59–60, Colima's indigenous population was so large that by the mid-sixteenth century, 112 Indian towns still existed in the area of initial Spanish occupation. Lecoin, "Intercambios," 124–25, 129, notes that according to the *Relaciones geográficas*, the Tarascan peasant communities of Michoacán who used to pay tribute to the Cazonci consented to pay it to the Spaniards instead. Until the decade of 1560 this included workers for the silver mines and, until 1576, the obligation to provide personal service in Spanish villages.

25. Gerhard, *North Frontier*, 10; Blázquez and Calvo, *Guadalajara*, 18.

26. Martínez, *Hernán Cortés*, 460–62.

27. Blázquez and Calvo, *Guadalajara*, 23.

28. Guzmán mistakenly asserts that he landed in Pánuco one year earlier, in his "Memoria de los servicios que había hecho Nuño de Guzmán desde que fue nombrado gobernador de Pánuco en 1525" (ca. 1538–39), in Blázquez and Calvo, *Guadalajara*, 53.

29. Blázquez and Calvo, *Guadalajara*, 19.

30. Particularly rough was the practice under Guzmán of enslaving Indians for the Caribbean slave trade. Marín Tamayo, *Nuño de Guzmán*, 32–34.

31. Guzmán, "Memoria de los servicios," in Blázquez and Calvo, *Guadalajara*, 65–66.

32. Letter from Omitlán, July 8, 1530, in José Luis Razo Zaragoza y Cortés, *Crónicas de la conquista del reino de Nueva Galicia en territorio de la Nueva España* (Guadalajara: Ayuntamiento de la Ciudad de Guadalajara, Instituto Jalisciense de Antropología e Historia, 1963), 25–59; also contained in Blázquez and Calvo, *Guadalajara*, 205–25. Letter to the empress, June 12, 1532, in Blázquez and Calvo, *Guadalajara*, 239–62; "Memoria de los servicios," in Blázquez and Calvo, *Guadalajara*, 53–73.

33. Accounts were written by Gonzalo López (1532), Juan de Sámano (1531), Pedro de Carranza (1532), Cristóbal Flores (undated), García del Pilar (1531), Francisco de Arceo (undated), Pedro de Guzmán (undated), and three anonymous authors whose *relaciones* also lack a date. All are contained in Razo Zaragoza y Cortés, *Crónicas*.

34. One *Relación geográfica* corresponds to Pátzcuaro, in the Tarascan plateau (Acuña, *Relaciones geográficas*, vol. 9), and nine correspond to principal towns in Nueva Galicia and their subjects. René Acuña, *Relaciones geográficas del siglo XVI*, vol. 10, *Nueva Galicia* (Mexico: Universidad Nacional Autónoma de México, 1988).

35. Antonio Tello, *Crónica miscelánea en que se trata de la conquista espiritual y temporal de la santa provincia de Xalisco en el Nuevo Reino de la Galicia y Nueva Vizcaya y el descubrimiento de Nuevo México* [ca. 1651] (Guadalajara: Imprenta de la República Literaria de Ciro L. Guevara, 1891). Tello is one of the most important sources concerning Guzmán's activities, although the first of his three original volumes is lost. Other colonial works on Nueva Galicia exist but contain little firsthand information on this early period: Antonio de la Mota y Escobar, *Descripción geográfica de los reynos de Nueva Galicia, Nueva Vizcaya y Nuevo León* [1605] (Guadalajara: Instituto Jalisciense de Antropología e Historia, 1966); Domingo Lázaro de Arregui, *Descripción de la Nueva Galicia* [1621], introduction by F. Chevalier (Guadalajara: Gobierno del Estado de Jalisco, 1980); Matías de la Mota y Padilla, *Historia de la conquista de la provincia de la Nueva Galicia* [1742] (Mexico: Sociedad Mexicana de Geografía y Estadística, 1870).

36. Razo Zaragoza y Cortés, *Crónicas*, 217.

37. Ibid., 25.

38. Ibid., 241–42.

39. "Primera relación anónima," ibid., 288.

40. Donald E. Chipman, *Nuño de Guzmán and the Province of Pánuco in New Spain, 1518–1533* (Glendale, Calif.: Arthur H. Clark, 1967), 231.

41. Castañeda Nájera, "Relación de la jornada," 63–65.

42. Marín Tamayo, *Nuño de Guzmán*, 114, argues there is not enough evidence to sustain this hypothesis.

43. Guzmán, "Memoria de los servicios," in Blázquez and Calvo, *Guadalajara*, 68. Pedro de Guzmán, "Relación," in Razo Zaragoza y Cortés, *Crónicas*, 283, calls the place Huxitipa. Also the "Segunda relación anónima," in Razo Zaragoza y Cortés, *Crónicas*, 326–27.

44. Razo Zaragoza y Cortés, *Crónicas*, 280, 321–22.

45. Berdan and Anawalt, *Essential Codex Mendoza*, 140–41.

46. Martínez, *Hernán Cortés*, 506–507.

47. For more detail on Oxitipa, particularly the conflict between Cortés and Guzmán over its jurisdiction, see Gerhard, *Guide*, 354–58; Chipman, *Nuño de Guzmán*, 88, 196–200; Marín Tamayo, *Nuño de Guzmán*, 43–47. See also Miguel Aguilar Robledo, "La territorialidad en el norte de Mesoamérica: El señorío de Oxitipa en el siglo XVI," *Tiempo de América* 10 (2003): 3–18.

48. Blázquez and Calvo, *Guadalajara*, 29.

49. "Relación de la ciudad de Pátzcuaro," in Acuña, *Relaciones geográficas*, 9:199; Cristóbal Flores, "Relación," in Razo Zaragoza y Cortés, *Crónicas*, 185.

50. Pedro de Carranza (in Razo Zaragoza y Cortés, *Crónicas*, 157) asserts that the death sentence the Indian monarch received was completely undeserved, as the ambush he was supposedly preparing proved nonexistent. In his letter to the king from Omitlán, Guzmán mentions the trial and execution only briefly (ibid., 26) and his "Memoria de los servicios," which omits the torture, argues that the Indian ruler had killed many Christians (in Blázquez and Calvo, *Guadalajara*, 63). The testimony Francisco de Arceo gave Gonzalo Fernández de Oviedo (in Razo Zaragoza y Cortés, *Crónicas*, 242–45) is also mute about the torture and asserts that in knowing his sentence, the Cazonci confessed that several Spaniards had been killed on his orders. The *relaciones* by Juan de Sámano (Razo Zaragoza y Cortés, *Crónicas*, 117), Cristóbal Flores (ibid., 185–89), and García del Pilar (ibid., 217–20) contain more detail about the cruel proceedings surrounding the Cazonci's imprisonment and death.

51. Tello, *Crónica miscelánea*, 31. Sources write this name differently: Cuisco, Cuiseo, or Cuyzco.

52. "Letter from Omitlán," in Razo Zaragoza y Cortés, *Crónicas*, 38-44.

53. Berdan, "Economic Dimensions"; Blázquez and Calvo, *Guadalajara*, 29.

54. "Letter from Omitlán," in Razo Zaragoza y Cortés, *Crónicas*, 47. El Teúl (Teblinchan in Guzmán's transliteration) was also called Tonanipan according to the second anonymous *relación*, in Razo Zaragoza y Cortés, *Crónicas*, 292.

55. "Letter from Omitlán"; Francisco de Arceo, "Relación"; and Gonzalo López, "Relación," in Razo Zaragoza y Cortés, *Crónicas*, 52-53, 83-85, 260.

56. San Miguel was originally founded on the Cihuatlán River, but the ninety-six Spaniards and numerous Tlaxcalans who remained in the village when Guzmán departed moved the entire settlement to the confluence of the Humaya and Tamazula rivers, where the city of Culiacán stands today. The enormous surrounding territory received the name of Sinaloa and was organized in two provinces (Chametla to the south and Culiacán to the north) subject to the authority of Nueva Galicia's governor. Sergio Ortega Noriega and Ignacio del Río, *Tres siglos de historia sonorense, 1530-1830* (Mexico: Universidad Nacional Autónoma de México, 1993), 28-30; Sergio Ortega Noriega, *Un ensayo de historia regional: el noroeste de México, 1530-1880* (Mexico: Universidad Nacional Autónoma de México, 1993), 38-42.

57. Gonzalo López, "Relación," in Razo Zaragoza y Cortés, *Crónicas*, 99-104; "Segunda relación anónima," in Razo Zaragoza y Cortés, *Crónicas*, 321; Ortega Noriega and del Río, *Tres siglos*, 28-30; Ortega Noriega, *Un ensayo*, 38-42; Bancroft, *Works*, 1-19.

58. Blázquez and Calvo, *Guadalajara*, 33-34.

59. Guzmán commissioned the founding of Espíritu Santo-Compostela to Francisco Verdugo in January 1531, when the army was still in the province of Chametla. The original name was Espíritu Santo but the Spanish empress ordered it be changed to Compostela. Guzmán, "Memoria de los servicios" and "Letter to the Empress," in Blázquez and Calvo, *Guadalajara*, 65-66, 239-40, 250-51.

60. Chipman, *Nuño de Guzmán*, 232, 243-45; Blázquez and Calvo, *Guadalajara*, 33, 44.

61. Razo Zaragoza y Cortés, *Crónicas*, 331.

62. Gonzalo López, "Relación," in Razo Zaragoza y Cortés, *Crónicas*, 70, 97; Juan de Sámano, "Relación," ibid., 72, 126, 129; "Letter from Omitlán," ibid., 38, 47; Francisco de Arceo, "Relación," ibid., 251.

63. Pedro de Carranza, "Relación," in Razo Zaragoza y Cortés, *Crónicas*, 159, 164, 171-72. The same tone of denunciation regarding Xalisco appears in the first anonymous *relación*, ibid., 294.

64. Bernard and Gruzinski, *Historia del Nuevo Mundo*, 1:341; Fernando Ocaranza, *Establecimientos franciscanos en el misterioso Reino de Nuevo México* (Mexico: n.p., 1934), 15-17.

65. *La relación que dio Alvar Núñez Cabeza de Vaca de lo acaescido en la Armada Donde iva por Gobernador Pámphilo de Narbáez desde el año de veinta y siete hasta el año de treinta y seis que bolvió a Sevilla con tres de su compagnía*. The British Library preserves one of the three extant copies of this edition and one of the thirteen copies that survive of the second edition (Valladolid 1555). For the history of this manuscript and its editions, see Danna Levin Rojo, "La configuración del fracaso en la obra y hazañas de Alvar Núñez Cabeza de Vaca," *Fuentes Humanísticas* 28 (1st semester 2004): 141-43.

66. The only known accounts written by the participants themselves are *Naufragios* and a short testimony by Cabeza de Vaca ending abruptly with the arrival at the island of Mal Hado (*Relación del viaje de Pánfilo de Narváez al Río de las Palmas hasta la Punta de la Florida, hecha por el tesorero Cabeza de Vaca, Año 1537*). This is preserved in the Archivo General de Indias and published in *CDIAO*, 14:269–79. In a letter to the empress dated February 11, 1537, Viceroy Mendoza mentions a report by the surviving Spaniards that he sent to Spain (*CDIAO*, 14:225), which may have been the one Oviedo summarized or another independent document. Neither has ever been found. See Luis Nicolau D'Olwer, *Cronistas de las culturas precolombinas* (Mexico: Fondo de Cultura Económica, 1963), 86; Henry Roy Wagner, *The Spanish Southwest, 1542–1794: An Annotated Bibliography*, pt. 1 (New York: Arno Press, 1967), 36.

67. The most extensive of these chronicles about the Narváez shipwreck survivors are by Francisco López de Gómara, *La conquista de México*, edited by J. L. de Rojas (Madrid: Historia 16, 1986), bk. 9, chap. 9; and Antonio de Herrera y Tordesillas, *Historia general de los hechos de los castellanos en las islas y tierra firme del Mar Océano* [1615], prologue by J. Natalicio González (Asunción, Paraguay: Editorial Guarania, 1945), decade 4, bk. 2, chap. 4, and bk. 4, chap. 4; decade 6, bk. 1, chaps. 3–7.

68. Gutiérrez, *When Jesus Came*, 41; Ortega Noriega and del Río, *Tres siglos*, 30.

69. In the nineteenth century it was believed the odyssey of Cabeza de Vaca and companions began east of the Mississippi River and that the wanderers traversed Arkansas and New Mexico. Today it is generally agreed that the last shipwreck occurred in Tampa Bay and the four survivors walked through Texas, part of Chihuahua, Sonora, and Sinaloa.

70. See Levin Rojo, "La configuración."

71. Adolph Bandelier, *The Discovery of New Mexico by the Franciscan Monk Friar Marcos de Niza in 1539* (Tucson: University of Arizona Press, 1981), 65–66.

72. Gerónimo de Mendieta, *Historia eclesiástica indiana* [1596–97], preliminary study by A. Rubial García (Mexico: Consejo Nacional para la Cultura y las Artes, 1997), 2:59–61.

73. Gerónimo de Zárate Salmerón, "Relaciones de todas las cosas que en el Nuevo México se han visto y sabido asi por mar como por tierra desde el año de 1538 hasta el de 1626" [ca. 1629], in *Documentos para servir a la historia de Nuevo México 1538–1778* (Madrid: Ediciones José Porrúa Turranzas, 1965), 120–21.

74. Mora, *Las siete ciudades*, 16.

75. Arthur S. Aiton, "Coronado's First Report on the Government of New Galicia," *Hispanic American Historical Review* 19, no. 3 (August 1939): 307–309.

76. Niza, "Relación," 148.

77. Janet Lecompte, "Coronado and Conquest," *New Mexico Historical Review* 64, no. 3 (1989): 285; Castañeda Nájera, "Relación de la jornada," 67–68.

78. Mora, *Las siete ciudades*, 76–77n. A "Relación" on Ruy Gómez de Villalobos's 1542 journey from New Spain to the Western Islands, written in Lisbon in 1548, includes in the list of survivors a man named Diego Sánchez de Cíbola (Garcia Descalante Alvarado, "Relación del viaje que hizo desde la Nueva España a las Islas del Poniente Ruy Gomez de Villalobos," in *CDIAO*, 5:205). This could have been a nickname for a soldier who had just been to the province of Cíbola with Vázquez de Coronado, or even a Zuñi Indian who accompanied Gómez de Villalobos either as a volunteer, servant, or slave.

79. Cortés was in California in 1535 and early 1536.

80. Niza, "Relación," 150.

81. Paul Horgan, *Conquistadors in North American History* (New York: Farrar, Straus and Giroux, 1963), 151, 162, 164; Ignacio del Río, *A la diestra mano de las Indias* (Mexico: Universidad Nacional Autónoma de México, 1990), 23; Martínez, *Hernán Cortés*, 732–33.

82. "Proceso-pleito entre el Marqués del Valle, Nuño de Guzmán, Diego de Guzmán, Pedro de Alvarado, Hernando de Soto y Lucas Vázquez de Ayllón sobre los Descubrimientos en Nueva Galicia y la Mar del Sur" (AGI, Patronato 21, no. 2, R. 4).

83. Martínez, *Documentos cortesianos*, 4:216–19.

84. "Asiento y capitulaciones entre el virrey de Nueva España, D. Antonio de Mendoza, y el adelantado, D. Pedro de Alvarado, para la prosecución del descubrimiento de tierra nueva, hecho por Fr. Marcos de Niza," in Mora, *Las siete ciudades*, 160–70.

85. The most important are published in Mora, *Las siete ciudades*; and Hammond and Rey, *Narratives*.

86. Lecompte, "Coronado," 286. See also Horgan, *Conquistadors*, 167–73.

87. Xavier Noguez, "El *Códice de Tlatelolco*: una nueva cronología," in X. Noguez and S. G. Wood, eds., *De tlacuilos y escribanos* (Mexico: El Colegio de Michoacán, 1998), 21; Perla Valle, "Estudio preliminar," in *Códice de Tlatelolco* (Mexico: Instituto Nacional de Antropología e Historia, Benemérita Universidad de Puebla, 1994), 59–60.

88. Frederick W. Hodge, *The First Discovered City of Cibola* (Washington, D.C.: Judd and Detweiler, printers, 1895), 3–9.

89. Castañeda Nájera, "Relación de la jornada," 75–106, recounts these events in detail; twice he mentions that gold was locally called *acochis* (88, 188). Other documentary references to the punishment for the Tiguex uprising are in Hammond and Rey, *Narratives*, 24, 225. For modern overviews of the period, see Forbes, *Apache*, 14–21; Cutter, *España*, 16–25; and Lecompte, "Coronado," 288–90.

90. Lecompte, "Coronado," 298–300.

91. Zárate Salmerón, "Relaciones de todas las cosas," 125–26, mentions only two friars, Juan de Padilla and Juan de la Cruz. Castañeda Nájera, "Relación de la jornada," 134–35, also records only two but instead of Juan de la Cruz he mentions a certain Friar Luis, asserting that Padilla stayed in Quivira and Luis in Cicuye. Carmen de Mora, *Las siete ciudades*, 134, 241, based on Matías de la Mota Padilla, affirms that this last friar was Luis de Ubeda. Cutter, *España*, 26, combines these assertions, concluding there were three friars: Juan de Padilla, Luis de Ubeda (Belda), and Juan de la Cruz.

92. Castañeda Nájera, "Relación de la jornada," 129, 142.

93. Richard G. Petersen, *The Lost Cities of Cibola* (Chicago: Franciscan Herald Press, 1980), 58; Bancroft, *Works*, 64–68; Beck, *New Mexico*, 46–48; Lecompte, "Coronado," 302–304; Cutter, *España*, 23–27.

94. E.g., Bancroft, *Works*; Herbert Bolton, *Coronado, Knight of Pueblos and Plains* (Albuquerque: University of New Mexico Press, 1949); Charles Di Peso, "History," in C. Di Peso, J. B. Rinaldo, and G. Fenner, eds., *Casas Grandes: A Fallen Trading Center of the Gran Chichimeca,* (Flagstaff, Ariz.: Amerind Foundation; Dragoon, Ariz.: Northland Press, 1974), 4:37–120; Carl O. Sauer, *The Road to Cibola* (Berkeley: University of California Press, 1932); and "The Credibility of the Fray Marcos Account," *New Mexico Historical Review* 16 (1940): 233–43; G. P. Winship, *The Coronado Expedition: Fourteenth Annual Report of the U.S. Bureau of American Ethnology* (Washington, D.C.: Bureau of

American Ethnology, 1896); Carroll L. Riley, "Early Spanish Indian Communication in the Greater Southwest," *New Mexico Historical Review* 46, no. 4 (1971): 285–314.

95. Daniel T. Reff, "Anthropological Analysis of Exploration Texts: Cultural Discourse and the Ethnological Import of Friar Marcos de Niza's Journey to Cibola," *American Anthropologist* 93 (1991): 636–37.

96. Charles Gibson, *The Aztecs under Spanish Rule, 1519–1810* (Stanford, Calif.: Stanford University Press, 1964), 32.

97. Reff, "Anthropological Analysis," 645–46. In a different article, Reff argues that in fact natives in northwestern Mexico accepted the Jesuits because sixteenth and seventeenth century epidemics had profoundly dislocated their systems with severe depopulation; "The Jesuit Mission Frontier in Comparative Perspective: The Reductions of the Rio de la Plata and the Missions of Northwestern Mexico, 1588–1700," in Guy and Sheridan, eds., *Contested Ground*, 17–18, 21.

98. "Memorial de Hernán Cortés a Carlos V acerca de los agravios que le hizo el virrey de la Nueva España, impidiéndole la continuación de los descubrimientos en la Mar del Sur," June 25, 1540, in Martínez, *Documentos cortesianos*, 4:210–12; Francisco Vázquez de Coronado to Viceroy Mendoza, August 3, 1540, in Hammond and Rey, *Narratives*, 170.

99. Bancroft, *Works*; Bandelier, *Discovery*; Horgan, *Conquistadors*; George J. Undreiner, "Fray Marcos de Niza and his Journey to Cibola," *The Americas* 3 (1947): 415–86; Reff, "Anthropological Analysis."

100. Henry Roy Wagner, "Fray Marcos de Niza," *New Mexico Historical Review* 9 (1934): 184–227.

101. Sauer, *Road to Cibola*.

102. Cleve Hallenbeck, *The Journey of Fray Marcos de Niza*, edited by D. J. Weber (Dallas, Tex.: Southern Methodist University Press, 1987). For an overview of the controversies the issue of Niza's truthfulness raised up through the 1980s, see Weber, *Myth and History*, 24–29; and Reff, "Anthropological Analysis," 636–45.

103. Reff, "Anthropological Analysis," 639–42.

104. Weber, *Myth and History*, 20–21.

105. Bandelier, *Discovery*, 100.

106. Reff, "Anthropological Analysis," 638, 640–42.

107. Niza, "Relación," 151–53.

108. Ibid., 158.

109. The system of raiding for Indian slaves went as far south as Texas, reaching its peak from 1575 to 1585. Forbes, *Apache*, 34.

110. Gerhard, *North Frontier*, 6–7; Wigberto Jiménez Moreno, *Estudios de historia colonial* (Mexico: Instituto Nacional de Antropología e Historia, 1958), 49; Gutiérrez, *When Jesus Came*, 45; Cutter, *España*, 29; Ignacio del Río, *Estudios históricos sobre la formación del norte de México* (Mexico: Universidad Nacional Autónoma de México, 2009), 62–63.

111. Radding, *Wandering Peoples*, 30–31. For a detailed study of Tlaxcalan colonies in the north, see Tomás Martínez Saldaña, *La diáspora tlaxcalteca: colonización agrícola del norte de México* (Tlaxcala: Gobierno del Estado de Tlaxcala, 1998). The policy of inducing natives from the south to settle in the north continued in New Spain throughout the seventeenth century. Viceroy Luis de Velasco, for instance, "gave" the Franciscans some Mexicans and Tlaxcalans "who were distributed throughout the said frontier so

the barbarians of this land, seeing the civility and good education of those from the Province of the Santo Evangelio de México, would adopt the same civility and education, which turned out to be a very useful remedy" ("Ynformacion juridica de los conventos, doctrinas y conversiones fundados por los padres de la provincia de Zacatecas. Conventos de Colotlan y Atotonilco. Yndios chichimecas y guachichiles. Alzamiento de Tepeguanes en 1617" [1622–23], Biblioteca Nacional de México, Nueva Vizcaya, caja 1, f. 9).

112. Lecoin, "Intercambios," 131. That a large number of native warriors from Michoacán and the valley of Mexico fought against the Chichimecas and then settled down in Zacatecas is clearly stated in the 1608 "Relación de Nuestra Señora de los Zacatecas" (BNE, 3064, Descripción de Indias 1, f. 85).

113. J. Ribera Bernárdez, *Compendio de las cosas más notables contenidas en los libros de cabildo de esta ciudad de Nuestra Señora de los Zacatecas desde el año de su descubrimiento 1546 hasta 1730* (Mexico: Academia Mexicana de la Historia, 1945), 2:9, 12; "Relación de Nuestra Señora de los Zacatecas," f. 84v.

114. I refer to Cristóbal de Oñate, Juan de Saldivar, and Vicente de Saldivar. Ribera Bernárdez, *Compendio*, 2:9; "Relación de Nuestra Señora de los Zacatecas," f. 84v.

115. For the exploration and conquest Francisco de Ibarra undertook in 1561–65, see "Memorial de los servicios que ha hecho el gobernador Francisco de Ybarra a Su Magestad en las conquistas y poblaciones que ha hecho en las provincias de Copala, Nueva Vizcaya, Chiametla, y los descubrimientos de minas, sacados de las ynformaciones que hicieron de oficio y a pedimento de parte que se presentaron en el Consejo año de 1574" (AGI, Patronato 21, no. 4, R. 2, fs. 1–2v). See also Robert H. Barlow and George T. Smisor, *Nombre de Dios, Durango: Two Documents in Nahuatl Concerning its Foundation. Memorial of the Indians Concerning Their Services, c. 1563. Agreement of the Mexicans and the Michoacanos, 1585* (Sacramento, Calif.: House of Tlaloc, 1943), xvi.

116. Baltasar de Obregón, born in Mexico City (1544) to a son of Rodrigo de Baeza, was one of the first settlers of New Spain. He joined Ibarra's army in Chiametla in 1566. Later on he wrote at length about this expedition in a chronicle describing the search for Nuevo México covering the period from Hernán Cortés (1521) to Antonio de Espejo (1582). He sent the manuscript to the Consejo de Indias in 1583 or 1584 but it was only published in 1924. Eva María Bravo, introduction to Obregón, *Historia de los descubrimientos*, 22–27; Rosa Camelo, "Baltasar de Obregón," *Estudios de Historia Novohispana* 7 (1981): 29.

117. A former soldier who had renounced the encomiendas he attained in the conquest of Mexico to become a monk, he was known as Friar Cintos (or Cindos) after receiving the Franciscan habit. Joaquín García Icazbalceta, *Nueva colección de documentos para la historia de México* (Mexico: Díaz de León, 1891), 3:xix–xx, 235–47.

118. Francisco de Ibarra to the Viceroy, Avino [in the modern-day state of Durango], June 6, 1562 (AGI, México 19, no. 27).

119. "Memorial de los servicios que ha hecho el gobernador Francisco de Ybarra" (AGI, Patronato 21, no. 4, R. 2:2–4); "Comisiones y provisiones del virrey Luis de Velasco a Francisco de Ibarra para descubrir y poblar Copala y Chiametla," July 24, 1562 (AGI, México 19, no. 49); "Memorial de los indios de Nombre de Dios, Durango, acerca de sus servicios al rey," ca. 1563 (in Barlow and Smisor, *Nombre de Dios*, 14–24). The "*Memoria de lo que pascimos los padres y nosotros los Mexicanos*," February 25, 1591 (in Barlow and Smisor, *Nombre de Dios*, 64–65) asserts the group departed from San Martín on June 3, 1562. The 1608 "Descripción de la villa de Nombre de Dios" (BNE, 3064, *Descripción*

de Indias, 1:115–24), elaborated by local authorities, provides a different date for the founding of Nombre de Dios: 1563, though it also mentions Pedro de Espinareda among the founders. In addition, it asserts that many natives from Tonalá had settled there, but most of the town's population at the time was still of Mexican and Tarascan origin. Regarding this date discrepancy, also noted by Barlow and Smisor (*Nombre de Dios*, xvii n6), Atanasio G. Saravia, *Obras: apuntes para la historia de la Nueva Vizcaya* (Mexico, Universidad Nacional Autónoma de México, 1978), 114–17, concluded that Nombre de Dios was established first as an Indian settlement in 1562 and then officially founded as a Spanish village in 1563. This is consistent with the chart that Viceroy Velasco issued on October 6, 1563, to confirm the founding of the village, published in Barlow and Smisor, *Nombre de Dios*, 67–69.

120. Francisco de Ibarra, "Relación de las cosas desta gobernación," ca. 1574 (AGI, Patronato 20, no. 5, R. 16). "Comisiones y provisiones del virrey Luis de Velasco a Francisco de Ibarra como gobernador y capitán general del descubrimiento y colonización de Copala," July 24, 1562, and "Confirmación del rey Felipe II para Francisco de Ibarra como gobernador y capitán general del descubrimiento y colonización de Copala," May 31, 1567 (AGI, México 19, no. 49).

121. Letter by Viceroy Luis de Velasco, May 26, 1563 (AGI, Patronato 21, no. 4, R. 3).

122. Apart from the letter quoted above, these events are related in a letter by Francisco de Ibarra to his uncle Diego, addressed on May 3, 1563, and another by Diego de Ibarra to the Viceroy, May 9, 1563 (both in AGI, Patronato 21, no. 4, R. 3). They also appear in "Memorial de los indios de Nombre de Dios" (in Barlow and Smisor, Nombre de Dios, 24–26), and in the "Relación de lo subcedido después que Francisco de Ybarra fue al descubrimiento y provincia de Copala asta que bolvio el real y el dicho Francisco de Ybarra al valle de San Juan, donde se avia salido, e onde al presente queda," ca. 1563 (AGI, Patronato 21, no. 4, R. 3). This account was published as "Relación de lo que descubrió Diego de Ibarra en la provincia de Copala llamada Topiamé; describiendo muy por menor, su viage y descubrimiento; y acompañando una carta escrita a S.M. por Don Luis de Velasco" in *CDIAO*, 14:555–59. In "Memorial de los servicios que ha hecho el gobernador Francisco de Ybarra, 1574" (AGI, Patronato 21, no. 4, R. 2:6–7), the episode is mentioned as an excursion to Topia.

123. "Relación de lo subcedido después que Francisco de Ybarra fue al descubrimiento y provincia de Copala" (AGI, Patronato 21, no. 4, R. 3).

124. Francisco de Ibarra, "Relación de las cosas desta gobernación" (AGI, Patronato 20, no. 5, R. 16); "Memorial de los servicios que ha hecho el gobernador Francisco de Ybarra" (AGI, Patronato 21, no. 4, R. 2); Obregón, *Historia de los descubrimientos*; Antonio Ruiz, *La relación de Antonio Ruiz (La conquista del noroeste)* [ca. 1595–1600], edited by A. Nakayama (Mexico: Instituto Nacional de Antropología e Historia, Centro Regional del Noroeste, 1974).

125. Ibarra and his men were perhaps the first Spaniards to see the magnificent ruins of Casas Grandes. The first written description of the site is contained in the chronicle by Baltasar de Obregón.

126. Death and desertion had caused a severe population drop in the whole coastal area since the 1530s. By 1550 only twenty-five of the ninety-six original Spanish colonists of Culiacán were still living there. Ortega Noriega, *Un ensayo*, 40–44; Jiménez Moreno, *Estudios*, 36–8, 61–62; Radding, *Wandering Peoples*, 32.

127. "Bulas y cédulas para el gobierno de Indias, siglo XVI" (BNE, 3017:281–301). A manuscript copy of the same document ("Ordenanzas de Felipe II para los

descubrimientos y poblaciones nuevas") is contained in a different compilation titled "Ordenanzas de la hacienda real en Indias" (BNE, 3035:282–316). The copier of this compilation mistakenly transcribed the issuing date of the document as 1563 instead of 1573.

128. "Ordenanzas y cédulas de Indias, S[iglo] XVI" (BNE, 3045:99–100).

129. The other soldiers in the expedition were Hernando Barrando, Pedro de Bustamante, Hernando Gallego, Pero Sánchez Chávez, Felipe de Escalante, Pedro de Herrera, Pero Sánchez de Fuensalida, and Juan Sánchez de Fuensalida. See Hernando Gallego, "Relacion de la entrada que hizo en el Nuevo México Francisco Sánchez Chamuscado en junio de 1581, traslado hecho por Joan de Aranda," 1602 (AGI, Patronato 22, R. 4:77–136), published with some related documents in *CDIAO*, 15:80–150, and also in Hammond and Rey, *Rediscovery*. Another report by Felipe de Escalante and Hernando Barrando dated October 1583 and consisting of only two pages exists in the Archivo General de Indias (AGI, Patronato 22, R. 4:1149–50). It is published in *Cartas de Indias* (Madrid: Ministerio de Fomento / Atlas, 1974), 1:230–33, and *CDIAO*, 15:146–50. More information is contained in "Relación de méritos y servicios de Hernán Gallego" (AGI, Patronato 77, no. 1, R. 7). Other early though secondhand accounts of this excursion appear in Obregón, *Historia de los descubrimientos*, 241–61; Zárate Salmerón, "Relaciones de todas las cosas," 125–28; and Carlos de Sigüenza y Góngora, *The Mercurio volante: An Account of the First Expedition of don Diego de Vargas into New Mexico in 1692* [1693], 3 vols., translated by I. A. Leonard (Los Angeles, Calif.: Quivira Society, 1932). Zárate Salmerón and Sigüenza y Góngora mistakenly register Friar Agustín Rodríguez's last name as Ruiz. For modern and succinct overviews, see Bancroft, *Works*, 75–81; Beck, *New Mexico*, 49–50; Forbes, *Apache*, 49–55; and Cutter, *España*, 31–33.

130. "Parecer de Rodrigo del Rio de Losa sobre la jornada de Nuebo Mexico," n.d. (AGI, México 20, no. 97); Viceroy Conde de la Coruña to the King, November 158[2] (AGI, México 20, no. 97). These documents, attached to one another in the same file, must be copies of the originals, because the letter's date of 1581 is clearly wrong.

131. Forbes, *Apache*, 55–56; Ocaranza, *Establecimientos franciscanos*, 7.

132. Beck, *New Mexico*, 50–51; Cutter, *España*, 32–34.

133. "Relación del viaje que yo, Antonio de Espejo, ciudadano de la ciudad de México, natural de la ciudad de Cordoba, hice, con catorce soldados y un religioso de la orden de San Francisco," October 1583 (*CDIAO*, 15:163–89).

134. Ocaranza, *Establecimientos franciscanos*, 7.

135. Pérez de Luxán, "Account," in Hammond and Rey, *Rediscovery*, 153–212.

136. AGI, México, 1064, Legajo 2, fs. 3r–v.

137. Bancroft, *Works*, 79–81, 94–97; Ocaranza, *Establecimientos franciscanos*, 7–9.

138. "Capitulación de Juan Baptista de Lomas con el marques de Billamanrique sobre la conquista del Nuebo Mexico, con una carta al rey" (AGI, Patronato 22, R. 8); "Capitulación hecha con Juan Bautista de Lomas sobre la jornada de Nuebo Mexico y presentada ante el marques de Villamanrique," February 15, 1589" (AGI, Patronato 22, R. 9).

139. Bancroft, *Works*, 92–100. On the Tlaxcalteca transfer, see Martínez Saldaña, *La diáspora*.

140. "Relación de Juan Morlete a Luis de Velasco sobre Castaño de Sosa," September 16, 1591 (AGI, Patronato 22, R. 10); "Traslado de las ynformaciones, autos y otras diligencias que se hizieron contra el capitan Gaspar Castaño de Sosa y sus soldados sobre aver ydo al Nuevo Mexico, 1592" (AGI, México 220, no. 27). Modern overviews are contained in Bancroft, *Works*, 100–107; and Forbes, *Apache*, 67–73.

141. Antonio Gutiérrez de Humaña according to Cutter, *España*, 36.

142. Bancroft, *Works*, 108, dates this incursion as 1594–96; Cutter, *España*, 35, dates it as 1593.

143. Bancroft, *Works*, 108–109. Cutter, *España*, 35–36, mentions a brief *relación* by an Indian survivor called Jusepe or José, which I have not found.

144. Zárate Salmerón, "Relaciones de todas las cosas," 155–56.

145. Juan Armando Niel, "Apuntamientos que a las memorias del P. Fray Gerónimo de Zárate Salmerón hizo el P. Juan Armando Niel de la Compañía de Jesús," 1710, in *Documentos para servir a la historia de Nuevo México, 1538–1778* (Madrid: José Porrúa Turranzas, 1965), 259–67, 273.

146. Horgan, *Conquistadors*, 215–16.

147. Marc Simmons, *The Last Conquistador: Juan de Oñate and the Settling of the Far Southwest* (Norman: University of Oklahoma Press, 1991), 3.

148. Gaspar de Villagrá, *Historia de la Nueva México* [1610], edited by F. del Paso y Troncoso (Mexico: Museo Nacional de México, 1900). Villagrá joined Oñate at the village of Llerena in June 1596 and was entrusted with important commissions. Like other captains he contributed a small company he recruited himself, paying seven thousand pesos of his own resources to buy horses, weapons, and clothes. His epic poem, published in Alcalá de Henares, Spain, in 1610, is one of the most important sources for Oñate's enterprise. Documents concerning his assignments are compiled in volume 2 of the 1900 edition.

149. "Traslado de la posesión que en nombre de Su Magestad tomó Don Juan de Oñate de los reynos y provincias de la Nueva México; y de las obediencias y vasallaje que los indios de algunos pueblos de los dichos reynos y provincias le dieron." Transcribed in Villagrá, *Historia de Nuevo México* [1610], edited by Mercedes Junquera (Madrid: Historia 16, 1989), 217–24, and also contained in *CDIAO*, 16:88–141. The other documents are "Memorial sobre el descubrimiento de Nuevo México y sus acontecimientos, años desde 1595 a 1602" (*CDIAO*, 16:188–227); "Discurso y proposición que se hace a vuestra magestad de lo tocante a los descubrimientos del Nuevo México por sus capítulos de puntos diferentes" (*CDIAO*, 16:38–66); "Discurso de las jornadas que hizo el campo de su magestad desde la Nueva España a la provincia de la Nueva México" (*CDIAO*, 16:228–76); "Relación cierta y verdadera de los subcesos que hubo en la entrada que hizo el adelantado y governador don Juan de Oñate," 1601 (AGI, Patronato 22, R. 12).

150. Villagrá, *Historia*, edited by M. Junquera, 126.

151. "Memorial sobre el descubrimiento de Nuevo México," *CDIAO*, 16:188.

152. José Ignacio Rubio Mañé, *El virreinato* (Mexico: Fondo de Cultura Económica, Universidad Nacional Autónoma de México, 1983), 1:134–35.

153. "Memorial sobre el descubrimiento de Nuevo México," *CDIAO*, 16:189.

154. Josiah Gregg, *Commerce of the Prairies* [1844], edited by M. L. Moorhead (Norman: University of Oklahoma Press, 1967), 109–10.

155. "Las capitulaciones que el virrey Don Luys de Velasco hizo con Don Juan de Oñate, governador y capitan general de las Provincias de la Nueva Mexico, en conformidad de las ordenanzas reales para semejantes descubrimientos, con las dichas ordenanzas, y las moderaciones del Virrey Conde de Monterrey," n.d. (AGI, Patronato 22, R. 12). In 1596 Gerónimo de Mendieta, *Historia eclesiástica*, 2:62–63, mentioned that Juan de Oñate's expedition was "under preparation." Other secondary but early sources are Torquemada, *Monarquía indiana*, 1:670ff.; Zárate Salmerón, "Relaciones de todas las cosas," 152–76; Francisco Javier Alegre, *Historia de la provincia de la compañía de Jesús*

en Nueva España [ca. 1770], edited by E. J. Burrus and F. Zubillaga (Rome: Jesuit Historical Institute,1956–60), 1:310–11; Niel, "Apuntamientos," 249–301; Antonio de Alcedo, *Diccionario geográfico-histórico de las Indias Occidentales ó América. Es a saber: de los reinos del Perú, Nueva España, Tierra Firme, Chile y Nuevo Reino de Granada* (Madrid: Imprenta de Benito Cano, 1786), 3:189; Ribera Bernárdez, *Compendio*, 31–34.

156. Simmons, *Last Conquistador*, 9.

157. Velázquez, *Establecimiento y pérdida*, 34–37.

158. Obregón, *Historia de los descubrimientos*, 202–204.

159. "Memorial sobre el descubrimiento de Nuevo México," *CDIAO*, 16:188–227. The Archivo General de Indias preserves an interesting document that systematically compares the capitulaciones signed by Oñate and Ponce de León to determine the most advantageous (AGI, Patronato 22, R. 12).

160. "Memorial sobre el descubrimiento de Nuevo México," *CDIAO*, 16:193.

161. "Discurso de las jornadas," *CDIAO*, 16:231–32; Villagrá, *Historia*, edited by M. Junquera, 164–75.

162. Cramaussel, "El camino real de tierra adentro de México a Santa Fe," in Chantal Cramaussel, ed., *Rutas de la Nueva España* (Zamora, Michoacán: El Colegio de Michoacán, 2006), 307–308.

163. Villagrá, *Historia*, edited by M. Junquera, 217–24.

164. "Discurso de las jornadas," *CDIAO*, 16:250–51.

165. Ibid., 247–52.

166. Horgan, *Conquistadors*, 228–29.

167. Florence H. Ellis, "The Long Lost City of San Gabriel del Yungue, Second Oldest European Settlement in the United States," in *When Cultures Meet: Remembering San Gabriel del Yunge Oweenge: Papers from the October 20, 1984, Conference Held at San Juan Pueblo, New Mexico* (Santa Fe, N.M.: Sunstone Press, 1987), 16–17.

168. "Discurso de las jornadas," *CDIAO*, 16:263.

169. Ibid., 264, 268. Villagrá, *Historia*, chaps. xvii–xix.

170. Gutiérrez, *When Jesus Came*, 52–53.

171. "Discurso de las jornadas," *CDIAO*, 16:268–72.

172. Documents sometimes refer to these two settlements as if they were one and the same. Archaeological research conducted in the late 1950s and early 1960s cleared up the confusion but the results have been slow to reach scholars, as the errors still committed by Horgan, *Conquistadors*, 243; Cutter, *España*, 42; and other authors show. For the results of that research see Ellis, "The Long Lost City."

173. Contained in *CDIAO*, 16:302–15.

174. Horgan, *Conquistadors*, 244–45, 247; Oñate, "Discurso y proposición que se hace a vuestra magestad de lo tocante a los descubrimientos del Nuevo México por sus capítulos de puntos diferentes" (*CDIAO*, 16:40–63).

175. Ocaranza, *Establecimientos franciscanos*, 27–29, includes a summary of the report that Friar Francisco de Escobar delivered about Oñate's exploration of the Colorado River and the natives living in the area.

176. For the last years of Oñate's government (1605–1609) and the following period up to the 1680 Pueblo Revolt, see Bancroft, *Works*, 148–57; Beck, *New Mexico*, 58–60; Gutiérrez, *When Jesus Came*, 54–55; Horgan, *Conquistadors*, 251–73; Fernando Ocaranza, *Crónicas y relaciones del occidente de México* (Mexico: Antigua Librería Robredo de José Porrúa e Hijos, 1937), 1:39–52; Cutter, *España*, 81–110; Martín González de la Vara, "La rebelión de los indios pueblos de Nuevo México, 1680–1693," in F. Castro, V. Guedea,

and J. L. Mirafuentes, eds., *Organización y liderazgo en los movimientos populares novohispanos* (Mexico: Universidad Nacional Autónoma de México, 1992), 11–18, 32–35.

Chapter 4. The Medieval Hypothesis

1. Danna Levin and Federico Navarrete, *Indios, mestizos y españoles: interculturalidad e historiografía en la Nueva España* (Mexico: Universidad Autónoma Metropolitana–Azcapotzalco, Universidad Nacional Autónoma de México, 2008). See chapters by Levin, Navarrete, Yukitaka Inoue Okubo, and Eduardo Natalino dos Santos.

2. References and a detailed review of these sources are provided in chapter 5.

3. See, for instance, Gandía, *Historia crítica*, 63; Irving Leonard, "Conquerors and Amazons in Mexico," *Hispanic American Historical Review* 24, no. 4 (1944): 561–79; Juan Gil, *Mitos y utopías del descubrimiento*, vol. 2, *El Pacífico* (Madrid: Alianza Editorial, 1989); Pastor Bodmer, *Armature*, 106–107.

4. Hanke, *Aristotle and the American Indians*, 3.

5. Edward G. Bourne, *Spain in America, 1450–1580* (New York: Harper, 1904); Claudio Sánchez Albornoz, *La edad media española y la empresa de América* [1934] (Madrid: Cultura Hispánica, 1983); Weckmann, "Middle Ages," 132; and *La herencia medieval*; Miguel Ángel Ladero Quesada, "Spain, circa 1492: Social Values and Structures," in Schwartz, ed., *Implicit Understandings*, 132–33.

6. Gandía, *Historia crítica*; Irving Leonard, *Books of the Brave: Being an Account of Books and of Men in the Spanish Conquest and Settlement of the Sixteenth-Century New World* [1949], introduction by R. Adorno (Berkeley: University of California Press, 1992); Ida Rodríguez Prampolini, *Amadises en América: la hazaña de Indias como empresa caballeresca* (Mexico: Junta Mexicana de Investigaciones Históricas, 1948); Mario Hernández Sánchez Barba, "La influencia de los libros de caballería sobre el conquistador," *Estudios Americanos: revista de la Escuela de Estudios Hispano-Americanos* 19, no. 102 (1960): 235–56; Pastor Bodmer, *Armature*.

7. The notion of mental baggage was coined by Lucien Fevre to designate the body of concepts and responses to the world that corresponds to each particular civilization, which is not universally valid for all times and societies and does not necessarily change according to linear progress. Chartier, *El mundo como representación*, 18–19.

8. Ainsa, *De la edad de oro*, 45–47, 80–83.

9. The events in the search for the Fountain of Youth are told by Fernández de Oviedo, *Historia general y natural de las Indias* [1535–52], edited by J. Pérez de Tudela y Bueso (Madrid: Atlas, 1959), bk. 15, chap. 11; Herrera y Tordesillas, *Historia general*; Garcilaso de la Vega, *La Florida del Inca* [1605], edited by S. L. Hilton (Madrid: Fundación Universitaria Española, 1982); and Francisco López de Gómara, *Historia general de las Indias* [1552] (Madrid: Espasa Calpe, 1941), chap. 104.

10. Leonardo Olschki, "Ponce de León's Fountain of Youth: History of a Geographical Myth," *Hispanic American Historical Review* 21, no. 3 (1941): 361–85; Gandía, *Historia crítica*, 49–56; Weckmann, "Middle Ages," 133; Pastor Bodmer, *Armature*, 106; Demetrio Ramos, *El mito de El Dorado* (Madrid: Colegio Universitario, Ediciones Istmo, 1988), 399–400.

11. Juan Gil, *Mitos y utopías del descubrimiento*, vol. 3, *El Dorado* (Madrid: Alianza Editorial, 1989), 151–53.

12. George Davidson, *The Origin and Meaning of the Name California: Calafia the Queen of the Island of California* (Los Angeles: Geographical Society of the Pacific,

1910); Ruth Putnam and H. I. Priestley, "California: The Name," *University of California Publications in History* 4, no. 4 (1917): 293-365; Leonard, "Conquerors and Amazons," 562-64; and *Books of the Brave*; Portillo y Diez de Sollano, *Descubrimientos*, 121-28; Gil, *Mitos y utopías*, 2:870-82; Pastor Bodmer, *Armature*, 153-68.

13. George P. Hammond, *The Search for the Fabulous in the Settlement of the Southwest* (Salt Lake City: Utah State Historical Society, 1956); Gandía, *Historia crítica*, 9-17, 59-61; Stephen Clissold, *The Seven Cities of Cibola* (London: Eyre and Spottiswoode, 1961), 24-26; Mora, *Las siete ciudades*, 34-36.

14. Gandía, *Historia crítica*, 63; Pastor Bodmer, *Armature*, 106-107.

15. Bernard and Gruzinski, *Historia del Nuevo Mundo*, 1;499.

16. Modern literature on El Dorado is abundant. This summary is based on Demetrio Ramos, *El mito*; Gil, *Mitos y utopías*, vol. 3; Ainsa, *De la edad de oro*, 121-25; and Wayland D. Hand, "The Effect of the Discovery on Ethnographical and Folklore Studies in Europe," in F. Chiappelli, ed., *First Images of America: The Impact of the New World on the Old* (Berkeley and Los Angeles: University of California Press, 1976), 1:50-51.

17. Fabiola Jara, "Monstruosité et altérité: Le mythe des Amazones des Indiens Kalina et Xikrin," *Circé: Cahiers du Centre de Recherche sur l'Imaginaire* 16-19 (1988): 49-79; Jalil Sued-Badillo, "El mito indoantillano de las mujeres sin hombres," *Boletín de Estudios Latinoamericanos y del Caribe* 40 (1986).

18. Putnam and Priestley, "California," 294-95.

19. Leonard, "Conquerors and Amazons," 564-65.

20. New editions of *Las sergas de Esplandián* were made in Toledo (1521), Salamanca (1525), Burgos (1526), and Seville (1526). Leonard, "Conquerors and Amazons," 566-67, observes that the period coincides with the conquest of Mexico by Hernán Cortés and the first expeditions he sent to locate gold and silver mines; in these expeditions, according to Leonard, Cortés sometimes gave further instructions about the verification of rumors concerning all-female tribes.

21. Partially reproduced in Marvin Lunenfeld, *1492: Discovery, Invasion, Encounter: Sources and Interpretations* (Lexington, Mass.: D. C. Heath, 1991), 39, 136.

22. Several authors have pointed out that Columbus's conviction that he had arrived in Asia probably predisposed him to interpret what he saw and heard in this manner. His will to find confirmation for the standard geographical knowledge of the period, embodied in tales of previous travelers like Marco Polo and in various treatises on cosmography, is discussed in detail by Samuel E. Morison, *Admiral of the Ocean Sea: A Life of Christopher Columbus* (Boston: Little, Brown, 1942); and O'Gorman, *La invención de América*. More recent assessments on the interpretations that Columbus and others gave to American reality include Tzvetan Todorov, *The Conquest of America: The Question of the Other* [1st French ed. 1982], foreword by A. Pagden, translated by R. Howard (Norman: University of Oklahoma Press, 1999); Hulme, *Colonial Encounters*; and "Tales of Distinction," 166-67; Greenblatt, *Marvelous Possessions*; and Rabasa, *Inventing America*.

23. Fragment from *Las sergas de Esplandián* quoted in Leonard, "Conquerors and Amazons," 565.

24. Mártir de Anglería, *Décadas del Nuevo Mundo*, 1:408, and 2:631.

25. Mason, "Imaginary Worlds," 57.

26. E.g., Weckmann, "Middle Ages," 132; Pastor Bodmer, *Armature*, 105-15.

27. Díaz del Castillo, *Historia verdadera*, 151 (written around 1555 but not published until 1632).

28. Greenblatt, *Marvelous Possessions*, 132-33.

29. Cortés, *Cartas*, 184.

30. In preconquest times Colima was split into different political units. One occupied the broad valley of Cihuatlán and apparently had an urban character and excelled in the quality of its weaving, cotton being one of the most important crops. Sauer, *Colima*.

31. Davidson, *Origin*, 28; Sauer, *Colima*; Cortés, *Cartas*, 176.

32. Gil, *Mitos y utopías*, 2:315–18; Cortés, *Cartas*, 199–200.

33. Davidson, *Origin*; Leonard, "Conquerors and Amazons"; and *Books of the Brave*; Río, *A la diestra mano*.

34. Putnam and Priestley, "California," 293–313, 351–54; Portillo, *Descubrimientos*, 111, 119, 130. All three authors considered it much likelier that the name derived from a misheard native word in one of several languages spoken locally that may have sounded similar to Calafia in the novel.

35. Río, *A la diestra mano*, 17–19.

36. Giovanni Battista Ramusio, *Delle navigationi et viaggi* (Venice, 1550–56), quoted in Portillo, *Descubrimientos*, 114–19.

37. Díaz, "Itinerario de la armada," in Vázquez, ed., *La conquista*, 37–57.

38. The first part of Oviedo's chronicle was published in Seville in 1535, and part 2, book 20 in 1552. The complete manuscript was only published in 1851.

39. See chapter 1, note 15, above.

40. Díaz, "Itinerario de la armada," in Vázquez, ed., *La conquista*, 42.

41. "Instrucciones de Diego Velázquez a Hernán Cortés," Isla Fernandina, October 23, 1518. In Martínez, *Documentos cortesianos*, 1:47–48, 53–54.

42. Ibid., 1:56.

43. In *CDIAO*, 16:153.

44. Quoted in Sauer, *Colima*, 20; and Leonard, "Conquerors and Amazons," 578. The document is reproduced in Francisco del Paso y Troncoso, *Papeles de Nueva España*, vol. 2 (Madrid: Establecimiento Tipográfico Sucesores de Rivadeneyra, 1905).

45. Razo Zaragoza y Cortés, *Crónicas*, 58. Also quoted in Leonard, "Conquerors and Amazons," 578.

46. Razo Zaragoza y Cortés, *Crónicas*, 300, 303–304.

47. Ibid., 93–94.

48. Ibid., 145. There is another similar reference in the second anonymous *relación*, ibid., 321–22.

49. Pedro Carranza, "Relacion," ibid., 173.

50. Cristóbal Flores, "Relación," ibid., 202.

51. "Relación hecha de viva voz por el Alferez Francisco de Arceo, al capitán e historiador Gonzalo Fernández de Oviedo," ibid., 265–67.

52. Frederick W. Hodge, *History of Hawikuh, New Mexico: One of the So-Called Cities of Cibola* (Los Angeles: Southwest Museum, 1937); Jiménez Moreno, *Estudios*, 49; Gandía, *Historia crítica*, 59–70; Clissold, *Seven Cities*, 74; Pastor Bodmer, *Armature*, 105; Mora, *Las siete ciudades*, 34; Bernard and Gruzinski, *Historia del Nuevo Mundo*, 2:346; Petersen, *Lost Cities*.

53. Herrera y Tordesillas, *Historia general*, 1:204

54. John L. Phelan, *The Millennial Kingdom of the Franciscans in the New World*, 1956 (Berkeley and Los Angeles: University of California Press, 1970), 70.

55. Bartolomé de las Casas, *Historia de las Indias* [1527–61], edited by A. Millares Carlo and L. Hanke (Mexico: Fondo de Cultura Económica, 1951), bk. 1, chap. 13.

56. Gandía, *Historia crítica*, 17.
57. Quoted in Wagner, *Discovery of Yucatan*, 42.
58. Martínez, *Documentos cortesianos*, 1:51–52.
59. Phelan, *Millennial Kingdom*, 69–71. Translation by Phelan.
60. Gandía, *Historia crítica*, 11–14, Clissold, *Seven Cities*, 25–26; Abulafia, *Discovery*, 25, 219. Transcriptions of letters and other documents related to the expeditions by Téllez and Duolmo are contained in *Alguns documentos do Archivo Nacional da Torre do Tombo acerca das navegações e conquistas portuguezas publicados ao celebrarse a commemoração quadricentaria do descobrimento da America*, preface by Jose Ramos Coelho (Lisbon: Academia das Ciencias de Lisboa, 1892), 38–41, 58–63.
61. Pastor Bodmer, *Armature*, 107; Mora, *Las siete ciudades*, 35.
62. Luis Weckmann, "The Alexandrine Bulls of 1493: Pseudo-Asiatic Documents," in Chiappelli, ed., *First Images of America*, 203.
63. Mora, *Las siete ciudades*, 34.
64. Ibid.; Gandía, *Historia crítica*, 9; Junquera, introduction, 14.
65. The globe is kept in Nuremberg. The quotation is taken from Gandía's transcription, *Historia crítica*, 18.
66. Gandía, *Historia crítica*, 59–60.
67. Ibid., 60
68. Ibid., 62–63, 68.
69. Gerónimo de Mendieta, *Historia eclesiástica*, 2:59–60, 394–95.
70. I refer to the following documents published in Mora, *Las siete ciudades*: "Letter from Vázquez de Coronado to the king," Tiguex, October 20, 1541; "Relación del suceso de la jornada que Francisco Vázquez hizo en el descubrimiento de Cíbola," 1541; "Traslado de las nuevas y noticias que dieron sobre el descubrimiento de una cibdad, que llamaron de Cíbola, situada en la tierra nueva," 1541; "Relación postrera de Sívola," 1541; and Castañeda Nájera, "Relación de la jornada."
71. "Relación que dio el capitán Juan Jaramillo de la jornada que hizo a la tierra nueva, de la que fue general Francisco Vázquez de Coronado," 1541, in Mora, *Las siete ciudades*, 194.
72. Castañeda Nájera, "Relación de la jornada," 88; Vázquez de Coronado, "Relación," in Mora, *Las siete ciudades*, 173–74.
73. About Gonzalo Guerrero, see Thomas, *Real Discovery*, 164.
74. Adolph Bandelier, *Contributions to the History of the South Western Portion of the United States* (Cambridge: Cambridge University Press, 1890), 6–12; Bourne, *Spain in America*, 169–70; Hodge and Lewis, *Spanish Explorers*; Bolton, *Spanish Exploration*.
75. A hint of this hypothesis had been posed, but not strongly argued, by Bandelier, *Contributions*, 6–9.
76. Robert Ricard, "Estebanico de Azamor et la légende des Sept Cités," *Journal de la Société des Américanistes de Paris*, n.s., 21 (1929); and "La diffusion de la légende des Sept Cités en Amérique," *Journal de la Société des Américanistes de Paris*, n.s., 27 (1936): 404–405.
77. Ainsa, *De la edad de oro*, 161–66.
78. To mention just a few: Horgan, *Conquistadors*, 151–60; Weckmann, "Middle Ages," 133; Hammond, *Search for the Fabulous*, 5–7; Clissold, *Seven Cities*, 75–76; Angélico Chávez, *Coronado's Friars* (Washington, D.C.: Academy of American Franciscan History, 1968), 11–12; Junquera, introduction, 14; Cutter, *España*, 14–15; Mora, *Las siete*

ciudades, 34–36; Stewart L. Udall, *To the Inland Empire: Coronado and Our Spanish Legacy* (Garden City, N.Y.: Doubleday, 1987), 64; Weber, *Myth and History*; and *Spanish Frontier*, 24.

79. Matthew Restall, *Seven Myths of the Spanish Conquest* (New York: Oxford University Press, 2003).

Chapter 5. From the North We Came Walking

1. West and Augelli, *Middle America*, 277.

2. For example, Carrasco, "Peoples"; Henry B. Nicholson, "Pre-Hispanic Central Mexican Historiography," in *Investigaciones contemporáneas sobre historia de México: memorias de la Tercera Reunión de Historiadores Mexicanos y Norteamericanos* (1969) (Mexico: Universidad Nacional Autónoma de México, El Colegio de México, University of Texas, 1971), 38–81; Carlos Martínez Marín, "Historiografía de la migración mexica," *Estudios de Cultura Náhuatl* 12 (1976): 121–36; Nigel Davies, *The Toltec Heritage: From the Fall of Tula to the Rise of Tenochtitlán* (Norman: University of Oklahoma Press, 1980); Christian Duverger, *L'origine des aztèques* (Paris: Éditions du Seuil, 1983); Michael Smith, "The Aztlan Migration of the Nahuatl Chronicles: Myth or History?" *Ethnohistory* 31, no. 3 (1984): 153–86; Enrique Florescano, "Mito e historia en la memoria nahua," *Historia Mexicana* 39, no. 3 (1990): 607–61; Federico Navarrete, "Las fuentes indígenas más allá de la dicotomía entre historia y mito," *Estudios de Cultura Náhuatl* 30 (1999): 231–56.

3. Anthropologists assign to Oto-Pamean languages such as Otomí, Mazahua, and Matlatzinca a temporal depth of two to three thousand years in the central highlands, whereas they agree that Náhuatl is a recent arrival in Mesoamerica. Náhuatl is the southernmost representative of the Uto-Aztecan linguistic family (also Yuto-Aztecan in some authors), a dialectal chain extending from California southeast to Nicaragua that includes many disappeared languages like Guachichil, Xixime, and Acaxee. See Leonardo Manrique Castañeda, "La historia del idioma de los mexica y sus congéneres," in D. Sierra Carrillo, ed., *Primer encuentro nahua: los nahuas de hoy* (Mexico: Instituto Nacional de Antropología e Historia, 1989), 18–23; R. Escalante Hernández, "Tres artes gramaticales de lenguas otomianas," in I. Guzmán Betancourt and E. Nansen Díaz, eds., *Memoria del coloquio "La obra de Antonio de Nebrija y su recepción en la Nueva España: quince estudios nebrisenses (1492-1992)"* (Mexico: Instituto Nacional de Antropología e Historia, 1997), 121; David Wright, "Linguistic Rights: A View from Central Mexico," paper presented at the World Conference on Linguistic Rights (Barcelona, 1996), 2–5. The most accepted classification (by Wick R. Miller, 1981) divides the Uto-Aztecan family into five branches, diversified as the speakers expanded over new territories: Númica, Tubatulabal, Tákika, Hopi, and Southern Uto-Azteca. Náhuatl belongs to the Aztecan group of the Southern Uto-Azteca branch, together with others like Pipil and Cazcán. While the language family as a whole seems to have begun its differentiation in the Great Basin of the United States around 3500–4000 years b.p, the Aztecan group only began to separate around 2500 years b.p. Manrique Castañeda, "La historia del idioma," 14–18, 24–26.

4. López Austin and López Luján, *El pasado*, 176–89; Noguez, "La zona del altiplano," 194–97, 201–204; Reyes García and Odena Güemes, "La zona del altiplano," 246.

5. López Austin and López Luján, *El pasado*, 262–71; Alfredo López Austin and Leonardo López Luján, *Mito y realidad de Zuyuá* (Mexico: Fondo de Cultura Económica, El Colegio de México, 1999).

6. About these ancestral migration traditions, see Dominique Michelet, "Apuntes para el análisis de las migraciones en el México prehispánico," in T. Calvo and G. López, eds., *Movimientos de población en el occidente de México* (Zamora: El Colegio de Michoacán, Centro de Estudios Mexicanos y Centroamericanos, 1988), 15–19; Carlos Martínez Marín, "Las migraciones de los grupos nahuas en el horizonte postclásico," in Sierra Carrillo, ed., *Primer encuentro nahua*, 27–30; Alfredo López Austin, "Mitos de una migración," *Arqueología Mexicana* 1, no. 4 (1993): 33–36; and "Tollan: Babel," *Universidad de México: revista de la UNAM* 528–29 (1995): 3–8. Gordon Brotherston, *Painted Books from Mexico: Codices in the UK Collections and the World They Represent* (London: British Museum Press, 1995), 62, 98, remarks that it was essentially the groups who claimed Chichimec or Toltec ancestry who represented their past in terms of migration from distant landmarks, whereas the Mixtecs depicted their ancestors as emerging from trees that stood closer to home.

7. López Austin, "Tollan: Babel," 3–4.

8. *Relación de Michoacán*, edited by L. Cabrero (Madrid: Historia 16, 1989), 59–61.

9. This and the following chapter keep the indigenous convention of using the term Aztec when referring to Mexica ancestors before the moment when, according to their own stories, their tutelary god instructed them to change their name, dropping that of Aztecs and adopting that of Mexicas.

10. *Popol Vuh*, *Memorial de Sololá*, and *Título de los señores de Totonicapán* use the term "Vucub Ziván" in combination with others, such as Tulán Zuivá, Vucub Pec, and Zuyuá, different names for the same place: the city where different peoples acquired the specific protection of particular tutelary gods, the site of the first human creation, where ancestors lived before migrating and before the language of each group became different from that of others. Due to lack of agreement on the alphabetic correspondence of Mayan language phonetics, different documents often spell the same word differently: "Wukub" may appear instead of "Vucub," whereas "Civán," "Siwán," or "Suywa" may appear instead of "Ziván" or "Zuyuá." Alfredo López Austin, *Hombre-dios: religión y política en el mundo náhuatl* (Mexico: Universidad Nacional Autónoma de México, 1989), 79–80.

11. Brotherston, *Painted Books*, 62; López Austin, *Hombre-dios*, 79, 84–85; and "Tollan: Babel," 2.

12. *Mapa de Cuauhtinchan no. 2* is reproduced in Keiko Yoneda, *Los mapas de Cuauhtinchan y la historia cartográfica prehispánica* (Mexico: Fondo de Cultura Económica, 1991), 119–38; *Historia Tolteca-Chichimeca* [ca.1533], edited by P. Kirchhoff, L. Odena Güemes, and L. Reyes García (Mexico: Centro de Investigaciones y Estudios Superiores en Antropología Social, Fondo de Cultura Económica, Gobierno del Estado de Puebla, 1989); *Codex Azcatitlan: Códice Azcatitlan*, introduction by M. Graulich, commentary by R. H. Barlow, translated by L. López Luján and D. Michelet (Paris: Bibliothèque Nationale de France, Société des Américanistes, 1995); *Codex Mexicanus*, in E. Menguin, ed., "Commentaire du Codex Mexicanus nos. 23–24 de la Bibliothèque Nationale de Paris," *Journal de la Société des Américanistes de Paris*, n.s., 41 (1952): 387–498, atlas.

13. López Austin and López Luján, *Mito y realidad*, 42–43.

14. Federico Navarrete, introduction to Cristóbal del Castillo, *Historia de la venida de los mexicanos y otros pueblos e historia de la conquista* (Mexico: Instituto Nacional de Antropología e Historia, 1991), 71; López Austin, *Tamoanchan*, 38.

15. For Indian allies of the Spaniards, see Matthew and Oudijk, eds., *Indian Conquistadors*, chapters by Ida Altman, "Conquest, Coersion, and Collaboration: Indian

Allies and the Campaigns in Nueva Galicia," 145–74; Stephanie Wood, "Nahua Christian Warriors in the Mapa Cuauhtlantzinco, Cholula Parish," 254–78; and Oudijk and Restall, "Mesoamerican Conquistadors," 46–48. See also Martínez Saldaña, *La diáspora*; and "La expansión cultural mesoamericana," in Andrés Fábregas Puig, Mario Alberto Nájera Espinoza, and José Francisco Román Gutiérrez, eds., *Regiones y esencias: estudios sobre la Gran Chichimeca* (Mexico: Seminario Permanente de Estudios de la Gran Chichimeca, 2008), 145–57.

16. The systematic study of native languages began in the 1530s in the Franciscan colleges in Tiripitío and Santa Cruz de Tlatelolco. By the end of the sixteenth century, grammatical rules and lexicons existed for several languages. Náhuatl received the most prolonged and fruitful attention, as reflected in the treatises and dictionaries by Andrés de Olmos (*Arte para aprender la lengua mexicana*, 1547), Alonso de Molina (*Vocabulario de la lengua castellana y mexicana*, 1555), and Antonio del Rincón (*Arte de la lengua mexicana*, 1595). See Ascensión Hernández de León Portilla, "Nebrija y las lenguas compañeras del imperio," in Guzmán Betancourt and Nansen Díaz, eds., *Memoria del coloquio*, 189–90. Later, in the Philippines a similar consideration drew the Spaniards to study and promote the use of the most widespread native language, Tagalog. See Rafael, *Contracting Colonialism*, 23–54.

17. Josefina Urquijo Durazo, "Perspectiva nacionalista y trabajo jesuítico: la ausencia de Nebrija en la acción lingüístico-educativa del noroeste," in Guzmán Betancourt and Nansen Díaz, eds., *Memoria del coloquio*, 165–66; Ignacio Guzmán Betancourt, "La lengua, compañera del imperio: destino de un presagio nebrisense en la Nueva España," ibid., 33–35.

18. H. R. Harvey, "The *Relaciones geográficas*, 1579–1586: Native Languages," in H. F. Cline, *Handbook of Middle American Indians*, vol. 12, *Guide to Ethnohistorical Sources*, pt. 1 (Austin: University of Texas Press, 1972), 313–14.

19. Lockhart, *Nahuas*, 1.

20. Several scholars categorize this sense of distinctiveness as "ethnic." For example, María Concepción Obregón Rodríguez, "La zona del altiplano central en el posclásico: la etapa de la triple alianza," in Manzanilla and López Luján, eds., *Historia antigua de México*, 3:282; Carmack, Gasco, and Gossen, *Legacy*; López Austin, *Tamoanchan*, 35–38.

21. Mary G. Hodge, "Land and Lordship in the Valley of Mexico: The Politics of Aztec Provincial Administration," in H. R. Harvey, ed., *Land and Politics*, 113.

22. The most ancient known historical records come from Oaxaca and the Maya area. They are glyphic texts integrated into public buildings in the form of sculpture and mural painting, or as decoration on ceramic artifacts. The link between this memorial practice, which recorded mostly calendrical and cosmogonic information as well as names, births, enthronements, and deaths of the elites, and later historiographical developments is not clear. Nevertheless, both the Mayas and the Mixtecs developed complex writing systems between the third and tenth centuries a.d. By the Post-Classic period, maps and scrolls of paper or animal hide were generally used throughout Mesoamerica to keep records of historical happenstance, tribute payments, religious ceremonies, calendar calculations, and other issues. Carlos Martínez Marín, "El registro de la historia," in Lombardo and Nalda, eds., *Temas mesoamericanos*, 397–418; Brotherston, *Painted Books*, 10–20; Michel Boccara, "Akab tsib, les lettres de nuit des Mayas," in A. Zali and A. Berthier, eds., *L'aventure des écritures naissantes* (Paris: Bibliothèque Nationale de France, 1997), 63–64.

23. Eloise Quiñones Keber, *Codex Telleriano-Remensis: Ritual, Divination, and History in a Pictorial Aztec Manuscript*, foreword by E. Le Roy Ladurie (Austin: University of Texas Press, 1995), 107.

24. Navarrete, "Las fuentes," 238–41.

25. Source selection was made on the basis of the following literature: Martínez Marín, "Historiografía"; Brotherston, *Painted Books*; Doris Heyden, *The Eagle, the Cactus, the Rock: The Roots of Mexico-Tenochtitlan's Foundation Myth and Symbol* (Oxford: British Archaeological Reports, 1989); Elizabeth Hill Boone, "Introduction: Writing and Recording Knowledge," in Boone and Mignolo, eds., *Writing without Words*, 3–26; "Aztec Pictorial Histories: Records without Words," in Boone and Mignolo, eds., *Writing without Words*, 50–76; and "Migration Histories as Ritual Performance," in D. Carrasco, ed., *To Change Place: Aztec Ceremonial Landscapes* (Boulder: University Press of Colorado, 1991), 121–51. The sample was cross-checked with the indexes by José Alcina Franch, "Fuentes indígenas de México: Ensayo de sistematización bibliográfica," *Revista de Indias* 6, nos. 61–62 (1955): 421–521; Manuel Carrera Stampa, "Códices, mapas y lienzos acerca de la cultura náhuatl," *Estudios de Cultura Náhuatl* 5 (1965): 165–220; John B. Glass and Donald Robertson, "A Census of Middle American Pictorial Manuscripts," in R. Wauchope and H. F. Cline, *Handbook of Middle American Indians*, vol. 14, *Guide to Ethnohistorical Sources*, pt. 3 (Austin: University of Texas Press, 1975), 81–252; and Charles Gibson and John B. Glass, "A Census of Middle American Prose Manuscripts in the Native Historical Tradition," in Wauchope and Cline, eds., *Handbook of Middle American Indians*, vol. 15, *Guide to Ethnohistorical Sources*, pt. 4 (Austin: University of Texas Press, 1975), 322–400. Federico Navarrete offers a detailed analysis of the migration narratives from the Valley of Mexico in *Los orígenes de los pueblos indígenas del valle de México: los altépetl y sus historias* (Mexico: Universidad Nacional Autónoma de México, 2010). Some of the sources he studied are absent from my sample because I am interested in identifying the most widespread indigenous views on the Mexica past that were still current in the contact period, while he aimed at comparing all the currently known migration histories of the different groups who lived in the Valley of Mexico before the Spanish conquest.

26. Eduardo Natalino Dos Santos, for example, has discussed how the structural function of the calendar in preconquest codices was gradually lost in colonial manuscripts, be they pictorial or alphabetic, giving way to documents thematically organized where the calendar, deities, and cosmogonies became separate topics much less intertwined. "Los ciclos calendáricos mesoamericanos en los escritos nahuas y castellanos del siglo XVI: De la función estructural al papel temático," in Levin and Navarrete, eds., *Indios, mestizos y españoles*, 225–62.

27. Martínez Marín, "El registro," 410–12; Gordon Brotherston, *La América indígena en su literatura: los libros del cuarto mundo*, translated by T. Ortega Guerrero and M. Utrilla (Mexico: Fondo de Cultura Económica, 1997), 69–109. The most influential classification elaborated in the first half of the twentieth century began from this native taxonomy and created overall categories based on thematic content and geographic provenance (Alcina Franch, "Fuentes indígenas"). Later indexes by Carrera Stampa ("Códices, mapas y lienzos") and Glass and Robertson ("Census") were more interested in providing a complete catalog with individual item descriptions, so they placed more emphasis on dates of elaboration, degrees of European stylistic influence, and other formal characteristics.

28. Boone, "Aztec Pictorial Histories," 55–67. See also Brotherston, *La América indígena*, 84, 119–40.

29. Manuel Orozco y Berra, José Fernando Ramírez, and Paul Radin deemed the *Códice Boturini* preconquest, but the stylistic analysis by Wigberto Jiménez Moreno established it as colonial. Still, it is the earliest example we have of a "year-count" book. Robertson, *Mexican Manuscript Painting of the Early Colonial Period: The Metropolitan Schools* [1958], foreword by E. H. Boone (Norman: University of Oklahoma Press, 1994), 63, 82–84. For a detailed description of the document and its editions see Glass and Robertson, "Census," 101; and Carrera Stampa, "Códices, mapas y lienzos," 174–76.

30. Robertson, *Mexican Manuscript Painting*, 83–84.

31. Ibid., 122–23.

32. Carrera Stampa, "Códices, mapas y lienzos," 212. Two modern facsimile editions of the *Tira de Tepechpan* exist, both accompanied by excellent studies: Xavier Noguez, *Tira de Tepechpan: códice colonial procedente del valle de México*, 2 vols. (Mexico: Instituto Mexiquense de Cultura del Estado de México, 1978); and Lori B. Diel, *The Tira de Tepechpan: Negotiating Place under Aztec and Spanish Rule* (Austin: University of Texas Press, 2008).

33. Glass and Robertson, "Census," 88–89; Carrera Stampa, "Códices, mapas y lienzos," 213–19. The original *Codex Aubin* manuscript is lost but three sixteenth century copies exist, one in the British Library.

34. Also known as *Fonds Mexicain 40* for its location in the National Library of France. Xóchitl Medina González, introduction to *Histoire mexicaine depuis 1221 jusq'en 1594: manuscrito no. 40 del Fondo de Manuscritos Mexicanos, Biblioteca Nacional de Francia* [ca.1700], introduction, paleography, and translation by X. Medina González (Mexico: Instituto Nacional de Antropología e Historia, 1998), 26.

35. Carrera Stampa, "Códices, mapas y lienzos," 183; Michel Graulich, introduction to *Codex Azcatitlan*, 16. Preserved in the National Library of France, this manuscript was first published by Robert Barlow in 1949.

36. Carrera Stampa, "Códices, mapas y lienzos," 203, said the *Codex Telleriano-Remensis* was completed in 1562–63, but this is only valid for the Spanish glosses, not the pictorial representation, which according to Robertson, *Mexican Manuscript Painting*, 110–11, should be dated at two different periods. A first campaign of work carried out by one single scribe ended in 1549, while the last years up to 1562 were drawn by one of the hands that glossed the manuscript, thus representing material added twelve years later.

37. *Codex Vaticano Rios* is also known as *Codex Vaticanus A* or *Vaticano Latino 3738*. These dates are provided by Robertson, *Mexican Manuscript Painting*, 111, but Carrera Stampa, "Códices, mapas y lienzos," 207, prefers 1563–70. The glosses, handwritten in Italian, are almost identical to those in *Codex Telleriano-Remensis*.

38. For a discussion of *Codex Huitzilopochtli* and its relation to codices *Vaticano Ríos* and *Telleriano-Remensis*, see Robertson, *Mexican Manuscript Painting*, 108–11; and Glass and Robertson, "Census," 136–39.

39. Robertson, *Mexican Manuscript Painting*, 94–96. The *Codex Mendoza* was painted in 1549, according to Carrera Stampa, "Códices, mapas y lienzos," 180. Intended as a gift to the king of Spain, it fell into the hands of French pirates before reaching Europe.

40. Boone, "Aztec Pictorial Histories," 60; and "Migration Histories," 123–24.

41. Yoneda, *Los mapas de Cuauhtinchan*, 15; John M. Pohl, "Mexican Codices, Maps, and Lienzos as Social Contracts," in Boone and Mignolo, *Writing without Words*, 145–47.

42. Nicholson, "Pre-Hispanic Central Mexican Historiography," 55.

43. Leibsohn, "Primers for Memory: Cartographic Histories and Nahua Identity," in Boone and Mignolo, eds., *Writing without Words*, 164; Yoneda, *Los mapas de Cuauhtinchan*, 19, 74.

44. Brotherston, *Painted Books*, 78–79; and *La América indígena*, 127, also calls the *Selden Roll* the *Tlahuixtlahuaca Roll* because it comes from the town of that name. Other interrelated lienzos showing Chicomoztoc as a place of origin have recently been located in different communities in the Coixtlahuaca valley.

45. Robert H. Barlow, "La Crónica X: Versiones coloniales de la historia de los mexica tenochca," *Revista Mexicana de Estudios Antropológicos*, 7 (1945): 65–87.

46. Christopher Couch, "The *Codex Ramirez*: Copy or Original?" *Estudios de Cultura Náhuatl* 21 (1991): 111.

47. Edmundo O'Gorman, prologue to José de Acosta, *Historia natural y moral de las Indias*, edited by E. O'Gorman (Mexico: Fondo de Cultura Económica, 1962), xiv–xxii; Martínez Marín, "Historiografía," 122, 126; Couch, "*Codex Ramirez*," 110–12; Jesús Monjarás Ruiz, "Fray Diego Durán, un conquistador conquistado," *Dimensión Antropológica* 1, no. 2 (1994): 49.

48. The manuscript, preserved in the National Library of France, is a later copy of the original text. Adrián León, introduction to Fernando Alvarado Tezozómoc, *Crónica mexicáyotl*, ix–xiv, xx.

49. The chronology of these writings was established by Edmundo O'Gorman, "Estudio preliminar," in Fernando de Alva Ixtlilxóchitl, *Obras históricas. Incluyen el texto completo de las llamadas relaciones e historia de la nación chichimeca en una nueva versión establecida con el cotejo de los manuscritos más antiguos que se conocen*, edited by E. O'Gorman (Mexico: Universidad Nacional Autónoma de México, 1985), 229–33.

50. Romero Galván, *Octava relación: obra histórica de Domingo Francisco de San Antón Muñón Chimalpahin Cuauhtlehuanitzin* (Mexico: Universidad Nacional Autónoma de México, 1983), 17.

51. The Chimalpahin manuscripts' history before they arrived in the National Library of France is obscure. Because eighteenth and nineteenth century references to Chimalpahin use many different titles, though sometimes similar ones, we do not know whether the extant documents are the remains of a single work that has lost many pages and their original order, or whether they are independent works, in which case we do not know which are complete and which are fragments of partly lost or unfinished works. Víctor M. Castillo Farreras, "Estudio preliminar," in Domingo Chimalpahin Cuauhtlehuanitzin, *Memorial breve acerca de la fundación de la ciudad de Culhuacán*, edited by V. M. Castillo Farreras (Mexico: Universidad Nacional Autónoma de México, 1991), xi, xxx. For more details see Silvia Rendón, "Introduction to Domingo Chimalpahin Cuauhtlehuanitzin," *Relaciones originales de Chalco Amaquemecan*, edited by S. Rendón (Mexico: Fondo de Cultura Económica, 1965), 9–13, 20–23; and Víctor M. Castillo Farreras, "Estudio preliminar," in Domingo Chimalpahin Cuauhtlehuanitzin, *Primer amoxtli libro: 3a relación de las Différentes histoires originales*, edited by V. M. Castillo Farreras (Mexico: Universidad Nacional Autónoma de México, 1997), v–xxi.

52. Paintings and writings on which Chimalpahin based his work were papers that he started gathering from his ancestors at least since 1606. His father had inherited some from Domingo Hernández Ayopochtzin, a noble of the local ruling lineage; others were given to him by different elders. Chimalpahin, *Las ocho relaciones*, 2:303–49.

53. Rendón, "Introduction to Domingo Chimalpahin Cuauhtlehuanitzin," 33–34.

54. Unlike Tezozómoc or Chimalpahin, who had inherited oral narratives and pictorial documents containing the historical discourse of their communities, Cristóbal del Castillo, being a commoner, did not have access to pictographic materials, which he was unable to read or interpret anyway. Navarrete, introduction, 67–68.

55. Ibid., 13–14, 18–19, 33–34, 88–100.

56. Náhuatl terms coined by missionaries to explain Christian concepts to the natives are *Tlacatecólotl* (demon) for the Mexica god Tetzauhtéotl, *Iztlacateteo* (false deities) for other people's gods, and *Tlaneltoquiliztli* (true faith) for Christianity (ibid., 93–94).

57. Both *Anales de Tlatelolco* manuscripts are preserved in the National Library of France. For a brief discussion of their authorship, content, and modern editions, see the introduction by Rafael Tena to *Anales de Tlatelolco*, paleography and translation by R. Tena (Mexico: Consejo Nacional para la Cultura y las Artes, 2004), 11–18.

58. Published in Ángel M. Garibay, ed., *Teogonía e historia de los mexicanos: tres opúsculos del siglo XVI* (Mexico: Porrúa, 1965), 23–66.

59. Ibid., 10–13.

60. Georges Baudot, *Utopía e historia en México: los primeros cronistas de la civilización mexicana (1520–1569)*, translated by V. González Loscertales (Madrid: Espasa Calpe, 1983), 196–219.

61. Ibid., 74–76.

62. *Histoire du Mechique* is contained in a manuscript written by Andrés Thevet on sixteenth century paper and preserved in the National Library of France. I use the standard Spanish translation by Ramón Rosales Mungía that Garibay published in *Teogonía e historia*, 91–120.

63. Ibid., 14–16.

64. Martínez Marín, "Historiografía," 127.

65. I use the 1945 translation by Primo Feliciano Velázquez, *Códice Chimalpopoca: anales de Cuauhtitlán y Leyenda de los soles*, prologue and translation from Náhuatl by P. F. Velázquez (Mexico: Universidad Nacional Autónoma de México, 1992).

66. Antonio Rubial, "Estudio preliminar," in Gerónimo de Mendieta, *Historia eclesiástica*, 46–47.

67. The awkward correspondences observed in Motolinía's *Memoriales* and *Historia de los indios de la Nueva España*, the few blatant errors that the *Historia* makes regarding Náhuatl language and culture, and the multiple references other sources make to a third manuscript by Motolinía have led scholars to presume that both derive from that manuscript, now lost. However, while they consider the *Memoriales* an incomplete copy of the lost piece, made by Motolinía himself and finished in 1541 (though supplemented later), they believe that the *Historia* is a summary made in Spain by someone else around 1565. For a discussion of this issue see Edmundo O'Gorman, "Estudio crítico," in Motolinía, *Historia*, edited by E. O'Gorman (Mexico: Porrúa, 1969).

68. Thomas Barfield, *The Dictionary of Anthropology* (Oxford: Blackwell, 1997), 152.

69. Frederick Barth, introduction to *Ethnic Groups and Boundaries: The Social Organization of Culture Difference* (Boston: Little, Brown, 1969), 14; Jonathan Okamura, "Situational Ethnicity," *Ethnic and Racial Studies* 4 (1981): 452–63; Marcus Banks, *Ethnicity: Anthropological Constructions* (London: Routledge, 1996), 11–48; Charles F. Keyes, "Towards a New Formulation of the Concept of Ethnic Group," *Ethnicity* 3 (1976): 202–13; G. Carter Bentley, "Ethnicity and Practice," *Comparative Studies in Society and History* 29 (January 1987): 24–55; Kevin A. Yelvington, "Ethnicity as Practice? A Comment on Bentley," *Comparative Studies in Society and History* 33, no. 1 (1991): 168.

70. López Austin and López Luján, *Mito y realidad*, 40–45.

71. López Austin, *Tamoanchan*, 38.

72. Reyes García and Güemes, "La zona del altiplano," 233; Obregón Rodríguez, "La zona del altiplano," 267; López Austin and López Luján, *El pasado*, 187–88.

73. Some scholars assert that the altepetl was also the basic unit of self-definition and affiliation: Ángel M. Garibay, "Relaciones internacionales en los pueblos de la meseta del Anahuac," *Estudios de Cultura Náhuatl* 3 (1962): 8; Castillo Farreras, *Estructura económica*, 58; Leibsohn, "Primers for Memory," 162; Carrasco, "La sociedad mexicana," 205; and "La triple alianza," in Lombardo and Nalda, eds., *Temas mesoamericanos*, 167; James Lockhart, "Postconquest Nahua Society and Concepts Viewed through Nahuatl Writings," *Estudios de Cultura Náhuatl* 20 (1990): 91–116; and *Nahuas*, 14. Others, like López Austin and Castillo Farreras, attribute this function to the calpulli.

74. Carrasco, "La sociedad mexicana," 205; Carmack, Gasco, and Gossen, *Legacy*, 81–82; Obregón Rodríguez, "La zona del altiplano," 283; Serge Gruzinski, *El poder sin límites: cuatro respuestas indígenas a la dominación española* (Mexico: Instituto Nacional de Antropología e Historia, 1989), 13–14; Lockhart, "Postconquest Nahua Society," 99–100; Hodge, "Land and Lordship," 12–13.

75. Carrasco, "La sociedad mexicana," 205–206; Gruzinski, *El poder sin límites*, 13–14.

76. Lockhart, "Postconquest Nahua Society," 99–100; and *Nahuas*, 14–20.

77. Carrasco, "La sociedad mexicana," 190–91, 207.

78. Castillo Farreras, *Estructura económica*; and Alfredo López Austin, "Organización política en el altiplano central de México durante el posclásico," in Monjarás Ruiz, Pérez Rocha, and Brambila, eds., *Mesoamérica y el centro*, 197–234.

79. Pedro Carrasco, "Peoples"; and "La organización social de los nahuas en la época prehispánica," in C. García Mora, ed., *La antropología en México: panorama histórico* (Mexico: Instituto Nacional de Antropología e Historia, 1988), 3:465–531; Lockhart, *Nahuas*, 16–20.

80. Lockhart, *Nahuas*, 15.

81. Stanley J. Tambiah, "A Reformulation of Geertz's Conception of the Theatre State," in S. J. Tambiah, ed., *Culture, Thought, and Social Action: An Anthropological Perspective* (Cambridge, Mass.: Harvard University Press, 1985), 321–24.

82. López Austin, "El texto sahaguntino," 324; Obregón Rodríguez, "La zona del altiplano," 282–83.

83. Obregón Rodríguez, "La zona del altiplano," 282–84; Bernal, "Formación y desarrollo," 150; Carrasco, "La sociedad mexicana," 174; Castillo Farreras, *Estructura económica*, 29.

84. Likewise, Clifford Geertz, *Negara: The Theatre State in Nineteenth-Century Bali* (Princeton, N.J.: Princeton University Press, 1980); and Shelly Errington, *Meaning and Power in a Southeast Asian Realm* (Princeton, N.J.: Princeton University Press, 1989), show that the control of people is the key to power in Southeast Asia.

85. Carrasco, "La sociedad mexicana," 187–89; Castillo Farreras, *Estructura económica*, 90–98, 132.

86. See, for example, Eric R. Wolf, "Closed Corporate Peasant Communities in Mesoamerica and Central Java," *Southwestern Journal of Anthropology* 13 (1957): 1–181; Jean Chesnaux et al., eds., *El modo de producción asiático* (Mexico: Grijalbo, 1969); Roger Bartra, *El modo de producción asiático* (Mexico: Era, 1975); Carrasco; "La organización social." Most of these works only touched on these similarities indirectly through the application of the Asiatic mode of production model. Although modeling and

comparison in the field of Native American studies at the close of the 1960s gave way to new perspectives seeking a deeper understanding of local forms of organization, oriental despotism continued to be discussed in relation to Mesoamerica and the Andes at least until the mid-1980s. George A. Collier, "In the Shadow of Empire: New Directions in Mesoamerican and Andean Ethnohistory," in G. A. Collier, R. I. Rosaldo, and J. D. Wirth, eds., *The Inca and Aztec States, 1400–1800: Anthropology and History* (New York: Academic Press, 1982), 1–8.

87. "They also said that hills . . . are filled with water, and they are made of earth on the outside. . . . For this reason they took to calling the towns where people live *altépetl*, meaning water hill, or hill filled with water." Sahagún, *Historia general*, vol. 2, bk. 11, chap. 12, parag. 1, p. 800.

88. Lockhart, *Nahuas*, 15.

89. José de Acosta, *Historia natural y moral de las Indias* [1590], prologue and appendix by E. O'Gorman (Mexico: Fondo de Cultura Económica, 1962), 320. Emphasis mine.

90. Diego Durán, *Historia de las Indias de Nueva España e islas de la tierra firme* [ca. 1579–81], prologue and notes by A. M. Garibay (Mexico: Porrúa, 1967), 2:18.

91. Ibid., 21. Emphasis mine.

92. Sahagún, *Historia general*, 2:671–76.

93. *Relación de la genealogía y linaje de los señores que han señoreado esta tierra de la Nueva España, después que se acuerdan haber gentes en estas partes* [ca. 1530–32], in *Relaciones de la Nueva España*, edited by Germán Vázquez (Madrid: Historia 16, 1990), 105–12; *Origen de los mexicanos* [ca. 1530–32], ibid., 131–39.

94. Motolinía, *Memoriales*, 126–29. The corresponding passage in Motolinía, *Historia*, 5–6, mentions seven brothers leading but only specifies the places that six of them populated. This version of the ancient settling of Central Mexico is substantially different from that included at the beginning of his *Memoriales*, cited in chapter 2. Contradictions of this kind are common in many colonial chronicles. Some stem from the fact that the authors are compiling information from different local historical traditions which, as stated before, were exclusivist in character; others are erroneous interpretations made by Spaniards of misunderstood native realities.

95. The original Náhuatl text says: "*ynan yta itzonteco mochiuhtica ynmochi yx yxquich yc nohuian altepetl yn yancuic Nueva España.*" Translated into Spanish by Adrián León as: "*madre, padre, cabeza que se está haciendo de todos cada uno de los* poblados *de todos lados de la reciente Nueva España.*" Alvarado Tezozómoc, *Crónica mexicáyotl*, 4. Emphasis mine.

96. Ibid., 6, 11, 21, 29, 33, 35.

97. Lockhart, *Nahuas*, 14.

98. Chiconcalpoltin, "the seven calpolli," from *ca* (indicative particle) + *chicome* (seven) + *calpolli*.

99. Alvarado Tezozómoc, *Crónica mexicáyotl*, 13, 15, 16, 24, 34.

100. Ibid., 13, 26, 32, 74.

101. *Histoire mexicaine.*

102. García Icazbalceta, *Nueva colección de documentos*, 3:263.

103. 1111 according to Berdan, *Aztecs*, 26.

104. Chimalpahin, *Las ocho relaciones*, 1:85, 179 (1064), 99 (1116), 191 (1168). The correlation between indigenous recorded dates and the Christian calendar is problematic. Chronological disparity between sources has been attributed to the simultaneous

use of different calendars in Mesoamerica—ten to thirteen in the basin of Mexico alone, according to Alfonso Caso, *Los calendarios prehispánicos* (Mexico: Universidad Nacional Autónoma de México, 1967); Wigberto Jiménez Moreno, "Diferente principio del año entre diversos pueblos y sus consecuencias para la cronología prehispánica," *El México Antiguo* 9 (1961): 146; and Paul Kirchhoff, "Calendarios tenochca, tlatelolca y otros," *Revista Mexicana de Estudios Antropológicos* 14, nos. 1–2 (1954–55): 257–67—but also to the chronological uncertainty structurally ingrained in the time-reckoning system they shared. The system combined two independent but interlocking cycles: A solar calendar (*xíhuitl*) ordering seasonal activities and the most important religious feasts, divided in eighteen 20-day units (months) to which five extra days (*nemontemi*) were added to make up a cycle of 365 days; and a divinatory almanac (*tonalpohualli*) combining 13 numerical coefficients and 20 signs to create a sequence of 260 different day-names. See Joyce Marcus, *Mesoamerican Writing Systems: Propaganda, Myth, and History in Four Ancient Civilizations* (Princeton, N.J.: Princeton University Press, 1992), 95–100. Built-in imprecision in the system resulted from the fact that each day of the *xíhuitl* was called by the name it had in the *tonalpohualli*, so in any given sequence of successive solar years the same day-name was repeated; for instance, on the first and 261st days of the first year, then on the 156th day of the second year, and so on. Moreover, solar years were named after the day on which they began, but for arithmetic reasons only four *tonalpohualli* day-signs were candidates to occupy this "year-bearer" position, succeeding each other in the order 1 Tochtli, 2 Acatl, 3 Tecpatl, 4 Calli, 5 Tochtli, 6 Acatl, etc., and restarting the cycle every 52 years, equivalent to 73 rounds of the 260-day cycle. The New Fire ceremony that marked the end/beginning of every "Year Binding" (52-year cycle) was used as a time marker in most indigenous historical records. This dating system is suited only to distinguish years within a short time-scale because the sequence of available year names is repeated identically every 52 years, and no system existed counting consecutively from a fixed zero point to label years with identical names that pertained to different revolutions of the cycle. See Nicholson, "Pre-Hispanic Central Mexican Historiography," 44–45; Duverger, *L'origine*, 40–47; Brotherston, *Painted Books*, 13–14; Hanns J. Prem, "The Chronological Dilemma," in J. Durand-Forest, ed., *The Native Sources and the History of the Valley of Mexico: Proceedings / 44th International Congress of Americanists* (Oxford: British Archaeological Reports, 1984), 6–7. Additional difficulties, Duverger and Brotherston observe, derive from the fact that in working out Christian date correlates for the events they wrote about, Spaniards took no account of the fact that different communities did not necessarily share the initial point from which to count successive years, so a year 1 Acatl of the Mexica-Tenochca calendar could well correspond to a year 12 Acatl in other calendars (e.g., Tilantongo), as was the case for the Christian year 1519.

105. Berdan and Anawalt, *Essential Codex Mendoza*, 6.

106. E.g., Fernando Alvarado Tezozómoc, *Crónica mexicana, escrita por Hernando Alvarado Tezozómoc hacia el año de 1598, anotada por Orozco y Berra y precedida por el Códice Ramírez, manuscrito del siglo XVI intitulado: relación del origen de los indios que habitan esta Nueva España según sus historias* (Mexico: Porrúa, 1980), 223; and *Crónica mexicáyotl*, 15. Chimalpahin, *Las ocho relaciones*, 1:65, 91, 179; *Histoire mexicaine*, 66.

107. Chimalpahin, *Las ocho relaciones*, 1:85.

108. Ibid., 85, 93; Castillo, *Historia de la venida*, 115–17; Alvarado Tezozómoc, *Crónica mexicáyotl*, 15; and *Crónica mexicana*, 223.

109. Alvarado Tezozómoc, *Crónica mexicana*, 223; Durán, *Historia de las Indias*, 2:28.

110. This is indicated in *Códice Boturini* and *Codex Mexicanus* according to Eduard Seler, "¿Dónde se encontraba Aztlan, la patria (original) de los aztecas?" in Monjarás Ruiz, Pérez Rocha, and Brambila, eds., *Mesoamérica y el centro*, 327–28.

111. Alvarado Tezozómoc, *Crónica mexicana*, 223.

112. Duverger, *L'origine*, 77–79.

113. Alvarado Tezozómoc, *Crónica mexicáyotl*, 15; *Códice Ramírez*, in Alvarado Tezozómoc, *Crónica mexicana*, 4.

114. Fernando de Alva Ixtlilxóchitl, *Obras históricas*, 2:28; Durán, *Historia de las Indias*, 2:18; *Histoire du Mechique*, in Garibay, *Teogonía e historia*, 96.

115. Seler, "¿Dónde se encontraba Aztlan?" 326.

116. Michel Graulich, "Las peregrinaciones aztecas y el ciclo de Mixcóatl," *Estudios de Cultura Náhuatl* 2 (1974): 337–44; and "Aspects mythiques des pérégrinations mexicas," in Durand-Forest, *Native Sources*, 26. Other authors with similar perspectives are Daniel Brinton, *American Hero-Myths: A Study in the Native Religions of the Western Continent* (Philadelphia: H. C. Watts, 1882); Barbara Price, "The Truth Is Not in Accounts but in Account Books: On the Epistemological Status of History," in E. B. Ross, *Beyond the Myth of Culture: Essays in Cultural Materialism* (New York: Academic Press, 1980), 155–80; Florescano, "Mito e historia"; Duverger, *L'origine*; Nigel Davies, "The Aztec Concept of History: Teotihuacan and Tula," in Durand-Forest, ed., *Native Sources*, 207–14.

117. Wigberto Jiménez Moreno, "La migración mexica," in *Atti del XL Congresso Internazionale degli Americanisti* (Rome-Geneva, September 1972), 1:169–70. Geneva, Switzerland: Tilgher, 1973).

118. Paul Kirchhoff, "¿Se puede localizar Aztlan?" in *Anuario de Historia* (Mexico: Universidad Nacional Autónoma de México, 1961), 64–67; and "El imperio tolteca y su caída," in Monjarás Ruiz, Pérez Rocha, and Brambila, eds., *Mesoamérica y el centro*, 258–59. A list of the principal locations scholars have proposed comes in Gutierre Tibón, *Historia del nombre y de la fundación de México* (Mexico: Fondo de Cultura Económica, 1980), 355.

119. Miguel Acosta Saignes, "Migraciones de los mexica," *Memorias de la Academia Mexicana de la Historia* 5, no. 2 (1946): 34–40.

120. Jiménez Moreno, "La migración"; Kirchhoff, "¿Se puede localizar Aztlan?" 59; Martínez Marín, "La cultura de los mexicas"; and "Las migraciones." For detailed discussions of these interpretive positions see Julio César Olivé Negrete, "Retos del patrimonio cultural: Aztlan," in B. Barba de Piña Chan, ed., *Estudios del México antiguo* (Mexico: Instituto Nacional de Antropología e Historia, 1996), 109–17; and Navarrete, "Las fuentes."

121. Alvarado Tezozómoc, *Crónica mexicáyotl*, 15–16; *Histoire du Mechique*, 96.

122. "Historia de los mexicanos por sus pinturas," in Garibay, *Teogonía e historia*, 39.

123. Castillo, *Historia de la venida*, 115–19.

124. *Códice Boturini, o, Tira de la peregrinación mexica* (Mexico: Librería Anticuaria G. M. Echániz, 1944); *Codex Mexicanus*; *Mapa Sigüenza*, in J. B. Glass, ed., *Catálogo de la colección de códices* (Mexico: Instituto Nacional de Antropología e Historia, 1964), 54–55; Chimalpahin, *Las ocho relaciones*, 1:85–59, 179–81; Torquemada, *Monarquía indiana*, 1:112. Sources like *Historia de Tlatelolco* and *Anales de Cuauhtitlán* adduce no reason for the departure from Aztlan. See *Anales de Tlatelolco: unos anales históricos de la nación mexicana y Códice de Tlatelolco, con un resumen de los anales y una interpretación del códice por Robert H. Barlow* [1528–32], notes and translation by H. Berlin (Mexico: Antigua Librería Robredo de José Porrúa e Hijos, 1948); and *Códice Chimalpopoca*.

125. *Histoire mexicaine; Códice Boturini; Codex Aubin*, in *Historia de la nación mexicana: reproducción a todo color del Códice de 1576 (Códice Aubin)*, edited and translated from Náhuatl by C. Dibble (Madrid: José Porrúa Turranzas, 1963). The episode is very obscure in Alvarado Tezozómoc, *Crónica mexicáyotl*, 19–20, because it mentions the tree and its rupture but omits the eight calpoltin from Colhuacan and the god's instruction to leave them behind. Thus it is only by consulting these codices and other sources like Chimalpahin, *Las ocho relaciones*, 1:185–87, that it becomes clear. See Edward E. Calneck, "The Analysis of Prehispanic Central Mexican Historical Texts," *Estudios de Cultura Náhuatl* 13 (1978): 246–47.

126. *Histoire mexicaine*, 70–71; *Codex Boturini*, plate 4; Alvarado Tezozómoc, *Crónica mexicáyotl*, 21–23; Chimalpahin, *Las ocho relaciones*, 1:187.

127. López Austin, *Hombre-dios*, 93–95; and *Los mitos del tlacuache*, 96.

128. Durán, *Historia de las Indias*, 2:31–34; Alvarado Tezozómoc, *Crónica mexicáyotl*, 30–36; and *Crónica mexicana*, 227–29; Torquemada, *Monarquía indiana*, 1:118–19.

129. *Anales de Tlatelolco*, 32; *Origen de los mexicanos* [ca. 1530–32], in *Relaciones de la Nueva España*, edited by Germán Vázquez (Madrid: Historia 16, 1990), 127–58.

130. "Historia de los mexicanos por sus pinturas," 43–44.

131. Sahagún, *Historia general*, 1:202–204.

132. *Relación de la genealogía*, in García Icazbalceta, ed., *Nueva colección de documentos*, 3:266.

133. Sahagún, *Historia general*, 1:208.

134. Ibid., 2:650–54.

135. Ibid., 1:209–18.

136. *Relación de la genealogía*, in García Icazbalceta, ed., *Nueva colección de documentos*, 3:263–67.

137. Noguez, "La zona del altiplano," 190–97, 201–204; López Austin and López Luján, *El pasado*, 182–87; Bernal, "Formación y desarrollo," 147.

138. Rudolf Zantwijk, "Quetzalcoatl y Huemac, mito y realidad azteca," in Magaña and Mason, eds., *Myth and the Imaginary*, 321–37.

139. *Historia Tolteca-Chichimeca*; and *Mapa de Cuauhtinchan no. 2*, in Yoneda, *Los mapas de Cuauhtinchan*, recount how these Tolteca-Chichimecas sought the alliance of seven Chichimeca groups from Chicomoztoc to expel the Olmeca-Xicallanca.

140. Noguez, "La zona del altiplano," 200–201; Carrasco, "Peoples," 459; María Esther Caamaño Panzi, "La importancia del linaje de Culhuacan en la formación de señoríos del posclásico en la cuenca de México," in R. Brambila and M. E. Caamaño Panzi, eds., *Apuntes de etnohistoria* (Mexico: Instituto Nacional de Antropología e Historia, 1992), 2:138; Reyes García and Güemes, "La zona del altiplano," 245–46; Brotherston, *Painted Books*, 73–74.

141. *Relación de la genealogía*, in *Relaciones de la Nueva España*, 117–19; *Origen de los mexicanos*, ibid., 131–47; *Anales de Cuauhtitlán*, in *Códice Chimalpopoca*, 14–17; Alva Ixtlilxóchitl, *Obras históricas*, 2:274–88.

142. Acosta, *Historia natural y moral*, 320; Motolinía, *Historia*, 2–3.

143. Carrasco, "Peoples," 465; Caamaño Panzi, "La importancia del linaje," 134; Reyes García and Güemes, "La zona del altiplano," 247–51.

144. *Anales de Cuauhtitlán*, 37; Alva Ixtlilxóchitl, *Obras históricas* 1:284, 342–47.

145. Garibay, "Relaciones internacionales," 9–10, 13; Obregón Rodríguez, "La zona del altiplano," 273–75, 281.

146. Durán, *Historia de las Indias*, 2:40; Alvarado Tezozómoc, *Crónica mexicáyotl*, 50–51.

147. The sacrificial victim was a Culhua maiden ("Historia de los mexicanos por sus pinturas," 54), sometimes the daughter of the Culhua ruler himself (Alvarado Tezozómoc, *Crónica mexicáyotl*, 54–56; Durán, *Historia de las Indias*, 2:41). Other sources assert the victims were Xochimilca captives: *Codex Aubin*, 40–41; Torquemada, *Monarquía indiana*, 1:131–32; *Anales de Tlatelolco*, 39–41.

148. Mexica sources claim the islet was uninhabited but excavations at the Great Temple of Tenochtitlan demonstrated otherwise (1975–79). Remains that unequivocally correspond to the period a.d. 900–1200 lie beneath the level of remains dated after 1200 that correspond to the Mexica occupation of the site, i.e., the city of Tenochtitlan. Duverger, *L'origine*, 350–51.

149. The Teocalli de la Guerra Sagrada is preserved in the Museo de Antropología in Mexico City.

150. This reading is based in Berdan and Anawalt, *Essential Codex Mendoza*, 4–5. Written records of the episode include Durán, *Historia de las Indias*, 2:44; Chimalpahin, *Las ocho relaciones*, 1:213–15; and Alvarado Tezozómoc, *Crónica mexicáyotl*, 62–68.

151. Robertson, *Mexican Manuscript Painting*, 98.

152. The Mexicas soon divided themselves into Mexica-Tenochcas and Mexica-Tlatelolcas, due to an early conflict over land that provoked a dissident faction to settle down separately on the adjacent islet of Tlatelolco.

153. Johanna Broda, "Consideraciones sobre historiografía e ideología mexicas: Las crónicas indígenas y el estudio de los ritos y sacrificios." *Estudios de Cultura Náhuatl* 13 (1978): 99; Navarrete, introduction, 70.

154. Obregón Rodríguez, "La zona del altiplano," 278.

155. Alva Ixtlilxóchitl, *Obras históricas*, 1:347.

156. Carrasco, "Peoples," 465; and "La sociedad mexicana," 174–75, 213–15, 218–21; Obregón Rodríguez, "La zona del altiplano," 278–82; Castillo Farreras, *Estructura económica*, 29; López Austin and López Luján, *El pasado*, 213.

157. Nigel Davies, *Los señoríos independientes del imperio azteca* (Mexico: Instituto Nacional de Antropología e Historia, 1968), 9–13; Carmack, Gasco, and Gossen, *Legacy*, 87–88.

Chapter 6. Your Past Is Our Future

1. See, for example, plates 10 and 13 of Diego Muñoz Camargo, "Descripción de la ciudad y provincia de Tlaxcala de la Nueva España e Indias del mar océano para el buen gobierno y ennoblecimie[nt]o dellas, mandada hacer por la S.C.R.M. del rey Don Felipe, nuestro señor" [1584–85], in R. Acuña, ed., *Relaciones geográficas del siglo XVI*, vol. 4, *Tlaxcala* (Mexico: Universidad Nacional Autónoma de México, Instituto de Investigaciones Antropológicas, 1984). They show the "burning and conflagration of the idolatrous temples of the province of Tlaxcala," and the "conflagration of all the clothes and books and attire of the idolatrous priests," respectively. Also *Relación de la genealogía*, in *Relaciones de la Nueva España*, 105, comments regretfully on this destruction: "And because we censure them and have burned their books, many things have now been difficult for us to know in truth; and if some books have survived they hide them secretly and do not dare show them to us."

2. See chapter 5, notes 89 and 114.

3. Obregón, *Historia de los descubrimientos*, 10.

4. Villagrá, *Historia*, edited by M. Junquera, 84–87.

5. Obregón, *Historia de los descubrimientos*, 14–15.

6. Literature quoted and discussed at length in chapter 4.

7. *Relación de la genealogía*, in *Relaciones de la Nueva España*, 106–107, 112; *Origen de los mexicanos*, ibid., 131–47.

8. Quote from "Origen de los mexicanos," in *Relaciones de la Nueva España*, 133. The next page of the document says the Mexicas were not originally of the same stock as the Culhuas because the former came from another place called Aztlá.

9. When Motolinía described for the king the different "books" that the Mexican Indians had, he remarked that only the annals were trustworthy, confident that their content qualified as legitimate, true knowledge. The others, he said, were the devil's work. Motolinía, *Memoriales*, 121.

10. Villagrá, *Historia*, edited by M. Junquera, 75.

11. Ibid., 74–87.

12. Ibid., 82–83.

13. *Códice Boturini* plate III; Alvarado Tezozómoc, *Crónica mexicáyotl*, 19–20.

14. Villagrá, *Historia*, edited by M. Junquera, 83–84.

15. Chimalpahin, "Memorial breve acerca de la fundación de la ciudad de Colhuacan," in *Las ocho relaciones*, 1:85.

16. Chimalpahin, ibid., 1:85–87.

17. Robert H. Barlow, commentary in *Codex Azcatitlan*, 62–66.

18. Durán, *Historia de las Indias*, 2:31–34; Alvarado Tezozómoc, *Crónica mexicáyotl*, 30–36; and *Crónica mexicana*, 227–29; Torquemada, *Monarquía indiana*, 1:118–19.

19. "Historia de los mexicanos por sus pinturas," 43–44; Sahagún, *Historia general*, 300–302.

20. For the Oñate family, see Donald Chipman, "The Oñate-Moctezuma-Zaldívar Families of Northern New Spain," New Mexico Historical Review 52, no. 4 (1977): 297–310.

21. Villagrá, *Historia*, edited by M. Junquera, 84–85. The large pieces of raw iron that are the object of Villagrá's speculation in this passage are the fragments of a meteorite. They were obviously an outstanding landmark at the time when Oñate led his army to Nuevo México. They still exist today, though not in the place where Villagrá saw them, that is, where the meteorite hit the ground, as they were removed for study in modern times (personal communication, Stephen Lekson, Curator of Anthropology, Museum of Natural History, University of Colorado, 2004).

22. Villagrá, *Historia*, edited by M. Junquera, 86–87.

23. Official documents concerning this petition are reproduced in Villagrá, *Historia*, edited by Francisco del Paso y Troncoso, 2:5–81.

24. Gordon Brotherston and Ana Gallegos, "El Lienzo de Tlaxcala y el Manuscrito de Glasgow (Hunter 242)," *Estudios de Cultura Náhuatl* 20 (1990): 117–40.

25. Manuscript number 242 of the Hunter Collection of the University of Glasgow. Published by René Acuña as Muñoz Camargo, "Descripción de la ciudad y provincia de Tlaxcala," in his two-volume edition of the *Relaciones geográficas del siglo XVI: Tlaxcala*.

26. Brotherston and Gallegos, "El Lienzo de Tlaxcala," 117–18.

27. Muñoz Camargo, "Descripción de la ciudad y provincia de Tlaxcala," [section 2], "Pinturas," 156.

28. Brotherston and Gallegos, "El Lienzo de Tlaxcala," 134–35.

29. Brotherston, *Painted Books*, 74.

30. *Códice de Tlatelolco*, preliminary study by P. Valle (Mexico: Instituto Nacional de Antropología e Historia, Benemérita Universidad de Puebla, 1994), plate 1. For a detailed analysis of this plate see the preliminary study by Perla Valle. See also Xavier Noguez, "El *Códice de Tlatelolco*: Una nueva cronología," in X. Noguez and S. G. Wood, eds., *De tlacuilos y escribanos* (Mexico: El Colegio de Michoacán, 1998), 15–32; and "Los códices de tradición náhuatl del centro de México en la etapa colonial," in C .A. Hoffmann, P. Schmidt, and X. Noguez, eds., *Libros y escritura de tradición indígena* (Mexico: El Colegio Mexiquense, Universidad Católica de Eichstätt, 2002), 159–83.

31. Francisco Acauzitli, "Relación sobre la guerra del Mixtón," AGN, Historia, vol. 4, no. 5, fols. 483–508.

32. Obregón, *Historia de los descubrimientos*, 39–41.

33. AGI, Patronato 21, no. 4, R. 3.

34. AGI, Patronato 20, no. 5, R. 16.

35. Jacinto de San Francisco to the king, Mexico, July 20, 1561. In García Icazbalceta, *Colección de documentos para la historia de México*, 2:241–43.

36. The document is published in *CDIAO*, 15:535–40, under the title "Toma de posesión de la Laguna de Nuevo México. Testimonio dado por el escribano Pedro de Valverde," November 8, 1568.

37. Jiménez Moreno, *Estudios*, 56–61; Ortega Noriega, *Un ensayo*, 43.

38. Durán, *Historia de las Indias*, 2:215–22.

39. Kirchhoff, *¿Se puede localizar Aztlan?*, 59.

40. This chart is preserved in the Bavarian State Library: "Terra Antipodv̆ Regis Castele inveta: a Xp̃oforo Colv̆bo: ian vĕsi," chart 12, *Portulanatlas Alte Welt und Terra Nova* by Fernão Vaz Dourado, 1580.

41. Translated for me into Spanish by Josefina Flores Estrella. English translation mine.

42. Chart 16, atlas attributed to Fernão Vaz Dourado, ca. 1576. Published by Armando Cortesão, ed., *Portugaliae Monumenta Cartographica* (Lisbon: Comissão para as Comemorações do V Centenário da Morte do Infante D. Henrique, 1960), 3:29–32. Available online at National Digital Library of Portugal.

43. "Toma de posesion de la Laguna de Nuevo México," Testimonio dado por el escribano Pedro de Valverde, November 8, 1568, *CDIAO*, 15:535–40.

44. *Memorial de los Indios de Nombre de Dios*, in Barlow and Smisor, *Nombre de Dios*, 14–24.

45. Friar Pedro de Espinareda to Orozco, judge of the Audiencia de Guadalajara, Nombre de Dios, January 20, 1567. AGI, Audiencia de Guadalajara, 51.

46. Obregón, *Historia de los descubrimientos*, 39–41.

47. See chapter 5.

48. Durán, *Historia de las Indias*, 2:44.

49. Obregón, *Historia de los descubrimientos*; Hernando Barrando, "Relación breve y berdadera," AGI, Patronato 22, R. 4, 1149–50.

50. Hernando Barrando, "Relación breve y berdadera," AGI, Patronato 22, R. 4, 1149–50.

51. Ibid.

52. Obregón, *Historia de los descubrimientos*, 251–53.

53. For example, Alvarado Tezozómoc, *Crónica Mexicáyotl*.
54. Personal communication, Federico Navarrete and José Rubén Romero.
55. Carlos Fernández Gómez, *Vocabulario de Cervantes* (Madrid: Real Academia Española, 1962, 716–17.
56. Navarrete, introduction, 71; Navarrete, *Los orígenes*, 12, 49–51.
57. Warriors from Tlalmanalco fighting on the Spanish side in the Mixtón War were led by their own cacique, Francisco Acauzitli (see his "Relación sobre la guerra del Mixtón"). Tlatelolca troops who went along with Vázquez de Coronado to Cíbola were commanded by the governor of Tlatelolco, Don Alonso Cuauhnochtli, and perhaps his successor Martín Cuauhtzin Tlacateccatl. Noguez, "El *Códice de Tlatelolco*," 21. See also Oudijk and Restall, "Mesoamerican Conquistadors," 42–57.
58. López Austin, "El texto sahaguntino," 327–30; and *Tamoanchan*, 48–51, 64–69.
59. Alva Ixtlilxóchitl, *Obras históricas*, 2:28.
60. *Relación de la genealogía*, in *Relaciones de la Nueva España*, 106–107, 112; *Origen de los mexicanos*, ibid., 131–47.
61. Hers, "Los chichimecas."
62. González de la Vara, "La rebelión," 24–25.
63. Peter Worsley, *The Trumpet Shall Sound: A Study of "Cargo" Cults in Melanesia* (New York: Schocken, 1968).
64. Norman Cohn, *The Pursuit of the Millennium: Revolutionary Messianism in the Middle Ages and its Bearing on Modern Totalitarian Movements*, 1957 (Oxford: Oxford University Press, 1970).
65. Ocaranza, *Establecimientos franciscanos*, 43.
66. Zárate Salmerón, "Relaciones de todas las cosas," 165, 190–94.
67. Taussig, *Mimesis and Alterity*, 64–65.
68. González de la Vara, "La rebelión," 26–29.

Conclusion

1. John H. Elliott, "Renaissance Europe and America: A Blunted Impact?" In F. Chiappelli, ed., *First Images of America: The Impact of the New World on the Old* (Berkeley and Los Angeles: University of California Press, 1976), 1:14–17, 21.
2. Schwartz, introduction, 2–3.
3. Bhabha, *Location*, 70.
4. Greenblatt, *Marvelous Possessions*, 7, 12–13.
5. McGrane, *Beyond Anthropology*, 7–26.
6. Mason, *Deconstructing America*, 21. Studies on the "implicit ethnographies" of Amerindian people had been done before the issue became an important question concerning Western constructions of the non-European world. Pioneering works were written by Miguel León Portilla, *La visión de los vencidos* [1959] (Mexico: Universidad Nacional Autónoma de México, 1984) and Nathan Wachtel, *The Vision of the Vanquished: The Spanish Conquest of Peru Through Indian Eyes, 1530–1570* (Sussex, U.K.: Harvester Press, 1977), who titled their respective books using the same expression alluding to conquered perceptions. León Portilla's book is a critical compilation of testimonies reflecting the indigenous view of the conquest of Mexico, whereas Wachtel's is a study on native perceptions of the Spanish conquest of the Andes.
7. John Comaroff and Jean Comaroff, *Of Revelation and Revolution*, 2:23, 25.

8. Ibid.
9. Bernand and Gruzinski, *De la idolatría*, 11–37, 40–56.
10. Greenblatt, *Marvelous Possessions*, 119–51.
11. For example, Said, *Orientalism*; James Clifford and George Marcus, eds., *Writing Culture: The Politics and Poetics of Ethnography* (Berkeley: University of California Press, 1986).
12. John Comaroff and Jean Comaroff, *Of Revelation and Revolution*, 2:24–25.
13. Jovita Baber, "Empire, Indians, and the Negotiation for the Status of City in Tlaxcala, 1521–1550." In E. Ruiz Medrano and S. Kellogg, eds., *Negotiation within Domination: New Spain's Indian Pueblos Confront the Spanish State* (Boulder: University Press of Colorado, 2010), 20–21.
14. See chapters 2 and 5.
15. Gordon Brotherston, "The Aztlan of the Codices, in Modern Mexican and Chicano Versions," *Indiana Journal of Hispanic Literatures* 12 (1998).
16. Comaroff and Comaroff, *Of Revelation and Revolution*, 2:19–29.
17. Bhabha, *Location*, 111–12, 116, 206–207.
18. Mignolo, "Signs and Their Transmission"; and *Darker Side*, 7.
19. Asad, *Genealogies of Religion*, 12–19.
20. Ortiz, *Cuban Counterpoint*, 97–103.
21. Goodman, *Ways of Worldmaking*, 7–17.

Bibliography

Archives

Archivo General de Indias, Seville, Spain (AGI)
Archivo General de la Nación, Mexico City, Mexico (AGN)
Biblioteca Nacional, Madrid, Spain (BNE)

Books and Articles

Abulafia, David. *The Discovery of Mankind: Atlantic Encounters in the Age of Columbus.* New Haven, Conn.: Yale University Press, 2008.
Acosta, José de. *Historia natural y moral de las Indias.* 1590. Prologue and appendix by Edmundo O'Gorman. Mexico: Fondo de Cultura Económica, 1962.
Acosta Saignes, Miguel. "Migraciones de los mexica." *Memorias de la Academia Mexicana de la Historia* 5, no. 2 (1946): 34–44.
Acuña, René, ed. *Relaciones geográficas del siglo XVI.* Vols. 4–5, *Tlaxcala.* Mexico: Universidad Nacional Autónoma de México, Instituto de Investigaciones Antropológicas, 1984.
———, ed. *Relaciones geográficas del siglo XVI.* Vol. 9, *Michoacán.* Mexico: Universidad Nacional Autónoma de México, Instituto de Investigaciones Antropológicas, 1987.
———, ed. *Relaciones geográficas del siglo XVI.* Vol. 10, *Nueva Galicia.* Mexico: Universidad Nacional Autónoma de México, Instituto de Investigaciones Antropológicas, 1988.
Aguilar, Francisco de. "Relación breve de la conquista de la Nueva España." ca. 1570. In Vázquez, *La conquista de Tenochtitlan,* 161–206.
Aguilar-Robledo, Miguel. "La territorialidad en el norte de Mesoamérica: el señorío de Oxitipa en el siglo XVI." *Tiempos de América: Revista de Historia, Cultura y Territorio,* no. 10 (2003). www.raco.cat/index.php/TiemposAmerica/article/view/105155.
Aguirre Beltrán, Gonzalo. *El proceso de aculturación en México.* Mexico: Universidad Iberoamericana, 1970.
Ainsa, Fernando. *De la edad de oro a El Dorado: génesis del discurso utópico americano.* Mexico: Fondo de Cultura Económica, 1992.
Aiton, Arthur S. "Coronado's First Report on the Government of New Galicia." *Hispanic American Historical Review* 19, no. 3 (August 1939): 307–309.
Alcedo, Antonio de. *Diccionario geográfico-histórico de las Indias Occidentales ó América. Es a saber: de los reinos del Perú, Nueva España, Tierra Firme, Chile y Nuevo Reino de Granada.* Vol. 3. Madrid: Imprenta de Benito Cano, 1786.

Alcina Franch, José. "Fuentes indígenas de México: ensayo de sistematización bibliográfica." *Revista de Indias* 6, nos. 61–62 (1955): 421–521.
Alegre, Francisco Javier. *Historia de la provincia de la compañía de Jesús en Nueva España*, edited by Ernest J. Burrus and Félix Zubillaga. ca. 1770. Vol. 1. Rome: Jesuit Historical Institute, 1956–60.
Alguns documentos do Archivo Nacional da Tarre do Tombo acerca das navegações e conquistas portuguezas publicados ao celebrarse a commemoração quadricentaria do descobrimento da America. Preface by Jose Ramos Coelho. Lisbon: Academia das Ciencias de Lisboa, 1892.
Altman, Ida. "Conquest, Coercion, and Collaboration: Indian Allies and the Campaigns in Nueva Galicia." In *Indian Conquistadors: Indigenous Allies in the Conquest of Mesoamerica*, edited by Laura Matthew and Michel R. Oudijk, 145–74. Norman: University of Oklahoma Press, 2007.
———. *The War for Mexico's West: Indians and Spaniards in New Galicia, 1524–1550*. Albuquerque: University of New Mexico Press, 2010.
Alva Ixtlilxóchitl, Fernando de. *Obras históricas. Incluyen el texto completo de las llamadas relaciones e historia de la nación chichimeca en una nueva versión establecida con el cotejo de los manuscritos más antiguos que se conocen*. ca. 1608–25. Edited by Edmundo O'Gorman. Mexico: Universidad Nacional Autónoma de México, Instituto de Investigaciones Históricas, 1985.
Alvar, Manuel. *Americanismos en la historia de Bernal Díaz del Castillo*. Madrid: Consejo Superior de Investigaciones Científicas, Revista de Filología Española, 1970.
Alvarado Tezozómoc, Fernando. *Crónica mexicana, escrita por Hernando Alvarado Tezozómoc hacia el año de 1598, anotada por Manuel Orozco y Berra y precedida por el Códice Ramírez, manuscrito del siglo XVI intitulado: Relación del origen de los indios que habitan esta Nueva España según sus historias*. 1598. Mexico: Editorial Porrúa, 1980.
———. *Crónica mexicáyotl*. ca. 1600–10. Introduction and translation from Náhuatl by Adrián León. Mexico: Universidad Nacional Autónoma de México, Instituto de Investigaciones Históricas, 1992.
Anales de Cuauhtitlán. See *Códice Chimalpopoca*.
Anales de Tlatelolco. Paleography and translation by Rafael Tena. Mexico: Consejo Nacional para la Cultura y las Artes, 2004.
Anales de Tlatelolco: unos anales históricos de la nación mexicana y Códice de Tlatelolco, con un resumen de los anales y una interpretación del códice por Robert H. Barlow. 1528–32. Notes and translation by Heinrich Berlin. Mexico: Antigua Librería Robredo de José Porrúa e Hijos, 1948.
Anderson, Benedict. *Imagined Communities: Reflections on the Origin and Spread of Nationalism*. London: Verso, 1983.
Anonymous. "Relación postrera de Sibola." In *Las siete ciudades de Cíbola: textos y testimonios sobre la expedición de Vázquez de Coronado*, edited by Carmen de Mora, 177–79. Seville: Alfar, 1992.
Arias, Santa, and Mariselle Meléndez. "Space and the Rhetorics of Power." In *Mapping Colonial Spanish America: Places and Commonplaces of Identity, Culture, and Experience*, edited by Santa Arias and Mariselle Meléndez, 14–16. Lewisbury, Penn.: Bucknell University, 2002.
Armillas, Pedro. "The Arid Frontier of Mexican Civilization." *Transactions of the New York Academy of Sciences*, 2nd ser., 31, no. 6 (1969): 697–704.

———. "Condiciones ambientales y movimientos de pueblos en la frontera septentrional de Mesoamérica." In *Homenaje a Fernando Márquez Miranda*, 62–82. Madrid: Universidad de Madrid, Seminario de Estudios Americanistas, 1964.

———. "Northern Mesoamerica." In *Prehistoric Man in the New World*, edited by J. D. Jennings and E. Norbeck, 291–329. Chicago: University of Chicago Press, 1964.

Arregui, Domingo Lázaro de. *Descripción de la Nueva Galicia*. 1621. Introduction by François Chevalier. Guadalajara: Gobierno del Estado de Jalisco, 1980.

Asad, Talal. Introduction to *Anthropology and the Colonial Encounter*, 9–19. London: Ithaca Press, 1973.

———. *Genealogies of Religion: Discipline and Reasons of Power in Christianity and Islam*. Baltimore, Md.: Johns Hopkins University Press, 1993.

Ascher, Marcia, and Robert Ascher. *Code of Quipu: A Study in Media, Mathematics, and Culture*. Ann Arbor: University of Michigan Press, 1981.

Aznárez, Carlos, and Néstor Norma, eds. *500 años después: ¿descubrimiento o genocidio?* Madrid: Nuer, 1992.

Baber, Jovita. "Empire, Indians, and the Negotiation for the Status of City in Tlaxcala, 1521–1550." In *Negotiation within Domination: New Spain's Indian Pueblos Confront the Spanish State*, edited by Ethelia Ruiz Medrano and Susan Kellogg, 19–44. Boulder: University Press of Colorado, 2010.

Bakhtin, Mikhail M. *The Dialogic Imagination: Four Essays*. Edited by Michael Holquist. Translated by Caryl Emerson and Michael Holquist. Austin: University of Texas Press, 1981.

Bancroft, Hubert H. *The Works of Hubert Howe Bancroft*. Vol. 17, *History of Arizona and New Mexico, 1530–1888*. San Francisco, Calif.: History Company, 1889.

Bandelier, Adolph. *Contributions to the History of the South Western Portion of the United States*. Cambridge: Cambridge University Press, 1890.

———. *The Discovery of New Mexico by the Franciscan Monk Friar Marcos de Niza in 1539*. Tucson: University of Arizona Press, 1981.

Banks, Marcus. *Ethnicity: Anthropological Constructions*. London: Routledge, 1996.

Barfield, Thomas. *The Dictionary of Anthropology*. Oxford, U.K.: Blackwell, 1997.

Barlow, Robert H. "La Crónica X: versiones coloniales de la historia de los mexica tenochca." *Revista Mexicana de Estudios Antropológicos* 7 (1945): 65–87.

Barlow, Robert H., and George T. Smisor, eds. *Nombre de Dios, Durango: Two Documents in Náhuatl Concerning Its Foundation. Memorial of the Indians Concerning Their Services, c. 1563. Agreement of the Mexicans and Michoacanos, 1585*. Sacramento, Calif.: House of Tlaloc, 1943.

Barth, Frederick. Introduction to *Ethnic Groups and Boundaries: The Social Organization of Culture Difference*, 1–38. Boston: Little, Brown, 1969.

Bartra, Roger. *El modo de producción asiático*. Mexico: Era, 1975.

———. *El salvaje en el espejo*. Mexico: Universidad Nacional Autónoma de México, Coordinación de Difusión Cultural, 1992.

Basso, Keith H. "History of Ethnological Research." In *Handbook of North American Indians*, vol. 9, *The Southwest*, edited by William C. Sturtevant, 14–21. Washington, D.C.: Smithsonian Institution, 1979.

Baudot, Georges. *Utopía e historia en México: los primeros cronistas de la civilización mexicana, 1520–1569*. 1977. Translated by. V. González Loscertales. Madrid: Espasa Calpe, 1983.

Beals, Ralph L. "Notes on Acculturation." In *Heritage of Conquest: The Ethnology of Middle America*, edited by Sol Tax, 225–32. Glencoe, Ill.: Free Press, 1952.
Beck, Warren. *New Mexico: A History of Four Centuries*. Norman: University of Oklahoma Press, 1969.
Benedict, Ruth. "Two Patterns of Indian Acculturation." *American Anthropologist*, n.s., 45 (April–June 1943): 207–12.
Benevolo, Leonardo. *The European City*. Translated by C. Ipsen. Oxford, U.K.: Blackwell, 1993.
Bentley, G. Carter. "Ethnicity and Practice." *Comparative Studies in Society and History* 29 (January 1987): 24–55.
Benz, Bruce F. "Maize in the Americas." In *Histories of Maize: Multidisciplinary Approaches to the Prehistory, Linguistics, Biogeography, Domestication, and Evolution of Maize*, edited by John E. Staller, Robert H. Tykot, and Bruce F. Benz, 9–18. Amsterdam: Elsevier Academic Press, 2006.
Berdan, Frances. *The Aztecs*. New York: Chelsea House, 1989.
———. "Economic Dimensions of Precious Metals, Stones, and Feathers: The Aztec State Society." *Estudios de Cultura Náhuatl* 22 (1992): 291–323.
———. "La organización del tributo en el imperio azteca." *Estudios de Cultura Náhuatl* 12 (1976): 185–95.
Berdan, Frances F., and Patricia R. Anawalt, eds. *The Essential Codex Mendoza*. Berkeley and Los Angeles: University of California Press, 1997.
Bernal, Ignacio. "Formación y desarrollo de Mesoamérica." In *Historia general de México*, vol. 1, edited by Daniel Cosío Villegas, 12–164. Mexico: El Colegio de México, 1977.
Bernand, Carmen, and Serge Gruzinski. *De la idolatría: una arqueología de las ciencias religiosas*. Translated by Diana Sánchez. Mexico: Fondo de Cultura Económica, 1992.
———. *Historia del Nuevo Mundo*. Vol. 1, *Del descubrimiento a la conquista: la experiencia europea, 1492–1550*. Translated by María A. Neira Bigorra. Mexico: Fondo de Cultura Económica, 1996.
———. *Historia del Nuevo Mundo*. Vol. 2, *Los mestizajes, 1550–1640*. Translated by María A. Neira Bigorra. Mexico: Fondo de Cultura Económica, 1999.
Bethell, Leslie, ed. *The Cambridge History of Latin America*. 11 vols. Cambridge: Cambridge University Press, 1984.
Bhabha, Homi K. *The Location of Culture*. London: Routledge, 1994.
Blázquez, Adrián, and Thomas Calvo. *Guadalajara y el Nuevo Mundo: Nuño Beltrán de Guzmán: semblanza de un conquistador*. Guadalajara, Spain: Institución Provincial de Cultura Marqués de Santillana, 1992.
Blosser, Bret. "By the Force of Their Lives and the Spilling of Blood: Flechero Service and Political Leverage on a Nueva Galicia Frontier." In *Indian Conquistadors: Indigenous Allies in the Conquest of Mesoamerica*, edited by Laura E. Matthew and Michel R. Oudijk, 289–316. Norman: University of Oklahoma Press, 2007.
Boccara, Michel. "Akab tsib, les lettres de nuit des Mayas." In *L'aventure des écritures: Naissances*, edited by Anne Zali and Annie Berthier, 61–73. Paris: Bibliothèque Nationale de France, 1997.
Bolton, Herbert E. *Coronado, Knight of Pueblos and Plains*. Albuquerque: University of New Mexico Press, 1949.
———*The Spanish Borderlands: A Chronicle of Old Florida and the Southwest*. New Haven, Conn.: Yale University Press, 1921.

———. *Spanish Exploration in the Southwest, 1542-1706*. New York: Charles Scribner's Sons, 1916.

Bonfiglioli, Carlo, Arturo Gutiérrez, and María Eugenia Olavarría, eds. *Las vías del noroeste I: una macrorregión indígena americana*. Mexico: Universidad Nacional Autónoma de México, Instituto de Investigaciones Antropológicas, 2006.

Bonfiglioli, Carlo, Arturo Gutiérrez, Marie-Areti Hers, and María Eugenia Olavarría, eds. *Las vías del noroeste II: propuestas para una perspectiva sistémica e interdisciplinaria*. Mexico: Universidad Nacional Autónoma de México, Instituto de Investigaciones Antropológicas, 2008.

Bonine, Michael E. *Atlas of Mexico*. Austin: Bureau of Business Research, University of Texas at Austin, 1970.

Boone, Elizabeth Hill. "Aztec Pictorial Histories: Records without Words." In Boone and Mignolo, *Writing without Words*, 50-76.

———. "Introduction: Writing and Recording Knowledge." In Boone and Mignolo, *Writing without Words*, 3-26.

———. "Migration Histories as Ritual Performance." In *To Change Place: Aztec Ceremonial Landscapes*, edited by Davíd Carrasco, 121-51. Boulder: University Press of Colorado, 1991.

Boone, Elizabeth Hill, and Walter D. Mignolo, eds. *Writing without Words: Alternative Literacies in Mesoamerica and the Andes*. Durham, N.C.: Duke University Press, 1994.

Borah, Woodrow W. *El siglo de la depresión en Nueva España*. Mexico: Secretaría de Educación Pública, 1975.

Bourne, Edward G. *Spain in America, 1450-1580*. New York: Harper, 1904.

Braniff Cornejo, Beatriz. "Arqueología del norte de México." In *Los pueblos y señoríos teocráticos*, vol. 1, edited by Ignacio Bernal, 217-78. Mexico: Secretaría de Educación Pública, Instituto Nacional de Antropología e Historia, 1975.

———. "El formativo en el norte de México." In *El preclásico o formativo: avances y perspectivas. Seminario de arqueología "Dr. Román Piña Chan" (Museo Nacional de Antropología)*, edited by Martha Carmona Macías, 443-60. Mexico: Museo Nacional de Antropología, Instituto Nacional de Antropología e Historia, 1989.

———. "La frontera septentrional de Mesoamérica." In Manzanilla and López Luján, *Historia antigua de México*, 1:113-43.

———, ed. *La Gran Chichimeca: el lugar de las rocas secas*. Mexico: Consejo Nacional para la Cultura y las Artes, 2001.

———. "Sistemas agrícolas prehispánicos en la Gran Chichimeca." In *Nómadas y sedentarios en el norte de México: homenaje a Beatriz Braniff*, edited by Marie-Areti Hers et al., 127-42. Mexico: Universidad Nacional Autónoma de México, Instituto de Investigaciones Estéticas, 2000.

Bravo, Eva María. Introduction to *Historia de los descubrimientos antiguos y modernos de la Nueva España*, by Baltasar de Obregón. Seville: Alfar, 1997.

Brinton, Daniel G. *American Hero-Myths: A Study in the Native Religions of the Western Continent*. Philadelphia: H. C. Watts, 1882.

———. *The American Race: A Linguistic Classification and Ethnographical Description of the Native Tribes of North and South America*. New York: N. D. C. Hodges, 1891.

Broda, Johanna. "Consideraciones sobre historiografía e ideología mexicas: las crónicas indígenas y el estudio de los ritos y sacrificios." *Estudios de Cultura Náhuatl* 13 (1978): 97-111.

Brooks, James F. *Captives and Cousins: Slavery, Kinship, and Community in the Southwest Borderlands*. Chapel Hill: University of North Carolina Press, 2002.

Brotherston, Gordon. *La América indígena en su literatura: los libros del cuarto mundo*. Translated by Teresa Ortega Guerrero and Mónica Utrilla. Mexico: Fondo de Cultura Económica, 1997.

———. "The Aztlan of the Codices, in Modern Mexican and Chicano Versions." *Indiana Journal of Hispanic Literatures* 12 (1998): 1–17.

———. *Painted Books from Mexico: Codices in UK Collections and the World They Represent*. London: British Museum Press, 1995.

Brotherston, Gordon, and Ana Gallegos. "El Lienzo de Tlaxcala y el Manuscrito de Glasgow (Hunter 242)." *Estudios de Cultura Náhuatl* 20 (1990): 117–40.

Brumfiel, Elizabeth M. "Agricultural Development and Class Stratification in the Southern Valley of Mexico." In *Land and Politics in the Valley of Mexico: A Two Thousand-Year Perspective*, edited by H. R. Harvey, 43–62. Albuquerque: University of New Mexico Press, 1991.

Burke, Kenneth. "What Are the Signs of What? (A Theory of Entitlement)." In *Language as Symbolic Action: Essays of Life, Literature, and Method*, 359–79. Berkeley: University of California Press, 1966.

Caamaño Panzi, María Esther. "La importancia del linaje de Culhuacan en la formación de señoríos del posclásico en la cuenca de México." In *Apuntes de etnohistoria*, vol. 2, edited by Rosa Brambila and María Esther Caamaño, 134–45. Mexico: Instituto Nacional de Antropología e Historia, 1992.

Cabrero García, María Teresa. "Algunas referencias al área del río Bolaños (Zacatecas y Jalisco) en los documentos del siglo XVI y XVII." *Anales de Antropología* 23 (1986): 105–26.

———. *El hombre y sus instrumentos en la cultura Bolaños*. Mexico: Universidad Nacional Autónoma de México, Instituto de Investigaciones Antropológicas, 2005.

Calnek, Edward E. "The Analysis of Prehispanic Central Mexican Historical Texts." *Estudios de Cultura Náhuatl* 13 (1978): 239–66.

Camelo, Rosa. "Baltasar de Obregón." *Estudios de Historia Novohispana* 7 (1981): 29–45.

Carmack, Robert M., Janine Gasco, and Gary H. Gossen. *The Legacy of Mesoamerica: History and Culture of a Native American Civilization*. Upper Saddle River, N.J.: Prentice Hall, 1996.

Carot, Patricia. "Cronología de la ocupación en Loma Alta, Zacapu, Michoacán, o los antecedentes de la cultura purépecha." In *Antropología e interdisciplina: homenaje a Pedro Carrasco, XXIII Mesa Redonda de la Sociedad de Antropología*, 2:46–63. Mexico, Sociedad Mexicana de Antropología, Universidad Nacional Autónoma de México, 1998.

———. *Le site de Loma Alta, lac de Zacapu, Michoacan, Mexique*. Oxford, U.K.: Archaeopress, 2001.

Carot, Patricia, and Marie-Areti Hers. "La gesta de los tolteca-chichimecas y los purépechas en la tierra de los Pueblos Ancestrales." In *Las vías del noroeste I: Una macrorregión indígena americana*, edited by Carlo Bonfiglioli, Arturo Gutiérrez, and María Eugenia Olavarría, 47–82. Mexico: Universidad Nacional Autónoma de México, Instituto de Investigaciones Antropológicas, 2006.

Carrasco, Pedro. "La organización social de los nahuas en la época prehispánica." In *La antropología en México, panorama histórico*, vol. 3, edited by Carlos García Mora, 465–531. Mexico: Instituto Nacional de Antropología e Historia, 1988.

---. *Los otomíes: cultura e historia prehispánicas de los pueblos de habla otomiana.* 1950. Mexico: Universidad Nacional Autónoma de México, Instituto Nacional de Antropología e Historia, 1976.

---. "La triple alianza." In Lombardo and Nalda, *Temas mesoamericanos,* 167–209.

Carrera Stampa, Manuel. "Códices, mapas y lienzos acerca de la cultura náhuatl." *Estudios de Cultura Náhuatl* 5 (1965): 165–220.

Cartas de Indias. Vol. 1. Madrid: Ministerio de Fomento, Atlas, 1974.

Casas, Bartolomé de las. *Historia de las Indias.* 1527–61. Edited by Agustín Millares Carlo and Lewis Hanke. Mexico: Fondo de Cultura Económica, 1951.

Caso, Alfonso. *Los calendarios prehispánicos.* Mexico: Universidad Nacional Autónoma de México, Instituto de Investigaciones Históricas, 1967.

Castañeda Nájera, Pedro de. "Relación de la jornada de Cíbola." 1560–65. In *Las siete ciudades de Cíbola: textos y testimonios sobre la expedición de Vázquez de Coronado,* edited by Carmen de Mora, 61–144. Seville: Alfar, 1992.

Castillo, Cristóbal del. *Historia de la venida de los mexicanos y otros pueblos e Historia de la conquista.* 1597–1600. Edited and translated from Náhuatl by Federico Navarrete. Mexico: Instituto Nacional de Antropología e Historia, 1991.

Castillo Farreras, Víctor M. *Estructura económica de la sociedad mexica, según las fuentes documentales.* Mexico: Universidad Nacional Autónoma de México, Instituto de Investigaciones Históricas, 1972.

---. "Estudio preliminar." In *Memorial breve acerca de la fundación de la ciudad de Culhuacán,* by Domingo Chimalpahin Cuauhtlehuanitzin, xi–xliv. Mexico: Universidad Nacional Autónoma de México, Instituto de Investigaciones Históricas, 1991.

---. "Estudio preliminar." In *Primer amoxtli libro: tercera relación de las différentes histoires originales,* by Domingo Chimalpahin Cuauhtlehuanitzin, v–lviii. Mexico: Universidad Nacional Autónoma de México, Instituto de Investigaciones Históricas, 1997.

CDIAO *[Colección de documentos inéditos, relativos al descubrimiento, conquista y organización de las antiguas posesiones españolas en América y Oceanía, sacados de los Archivos del Reino y muy especialmente del de Indias, por Luis Torres de Mendoza. Abogado de los Tribunales, ex-diputado á Córtes. Con la cooperación competente. Autorizada por el Ministerio de Ultramar, según Real órden de 10 de julio de 1862].* Vols. 4–5. Madrid: Imprenta de Frías y Compañía, 1865–66.

CDIAO *[Colección de documentos inéditos, relativos al descubrimiento, conquista y organización de las antiguas posesiones españolas en América y Oceanía, sacados de los Archivos del Reino y muy especialmente del de Indias. Competentemente autorizada].* Vols. 14–15. Madrid: Imprenta de José María Pérez, 1870–71.

CDIAO *[Colección de documentos inéditos, relativos al descubrimiento, conquista y organización de las antiguas posesiones españolas en América y Oceanía, sacados de los Archivos del Reino y muy especialmente del de Indias. Competentemente autorizada].* Vol. 16. Madrid: Imprenta del Hospicio, 1871.

Chanock, Martin. *Law, Custom, and Social Order: The Colonial Experience in Malawi and Zambia.* Cambridge: Cambridge University Press, 1985.

Chapman, Anne. "Mesoamérica: ¿estructura o historia?" In *La validez teórica del concepto de Mesoamérica,* edited by Antonio Guzmán and Lourdes Martínez, 21–29. Mexico: Instituto Nacional de Antropología e Historia, Sociedad Mexicana de Antropología, 1990.

Chartier, Roger. *El mundo como representación: historia cultural, entre práctica y representación.* Translated by C. Ferrari. Barcelona: Gedisa, 1995.

Chávez, Angélico. *Coronado's Friars.* Washington, D.C.: Academy of American Franciscan History, 1968.

Chesneaux, Jean, et al. *El modo de producción asiático.* Mexico: Grijalbo, 1969.

Chiappelli, Fredi, ed. *First Images of America: The Impact of the New World on the Old.* 2 vols. Berkeley and Los Angeles: University of California Press, 1976.

Chiaramonte, José Carlos, Carlos Marichal, and Aimer Granados, eds. *Crear la nación: los nombres de los países de América Latina.* Buenos Aires: Editorial Sudamericana, 2008.

Chimalpahin, Domingo. *Las ocho relaciones y el memorial de Colhuacan.* 2 vols. ca. 1620–31. Paleography and translation from Náhuatl by Rafael Tena. Mexico: Consejo Nacional para las Culturas y las Artes, 1998.

Chipman, Donald E. *Nuño de Guzmán and the Province of Pánuco in New Spain, 1518–1533.* Glendale, Calif.: Arthur H. Clark, 1967.

———. "The Oñate-Moctezuma-Zaldívar Families of Northern New Spain." *New Mexico Historical Review* 52, no. 4 (1977): 297–310.

Clavijero, Francisco Javier. *Historia antigua de México.* 1781. Edited by Mariano Cuevas. Mexico: Porrúa, 1964.

Clifford, James, and George Marcus, eds. *Writing Culture: The Politics and Poetics of Ethnography.* Berkeley: University of California Press, 1986.

Cline, Howard F. "Ethnohistorical Regions of Middle America." In *Handbook of Middle American Indians,* vol. 12, *Guide to Ethnohistorical Sources,* edited by Howard F. Cline, pt. 1, 166–82. Austin: University of Texas Press, 1971.

Clissold, Stephen. *The Seven Cities of Cibola.* London: Eyre and Spottiswoode, 1961.

Codex Aubin. In *Historia de la nación mexicana: reproducción a todo color del Códice de 1576 (Códice Aubin).* Edited and translated from Náhuatl by Charles Dibble. Madrid: José Porrúa Turranzas, 1963.

Codex Azcatitlan / Códice Azcatitlan. Introduction by Michel Graulich, commentary by Robert H. Barlow, translated by Leonardo López Luján and Dominique Michelet. Paris: Bibliothèque Nationale de France, Société des Américanistes, 1995.

Codex Mendoza. See Berdan and Anawalt.

Codex Mexicanus. In "Commentaire du Codex Mexicanus nos. 23–24 de la Bibliothèque Nationale de Paris," edited by E. Mengin. *Journal de la Société des Américanistes de Paris,* n.s., 41 (1952): 387–498, atlas.

Codex Telleriano-Remensis. See Quiñones Keber.

Codex Vaticano Ríos. In *Il Manoscritto Messicano Vaticano 3738, detto il Codice Rio.* Rome: Biblioteca Vaticana, 1960.

Códice Boturini, o, Tira de la Peregrinación Mexica. Mexico: Librería Anticuaria G. M. Echániz, 1944.

Códice Chimalpopoca: anales de Cuauhtitlán y leyenda de los soles. Prologue and translation from Náhuatl by Primo F. Velázquez. Mexico: Universidad Nacional Autónoma de México, Instituto de Investigaciones Históricas, 1992.

Códice de Tlatelolco. Introduction by Perla Valle. Mexico: Instituto Nacional de Antropología e Historia, Benemérita Universidad de Puebla, 1994.

Códice Ramírez. See Alvarado Tezozómoc, *Crónica mexicana.*

Cohn, Bernard S. *An Anthropologist among the Historians, and Other Essays.* Delhi and Oxford: Oxford University Press, 1990.

Cohn, Norman. *The Pursuit of the Millennium: Revolutionary Messianism in the Middle Ages and its Bearing on Modern Totalitarian Movements*. 1957. Oxford: Oxford University Press, 1970.

Collier, George A. "In the Shadow of Empire: New Directions in Mesoamerican and Andean Ethnohistory." In *The Inca and Aztec States, 1400–1800: Anthropology and History*, edited by George A. Collier, Renato I. Rosaldo, and J. D. Wirth, 1–20. New York: Academic Press, 1982.

Comaroff, Jean. *Body of Power, Spirit of Resistance: The Culture and History of a South African People*. Chicago: University of Chicago Press, 1985.

Comaroff, John L. "Images of Empire, Contests of Conscience." In *Tensions of Empire: Colonial Cultures in a Bourgeois World*, edited by Frederick Cooper and Ann L. Stoler, 163–97. Berkeley and Los Angeles: University of California Press, 1997.

Comaroff, John L., and Jean Comaroff. *Of Revelation and Revolution*. Vol. 1, *Christianity, Colonialism, and Consciousness in South Africa*. Chicago: University of Chicago Press, 1991.

———. *Of Revelation and Revolution*. Vol. 2, *The Dialectics of Modernity on a South African Frontier*. Chicago: University of Chicago Press, 1997.

Conquistador anónimo. *Relación de la Nueva España*. Edited by J. Bustamante. Madrid: Polifemo, 1986.

Cook, Sherburne F., and Woodrow W. Borah. *Essays in Population History*. Vol. 1. Berkeley and Los Angeles: University of California Press, 1971.

Cooper, Frederick, and Ann Laura Stoler. "Between Metropole and Colony: Rethinking a Research Agenda." In *Tensions of Empire: Colonial Cultures in a Bourgeois World*, edited by Frederick Cooper and Ann Laura Stoler, 1–56. Berkeley and Los Angeles: University of California Press, 1997.

———. Introduction to "Tensions of Empire: Colonial Control and Visions of Rule." Special issue, *American Ethnologist* 16 (1989): 609–21.

———, eds. *Tensions of Empire: Colonial Cultures in a Bourgeois World*. Berkeley: University of California Press, 1997.

Corbey, Raymond, and Joseph Leersen. "Studying Alterity: Backgrounds and Perspectives." In *Alterity, Identity, Image: Slaves and Others in Society and Scholarship*, vi–xviii. Amsterdam and Atlanta: Rodopi, 1991.

———, *Alterity, Identity, Image: Slaves and Others in Society and Scholarship*. Atlanta: Rodopi, 1991.

Cordell, Linda S. *Archaeology of the Southwest*. 2nd ed. San Diego, Calif.: Academic Press, 1997.

———. "Prehistory: Eastern Anasazi." In *Handbook of North American Indians*, vol. 9, *The Southwest*, edited by William C. Sturtevant, 131–51. Washington, D.C.: Smithsonian Institution, 1979.

Cordell, Linda S., and Bruce D. Smith. "Indigenous Farmers." In *The Cambridge History of the Native Peoples of the Americas*, vol. 1., *North America*, edited by Bruce G. Trigger and W. E. Washburn, pt. 1, 201–67. Cambridge: Cambridge University Press, 1996.

Corfield, Penelope. "Urban Development in England and Wales in the XVI and XVII Centuries." In *The Tudor and Stuart Town: A Reader in English Urban History, 1530–1668*, edited by Jonathan Barry, 35–62. London: Longman, 1990.

Coronil, Fernando. Introduction to *Cuban Counterpoint: Tobacco and Sugar*, by Fernando Ortiz, ix–lvi. Durham, N.C.: Duke University Press, 1995.

Cortés, Hernán. *Cartas de relación*. Mexico: Porrúa, 1994.

Couch, Christopher. "The *Codex Ramirez*: Copy or Original?" *Estudios de Cultura Náhuatl* 21 (1991): 109–25.

Cramaussel, Chantal. "El camino real de tierra adentro de México a Santa Fe." In *Rutas de la Nueva España*, edited by Chantal Cramaussel, 299–327. Zamora: El Colegio de Michoacán, 2006.

Cummins, Tom. "Representation in the Sixteenth Century and the Colonial Image of the Inca." In Boone and Mignolo, *Writing without Words*, 188–219.

Cutter, Donald. *España en Nuevo México*. Madrid: Mapfre, 1992.

Dahlgren, Barbro, and Maria D. Soto de Archavaleta, eds. *Arqueología del norte y del occidente de México: homenaje al Dr. J. Charles Kelley*. Mexico: Universidad Nacional Autonoma de Mexico, Instituto de Investigaciones Antropologicas, 1995.

Darnton, Robert. *The Great Cat Massacre and Other Episodes in French Cultural History*. New York: Vintage, 1985.

Davidson, George. *The Origin and Meaning of the Name California: Calafia the Queen of the Island of California*. Los Angeles: Geographical Society of the Pacific, 1910.

Davies, Nigel. "The Aztec Concept of History: Teotihuacan and Tula." In *The Native Sources and the History of the Valley of Mexico: Proceedings / 44th International Congress of Americanists*, edited by Jacqueline Durand-Forest, 207–14. Oxford: British Archaeological Reports, 1984.

———. *Los señoríos independientes del imperio azteca*. Mexico: Instituto Nacional de Antropología e Historia, 1968.

———. *The Toltec Heritage: From the Fall of Tula to the Rise of Tenochtitlán*. Norman: University of Oklahoma Press, 1980.

Deeds, Susan M. *Defiance and Deference in Mexico's Colonial North: Indians under Spanish Rule in Nueva Vizcaya*. Austin: University of Texas Press, 2003.

———. "Indigenous Rebellions on the Northern Mexican Mission Frontier: From First-Generation to Later Colonial Responses." In *Contested Ground: Comparative Frontiers on the Northern and Southern Edges of the Spanish Empire*, edited by D. J. Guy and T. E. Sheridan, 32–51. Tucson: University of Arizona Press, 1998.

Di Peso, Charles. "History." In *Casas Grandes: A Fallen Trading Center of the Gran Chichimeca*, vol. 4, by Charles Di Peso, John B. Rinaldo, and Gloria Fenner, 37–120. Flagstaff, Ariz.: Amerind Foundation; Dragoon, Ariz.: Northland Press, 1974.

———. "Prehistory: Southern Periphery." In *Handbook of North American Indians*, vol. 9, *The Southwest*, edited by William C. Sturtevant, 152–61. Washington, D.C.: Smithsonian Institution, 1979.

Díaz, Juan. "Itinerario de la armada del Rey Católico a la isla de Yucatán, en la India, en el año 1518, en la que fue por Comandante y Capitán General Juan de Grijalva." In Vázquez, *La conquista de Tenochtitlan*, 37–57.

Díaz del Castillo, Bernal. *Historia verdadera de la conquista de la Nueva España*. ca. 1555. Edited by Carmelo Sáenz de Santa María. Madrid: Instituto Gonzalo Fernández de Oviedo, Consejo Superior de Educación Científica, 1982.

Diel, Lori Boornazian. *The Tira de Tepechpan: Negotiating Place under Aztec and Spanish Rule*. Austin: University of Texas Press, 2008.

Dirks, Nicholas. Introduction to *Colonialism and Culture*, 1–25. Ann Arbor: University of Michigan Press, 1992.

———. "The Original Caste: Power, History, and Hierarchy in South Asia." *Contributions to Indian Sociology* 23, no. 1 (January 1989): 59–77.

Dos Santos, Eduardo Natalino, "Los ciclos calendáricos mesoamericanos en los escritos nahuas y castellanos del siglo XVI: de la función estructural al papel temático." In *Indios, mestizos y españoles: interculturalidad e historiografía en la Nueva España*, edited by Danna Levin and Federico Navarrete, 225-62. Mexico: Universidad Autónoma Metropolitana-Azcapotzalco, Universidad Nacional Autónoma de México, Instituto de Investigaciones Históricas, 2007.

Douglas, Mary. Foreword to *The Gift: The Form and Reason for Exchange in Archaic Societies*, by Marcel Mauss, vii–xviii. Translated by W. D. Halls. New York: W. W. Norton, 1990.

Driver Harold E., and Wilhelmine Driver. *Ethnography and Acculturation of the Chichimeca Jonaz of Northeast Mexico*. Bloomington: Indiana University Press, 1963.

Durán, Diego. *Historia de las Indias de Nueva España e islas de la Tierra Firme*. ca. 1579–81. 2 vols. Edited by Ángel M. Garibay K. Mexico: Porrúa, 1967.

Dutton, Bertha P. *American Indians of the Southwest*. Albuquerque: University of New Mexico Press, 1983.

Duverger, Christian. *L'origine des Aztèques*. Paris: Éditions du Seuil, 1983.

Eggan, Fred. "Pueblos: Introduction." In *Handbook of North American Indians*, vol. 9, *The Southwest*, edited by William C. Sturtevant, 224–35. Washington, D.C.: Smithsonian Institution, 1979.

Elliott, John H. "Renaissance Europe and America: A Blunted Impact?" In *First Images of America: The Impact of the New World on the Old*, vol. 1, edited by Fredi Chiappelli, 11–23. Berkeley and Los Angeles: University of California Press, 1976.

———. "Spain and America in the Sixteenth and Seventeenth Centuries." In Bethell, *Cambridge History of Latin America*, 1:287–339.

———. "The Spanish Conquest and the Settlement of America." In Bethell, *Cambridge History of Latin America*, 1:149–206.

Ellis, Florence H. "The Long Lost 'City' of San Gabriel del Yunque, Second Oldest European Settlement in the United States." In *When Cultures Meet: Remembering San Gabriel del Yunge Oweenge. Papers from the October 20, 1984, Conference Held at San Juan Pueblo, New Mexico*, edited by Florence H. Ellis, Myra E. Jenkins, and Richard Ford, 10–38. Santa Fe, N.M.: Sunstone Press, 1987.

Errington, Shelly. *Meaning and Power in a Southeast Asian Realm*. Princeton, N.J.: Princeton University Press, 1989.

Escalante Hernández, Roberto. "Tres artes gramaticales de lenguas otomianas." In Guzmán and Nansen, *Memoria del coloquio "La obra de Antonio de Nebrija y su recepción en la Nueva España,"* 121–34.

Estrada, Juan Antonio. *¿Quinto centenario de qué?* Santander, Spain: Sal Terrae, 1992.

Fabian, Johannes. *Time and the Other: How Anthropology Makes Its Object*. New York: Columbia University Press, 1983.

Fábregas Puig, Andrés, Mario A. Nájera Espinoza, and Claudio Esteva Fabregat, eds. *Continuidad y fragmentación de la Gran Chichimeca*. Mexico: Seminario Permanente de Estudios de la Gran Chichimeca, 2008.

Ferguson, Thomas J., and E. Richard Hart. *A Zuni Atlas*. Norman: University of Oklahoma Press, 1990.

Fernández de Oviedo, Gonzalo. *Historia general y natural de las Indias*. 1535–52. Edited by J. Pérez de Tudela y Bueso. Madrid: Atlas, 1959.

Fernández Gómez, Carlos. *Vocabulario de Cervantes*. Madrid: Real Academia Española, 1962.

Flannery, Kent V. *Guilá Naquitz: Archaic Foraging and Early Agriculture in Oaxaca, Mexico.* New York: Academic Press, 1986.

———. "The Origins of Agriculture." *Annual Review of Anthropology* 2 (October 1973): 271–310.

Florescano, Enrique. "Mito e historia en la memoria nahua." *Historia Mexicana* 39, no. 3 (1990): 607–61.

Forbes, Jack D. *Apache, Navaho, and Spaniard.* Norman: University of Oklahoma Press, 1960.

Foucault, Michel. *Historia de la locura en la época clásica.* 1964. Translated by José J. Utrilla. 2 vols. Mexico: Fondo de Cultura Económica, 1976.

Gandía, Enrique de. *Historia crítica de los mitos de la conquista americana.* Madrid: Sociedad General Española de Librería, 1929.

García Icazbalceta, Joaquín. *Colección de documentos para la historia de México.* 2 vols. Mexico: Librería de J. M. Andrade, 1858–89.

———. *Nueva colección de documentos para la historia de México.* Vol. 3. Mexico: Díaz de León, 1891.

Garibay K., Ángel M. "Relaciones internacionales en los pueblos de la meseta del Anahuac." *Estudios de Cultura Náhuatl* 3 (1962): 7–21.

———, ed. *Teogonía e historia de los mexicanos: tres opúsculos del siglo XVI.* Mexico: Porrúa, 1965.

Geertz, Clifford. *The Interpretation of Cultures: Selected Essays.* 1973. London: Fontana Press, 1993.

———. *Negara: The Theatre State in Nineteenth-Century Bali.* Princeton, N.J.: Princeton University Press, 1980.

Gerhard, Peter. *A Guide to the Historical Geography of New Spain.* Cambridge: Cambridge University Press, 1972.

———. *The North Frontier of New Spain.* Princeton, N.J.: Princeton University Press, 1982.

Gibson, Charles. *The Aztecs under Spanish Rule, 1519–1810.* Stanford, Calif.: Stanford University Press, 1964.

———. "Indian Societies under Spanish Rule." In Bethell, *Cambridge History of Latin America*, 2:381–421.

Gibson, Charles, and John B. Glass. "A Census of Middle American Prose Manuscripts in the Native Historical Tradition." In *Handbook of Middle American Indians*, vol. 15, *Guide to Ethnohistorical Sources*, edited by Robert Wauchope and Howard F. Cline, pt. 4, 322–400. Austin: University of Texas Press, 1975.

Gil, Juan. *Mitos y utopías del descubrimiento.* Vol. 2, *El Pacífico.* Madrid: Alianza Editorial, 1989.

———. *Mitos y utopías del descubrimiento.* Vol. 3, *El Dorado.* Madrid: Alianza Editorial, 1989.

Ginzburg, Carlo. *The Cheese and the Worms: The Cosmos of a Sixteenth-Century Miller.* Translated by John A. Tedeschi and Mary Tedeschi. Baltimore, Md.: Johns Hopkins University Press, 1980.

Glass, John B., and Donald Robertson. "A Census of Middle American Pictorial Manuscripts." In *Handbook of Middle American Indians*, vol. 14, *Guide to Ethnohistorical Sources,* edited by Robert Wauchope and Howard F. Cline, pt. 3, 81–252. Austin: University of Texas Press, 1975.

Gómez Serrano, Jesús. "El exterminio de los chichimecas en el norte de la Nueva Galicia y los criterios de repoblación indígena." In *Continuidad y fragmentación de la Gran Chichimeca*, edited by Andrés Fábregas Puig, Mario A. Nájera Espinoza, and Claudio Esteva Fabregat, 185–220. Mexico: Seminario Permanente de Estudios de la Gran Chichimeca, 2008.

González de la Vara, Martín. "La rebelión de los indios pueblos de Nuevo México, 1680–1693." In *Organización y liderazgo en los movimientos populares novohispanos*, edited by Felipe Castro, Virginia Guedea, and José L. Mirafuentes, 11–36. Mexico: Universidad Nacional Autónoma de México, Instituto de Investigaciones Históricas, 1992.

Goodman, Nelson. *Ways of Worldmaking*. Ann Arbor, Mich.: Harvester, 1978.

Graulich, Michel. "Aspects mythiques des pérégrinations mexicas." In *The Native Sources and the History of the Valley of Mexico: Proceedings / 44th International Congress of Americanists*, edited by Jacqueline Durand-Forest, 25–71. Oxford: British Archaeological Reports, 1984.

———. Introduction to *Codex Azcatitlan / Códice Azcatitlan*, 8–31. Paris: Bibliothèque Nationale de France, Société des Américanistes, 1995.

———. "Las peregrinaciones aztecas y el ciclo de Mixcóatl." *Estudios de Cultura Náhuatl* 2 (1974): 311–54.

Greenblatt, Stephen. *Marvelous Possessions: The Wonder of the New World*. Chicago: University of Chicago Press, 1991.

———, ed. *New World Encounters*. Berkeley and Los Angeles: University of California Press, 1993.

Gregg, Josiah. *Commerce of the Prairies*. 1844. Edited by Max L. Moorhead. Norman: University of Oklahoma Press, 1990.

Gruzinski, Serge. *La colonización de lo imaginario: sociedades indígenas y occidentalización en el México español, siglos XVI–XVIII*. 1988. Translated by Jorge Ferreiro. Mexico: Fondo de Cultura Económica, 1991.

———. *La guerra de las imágenes: de Cristóbal Colón a Blade Runner (1492–2019)*. Translated by José J. Utrilla. Mexico: Fondo de Cultura Económica, 1994.

———. *El poder sin límites: cuatro respuestas indígenas a la dominación española*. Mexico: Instituto Nacional de Antropología e Historia, 1989.

Güemes, Lina Odena. "La composición étnica en el posclásico y la cuestión chichimeca." In *Mesoamérica y el norte de México, siglos IX–XII*, edited by Federica Sodi Miranda, 2:451–58. Mexico: Instituto Nacional de Antropología e Historia, 1990.

Guevara, Arturo. *Apuntes para la arqueología de Chihuahua*. Mexico: Centro Regional de Chihuahua del Instituto Nacional de Antropología e Historia, 1985.

———. "Oasisamérica en el posclásico: la zona de Chihuahua." In Manzanilla and López Luján, *Historia antigua de México*, 3:329–54.

Gutiérrez, Ramón A. *When Jesus Came, the Corn Mothers Went Away: Marriage, Sexuality, and Power in New Mexico, 1500–1846*. Stanford, Calif.: Stanford University Press, 1991.

Guy, Donna J., and Thomas E. Sheridan, eds. *Contested Ground: Comparative Frontiers on the Northern and Southern Edges of the Spanish Empire*. Tucson: University of Arizona Press, 1998.

Guzmán Betancourt, Ignacio. "La lengua, compañera del imperio: destino de un presagio nebrisense en la Nueva España." In Guzmán and Nansen, *Memoria del coloquio "La obra de Antonio de Nebrija y su recepción en la Nueva España,"* 23–37.

Guzmán Betancourt, Ignacio, and Eréndira Nansen Díaz, eds. *Memoria del coloquio "La obra de Antonio de Nebrija y su recepción en la Nueva España": quince estudios nebrisenses (1492–1992)*. Mexico: Instituto Nacional de Antropología e Historia, 1997.

Hall, Thomas D. *Social Change in the Southwest, 1530–1880*. Lawrence: University Press of Kansas, 1989.

Hallenbeck, Cleve. *The Journey of Fray Marcos de Niza*. Edited by David J. Weber. Dallas, Tex.: Southern Methodist University Press, 1987.

Hammond, George P. *The Search for the Fabulous in the Settlement of the Southwest*. Salt Lake City: Utah State Historical Society, 1956.

Hammond, George P., and Agapito Rey, eds. *Don Juan de Oñate, Colonizer of New Mexico, 1595–1628*. Albuquerque: University of New Mexico Press, 1953.

———, eds. *Narratives of the Coronado Expedition, 1540–1542*. Albuquerque: University of New Mexico Press, 1940.

———. *The Rediscovery of New Mexico, 1580–1594: The Explorations of Chamuscado, Espejo, Castaño de Sosa, Morlete, and Leyva de Bonilla and Humaña*. Albuquerque: University of New Mexico Press, 1966.

Hand, Wayland D. "The Effect of the Discovery on Ethnographical and Folklore Studies in Europe." In *First Images of America: The Impact of the New World on the Old*, edited by Fredi Chiappelli, 1:45–55. Berkeley and Los Angeles: University of California Press, 1976.

Hanke, Lewis. *Aristotle and the American Indians. A Study in Race Prejudice in the Modern World*. Bloomington: Indiana University Press, 1959.

Harvey, H. R. "The relaciones geográficas, 1579–1586: Native Languages." In *Handbook of Middle American Indians*, vol. 12, *Guide to Ethnohistorical Sources*, edited by Howard F. Cline, pt. 1, 279–316. Austin: University of Texas Press, 1972.

———, ed. *Land and Politics in the Valley of Mexico: A Two Thousand-Year Perspective*. Albuquerque: University of New Mexico Press, 1991.

Haskett, Robert. *Indigenous Rulers: An Ethnohistory of Town Government in Colonial Cuernavaca*. Albuquerque: University of New Mexico Press, 1991.

Hassig, Ross. *Trade, Tribute, and Transportation: The Sixteenth-Century Political Economy of the Valley of Mexico*. Norman: University of Oklahoma Press, 1985.

Haury, Emil W. "The Problem of Contacts between the Southwestern United States and Mexico." *Southwestern Journal of Anthropology* 1, no. 1 (1945): 55–74.

Hernández de León Portilla, Ascensión. "Nebrija y las lenguas compañeras del imperio." In Guzmán and Nansen, *Memoria del coloquio "La obra de Antonio de Nebrija y su recepción en la Nueva España,"* 185–95.

Hernández Sánchez Barba, Mario. "La influencia de los libros de caballería sobre el conquistador." *Estudios Americanos: Revista de la Escuela de Estudios Hispano-Americanos* 19, no. 102 (1960): 235–56.

Herrera y Tordesillas, Antonio de. *Historia general de los hechos de los castellanos en las islas y tierra firme del Mar Océano*. 1615. Prologue by J. Natalicio González. Asunción, Paraguay: Editorial Guarania, 1945.

Hers, Marie-Areti. "Los chichimecas: ¿nómadas o sedentarios?" In *Continuidad y fragmentación de la Gran Chichimeca*, edited by Andrés Fábregas Puig, Mario A. Nájera Espinoza, and Claudio Esteva Fabregat, 33–59. Mexico: Seminario Permanente de Estudios de la Gran Chichimeca, 2008.

———. "Las salas de las columnas en La Quemada." In *Arqueología del norte y del occidente de México: homenaje al Dr. J. Charles Kelley*, edited by Barbro Dahlgren and

María D. Soto de Arechavaleta, 93–113. Mexico: Universidad Nacional Autónoma de México, Instituto de Investigaciones Antropológicas, 1995.

———. "La sierra tepehuana: imágenes y discordancias sobre su pasado prehispánico." In *La sierra tepehuana: asentamientos y movimientos de población*, edited by Chantal Cramaussel and Sara Ortelli, 17–44. Zamora, Michoacán: El Colegio de Michoacán, Universidad Juárez del Estado de Durango, 2006.

———. *Los toltecas en tierras chichimecas*. Mexico: Universidad Nacional Autónoma de México, Instituto de Investigaciones Estéticas, 1989.

Hers, Marie-Areti, and María de los Dolores Soto. "La obra de Beatriz Braniff y el desarrollo de la arqueología del norte de México." In *Nómadas y sedentarios en el norte de México: homenaje a Beatriz Braniff*, edited by Marie-Areti Hers et al., 37–53. Mexico: Universidad Nacional Autónoma de México, Instituto de Investigaciones Estéticas, 2000.

Hers, Marie-Areti, et al., eds. *Nómadas y sedentarios en el norte de México: homenaje a Beatriz Braniff*. Mexico: Universidad Nacional Autónoma de México, Instituto de Investigaciones Estéticas, 2000.

Heyden, Doris. *The Eagle, the Cactus, the Rock: The Roots of Mexico-Tenochtitlan's Foundation Myth and Symbol*. Oxford: British Archaeological Reports, 1989.

Hillgarth, J. N. *The Spanish Kingdoms, 1250–1516*. Vol. 2, *1410–1516*. Oxford, U.K.: Clarendon Press, 1978.

Histoire mexicaine depuis 1221 jusq'en 1594: manuscrito no. 40 del Fondo de Manuscritos Mexicanos, Biblioteca Nacional de Francia. ca. 1700. Introduction, paleography, and translation by Xóchitl Medina González. Mexico: Instituto Nacional de Antropología e Historia, 1998.

Historia tolteca-chichimeca. ca. 1533. Edited by Paul Kirchhoff, Lina Odena Güemes, and Luis Reyes García. Mexico: Centro de Investigaciones y Estudios Superiores en Antropología Social, Fondo de Cultura Económica, Estado de Puebla, 1989.

Hodge, Frederick W. *The First Discovered City of Cibola*. 1890. Washington, D.C.: Judd and Detweiler, printers, 1895.

———. *History of Hawikuh, New Mexico: One of the So-Called Cities of Cibola*. Los Angeles: Southwest Museum, 1937.

Hodge, Frederick W., and Theodore H. Lewis. *Spanish Explorers in the Southern United States, 1528–1543*. New York: Scribner, 1907.

Hodge, Mary G. "Land and Lordship in the Valley of Mexico: The Politics of Aztec Provincial Administration." In *Land and Politics in the Valley of Mexico: A Two Thousand-Year Perspective*, edited by H. R. Harvey, 113–39. Albuquerque: University of New Mexico Press, 1991.

Horgan, Paul. *Conquistadors in North American History*. New York: Farrar, Straus and Giroux, 1963.

Huckell, Lisa W. "Ancient Maize in the American Southwest: What Does It Look Like and What Can It Tell Us?" In *Histories of Maize: Multidisciplinary Approaches to the Prehistory, Linguistics, Biogeography, Domestication, and Evolution of Maize*, edited by John E. Staller, Robert H. Tykot, and Bruce F. Benz, 97–109. Amsterdam: Elsevier Academic Press, 2006.

Hulme, Peter. *Colonial Encounters: Europe and the Native Caribbean, 1492–1797*. New York: Methuen, 1986.

———. "Tales of Distinction: European Ethnography and the Caribbean." In *Implicit Understandings: Observing, Reporting, and Reflecting on the Encounters between*

Europeans and Other Peoples in the Early Modern Era, edited by Stuart B. Schwartz, 157–97. Cambridge: Cambridge University Press, 1994.

Ileto, Reynaldo. *Pasyon and Revolution: Popular Movements in the Philippines, 1840–1910.* Quezon City, Philippines: Ateneo de Manila University Press, 1979.

Iltis, Hugh. "Origin of Polystichy in Maize." In *Histories of Maize: Multidisciplinary Approaches to the Prehistory, Linguistics, Biogeography, Domestication, and Evolution of Maize,* edited by John E. Staller, Robert H. Tykot, and Bruce F. Benz, 22–50. Amsterdam: Elsevier Academic Press, 2006.

Izada, Roger. *¿500 años de qué?* Lima, Peru: Universidad Nacional Mayor de San Marcos, 1992.

Jackson, Robert H., ed. *New Views of Borderlands History.* Albuquerque: University of New Mexico Press, 1998.

Jaffe, Abram J. *The First Immigrants from Asia: A Population History of the North American Indians.* New York: Plenum, 1992.

Jara, Fabiola. "Monstruosité et altérité: le mythe des Amazones des Indiens Kalina et Xikrin." *Circé: Cahiers du Centre de Recherche sur l'Imaginaire* 16–19 (1988): 49–79.

Jaramillo Luque, Ricardo. "Consideraciones sobre la arqueología del valle de Valparaíso, Zacatecas, occidente y norte de México." In *Arqueología del norte y del occidente de México: homenaje al Dr. J. Charles Kelley,* edited by Barbro Dahlgren and María D. Soto de Arechavaleta, 173–79. Mexico: Universidad Nacional Autónoma de México, Instituto de Investigaciones Antropológicas, 1995.

Jiménez Betts, Peter. "Algunas observaciones sobre la dinámica cultural de la arqueología de Zacatecas." In *Arqueología del norte y del occidente de México: homenaje al Dr. J. Charles Kelley,* edited by Barbro Dahlgren and María D. Soto de Arechavaleta, 35–63. Mexico: Universidad Nacional Autónoma de México, Instituto de Investigaciones Antropológicas, 1995.

Jiménez Moreno, Wigberto. "La colonización y evangelización de Guanajuato en el siglo XVI." *Cuadernos Americanos* 1, no. 3 (1944): 6–29.

———. "Diferente principio del año entre diversos pueblos y sus consecuencias para la cronología prehispánica." *El México Antiguo* 9 (1961): 137–52.

———. *Estudios de historia colonial.* Mexico: Instituto Nacional de Antropología e Historia, 1958.

———. "La migración mexica." In *Atti del XL Congresso Internazionale degli Americanisti* (Rome-Geneva, September 1972), 1:167–72. Geneva, Switzerland: Tilgher, 1973.

———. "Tribus e idiomas del norte de México." In *El norte de México y el sur de Estados Unidos: tercera reunión de la mesa redonda sobre problemas antropológicos de México y Centro América,* 121–33. Mexico: Sociedad Mexicana de Antropología, 1943.

Junquera, Mercedes. Introduction to *Historia de la Nueva México,* by Gaspar de Villagrá, 7–69. Madrid: Historia 16, 1989.

Karskens, Machiel. "Alterity as Defect: On the Logic of the Mechanism of Exclusion." In *Alterity, Identity, Image: Slaves and Others in Society and Scholarship,* edited by Raymond Corbey and Joseph Leersen, 75–90. Amsterdam and Atlanta: Rodopi, 1991.

Kelley, J. Charles. "Archaeology of the Northern Frontier: Zacatecas and Durango." In *Handbook of Middle American Indians,* vol. 11, *Archaeology of Northern Mesoamerica,* edited by Gordon F. Ekholm and Ignacio Bernal, pt. 2, 768–801. Austin: University of Texas Press, 1971.

———. "Mesoamerica and the Southwestern United States." In *Handbook of Middle American Indians,* vol. 4, *Archaeological Frontiers and External Connections,* edited by

Gordon F. Ekholm and Gordon R. Willey, 95–110. Austin: University of Texas Press, 1966.

———. "Mesoamerican Colonization of Zacatecas-Durango: The Loma–San Gabriel and Chalchihuites Cultures." In *Homenaje al Dr. John Charles Kelley (1913-1997)*, edited by María T. Cabrero, Jaime Litvak King, and Peter Jiménez Betts, 83–98. Mexico: Universidad Nacional Autónoma de México, Instituto de Investigaciones Antropológicas, 2002.

———. "Settlement Patterns in North-Central Mexico." In *Prehistoric Settlement Patterns in the New World*, edited by Gordon R. Willey, 128–39. New York: Wenner-Gren Foundation for Anthropological Research, 1956.

———. "Speculations on the Culture History of Northwestern Mesoamerica." In *The Archaeology of West Mexico*, edited by Betty Bell, 19–39. Ajijic, Jalisco: West Mexican Society for Advanced Study, 1974.

Keyes, Charles F. "Towards a New Formulation of the Concept of Ethnic Group." *Ethnicity* 3 (1976): 202–13.

Kirchhoff, Paul. "Calendarios tenochca, tlatelolca y otros." *Revista Mexicana de Estudios Antropológicos* 14, nos. 1–2 (1954–55): 257–67.

———. "Gatherers and Farmers in the Greater Southwest: A Problem in Classification." *American Anthropologist* 56, no. 4 (1954): 529–60.

———. "El imperio tolteca y su caída." In *Mesoamérica y el centro de México*, edited by Jesús Monjarás Ruiz, Emma Pérez Rocha, and Rosa Brambila, 249–72. Mexico: Instituto Nacional de Antropología e Historia, 1985.

———. "Mesoamérica: sus límites geográficos, composición étnica y caracteres culturales." *Acta Americana* 1, no. 1 (1943): 92–107.

———. "Los recolectores cazadores del norte de México." In *El norte de México y el sur de Estados Unidos: tercera reunión de la mesa redonda sobre problemas antropológicos de México y Centro América*, 133–44. Mexico: Sociedad Mexicana de Antropología, 1943.

———. "¿Se puede localizar Aztlan?" In *Anuario de Historia*, 59–67. Mexico: Universidad Nacional Autónoma de México, 1961.

Krickeberg, Walter. *Etnología de América*. Translated by Pedro Hendrich. Mexico: Fondo de Cultura Económica, 1946.

Kroeber, Alfred L. *Anthropology: Race, Language, Culture, Psychology, Pre-History*. 1923. New York: Harcourt, Brace, 1948.

———. *Cultural and Natural Areas of Native North America*. Berkeley: University of California Press, 1939.

———. *Native Culture of the Southwest*. Berkeley: University of California Press, 1928.

Ladero Quesada, Miguel Ángel. "Spain, circa 1492: Social Values and Structures." In *Implicit Understandings: Observing, Reporting, and Reflecting on the Encounters between Europeans and Other Peoples in the Early Modern Era*, edited by Stuart B. Schwartz, 96–133. Cambridge: Cambridge University Press, 1994.

Lamar, Howard R., and Sam Truett. "The Greater Southwest and California from the Beginning of European Settlement to the 1880s." In *The Cambridge History of the Native Peoples of the Americas*, vol. 1, *North America*, edited by B. G. Trigger and W. E. Washburn, pt. 2, 57–115. Cambridge: Cambridge University Press, 1997.

Le Goff, Jacques. "Les mentalités: une histoire ambigue." In *Faire de l'histoire*, vol. 3, edited by Jacques Le Goff and Pierre Nora, 76–94. Paris: Gallimard, 1974.

Lecoin, Sylvie. "Intercambios, movimientos de población y trabajo en la diócesis de Michoacán en el siglo XVI: un aspecto de las relaciones geográficas de 1580." In

Movimientos de población en el occidente de México, edited by Thomas Calvo and Gustavo López, 123–37. Zamora, Michoacán: El Colegio de Michoacán, Centro de Estudios Mexicanos y Centroamericanos, 1988.

Lecompte, Janet. "Coronado and Conquest." *New Mexico Historical Review* 64, no. 3 (1989): 279–304.

Leibsohn, Dana. "Primers for Memory: Cartographic Histories and Nahua Identity." In Boone and Mignolo, *Writing without Words*, 161–87.

León, Adrián. Introduction to *Crónica mexicáyotl*, by Fernando Alvarado Tezozómoc, vii–xxviii. Mexico: Universidad Nacional Autónoma de México, Instituto de Investigaciones Históricas, 1992.

León Portilla, Miguel. "El proceso de aculturación de los chichimecas de Xólotl." *Estudios de Cultura Náhuatl* 7 (1967): 59–86.

———. *La visión de los vencidos*. 1959. Mexico: Universidad Nacional Autónoma de México, 1984.

Leonard, Irving. *Books of the Brave: Being an Account of Books and of Men in the Spanish Conquest and Settlement of the Sixteenth-Century New World*. 1949. Introduction by R. Adorno. Berkeley: University of California Press, 1992.

———. "Conquerors and Amazons in Mexico." *Hispanic American Historical Review* 24, no. 4 (1944): 561–79.

Levin, Danna, and Federico Navarrete, eds. *Indios, mestizos y españoles: interculturalidad e historiografía en la Nueva España*. Mexico: Universidad Autónoma Metropolitana–Azcapotzalco, Universidad Nacional Autónoma de México, Instituto de Investigaciones Históricas, 2007.

Levin Rojo, Danna A. "La búsqueda del Nuevo México: un proceso de-migratorio en la América Española del siglo XVI." In *Las vías del noroeste I: una macrorregión indígena americana*, edited by Carlo Bonfiglioli, Arturo Gutiérrez, and María Eugenia Olavarría, 133–68. Mexico: Universidad Nacional Autónoma de México, Instituto de Investigaciones Antropológicas, 2006.

———. "La configuración del fracaso en la obra y hazañas de Alvar Núñez Cabeza de Vaca." *Fuentes Humanísticas* 28 (1st Semester 2004): 135–51.

———. "Nuevos nombres viejos lugares: España y México reproducidos como topónimos en el Nuevo Mundo." *Secuencia* 57 (September–December 2003): 7–36.

———. "The Road to Aztlan Ends in New Mexico." In *The Road to Aztlan: The Art of a Mythic Homeland*, edited by Virginia M. Fields and Víctor Zamudio-Taylor, 248–61. Los Angeles: Los Angeles County Museum of Art, 2001.

Levinas, Emmanuel. *Time and the Other*. Pittsburgh, Pa.: Duquense University Press, 1987.

———. *Totality and Infinity: An Essay on Metaphysics*. Pittsburgh, Pa.: Duquense University Press, 1969.

Leyenda de los soles. See *Códice Chimalpopoca*.

Linton, Ralph, ed. *Acculturation in Seven American Indian Tribes*. New York: Appleton-Century, 1940.

Litvak King, Jaime. "En torno al problema de la definición de Mesoamérica." *Anales de Antropología* 12 (1975): 171–95.

Lockhart, James. "Double Mistaken Identity: Some Nahua Concepts in Postconquest Guise." In *Of Things of the Indies: Essays Old and New in Early Latin American History*, 98–119. Stanford, Calif.: Stanford University Press, 1999.

———. *The Nahuas after the Conquest: A Social and Cultural History of the Indians of Central Mexico, Sixteenth through Eighteenth Centuries*. Stanford, Calif.: Stanford University Press, 1992.

———. "Postconquest Nahua Society and Concepts Viewed through Nahuatl Writings." *Estudios de Cultura Náhuatl* 20 (1990): 91–116.

Lombardo, Sonia, and Enrique Nalda, eds., *Temas mesoamericanos*. Mexico: Instituto Nacional de Antropología e Historia, 1996.

Long, Charles H. "Primitive Religion." In *A Reader's Guide to the Great Religions*, edited by Charles J. Adams, 1–39. New York: Free Press, 1977.

López Austin, Alfredo. "El fundamento mágico religioso del poder." *Estudios de Cultura Náhuatl* 12 (1976): 197–240.

———. *Hombre-dios: religión y política en el mundo náhuatl*. Mexico: Universidad Nacional Autónoma de México, Instituto de Investigaciones Históricas, 1989.

———. "Mitos de una migración." *Arqueología Mexicana* 1, no. 4 (1993): 33–36.

———. *Los mitos del tlacuache: caminos de la mitología mesoamericana*. Mexico: Alianza Editorial, 1990.

———. "Organización política en el altiplano central de México durante el posclásico." In *Mesoamérica y el centro de México*, edited by Jesús Monjarás Ruiz, Emma Pérez Rocha, and Rosa Brambila, 197–234. Mexico: Instituto Nacional de Antropología e Historia, 1985.

———. "La religión, la magia y la cosmovisión." In Manzanilla and López Luján, *Historia antigua de México*, 3:419–58.

———. *Tamoanchan y Tlalocan*. Mexico: Fondo de Cultura Económica, 1994.

———. "El texto sahaguntino sobre los mexicas." *Anales de Antropología* 22 (1985): 287–335.

———. "Tollan: Babel." *Revista de la UNAM* 528–29 (1995): 3–8.

López Austin, Alfredo, and Leonardo López Luján. *Mito y realidad de Zuyuá*. Mexico: Fondo de Cultura Económica, El Colegio de México, 1999.

———. *El pasado indígena*. Mexico: Fondo de Cultura Económica, El Colegio de México, 1996.

López de Gómara, Francisco. *La conquista de México*. Edited by José L. de Rojas. Madrid: Historia 16, 1986.

———. *Historia general de las Indias*. 1552. Madrid: Espasa Calpe, 1941.

Lorenzo, Carmen. "La circulación." In Manzanilla and López Luján, *Historia antigua de México*, 3:355–418.

Lunenfeld, Marvin. *1492: Discovery, Invasion, Encounter: Sources and Interpretations*. Lexington, Mass.: D. C. Heath, 1991.

Manrique Castañeda, Leonardo. "La historia del idioma de los mexica y sus congéneres." In *Primer encuentro nahua: los nahuas de hoy*, edited by Dora Sierra Carrillo, 13–26. Mexico: Instituto Nacional de Antropología e Historia, 1989.

Manzanilla, Linda, and Leonardo López Luján, eds. *Historia antigua de México*. Vol. 1, *El México antiguo, sus áreas culturales, los orígenes y el horizonte preclásico*. Mexico: Instituto Nacional de Antropología e Historia, Universidad Nacional Autónoma de México, Porrúa, 1994.

———, eds. *Historia antigua de México*. Vol. 3, *El horizonte posclásico y algunos aspectos intelectuales de las culturas mesoamericanas*. Mexico: Instituto Nacional de Antropología e Historia, Universidad Nacional Autónoma de México, Porrúa, 1995.

Mapa Sigüenza. 16th c. In *Catálogo de la colección de códices*, ed. J. B. Glass, 54–55. Mexico: Instituto Nacional de Antropología e Historia, 1964.

Marcus, Joyce. *Mesoamerican Writing Systems: Propaganda, Myth, and History in Four Ancient Civilizations*. Princeton, N.J.: Princeton University Press, 1992.

Marín Tamayo, Fausto. *Nuño de Guzmán*. Mexico: Siglo XXI, 1992.

Martin, Paul S., George I. Quimby, and Donald Collier. *Indians before Columbus: Twenty Thousand Years of North American History Revealed by Archaeology*. Chicago: University of Chicago Press, 1947.

Martínez, José Luis, ed. *Documentos cortesianos*. 4 vols. Mexico: Universidad Nacional Autónoma de México, Fondo de Cultura Económica, 1990–92.

———. *Hernán Cortés*. Mexico: Universidad Nacional Autónoma de México, Fondo de Cultura Económica, 1990.

Martínez Caraza, Leopoldo. *El norte bárbaro de México*. Mexico: Panorama Editorial, 1983.

Martínez Marín, Carlos. "La cultura de los mexicas durante la migración: nuevas ideas." In *De Teotihuacán a los aztecas: antología de fuentes e interpretaciones históricas*, edited by Miguel León-Portilla, 247–55. Mexico: Universidad Nacional Autónoma de México, Instituto de Investigaciones Históricas, 1971.

———. "Historiografía de la migración mexica." *Estudios de Cultura Náhuatl* 12 (1976): 121–36.

———. "Las migraciones de los grupos nahuas en el horizonte postclásico." In *Primer encuentro nahua: los nahuas de hoy*, edited by Dora Sierra Carrillo, 27–35. Mexico: Instituto Nacional de Antropología e Historia, 1989.

———. "El registro de la historia." In Lombardo and Nalda, *Temas mesoamericanos*, 397–418.

Martínez Saldaña, Tomás. *La diáspora tlaxcalteca: colonización agrícola del norte de México*. Tlaxcala: Gobierno del Estado de Tlaxcala, 1998.

———. "La expansión cultural mesoamericana." In *Regiones y esencias: estudios sobre la Gran Chichimeca*, edited by Andrés Fábregas Puig, Mario Alberto Nájera Espinoza, and José Francisco Román Gutiérrez, 145–57. Mexico: Seminario Permanente de Estudios de la Gran Chichimeca, 2008.

Mártir de Anglería, Pedro. *Cartas sobre el Nuevo Mundo*. Translated by Julio Bauzano. Introduction by Ramón Alba. Madrid: Polifemo, 1990.

———. *Décadas del Nuevo Mundo por Pedro Mártir de Anglería, primer cronista de Indias*. Edited by Edmundo O'Gorman. Translated by Agustín Millares Carlo. Mexico: José Porrúa e Hijos, 1964–65.

Mason, Otis T. "Environment." In *Handbook of American Indians North of Mexico*, edited by Frederick W. Hodge, 427–30. Washington, D.C.: Bureau of American Ethnology, 1907.

Mason, Peter. "Continental Incontinence: Horror Vacui and the Colonial Supplement." In *Alterity, Identity, Image: Slaves and Others in Society and Scholarship*, edited by Raymond Corbey and Joseph Leersen, 151–90. Amsterdam and Atlanta: Rodopi, 1991.

———. *Deconstructing America: Representations of the Other*. London: Routledge, 1990.

———. "Imaginary Worlds, Counterfact and Artefact." In *Myth and the Imaginary in the New World*, edited by Edmundo Magaña and Peter Mason, 43–71. Amsterdam: Centrum voor Studie en Documentatie van Latijns-Amerika, 1986.

Matos Moctezuma, Eduardo. "Mesoamérica." In Manzanilla and López Luján, *Historia antigua de México*, 1:49–73.

———. "El proceso de desarrollo en Mesoamérica." *Boletín de Antropología Americana* 5 (1982): 117–31.

Matthew, Laura, and Michel R. Oudijk. *Indian Conquistadors: Indigenous Allies in the Conquest of Mesoamerica*. Norman: University of Oklahoma Press, 2007.

McGrane, Bernard. *Beyond Anthropology: Society and the Other*. New York: Columbia University Press, 1989.

Medina, José Humberto, and Baudelina L. García Uranga, eds. *A 100 años de su descubrimiento: Alta Vista*. Mexico: Consejo Nacional para la Cultura y las Artes, Instituto Nacional de Antropología e Historia, 2010.

Medina González, Xóchitl. Introduction to *Histoire mexicaine depuis 1221 jusq'en 1594: Manuscrito núm. 40 del Fondo de Manuscritos Mexicanos, Biblioteca Nacional de Francia*, 13–61. Mexico: Instituto Nacional de Antropología e Historia, 1998.

Mendieta, Gerónimo de. *Historia eclesiástica indiana*. 1596–97. Edited by Antonio Rubial García. 2 vols. Mexico: Consejo Nacional para la Cultura y las Artes, 1997.

Merrill, William L., et al. "The Diffusion of Maize to the Southwestern United States and Its Impact." *Proceedings of the National Academy of Sciences* 106, no. 50 (December 15, 2009): 21019–26.

Michelet, Dominique. "Apuntes para el análisis de las migraciones en el México prehispánico." In *Movimientos de población en el occidente de México*, edited by Thomas Calvo and Gustavo López, 13–23. Zamora, Michoacán: El Colegio de Michoacán, Centro de Estudios Mexicanos y Centroamericanos, 1988.

Mignolo, Walter D. *The Darker Side of the Renaissance: Literacy, Territoriality, and Colonization*. Ann Arbor: University of Michigan Press, 1995.

———. "The Movable Center: Geographical Discourses and Territoriality during the Expansion of the Spanish Empire." In *Coded Encounters: Writing, Gender, and Ethnicity in Colonial Latin America*, edited by Francisco J. Cevallos-Candau et al., 15–45. Amherst: University of Massachusetts Press, 1994.

———. "Signs and Their Transmission: The Question of the Book in the New World." In Boone and Mignolo, *Writing without Words*, 220–70. .

Minnis, Paul E., and Charles L. Redman. *Perspectives on Southwestern Prehistory*. Boulder, Colo.: Westview Press, 1990.

Monjarás Ruiz, Jesús. "Fray Diego Durán, un conquistador conquistado." *Dimensión Antropológica* 1, no. 2 (1994): 43–56.

Monjarás Ruiz, Jesús, Emma Pérez Rocha, and Rosa Brambila, eds. *Mesoamérica y el centro de México*. México: Instituto Nacional de Antropología e Historia, 1985.

Moore, Jerry D. *Visions of Culture. An Introduction to Anthropological Theories and Theorists*. Walnut Creek, Calif.: Altamira Press, 1997.

Mora, Carmen de. *Las siete ciudades de Cíbola: textos y testimonios sobre la expedición de Vázquez de Coronado*. Seville: Alfar, 1992.

Morison, Samuel E. *Admiral of the Ocean Sea: A Life of Christopher Columbus*. Boston: Little, Brown, 1942.

Mota y Escobar, Antonio de la. *Descripción geográfica de los reynos de Nueva Galicia, Nueva Vizcaya y Nuevo León*. 1605. Guadalajara, Jalisco: Instituto Jalisciense de Antropología e Historia, 1966.

Mota y Padilla, Matías de la. *Historia de la conquista de la provincia de la Nueva Galicia*. 1742. Mexico: Sociedad Mexicana de Geografía y Estadística, 1870.

Motolinía, Toribio de Benavente. *Historia de los indios de la Nueva España*. 1565. Edited by Edmundo O'Gorman. Mexico: Porrúa, 1969.

———. *Memoriales: libro de oro (MS JGI 31)*. 1541. Edited by N. J. Dyer. Mexico: El Colegio de México, 1996.

Muñoz Camargo, Diego. "Descripción de la ciudad y provincia de Tlaxcala de la Nueva España e Indias del mar océano para el buen gobierno y ennoblecimie[nt]o dellas, mandada hacer por la S.C.R.M. del rey Don Felipe, nuestro señor." In *Relaciones geográficas del siglo XVI*, vols. 4–5, *Tlaxcala*, edited by René Acuña, 25–286. Mexico: Universidad Nacional Autónoma de México, Instituto de Investigaciones Antropológicas, 1984.

———. *Historia de Tlaxcala (Ms. 210 de la Biblioteca Nacional de París)*. Paleography, introduction, and notes by Luis Reyes García and Javier Lira Toledo. Mexico: Gobierno del Estado de Tlaxcala, Centro de Investigaciones y Estudios Superiores en Antropología Social, Universidad Autónoma de Tlaxcala, 1998.

Murra, John V. "Did Tribute and Markets Prevail in the Andes before the European Invasion?" In *Ethnicity, Markets, and Migration in the Andes: At the Crossroads of History and Anthropology*, edited by Brooke Larson and Olivia Harris, 57–72. Durham, N.C.: Duke University Press, 1995.

Nalda, Enrique. "La frontera norte de Mesoamérica." In Lombardo and Nalda, *Temas mesoamericanos*, 255–76.

Nárez, Jesús. "Aridamérica y Oasisamérica." In Manzanilla and López Luján, *Historia antigua de México*, 1:75–111.

Navarrete, Federico. "Las fuentes indígenas más allá de la dicotomía entre historia y mito." *Estudios de Cultura Náhuatl* 30 (1999): 231–56.

———. Introduction to *Historia de la venida de los mexicanos y otros pueblos e Historia de la conquista*, by Cristóbal del Castillo, 13–107. Mexico: Instituto Nacional de Antropología e Historia, 1991.

———. *Los orígenes de los pueblos indígenas del valle de México: los altépetl y sus historias*. Mexico: Universidad Nacional Autónoma de México, 2010.

Nicholson, Henry B. "Pre-Hispanic Central Mexican Historiography." In *Investigaciones contemporáneas sobre historia de México: memorias de la tercera reunión de historiadores mexicanos y norteamericanos (1969)*, 38–81. Mexico: Universidad Nacional Autónoma de México, El Colegio de México, University of Texas, 1971.

Nicolau D'Olwer, Luis. *Cronistas de las culturas precolombinas*. Mexico: Fondo de Cultura Económica, 1963.

Niederberger, Christine. *Páleopaysages et archeologie pré-urbaine du bassin de Mexico*. Mexico: Centro de Estudios Mexicanos y Centroamericanos, 1987.

Niel, Juan Armando. "Apuntamientos que a las memorias del P. Fray Gerónimo de Zárate Salmerón hizo el P. Juan Armando Niel de la Compañía de Jesús." 1710. In *Documentos para servir a la historia de Nuevo México, 1538–1778*, 209–304. Madrid: José Porrúa Turranzas, 1965.

Noguera, Eduardo. *La Quemada: Chalchihuites*. Mexico: Instituto Nacional de Antropología e Historia, 1970.

———. "Sitios de ocupación en la periferia de Tenochtitlan y su significado histórico-arqueológico." *Anales de Antropología* 11 (1974): 53–88.

Noguez, Xavier. "El *Códice de Tlatelolco*: una nueva cronología." In *De tlacuilos y escribanos*, edited by Xavier Noguez and Stephanie G. Wood, 15–32. Mexico: El Colegio de Michoacán, 1998.

———. "La zona del altiplano central en el posclásico: la etapa tolteca." In Manzanilla and López Luján, *Historia antigua de México*, 3:189–224.

———. "Los códices de tradición náhuatl del centro de México en la etapa colonial." In *Libros y escritura de tradición indígena*, edited by Carmen A. Hoffmann, Peter Schmidt, and Xavier Noguez, 159–83. Mexico: El Colegio Mexiquense, Universidad Católica de Eichstätt, 2002.

Núñez Cabeza de Vaca, Alvar. *Relación de los naufragios y comentarios de Alvar Núñez Cabeza de Vaca, adelantado y gobernador del Río de la Plata*. 1542. Edited by Manuel Serrano y Sanz. Madrid: Librería General de Victoriano Suárez, 1906.

O'Gorman, Edmundo. "Estudio crítico." In Motolinía, Toribio de Benavente. *Historia de los indios de la Nueva España*, edited by Edmundo O'Gorman, vii–xix. Mexico: Porrúa, 1969.

———. "Estudio preliminar." In *Obras históricas. Incluyen el texto completo de las llamadas relaciones e historia de la nación chichimeca en una nueva versión establecida con el cotejo de los manuscritos más antiguos que se conocen*, by Fernando de Alva Ixtlilxóchitl, edited by Edmundo O'Gorman. Mexico: Universidad Nacional Autónoma de México, Instituto de Investigaciones Históricas, 1985.

———. "La falacia histórica de Miguel León Portilla sobre el encuentro del Viejo y del Nuevo Mundo." *Quinto Centenario* 12 (1987): 17–31.

———. *La invención de América: investigación acerca de la estructura histórica del Nuevo Mundo y del sentido de su devenir*. 1958. Mexico: Fondo de Cultura Económica, Secretaría de Educación Pública, 1984.

———. Prologue to *Historia natural y moral de las Indias*, by José de Acosta, edited by Edmundo O'Gorman. Mexico: Fondo de Cultura Económica, 1962.

Obregón, Baltasar de. *Historia de los descubrimientos antiguos y modernos de la Nueva España*. ca. 1584. Mexico: Secretaria de Educación Pública, 1924.

Obregón Rodríguez, María Concepción. "La zona del altiplano central en el posclásico: la etapa de la triple alianza." In Manzanilla and López Luján, *Historia antigua de México*, 3:265–306.

Ocaranza, Fernando. *Crónicas y relaciones del occidente de México*. Vol. 1. Mexico: Antigua Librería Robredo de José Porrúa e Hijos, 1937.

———. *Establecimientos franciscanos en el misterioso reino de Nuevo México*. Mexico: n.p., 1934.

Okamura, Jonathan. "Situational Ethnicity." *Ethnic and Racial Studies* 4 (1981): 452–63.

Olivé Negrete, Julio César. "Estado, formación socioeconómica y periodificación de Mesoamérica." In *Mesoamérica y el centro de México*, edited by Jesús Monjarás Ruiz, Emma Pérez Rocha, and Rosa Brambila, 81–114. Mexico: Instituto Nacional de Antropología e Historia, 1985.

———. "Retos del patrimonio cultural: Aztlan." In *Estudios del México antiguo*, edited by Beatriz Barba de Piña Chan, 109–17. Mexico: Instituto Nacional de Antropología e Historia, 1996.

Olschki, Leonardo. "Ponce de León's Fountain of Youth: History of a Geographical Myth." *Hispanic American Historical Review* 21, no. 3 (1941): 361–85.

Origen de los mexicanos. ca. 1530–32. In *Relaciones de la Nueva España*, edited by Germán Vázquez, 127–58. Madrid: Historia 16, 1990.

Ortega Noriega, Sergio. *Un ensayo de historia regional: el noroeste de México, 1530–1880*. Mexico: Universidad Nacional Autónoma de México, 1993.

Ortega Noriega, Sergio, and Ignacio del Río. *Tres siglos de historia sonorense, 1530–1830*. Mexico: Universidad Nacional Autónoma de México, Instituto de Investigaciones Históricas, 1993.

Ortiz, Alfonso. Introduction to *Handbook of North American Indians*, vol. 9, *The Southwest*, edited by William C. Sturtevant, pt. 1, 4. Washington, D.C.: Smithsonian Institution, 1979.

Ortiz, Fernando. *Cuban Counterpoint: Tobacco and Sugar*. 1940. Translated by Harriet de Onís, introduction by Bronislaw Malinowski, with a new introduction by Fernando Coronil. Durham, N.C.: Duke University Press, 1995.

Oudijk, Michel R., and Matthew Restall, "Mesoamerican Conquistadors in the Sixteenth Century." In *Indian Conquistadors: Indigenous Allies in the Conquest of Mesoamerica*, edited by Laura E. Matthew and Michel R. Oudijk, 28–63. Norman: University of Oklahoma Press, 2007.

Pagden, Anthony. *The Fall of Natural Man: The American Indian and the Origins of Comparative Ethnology*. Cambridge: Cambridge University Press, 1982.

Palkovich, Ann M. "Historic Population of the Eastern Pueblos, 1540–1910." *Journal of Anthropological Research* 41, no. 4 (1985): 401–22.

Pané, Ramón. *Relación acerca de las antigüedades de los indios*. ca. 1498. Introduction and notes by J. J. Arrom. Mexico: Siglo XXI, 1974.

Parry, John H. *The Spanish Seaborne Empire*. London: Hutchinson, 1967.

Parsons, Jeffrey R. "Political Implications of Prehispanic Chinampa Agriculture in the Valley of Mexico." In *Land and Politics in the Valley of Mexico: A Two Thousand-Year Perspective*, edited by H. R. Harvey, 17–42. Albuquerque: University of New Mexico Press, 1991.

Paso y Troncoso, Francisco del. *Papeles de Nueva España: geografía y estadística*. Vol. 2. Madrid: Establecimiento Tipográfico Sucesores de Rivadeneyra, 1905.

Pastor Bodmer, Beatriz. *The Armature of Conquest: Spanish Accounts of the Discovery of America, 1492–1589*. Stanford, Calif.: Stanford University Press, 1992.

Pérez de Luxán, Diego. "Account of the Antonio de Espejo Expedition into New Mexico, 1582." In *The Rediscovery of New Mexico, 1580–1594: The Explorations of Chamuscado, Espejo, Castaño de Sosa, Morlete, and Leyva de Bonilla and Humaña*, edited by George P. Hammond and Agapito Rey, 153–212. Albuquerque: University of New Mexico Press, 1966.

Pérez de Oliva, Hernán. *Historia de la invención de las Indias*, 1525–1528. Edited by José J. Arrom. Mexico: Siglo XXI, 1991.

Pericot y García, Luis. *América indígena*. Vol. 1, *El hombre americano y los pueblos de América*. Barcelona: Salvat, 1961.

Petersen, Richard G. *The Lost Cities of Cibola*. Chicago: Franciscan Herald Press, 1980.

Phelan, John L. *The Millennial Kingdom of the Franciscans in the New World*. 1956. Berkeley and Los Angeles: University of California Press, 1970.

Pietz, William. "The Problem of the Fetish, I." *Res: Anthropology and Aesthetics* 9 (Spring 1985): 5–17.

———. "The Problem of the Fetish, II." *Res: Anthropology and Aesthetics* 13 (Spring 1987): 23–45.

Plunket, Patricia, and Gabriela Uruñuela. "Social and Cultural Consequences of a Late Holocene Eruption of Popocatepetl in Central Mexico." *Quaternary International* 51 (July 2006): 19–28.

Pohl, John M. "Mexican Codices, Maps, and Lienzos as Social Contracts." In Boone and Mignolo, *Writing without Words*, 137–60.

Polanyi, Karl. "The Economy as Instituted Process." In *Trade and Markets in the Early Empires*, edited by Karl Polanyi, Conrad Arensberg, and Harry Pearson, 243–70. Glencoe, Ill.: Free Press, 1957.

Portillo y Diez de Sollano, Álvaro del. *Descubrimientos y exploraciones en las costas de California*. Madrid: Escuela de Estudios Hispanoamericanos de Sevilla, 1947.

Powell, Philip W. *La Guerra chichimeca*. Translated by Juan José Utrilla. Mexico: Fondo de Cultura Económica, 1977.

Prem, Hanns J. "The Chronological Dilemma." In *The Native Sources and the History of the Valley of Mexico: Proceedings / 44th International Congress of Americanists*, edited by Jacqueline Durand-Forest, 5–24. Oxford: British Archaeological Reports, 1984.

Price, Barbara. "The Truth Is Not in Accounts but in Account Books: On the Epistemological Status of History." In *Beyond the Myth of Culture: Essays in Cultural Materialism*, edited by Eric B. Ross, 155–80. New York: Academic Press, 1980.

Putnam, Ruth, and H. I. Priestley. "California: The Name." *University of California Publications in History* 4, no. 4 (1917): 293–365.

Quiñones Keber, Eloise. *Codex Telleriano-Remensis: Ritual, Divination, and History in a Pictorial Aztec Manuscript*. Foreword by Emmanuel Le Roy Ladurie. Austin: University of Texas Press, 1995.

Rabasa, José. *Inventing America: Spanish Historiography and the Formation of Eurocentrism*. Norman: University of Oklahoma Press, 1993.

Radding, Cynthia. "The Colonial Pact and Changing Ethnic Frontiers in Highland Sonora, 1740–1840." In *Contested Ground: Comparative Frontiers on the Northern and Southern Edges of the Spanish Empire*, edited by Donna J. Guy and Thomas E. Sheridan, 52–66. Tucson: University of Arizona Press, 1998.

———. *Landscapes of Power and Identity: Comparative Histories in the Sonoran Desert and the Forests of Amazonia from Colony to Republic*. Durham, N.C.: Duke University Press, 2005.

———. *Wandering Peoples: Colonialism, Ethnic Spaces, and Ecological Frontiers in Northwestern Mexico, 1700–1850*. Durham, N.C.: Duke University Press, 1997.

Rafael, Vicente L. *Contracting Colonialism: Translation and Christian Conversion in Tagalog Society under Early Spanish Rule*. Durham, N.C.: Duke University Press, 1993.

Ramos, Demetrio. *El mito de El Dorado*. Madrid: Colegio Universitario, Ediciones Istmo, 1988.

Ranger, Terence. "The Invention of Tradition in Colonial Africa." In *The Invention of Tradition*, edited by Eric Hobsbawm and Terence Ranger, 211–62. Cambridge: Cambridge University Press, 1983.

Rapport, Nigel, and Joanna Overing. *Social and Cultural Anthropology: The Key Concepts*. London: Routledge, 2000.

Razo Zaragoza y Cortés, José Luis, ed. *Crónicas de la conquista del reino de Nueva Galicia en territorio de la Nueva España*. Guadalajara, Jalisco: Ayuntamiento de la Ciudad de Guadalajara, Instituto Jalisciense de Antropología e Historia, 1963.

Real Academia Española. *Diccionario de autoridades*. 1732. Madrid: Gredos, 1984.

Redfield, Robert, Ralph Linton, and Melville J. Herskovitz. "Memorandum for the Study of Acculturation." *American Anthropologist* 38 (1936): 149–52.

Reff, Daniel T. "Anthropological Analysis of Exploration Texts: Cultural Discourse and the Ethnological Import of Friar Marcos de Niza's Journey to Cibola." *American Anthropologist* 93 (1991): 636–55.

———. "The Jesuit Mission Frontier in Comparative Perspective: The Reductions of the Rio de la Plata and the Missions of Northwestern Mexico, 1588–1700." In *Contested Ground: Comparative Frontiers on the Northern and Southern Edges of the Spanish Empire*, edited by Donna J. Guy and Thomas E. Sheridan, 16–31. Tucson: University of Arizona Press, 1998.

Relación de la genealogía y linaje de los señores que han señoreado esta tierra de la Nueva España, después que se acuerdan haber gentes en estas partes. ca. 1530–32. In *Relaciones de la Nueva España*, edited by Germán Vázquez, 101–25. Madrid: Historia 16, 1990.

Relación de la genealogía y linaje de los señores que han señoreado esta tierra de la Nueva España. In *Nueva colección de documentos para la historia de México*, edited by Joaquín García Icazbalceta, 3:256–80. Mexico: Imprenta de Francisco Díaz de León, 1891.

Relación de Michoacán. Edited by L. Cabrero. Madrid: Historia 16, 1989.

Relaciones de la Nueva España. Edited by Germán Vázquez. Madrid: Historia 16, 1990.

Rendón, Silvia. Introduction to *Relaciones originales de Chalco Amaquemecan*, by Domingo Chimalpahin Cuauhtlehuanitzin, edited by Silvia Rendón, 9–35. Mexico: Fondo de Cultura Económica, 1965.

Restall, Matthew. *Seven Myths of the Spanish Conquest*. New York: Oxford University Press, 2003.

Reyes García, Luis, and Odena Güemes. "La zona del altiplano central en el posclásico: la etapa chichimeca." In Manzanilla and López Luján, *Historia antigua de México*, 3:225–64.

Ribera Bernárdez, José. *Compendio de las cosas más notables contenidas en los libros de cabildo de esta ciudad de Nuestra Señora de los Zacatecas desde el año de su descubrimiento 1546 hasta 1730*. Vol. 2. Mexico: Academia Mexicana de la Historia, 1945.

Ricard, Robert. "La diffusion de la légende des Sept Cités en Amérique." *Journal de la Société des Américanistes de Paris*, n.s., 27 (1936): 404–405.

———. "Estebanico de Azamor et la légende des Sept Cités." *Journal de la Société des Américanistes de Paris*, n.s., 21 (1929): 414.

Riley, Carroll L. *Becoming Aztlan: Mesoamerican Influence in the Greater Southwest, A.D. 1200–1500*. Salt Lake City: University of Utah Press, 2005.

———. "Early Spanish-Indian Communication in the Greater Southwest." *New Mexico Historical Review* 46, no. 4 (1971): 285–314.

Río, Ignacio del. *A la diestra mano de las Indias*. Mexico: Universidad Nacional Autónoma de México, Instituto de Investigaciones Históricas, 1990.

———. *Estudios históricos sobre la formación del norte de México*. Mexico: Universidad Nacional Autónoma de México, 2009.

Robertson, Donald. *Mexican Manuscript Painting of the Early Colonial Period: The Metropolitan Schools*. 1958. Foreword by Elizabeth Hill Boone. Norman: University of Oklahoma Press, 1994.

Rodríguez Prampolini, Ida. *Amadises en América: la hazaña de Indias como empresa caballeresca*. Mexico: Junta Mexicana de Investigaciones Históricas, 1948.

Rojas, José Luis de. *México Tenochtitlan: economía y sociedad en el siglo XVI*. Mexico: El Colegio de Michoacán, Fondo de Cultura Económica, 1986.

Romero Galván, José Rubén. *Octava relación: obra histórica de Domingo Francisco de San Antón Muñón Chimalpahin Cuauhtlehuanitzin*. Mexico: Universidad Nacional Autónoma de México, Instituto de Investigaciones Históricas, 1983.

Rubial, Antonio. "Estudio preliminar." In *Historia eclesiástica indiana*, by Gerónimo de Mendieta, edited by Antonio Rubial, 15–91. Mexico: Consejo Nacional Para la Cultura y las Artes, 1997.

Rubio Mañé, José Ignacio. *El virreinato*. Vol. 1. Mexico: Fondo de Cultura Económica, Universidad Nacional Autónoma de México, 1983.

Ruiz, Antonio. *La relación de Antonio Ruiz (La conquista del noroeste)*. ca. 1595–1600. Edited by Antonio Nakayama. Mexico: Instituto Nacional de Antropología e Historia, Centro Regional del Noroeste, 1974.

Ruiz Medrano, Ethelia. *Mexico's Indigenous Communities: Their Lands and Histories, 1500 to 2010*. Translated by Russ Davidson. Niwot: University Press of Colorado, 2010.

Sahagún, Bernardino de. *Historia general de las cosas de Nueva España: primera versión íntegra del texto castellano del manuscrito conocido como Códice Florentino*. ca. 1558–77. Introduction and paleography by Alfredo López Austin and Josefina García Quintana. Mexico: Consejo Nacional para la Cultura y las Artes, Alianza Editorial, 1989.

Sahlins, Marshall. *How "Natives" Think: About Captain Cook, for Example*. Chicago: University of Chicago Press, 1995.

Said, Edward W. *Orientalism: Western Conceptions of the Orient*. 1978. London: Penguin, 1995.

Sánchez Albornoz, Claudio. *La edad media española y la empresa de América*. 1934. Madrid: Cultura Hispánica, 1983.

Saravia, Atanasio G. *Obras: apuntes para la historia de la Nueva Vizcaya*. Mexico: Universidad Nacional Autónoma de México, Instituto de Investigaciones Históricas, 1978.

Sauer, Carl O. *Aboriginal Population of Northwestern Mexico*. Berkeley: University of California Press, 1935.

———. *Colima of New Spain in the XVI Century*. Berkeley: University of California Press, 1948.

———. "The Credibility of the Fray Marcos Account." *New Mexico Historical Review* 16 (1940): 233–43.

———. *The Road to Cibola*. Berkeley: University of California Press, 1932.

Schroeder, Albert. "History of Archaeological Research." In *Handbook of North American Indians*, vol. 9, *The Southwest*, edited by William C. Sturtevant, 5–13. Washington, D.C.: Smithsonian Institution, 1979.

Schwartz, Stuart B. Introduction to *Implicit Understandings: Observing, Reporting, and Reflecting on the Encounters between Europeans and Other Peoples in the Early Modern Era*, edited by Stuart B. Schwartz, 1–19. Cambridge: Cambridge University Press, 1994.

Scully, Pamela. "Rape, Race, and Colonial Culture: The Sexual Politics of Identity in the Nineteenth-Century Cape Colony, South Africa." *American Historical Review* 100 (1995): 335–59.

Sego, Eugene. *Aliados y adversarios: los colonos tlaxcaltecas en la frontera septentrional de Nueva España*. San Luis Potosí, Mexico: El Colegio de San Luis, 1998.

Seler, Eduard. "¿Dónde se encontraba Aztlan, la patria (original) de los aztecas?" 1894. In *Mesoamérica y el centro de México*, edited by Jesús Monjarás Ruiz, Emma Pérez Rocha, and Rosa Brambila, 309–30. Mexico: Instituto Nacional de Antropología e Historia, 1985.

Sheridan, Alan. *Michel Foucault: The Will to Truth*. London: Tavistock, 1980.
Sheridan, Cecilia. "Social Control and Native Territoriality in Northeastern New Spain." In *Choice, Persuasion, and Coercion: Social Control on Spain's North American Frontiers*, edited by Jesús F. de la Teja and Ross Frank, 121–48. Albuquerque: University of New Mexico Press, 2005.
Sigüenza y Góngora, Carlos. *The Mercurio Volante: An Account of the First Expedition of don Diego de Vargas into New Mexico in 1692*. 1693. 3 vols. Translated by Irving A. Leonard. Los Angeles: Quivira Society, 1932.
Simmons, Marc. *The Last Conquistador: Juan de Oñate and the Settling of the Far Southwest*. Norman: University of Oklahoma Press, 1991.
Smith, Bruce D. *The Emergence of Agriculture*. New York: Scientific American Library, 1995.
Smith, Michael. "The Aztlan Migrations of the Nahuatl Chronicles: Myth or History?" *Ethnohistory* 31, no. 3 (1984): 153–86.
Sodi, Demetrio. "Consideraciones sobre el origen de la Toltecáyotl." *Estudios de Cultura Náhuatl* 3 (1962): 55–73.
Spicer, Edward H. *Cycles of Conquest: The Impact of Spain, Mexico, and the United States on the Indians of the Southwest, 1533–1960*. 1962. Tucson: University of Arizona Press, 1981.
Staller, John E., Robert H. Tykot, and Bruce F. Benz, eds. *Histories of Maize: Multidisciplinary Approaches to the Prehistory, Linguistics, Biogeography, Domestication, and Evolution of Maize*. Amsterdam: Elsevier Academic Press, 2006.
Stern, Peter. "Marginals and Acculturation in Frontier Society." In *New Views of Borderlands History*, edited by Robert H. Jackson, 157–88. Albuquerque: University of New Mexico Press, 1998.
Stoler, Ann Laura. "Rethinking Colonial Categories: European Communities and the Boundaries of Rule." *Comparative Studies in Society and History* 13, no. 1 (1989): 134–61.
Subirats, Eduardo. *El continente vacío: la conquista del Nuevo Mundo y la conciencia moderna*. Mexico: Siglo XXI, 1994.
Sued-Badillo, Jalil. "El mito indoantillano de las mujeres sin hombres." *Boletín de Estudios Latinoamericanos y del Caribe* 40 (1986).
Tambiah, Stanley J. "A Reformulation of Geertz's Conception of the Theatre State." In *Culture, Thought, and Social Action: An Anthropological Perspective*, edited by Stanley J. Tambiah, 321–24. Cambridge, Mass.: Harvard University Press, 1985.
Taussig, Michael. "Culture of Terror, Space of Death: Roger Casement's Putumayo Report and the Explanation of Torture." *Comparative Studies in Society and History* 26 (1984): 467–97.
———. *Mimesis and Alterity: A Particular History of the Senses*. London: Routledge, 1993.
Teja, Jesús F. de la, and Ross Frank, eds. *Choice, Persuasion, and Coercion: Social Control on Spain's North American Frontiers*. Albuquerque: University of New Mexico Press, 2005.
Tello, Antonio. *Crónica miscelánea en que se trata de la conquista espiritual y temporal de la santa provincia de Xalisco en el nuevo reino de la Galicia y Nueva Vizcaya y el descubrimiento de Nuevo México*. ca. 1651. Guadalajara: Imprenta de la República Literaria de Ciro L. Guevara, 1891.

———. "Fragmentos de una historia de la Nueva Galicia, escrita hacia 1650." In *Colección de documentos para la historia de México*, edited by Joaquín García Icazbalceta. Mexico: Porrúa, 1973.

Thomas, Hugh. *The Conquest of Mexico*. London: Pimlico, 1993.

———. *The Real Discovery of America: Mexico, November 8, 1519*. New York: Moyer Bell, 1992.

Thomas, Nicholas. *Colonialism's Culture: Anthropology, Travel, and Government*. Cambridge, U.K.: Polity Press, 1994.

———. *Entangled Objects: Exchange, Material Culture, and Colonialism in the Pacific*. Cambridge, Mass.: Harvard University Press, 1991.

Tibón, Gutierre. *Historia del nombre y de la fundación de México*. Mexico: Fondo de Cultura Económica, 1980.

Tira de Tepechpan: códice colonial procedente del valle de México. Facsimilar edition by Xavier Noguez. Mexico: Instituto Mexiquense de Cultura, 1978.

Todorov, Tzvetan. *The Conquest of America: The Question of the Other*. 1st French ed. 1982. Foreword by Anthony Pagden, translated by Richard Howard. Norman: University of Oklahoma Press, 1999.

Torquemada, Juan de. *Monarquía indiana. De los veinte y un libros rituales y monarquía indiana, con el origen y guerras de los indios occidentales, de sus poblazones, descubrimiento, conquista, conversión y otras cosas maravillosas de la mesma tierra*. 7 vols. 1615. Mexico: Universidad Nacional Autónoma de México, Instituto de Investigaciones Históricas, 1975–83.

Udall, Stuart. *To the Inland Empire: Coronado and Our Spanish Legacy*. Garden City, N.Y.: Doubleday, 1987.

Undreiner, George J. "Fray Marcos de Niza and his Journey to Cibola." *The Americas* 3 (1947): 415–86.

Urquijo Durazo, Josefina. "Perspectiva nacionalista y trabajo jesuítico: la ausencia de Nebrija en la acción lingüístico-educativa del noroeste." In Guzmán and Nansen, *Memoria del coloquio "La obra de Antonio de Nebrija y su recepción en la Nueva España,"* 163–75.

Valle, Perla. "Estudio preliminar." In *Códice de Tlatelolco*, 19–85. Mexico: Instituto Nacional de Antropología e Historia, Benemérita Universidad de Puebla, 1994.

Vázquez, Germán, ed. *La conquista de Tenochtitlan*, by Juan Díaz, Andrés de Tapia, Bernardino Vázquez de Tapia, and Francisco de Aguilar. Madrid: Historia 16, 1988.

Vega, Garcilaso de la. *La Florida del Inca*. 1605. Edited by Sylvia L. Hilton. Madrid: Fundación Universitaria Española, 1982.

Velázquez, María del Carmen. *Establecimiento y pérdida del septentrión de Nueva España*. Mexico: El Colegio de México, 1974.

Villagrá, Gaspar de. *Historia de la Nueva México*. 1610. Edited by Mercedes Junquera. Madrid: Historia 16, 1989.

———. *Historia de la Nueva México*. 1610. Edited by Francisco del Paso y Troncoso. Mexico: Museo Nacional de México, 1900.

Wachtel, Nathan. "La aculturación." In *Hacer la historia*, vol. 1, edited by Jacques Le Goff and Pierre Nora, 135–55. Translated by Jem Cabanes. Barcelona: Laia, 1978.

———. *The Vision of the Vanquished: The Spanish Conquest of Peru through Indian Eyes, 1530–1570*. Translated by Ben Reynolds and Sian Reynolds. Sussex, U.K.: Harvester Press, 1977.

Wagner, Henry R. *The Discovery of Yucatan by Francisco Hernández de Córdoba: A Translation of the Original Texts.* Berkeley, Calif.: Cortes Society, 1942.

———. "Fray Marcos de Niza." *New Mexico Historical Review* 9 (1934): 184–227.

———. *The Spanish Southwest, 1542–1794: An Annotated Bibliography.* Pt. 1. New York: Arno Press, 1967.

Warren, J. Benedict. *La conquista de Michoacán, 1521–1530.* Translated by Agustín García Alcaraz. Morelia, Michoacán: Fimax Publicistas, 1979.

Weber, David J. *Myth and the History of the Hispanic Southwest.* Albuquerque: University of New Mexico Press, 1987.

———, ed. *New Spain's Far Northern Frontier: Essays on Spain in the American West, 1540–1821.* Albuquerque: University of New Mexico Press, 1979.

———. *The Spanish Frontier in North America.* New Haven, Conn.: Yale University Press, 1992.

Weckmann, Luis. "The Alexandrine Bulls of 1493: Pseudo-Asiatic Documents." In *First Images of America: The Impact of the New World on the Old*, vol. 1, edited by Fredi Chiappelli, 200–209. Berkeley and Los Angeles: University of California Press, 1976.

———. *La herencia medieval de México.* Mexico: El Colegio de México, 1984.

———. "The Middle Ages in the Conquest of America." *Speculum* 26, no. 1 (1951): 130–41.

Weigand, Phil C. "Architectural Principles Illustrated in Archaeology: A Case Study from Western Mesoamerica." In *Arqueologia del norte y del occidente de México: homenaje al Dr. J. Charles Kelley*, edited by Barbro Dahlgren and María D. Soto de Arechavaleta, 159–72. Mexico: Universidad Nacional Autónoma de México, Instituto de Investigaciones Antropológicas, 1995.

———. "La prehistoria del estado de Zacatecas: una interpretación." *Anuario de Historia* 1 (1978): 203–48.

West, Robert C., and John Augelli. *Middle America: Its Lands and Peoples.* Englewood Cliffs, N.J.: Prentice Hall, 1976.

Whitecotton, Joseph, and Richard Pailes. "New World Precolumbian World Systems." In *Ripples in the Chichimec Sea*, edited by Frances Joan Mathien and Randall McGuire, 183–204. Carbondale: Southern Illinois University Press, 1986.

Whiteley, Peter M. "Unpacking Hopi Clans: Another Vintage Model Out of Africa?" *Journal of Anthropological Research* 41, no. 4 (1985): 359–74.

Wills, Wirt H. "Patterns of Prehistoric Food Production in West-Central New Mexico." *Journal of Anthropological Research* 45, no. 3 (1989): 139–53.

Winship, George P. *The Coronado Expedition: Fourteenth Annual Report of the U.S. Bureau of American Ethnology.* Washington, D.C.: Bureau of American Ethnology, 1896.

Wissler, Clark. *The American Indian: An Introduction to the Anthropology of the New World.* 1917. Gloucester, Mass.: Peter Smith, 1938.

Wolf, Eric R. "Closed Corporate Peasant Communities in Mesoamerica and Central Java." *Southwestern Journal of Anthropology* 13 (1957): 1–18.

———. *Europe and the People without History.* Berkeley: University of California Press, 1982.

Wood, Stephanie. "Nahua Christian Warriors in the Mapa Cuauhtlantzinco, Cholula Parish." In *Indian Conquistadors: Indigenous Allies in the Conquest of Mesoamerica*, edited by Laura Matthew and Michel R. Oudijk, 254–88. Norman: University of Oklahoma Press, 2007.

———. *Transcending Conquest: Nahua Views of Spanish Colonial Mexico*. Norman: University of Oklahoma Press, 2003.

Woodbury, Richard B. "Prehistory: Introduction." In *Handbook of North American Indians*, vol. 9, *The Southwest*, edited by William C. Sturtevant, 22–30. Washington, D.C.: Smithsonian Institution, 1979.

Worsley, Peter. *The Trumpet Shall Sound: A Study of "Cargo" Cults in Melanesia*. New York: Schocken, 1968.

Wright, David. "Linguistic Rights: A View from Central Mexico." Paper presented at the World Conference on Linguistic Rights, organized by the International Association of Poets, Playwrights, Editors, Essayists, and Novelists (PEN International) and the Escarro International Center for Ethnic Minorities and Nations (CIEMEN), Barcelona, June 7, 1996.

Yelvington, Kevin A. "Ethnicity as Practice? A Comment on Bentley." *Comparative Studies in Society and History* 33, no. 1 (1991): 158–68.

Yoneda, Keiko. *Los mapas de Cuauhtinchan y la historia cartográfica prehispánica*. Mexico: Fondo de Cultura Económica, 1991.

Zantwijk, Rudolf. "Quetzalcoatl y Huemac, mito y realidad azteca." In *Myth and the Imaginary in the New World*, edited by Edmundo Magaña and Peter Mason, 321–58. Amsterdam: Centrum voor Studie en Documentatie van Latijns-Amerika, 1986.

Zárate Salmerón, Gerónimo de. "Relaciones de todas las cosas que en el Nuevo México se han visto y sabido así por mar como por tierra desde el año de 1538 hasta el de 1626." ca. 1629. In *Documentos para servir a la historia de Nuevo México, 1538–1778*, 114–204. Madrid: José Porrúa Turranzas, 1965.

Index

Page numbers in italic type indicate plates, figures, or maps.

Abbot, Ellen, 48
Acauzitli, Francisco, 185, 261n57
Acculturation, 10–11, 111, 203
Acolhuas, 116, 121, 123, 130
Acoma, 73, 79, 84–85
Acoma rebellion (1599), 84–85
Acosta, José de, 116, 122–23, 126
Acosta Saignes, Miguel, 126
Aeneas Sylvius, 31
Agriculture, 32–33, 53, 54, 222n46; irrigation in, 42, 45–46, 75, 122; in Mesoamerica, 38, 41–42, 43–44, 46–47
Aguacatlán, 55, 57, 67
Aguilar, Francisco de, 28–29, 213n31, 214n36
Aguilar, Jerónimo de, 32
Ahumada, Pedro de, 77
Ainsa, Fernando, 92, 107
Alarcón, Hernando de, 72, 73
Altepetl, 111, 121, 124, 127, 130, 131–32; as basic political unit, 119–20, 253n73; Spanish conception of, 120, 122, 124–25, 254n87
Alterity, 8–9, 16, 32, 197, 200, 203, 211n3
Alva Ixtilxóchitl, Fernando de, 116, 126, 129, 194
Alvarado, Pedro de, 63, 72, 98, 215n56
Alvarado Tezozómoc, Hernando, 116, 124–25, 126, 128, 131, 182, 192
Amazons legend, 91, 94–100; Columbus and, 93, 95; Cortés and, 93, 96, 98–99
Anales de Cuauhtitlán, 118, 129
Anales de Tlatelolco, 117, 128, 252n57
Anonymous Conqueror, 28–29

Anthropological history, 3–4, 206n9
Antillia, 94, 100–107
Apaches, 52, 54, 226n82
Arceo, Francisco de, 66, 100, 231n33, 232n50
Arias, Santa, 3
Aridamerica, 58–59, *160*; as analytical model, 50–51, 53–54, 224–25n71; as culture area, 2, 37, 38, 58
Armillas, Pedro, 46, 48
Arricuita, Juan Domingo, 70–71
Ascensión, Juan de la, 71
Astatlán (Aztatlán), 99
Athabascans, 52, 84, 226n82
Atlantis legend, 93, 103
Aurea Chersonesus, 94
Avalos, Juan de, 63
Ayala, Pedro de, 102–103
Ayllón, Lucas Vázquez de, 106, 230n19
Azcapotzalco, 130, 131, 132, *162*
Aztatlán region and cultural complex, 49, 68, 71, *160*
Aztec empire, 30, 45–46, 102, 109, 121; limits of, 2, 65; Mexico-Tenochtitlan and, 15, 32, 63, 205n3, 213n19; Spanish conquest of, 102, 175; Triple Alliance and, 115, 132, 192
Aztec/Mexicas, 110; group identity of, 118–25; history of in alphabetic sources, 115–18, 192; migrations by, 2, 91, 112, 123, 125–32; Nuevo México as chimerical realm of, 1–2, 187–92; pictorial codices of, 56, 113–15, 131, *138*, *145*, *147*, *168*, *169*,

295

Aztec/Mexicas (*continued*)
177, 180; rulership among, 19–20, 22–23, 111, 121, 132; usage of terms, 119, 205n2, 247n9. *See also* Nahua migration narratives; Tenochtitlan

Aztlan, 35, 40, 124, 178, 181; Mexico-Tenochtitlan and, 125–32, 186–87, 188–89; name and characteristics of, 125–27; Nuevo México linked to, 3, 123, 174–76, 183–84, 185–88, 190, 192, 198; pictorial depictions of, *140*, *141*, *142–43*, *144*, *169*; as sign of cultural resistance, 202–3; *Yancuic Mexico* as, 191

Baber, Jovita, 202
Baja California, 71, 97–98, 234n79
Bakhtin, Mikhail, 11
Bancroft, Hubert H., 7, 74
Bandelier, Adolph F., 74, 75, 106
Barlow, Robert, 115
Barth, Frederick, 118
Batista Ramusio, Giovanni, 216n65
Beals, Ralph L., 53
Becerra, Diego de, 97
Bedario, 103
Behaim, Martin, 104
Beltrán, Bernardino, 80, 190–91
Benincasa, Grazioso, 103
Bernand, Carmen, 21, 199
Bhabha, Homi, 9, 196, 203
Bianco, Andrea, 103
Bimini Regio, 188
Bolton, Herbert E., 7, 106
Boone, Elizabeth Hill, 113
Borah, Woodrow, 64
Bourne, Edward G., 106
Braniff, Beatriz, 6, 48, 58
Brinton, Daniel G., 41
Brooks, James, 10
Brotherston, Gordon, 184, 251n44, 255n104

Cabeza de Vaca, Alvar Núñez, 7, 79, 174; expedition of, 33, 69, 70, *164*, 217n86, 234n66, 234n69; reports of indigenous cities by, 60, 61, 101, 182
Cabrero, María Teresa, 6

Caciques, 20, 22–23, 199
Cadena, Diego de la, 78
Cahitas, 52, 54
Caicedo, Antonio, 63
Calendar, 42, 113, 249n26, 254–55n104
California, 83, 94–98
Calpulli (Hispanicized plural form of calpolli), 42, 111, 120–21, 124–25
Campo, Andrés do, 74
Cano, Francisco, 186, 188
Cano, Juan, 117
Cape Mendocino, 25, 215n50
Capitulaciones, 17–18, 80, 82, 83
Caribs, 34, 217–18n88; Caribbean peoples as uncivilized, 21–22, 31, 33–34, 199
Carot, Patricia, 6
Carranza, Pedro de, 69, 100, 231n33, 232n50
Carta del Cabildo, 18, 22, 31, 212n13
Cartagena de Indias as place-name, 25, 26
Cartography, 101, 103, 187, 190
Casa de Contratción de Sevilla, 17
Casas, Bartolomé de las, 8, 101
Castañeda Nájera, Pedro de, 66, 67, 71, 72
Castaño de Sosa, Gaspar, 81, 84
Castilla del Oro, as place-name, 25
Castillo, Cristóbal del, 116–17, 252n54
Castillo Maldonado, Bernardino del, 70
Catholicism, 23, 101, 102, 174, 195
Cazorla, Pedro, 81
Central Mexico sub-area, 2, 43, 45
Central Plateau, Mexican, 17, 36–37, 44, 46, 48, 50, 54
Chalchihuites, 47, 48–49, 77, *160*, 223n53, 223n55, 224n56
Chalchiuhtlatónac, 181
Chalco, 121, 130
Chalco Amaquemecan, 116
Chametla, 68, 69, 78, 233n56
Chapultepec, 128, 130, *167*
Chichén Itzá, 50
Chichimecas, 34, 56–58, 130, 190; ambiguity of term, 6, 39, 54–55, 129–30, 217n85; and group identity, 6, 119, 122–23; as hunter-gatherers, 39, 54, 55–56, 57, 122; and migration, 123, 129, 247n6; native meanings for, 57; Spanish use of term, 6, 33, 39, 40, 55

Chichimeca War, 76, 237n112
Chicomoztoc, 124, 193; depictions of, *135, 136, 137, 165, 166,* 187; and Nahua origin myth, 2, 35, 104–107, 109, 110, 112–13, 123–25, 127, 178–81
Chihuahua, 38, 52, 53, 54, 61, 174
Chimalpahin Cuauhtlehuanitzin, Domingo, 116, 125, 180–81, 192, 251nn51–52
Chipman, Donald, 66
Chirino, Peralmíndez, 68
Chivalric literature, 92, 93, 96, 101
Cholula, 24, 115
Cíbola, 7, 31–35, 62–86, 93, 182, 190; first use of term, 71, 234n78; Guzmán expedition and, 67, 176; Niza and legend of, 33, 60, 71–72, 74–76, 93, 101, 104, 105; Nuevo México initially called, 2, 33, 60, 79, 80; possible inspirations for, 73, 105, 106–107; and seven bishops legend, 104, 106; *Tlaxcala Codex,* depiction of, *172.* See also Nuevo México
Cihuatlán, 96, 97, 99, 100, 244n30
Cintos, Friar, 77, 237n117. *See also* San Francisco, Jacinto de
Ciudad Rodrigo, Antonio de, 70
Civilization, 210–11n2, 212–13n19; Spanish conquerors' view of, 15, 19, 21–22, 23, 191–92
Classic Horizon, 45, 46
Clavijero, Francisco Javier, 49
Climate change, 48
Coahuila, 50, 54, 61, 186
Coatepec, 128, *150*
Coatlinchan, 130, 132
Codex Aubin (Códice de 1576), 114, 126, 131, 186–87; depictions from, *139, 140, 141, 147, 165*
Codex Azcatitlan, 109, 114, 125, 126, 128, 131, 182, 188; depictions from, *142–43, 148–49, 150, 168*
Codex Huitzilopochtli, 115
Codex Mendoza, 30, 67, 115, 126, 131, 250n39; depictions from, *145*
Codex Mexicanus, 109, 114, 125, 126; depictions from, *137, 140*
Codex Vaticano Ríos, 114–15, 250n37

Códice Boturini, 113–14, 126, 179, 188, 250n29; depictions from, *167, 169, 170, 171*
Códice Chimalpopoca, 118
Códice de Tlatelolco, 73, *153,* 184–85
Códice Florentino (Sahagún), 56, 122, 123, 228n102
Códice Ramírez, 116, 126
Cognition and alterity, 6, 10–11, 15, 16, 22, 26, 27, 62, 173, 187, 196, 200, 206n16; Cohn, Bernard, 3, 10
Cohn, Norman, 195
Colhuacan, 19, 28, 127, *148–49,* 213n19. *See also* Culhuacan
Colima, 43, 64, 244n30; conquest of, 63, 65, 96
Colonial appropriation, 2–3, 8, 16, 22, 24, 26, 197, 199
Colonial discourse, 9–10, 196–97
Colonial knowledge, 38–39
Colonial place-names, 15–16, 25–26, 211n3
Colonial semiosis, 11–12, 16, 203, 211n7
Colorado River and Plateau, 36, 73
Columbus, Christopher, 20, 31, 95, 243n22; and Amazons, 93, 95; and Antillia legend, 101–102; and Hispaniola, 16, 26
Columbus, Ferdinand, 100
Comaroff, John and Jean, 9–10, 198, 201, 203
Concho Indians, 54
Conchos River, 79, 83, 190
Copala, 77, 78, 190; and Nuevo México name, 185, 189, 190; Spanish search for, 78, 185
Cópil, 128, 130, 131, *168*
Corbey, Raymond, 16
Coronil, Fernando, 11
Cortés, Francisco, 63, 67, 99
Cortés, Hernán, 30, 61, 64, 69, 70; and Amazons legend, 93, 96, 98–99; astonishment and awe by, 15, 23–24, 27; in Baja California, 71, 234n79; and Carta del Cabildo, 18, 22; and early conquests in New Spain, 62–63; expedition toward Valley of Mexico by, 27, 31, 32, 72, 102, *158–59,* 174,

Cortés, Hernán (*continued*)
217n81; and Mexico-Tenochtitlan, 15, 18, 19–20, 27, 28, 216n545; and Moctezuma, 19–20, 32, 62–63; and naming of Nueva España, 5, 18, 19, 212n13; and Pánuco-Oxitipa, 64–65, 67; Pacific navigation program of, 97; and Vázquez de Coronado, 72, 75
Coyolxauhqui, 128, 182
Crónica del Rey Don Rodrigo y la destrucción de España, 10
Crónica mexicana (Alvarado Tezozómoc), 116
Crónica mexicáyotl (Alvarado Tezozómoc), 116, 124–25
Crónica X, 115, 116
Cross-cultural interaction, 3, 9, 22, 39, 90, 175–76, 187–88, 194, 197–98; contemporary models of, 7–8, 203; as dialectical process, 10, 92; and "double mistaken identity," 24; intersubjectivity in, 201–202; in quest for Nuevo México, 62, 200–201; transformations resulting from, 4, 39
Cruz, Juan de la, 235n91
Cuauhnochtli, Alonso, 72–73
Cuauhtlequetzqui, 109
Cuauhtzin, Martín, 73
Cuba, 25, 31–32, 204
Cuextecachichimeca, 58, 229n111
Cuitzeo, 37, 68
Culhuacan, 123, 130, 132, 176. See also Colhuacan
Culhuas, 56, 131, 176, 259n8; as Mexicas' ancestors (Culguas Mexicanos), 61, 78, 175, 185, 191; and Toltec ancestry, 129–30, 132
Culiacán, 68, 73, 74, 233n56, 238n126
Culture areas, 2, 6, 37, 38, 53–54, 58; concept of, 40–41; Southwest as, 51

D'Ailly, Pierre, 31
Darnton, Robert, 4
Deeds, Susan, 37–38
De Orbe Novo Decades (Mártir de Anglería), 20, 213n22
Desert Culture, 46, 47

Díaz, Juan, 19, 31, 98, 212n15
Díaz del Castillo, Bernal, 22, 28, 32, 96, 98, 216n65
Díaz de Vargas, Francisco, 80
Di Peso, Charles, 58
Dorantes, Andrés, 70
"Double mistaken identity," 24
Douglas, Mary, 206n9
Dourado, Fernão Vaz, *154–55*, 187–88
Durán, Diego, 116, 123, 128, 131, 182, 189
Durango, 6, 38, 48–49, 52–53, 61, 78, 174, 186; in Spanish empire, 78, 80
Durkheim, Emile, 206n9
Duverger, Christian, 126, 255n104

El Dorado legend, 94
Elliott, John, 196, 197
El Teúl, 49, 68
England, 64, 83
Enríquez, Martín, 55
Espejo, Antonio de, 80, 174, 190
Espinareda, Pedro de, 78, 189, 238n119
Espíritu Santo (Compostela), 68, 76, 233n59
Esteven (Moorish slave), 70, 71, 72, 75
Estreito, Juan Alfonso del, 103
Ethnicity, 34, 59, 91, 111, 118, 119

Fabian, Johannes, 8
Fetish, 21, 200. See also Zemes
First Images of America, 196
Flores, Cristóbal, 100, 231n33
Florida, 63, 64, 73, 93, 106, 230–31n18
Foucault, Michel, 8, 16
Fountain of Youth, 91, 93, 188
France, 64, 83, 230n21
Frías Salazar, Juan de, 83

Galactic polity, 121–22
Galicia Chimalpopoca, Faustino, 118
Gallego, Hernando, 79
Gallegos, Ana, 184
Gandía, Enrique de, 93, 104, 105, 107, 175
Garay, Francisco de, 64
Garibay, K., 117–18
Geertz, Clifford, 45
Gibson, Charles, 74

Ginés de Sepúlveda, Juan, 8
Goddard, Pliny E., 51
Gold and silver, 64, 68, 76–77, 81, 92
Gómez de Villalobos, Ruy, 234n78
Goodman, Nelson, 204
Graulich, Michel, 126
Greenblatt, Stephen, 96, 196–97, 200
Gregg, Josiah, 82
Grijalva, Hernando de, 97
Grijalva, Juan de, 18–19, 21, 32, 98, 212n15
Gruzinski, Serge, 21, 199
Guachichiles, 54, 55, 76
Guamares, 55, 76
Guanajuato, 47, 50, 68, 76, 126, 129
Guerrero, Gonzalo, 106
Guzmán, Nuño de, 65, 93; execution of cazonci by, 68, 232n50; expedition of conquest by, 49, 59, 63, 66–69, 72, 99, *164*
Guzmán, Pedro de, 67

Hale, Edward Everett, 97
Hallenbeck, Cleve, 75
Hanke, Lewis, 92
Harvey, H. R., 111
Haskett, Robert, 23
Hassig, Ross, 30, 211n8
Hawikuh (Zuñi), 73
Heredia, Pedro de, 80
Hernández de Córdoba, Francisco, 21, 31, 102, 217n81, 230n19
Hernández Portocarrrero, Alonso, 212n13, 213n20
Herrera, Antonio de, 101, 104, 105
Hers, Marie-Areti, 6, 49–50, 57, 194, 222n46
Herskovitz, Melville J., 10
Hieroglyphics, 42, 177, 180
Hispania victrix (López de Gómara), 101–102
Hispaniola, 16, 20, 21, 26, 215n54
Histoire du Mechique, 117, 126, 252n62
Histoire mexicaine depuis 1221 jusqu'en 1595, 114, 125, 126, 131, *169*, 186–87
Historia de la invención de las Indias (Pérez de Oliva), 21

Historia del Almirante Cristóbal Colón (F. Columbus), 100
Historia de la nación chichimeca (Alva Ixtilxóchitl), 116, 194
Historia de la Nueva México (Villagrá), 82, 174, 178–84, 240n148, 259n21
Historia de las Indias de Nueva España e islas de la tierra firme (Durán), 116
Historia de la venida de los mexicanos y de otros pueblos (Castillo), 116–17
Historia de los descubrimientos antiguos y modernos de la Nueva España (Obregón), 61, 78, 83, 174, 217n88, 226n76
Historia de los indios de la Nueva España (Motolinía), 55–56, 57, 58, 118, 252n67, 254n94
Historia de los mexicanos por sus pinturas, 117–18, 128, 182
Historia de Tlaxcala (Muñoz Camargo), *172*, 184, 192
Historia eclesiástica indiana (Mendieta), 118
Historia general de las cosas de Nueva España (Sahagún), 118, 129, 193, 254n87
Historia general de las Indias (López de Gómara), 102
Historia general y natural de las Indias (Oviedo), 70, 98, 234n66, 244n38
Historia natural y moral de las Indias (Acosta), 116, 122–23, 126
Historia Tolteca-Chichimeca, 109, 115, *136*, 187
Historiography of New Mexico, standard, 2, 60–62, 77, 191, 201
History: and anthropology, 3–4, 206n9; indigenous narratives and, 56, 109, 110, 112, 119–20, 177, 184, 248n22, 259n9; political geography and, 60
Hodge, Frederick W., 73, 106
Homer, 93
Hopi, 52, 73
Horgan, Paul, 74, 84
Huasteco, 58
Huexotzincas, 130, 132
Huitzilíhuitl, 132

Huitzilopochtli, 109, 178; and Aztec/Mexicas migration, 127, 128, 130, 131, 192; depiction of, *150*, 182; temple-pyramids dedicated to, 28, 131
Huixtotin, 57
Hulme, Peter, 8, 215n54
Humaña, Juan de, 81
Human sacrifice, 131, *171*, 258n147
Hunter-gatherers, 43–44, 46, 52, 53, 54, 55–56, 57
Hybridity, 9, 11, 203

Ibarra, Diego de, 61, 76
Ibarra, Francisco de, 61, 76–78, 174, 185, 189, 238n122
Idolatry, 20–22, 23, 191, 199
Imaginary world: concept of, 1, 205n1; Nuevo México as, 1–2, 7, 60, 62, 177, 185–86, 188, 198
Incas, 17, 220n23
Indigenous agency, 9, 10, 66, 92, 201
Indigenous revolts, 64, 69; Acoma rebellion, 84–85; Chichimeca War, 76, 237n112; Mixtón War, 69, 72, 76, 184, 261n57; Pueblo Revolt, 86, 194–95, 202; Tiguex uprising, 73, 235n89; Zacateco-Guahichil rebellion, 77
Intersubjectivity, 10, 176, 198, 201–202
La invención de América (O'Gorman), 15
Isabel (queen of Portugal), 65
Ixtlilxóchitl, Fernando de Alva, 202
Iztaccíhuatl, 37

Jalisco, 43, 49, 63, 68, 69, 111, 129
Jaramillo, Juan, 72, 105, 106
Jiménez, Lázaro, 85–86
Jiménez Moreno, Wigberto, 126–27, 186
Jusepe, 81

Kelley, Charles, 48
Keres (Queres), 52
Kinship, 119, 120, 206n9
Kiowa-Tanoan, 52
Kirchhoff, Paul, 37, 40–41, 43, 58, 126–27, 187, 224n71
Knight of Elvas, 73
Kroeber, Alfred, 41

Laguna Grande de Coahuila (Ciénaga de Patos), 186
La invención de América (O'Gorman), 15
Lake Chapala, 37, 46, 68
Lake Copala, 186
Lake Pátzcuaro, 37, 109, 128
Lake Tetzcoco, 27–28, 131, *162*
Lake Xochimilco, 27–28, *162*
Language, 40–41, 108, 220n15, 246n3; and group identity, 119, 122, 124; Mayan, 25, 42, 247n10; Náhuatl, 43, 45, 49, 52, 56, 58, 108, 110–11, 117, 126, 191, 246n3, 248n16, 252n56; Oto-Manguean family, 43, 246n3; Otomí, 2, 43, 108, 119, 124, 246n3; Shoshone, 52; Tanoan, 52; Uto-Aztecan family, 43, 52, 246n3
Las sergas de Esplandián (Montalvo), 93, 94–95, 97, 100, 243n20
La Quemada, 48, 49, 68, 77, 183
Leach, Edmund, 118
Lecompte, Janet, 73–74
Leonard, Irving, 95, 175
Lerma River, 37, 68
Levinas, Emmanuel, 8
Lewis, Theodore H., 106
Leyenda de los soles, 118
Leyva Bonilla, Francisco, 81
Lienzo de Tlaxcala, 72, 184, 192
Linton, Ralph, 10
Lisuarte de Grecia, 93
Lockhart, James, 10, 24, 120–21, 122, 198
Lomas y Colmenares, Juan Bautista de, 80
López, Francisco, 79
López, Gonzalo, 69, 99–100, 231n33
López, Jerónimo, 99
López Austin, Alfredo, 45, 108, 109, 110, 119, 127–28, 193–94
López de Gómara, Francisco, 25, 101–102, 105–106
López Luján, Leonardo, 108, 110
Los toltecas en tierras chichimecas (Hers), 57
Luna y Arellano, Tristán, 231–32nn19–20

Maize, 44, 222nn36–38
Malinalco, 128

Malintzin, 32
Mandeville, Sir John, 93, 104
Manso Indians, 84
Mapa de Cuauhtinchan no. 2, 109, 115, *135*, 187
Mapa Sigüenza, 115, 126, *141*, 186–87
Martín, Cristóbal, 80, 81
Martínez, José Luis, 19
Martínez Marín, Carlos, 118, 126–27
Mártir de Anglería, Pedro, 19, 25, 95, 212–13n19; *De Orbe Novo Decades*, 20, 213n22
Mason, Otis T., 51
Mason, Peter, 1, 8, 9, 197
Matlatzinca, 43, 119, 246n3
Matos, Eduardo, 42
Mauro, Fra, 103
Mauss, Marcel, 206n9Mayas, 32, 45, 108, 109; language of, 25, 42, 247n10
Mazahua (Mazahuaque), 43, 57, 108, 246n3
McGrane, Bernard, 8, 197
Mechoacan, 128
Medea (Seneca), 92, 93
Medieval hypothesis, 7, 89–107, 175; cross-cultural exchange versus, 197; summarized, 92–94
Meléndez, Mariselle, 3
Memorial breve acerca de la fundación de la ciudad de Culhuacan (Chimalpahin Cuauhtlehuanitzin), 116, 180–81, 251n51
Memoriales (Motolinía), 118, 252n67, 254n94
Mendieta, Gerónimo de, 70, 102, 105, 118
Mendoza, Antonio de, 33, 72, 76, 115, 174; exploration and conquest mission by, 68–69; and Narváez expedition, 70, 217n86, 234n66; and Niza exploration, 61, 71, 230n4
Mendoza, Gerónimo de, 78
Menéndez de Avilés, Pedro, 83, 231n20
Mental baggage, 92, 106, 175; concept by Lucien Fevre, 242n7
Mercator, Gerhard, 103
Mérida, 25

Mesoamerica, 41–50; agriculture and sedentism in, 38, 41–44, 46–47, 55, 57, 227n94; architecture of, 47, 49, 223n53; boundaries of, 47, 58–59, *160*; class structure of, 24, 42–43; and cross-cultural interaction, 3, 173; as culture area, 2, 37, 38, 41, 58; enlargement and shrinkage of, 47–48, 194; historical tradition and memory in, 42, 112, 119–20, 248n22; hunter-gatherers in, 38, 43–44, 46; indigenous group identity in, 119; languages spoken in, 108, 246n3; and migration, 49, 108–109, 110, 247n6; pictorial writing in, 42, 113–15, 249nn26–27; sociopolitical organization in, 23, 38, 42, 132; Spanish conquest of, 62; Spanish view of, 22, 199, 214n36; time periods of, 46–47, 223n53
Mexicas, 123, 131–32, 179. *See also* Aztec/Mexicas
Mexico, 191
Mexico City, 28; Niza reports on, 75–76
Mexico-Tenochtitlan. *See* Tenochtitlan
Mezcaleros, 226n82
Micchuaque, 57
Michoacán, 43, 59, 62, 63, 76, 96
Mignolo, Walter, 11, 16, 203, 211n7
Migration, 6–7, 108, 124. *See also* Aztec/Mexicas, migrations by; Nahua migration narratives
Missionaries, 79, 117, 195, 252n56
Mixtecs, 108, 124, 127, 247n6
Mixtón War (Cazcán rebellion), 69, 72, 76, 184, 261n57
Moctezuma, Isabel, 117
Moctezuma I, 187
Moctezuma II, 177; defeat and death of, 59, 63; dominion over Mexico-Tenochtitlan by, 19–20, 214n36; Spanish conquerors and, 22, 23, 32, 62–63, 214n36, 217n81; tribute paid to, 32, 67
Molina, Alonso de, 122
Moluccas (Spice Islands), 97
Monarquía indiana (Torquemada), 49

Montalvo, Garci Rodríguez de, 94–95, 97, 100, 243n20
Montejo, Francisco de, 212n13, 213n20
Morgan, Lewis H., 206n9
Morlete, Juan, 81
Motolinía (Toribio de Benavente), 55–56, 57, 58, 118, 124, 252n67, 254n94
Muñoz Camargo, Diego, *172,* 184, 192

Nadal, Pedro, 71
Nahuachichimeca, 58, 58n111
Nahua migration narratives, 2, 6–7, 93, 108–32; broken tree episode in, 127–28, *170,* 257n125; controversial interpretations of, 193–94; historical memory in, 56, 91, 109, 110, 112, 119–20, 177, 184, 248n22, 259n9; ideological function of, 110, 193; and Nahua identity, 123–24; native sources on, 91, 112–18, 249n25; Nuevo México linked to, 33, 60, 79–86, 174–76; relevance of, 202; and Seven Caves of Chicomoztoc, 104, 105, 107, 109, 110, 124–25, 178; Spanish credence to, 5–6, 175–76, 177–86, 190, 191–92. *See also* Aztec/Mexicas, migrations by
Náhuatl language, 45, 49, 52, 56, 58, 108, 246n3; dominance of, 43, 111; missionaries and, 117, 252n56; Spanish adoption as lingua franca, 110–11; known as lengua Mexicana, 191, 248n16; word composition in, 126
Narváez, Pánfilo de, 60, 69–70, 106, 233–34nn65–69
Naufragios (Cabeza de Vaca), 70, 233–34nn65–66
Navaho, 226n82
Nayarit, 43, 57, 63, 65, 111, 126
Niel, Juan Armando, 81
Niza, Marcos de, 2, 7, 60–61, 73, 84, 117–18, 174; historical debate over, 74–75; route taken by, 71–72, *164;* and seven cities of Cíbola legend, 33, 75–76, 93, 101, 104, 105
Nombre de Dios, 77–78, 185, 189, 192, 238n119
Nonoalcas, 49, 57, 129, 228n105
Nueva España, 22, 23, 69, 124, 191, 199; administration of, 65; Amazons legend and, 94–100; boundaries of, 63–64; and colonial knowledge, 38–39; early settlement and exploration of, 62–79; imaginary geography of, 176–77, 189–90; influence on Spain of, 199, 200–201; map of, *158;* naming of, 5, 15–16, 18–19, 24, 25–26, 30–31, 32, 33, 199; natives' cities and buildings in, 21, 213–14n31; pacification program for, 79; population of, 17, 64–65, 211–12n8; Spanish conceptualization of, 184. *See also* Nuevo México expeditions
Nueva Galicia, 61, 74, *158;* conquest expedition of, 49, 65, 66, 69, 70, 99, 232n35
Nueva Vizcaya, 79, 81, *158,* 192; Ibarra conquest of, 61, 77, 78, 185
Nuevo México: Aztlan linked to, 3, 123, 174–76, 183–84, 185–88, 190, 192, 198; Cíbola reappearance as, 2, 33, 60, 79–86, 80; colonial appropriation of, 2–3; Copala seen as former name of, 185, 189, 190; economy of, 32–33, 37–38; as imaginary world, 1–2, 7, 60, 62, 177, 185–86, 188, 198; as land of wonder, 33, 35; map, *158;* quest for, 9, 32, 33–34, 36, 40, 194, 201, 204; reification of, 5, 62, 77, 198; sociopolitical forms in, 37, 199; Spanish consolidation of, 17, 35, 194; standard historiography of, 2, 60–61, 191, 201; topography of, 36–37; toponym of, 6, 15–16, 26–27, 32, 61, 80, 178, 191, 199; and transculturation, 60, 198, 204
Nuevo México expeditions, 79–80, 239n129; Cabeza de Vaca, 33, 69, 70, *164,* 217n86, 234n66, 234n69; Espejo, 80, 174; Guzmán, 49, 59, 63, 66–69, 72, 99, *164;* Ibarra, 76–78, 174, 185, 238n122; Niza, 7, 33, 61, 71–72, 84, 174, 230n4; Oñate, 7, 62, 80, 81–85, *164,* 174, 240n148, 240–41n155; Rodríguez and Sánchez

Chamuscado, 61, 79–80, 174, 190–91; Vázquez de Coronado, 7, 17, 33, 72–74, 84, *164*, 174, 184

Oasisamerica, 40, 54, 59, *160*; as analytical model, 50–51, 53–54, 224–25n71; as culture area, 2, 37, 38, 58
Obregón, Baltasar de, 78, 79, 80, 185, 190–91, 217n88, 226n76; biographical information, 237n116; on reasons for Ibarra's expedition, 61, 77, 174, 175, 178
Ochoa de Lejalde, Juan, 18
O'Gorman, Edmundo, 9, 10, 15
Olid, Cristóbal de, 63, 64–65, 96, 98
Olmecas, 43, 57, 228n105
Olmen, Van, 103
Olmos, Andrés de, 117, 118
Oñate, Cristóbal de, 68
Oñate, Juan de, 60, 182, 194; expedition of, 7, 62, 80, 81–85, *164*, 174, 240n148, 240–41n155
Opata, 52, 54
Ordaz, Diego de, 27
Ordinances for New Discovery and Settlement, 79, 238–39n127
Ordóñez, Isidro, 85–86
Orellana, Francisco de, 93
Oriental despotism, 122, 253–54n86
Origen de los mexicanos, 117, 128, 129, 176, 194, 202
Origin myths. *See* Nahua migration narratives
Ortega, Sergio, 186
Ortelius, Abraham, 103
Ortiz, Fernando, 11, 203–204
Otermín, Antonio de, 86
Oto-Manguean language family, 43, 246n3
Otomí, 55, 56, 127, 130; and Chichimecas, 55, 57, 58; language of, 2, 43, 108, 119, 124, 246n3
Otonchichimeca, 58, 229n111
Oviedo, Gonzalo Fernández de, 70, 98, 100, 217n86, 232n50, 244n38
Oxitipa (Santiago de los Valles in the Huasteca Potosina), 66–68, 75

Padilla, Juan de, 74, 235n91
Paez, Juan, 98
Pagden, Anthony, 8
Palencia, Pedro de, 97
Pames, 54, 55, 76, 108
Pané, Ramón, 20, 21
Pánuco, 63, 64, 65, 67, 69, 123, *164*
Pánuco-Moctezuma river system, 37
Panutla, 193
Papago, 54
Paquimé (Casas Grandes), 52, 78
Pareto, Bartolomé, 103
Pastor Bodmer, Beatriz, 93
Peñalosa, Diego de, 85
Peralta, Pedro de, 86
Pérez de Luxán, Diego, 80
Pérez de Oliva, Hernán, 20, 21
Phelan, John, 102
Philippines, 25, 215n50, 248n16
Piaxtla, 68
Pietz, William, 21, 200
Pilar, García del, 66, 231n33
Pima, 52, 54
Piña Chan, Román, 48
Pizzigani brothers, 103
Pizzigano, Zuane, 103
Plato, 93, 103
Pliny the Elder, 31
Polo, Marco, 31, 93
Ponce de León, Juan, 64, 93, 106, 188, 230n19
Ponce de León, Luis, 65
Ponce de León, Pedro, 83
Popé, 194–95, 202
Popocatépetl, 27, 37
Popular culture, 92, 175
Population: of indigenous peoples, 16–17, 29, 211–12n8, 216n72; of Spanish colonists, 64–65, 238n126
Portilla, Miguel León, 261n6
Portillo y Diez de Sollano, Álvaro, 97
Portugal, 65, 231n20
Post-Classic Horizon, 45, 47, 108
Post functionalism, 4, 206n14
Prester John legend, 107
Priestley, H. I., 97
Ptolemy, 94, 104

Puebla-Tlaxcala valley, 110, 111, 123, 132, 191, 223n53
Pueblo Indians, 2, 58, 74; eastern and western, 52; economy of, 51–52, 226n77; as "ethnologic" category, 40, 51; housing among, 225–26n76; settlements of, 33, 40, 51–52; social structures of, 52, 54
Pueblo Revolt (1680), 86, 194–95, 202
Punta de Santa Elena, 63–64, 231n20
Putnam, Ruth, 97
Pyramids, 21, 28, 42, *168*, 182, 214n33

Quivira, 73–74, 81, 84–85, 105, 117–18, 126, 190
Qwapaw Indians, 73

Rancherías, 38, 51, 77, 186
Real y Supremo Consejo de Indias, 17
Redfield, Robert, 10
Reff, Daniel, 74, 75, 236n97
Relación breve y berdadera del descubrimiento del Nuevo Mexico (Obregón), 190–91
Relación de la genealogía, 117, 125, 129, 176, 185, 194, 202
Relación de Michoacán, 63, 109
Relaciones geográficas, 65, 111, 231n34
Religion, 20–22, 23, 191, 199
Representation: colonial, 9, 39, 173, 190, 196–97; cross-cultural, 62, 201–202; culture and, 4, 196
Restall, Matthew, 107
Ricard, Robert, 106–107
Río de Losa, Rodrigo del, 80
Rio Grande (Rio Bravo), 36, 79, 84
Ríos, Pedro de los, 115
Rocky Mountains, 36, 52
Rodríguez, Agustín, 61, 79, 80, 174, 190–91
Rodríguez Cabrillo, Juan, 98
Rodríguez Prampolini, Ida, 175
Rodríguez Villafuerte, Juan, 63
Rojas, José Luis de, 28
Ruiz, Antonio, 78
Ruiz Medrano, Ethelia, 16
Rulership, indigenous, 108, 121–22, 124, 199

Ruysch, Jan, 103

Saavedra, Álvaro de, 97
Sahagún, Bernardino de: *Códice Florentino*, 56, 122, 123, 228n102; *Historia general de las cosas de Nueva España*, 118, 129, 193, 254n87
Said, Edward, 196
Saldívar, Juan de, 84–85
Saldívar, Vicente de, 84, 85
Sámano, Juan de, 69, 231n33
Sánchez, Alonso, 81
Sánchez Chamuscado, Juan, 61
Sánchez Chamuscado, Francisco, 79
Sandoval, Gonzalo de, 63, 96, 99
San Francisco, Jacinto de, 33, 78, 189. *See also* Cintos, Friar
San Juan (Okeh Oweenge), 85, 241n172
San Juan Bautista de Cialoa, 78
San Juan de los Caballeros, 84
San Martín, 77, 78, 189
San Miguel de Culiacán, 68, 78, 233n56
Santa Bárbara (modern Parral, Chihuahua), 78, 79–80, 82, 83, *164*, 190
Santa Cruz (first name for the peninsula of California), 97, 102, 244n34
Santa María, Juan de, 79
Santo Domingo, 17, 25
Sauer, Carl O., 74–75
Sayavedra, Hernando de, 63
Schöner, Johannes, 103
Schwartz, Stuart B., 196
Sedentism, 43–44, 52, 54, 55, 227n94
Selden Roll, 109, 115, *166*, 251n44
Seneca, 92, 93
Las sergas de Esplandián (Montalvo), 93, 94–95, 97, 100, 243n20
Seven Caves, 104, 105, 107, 109, 110, 123, 124–25, 178. *See also* Chicomoztoc
Seven Cities myth. *See* Cíbola
Seven Myths of the Spanish Conquest (Restall), 107
Seven Portuguese Bishops myth, 94, 100–107, 175
Shoshone language, 52
Sierra Madre Occidental, 36–37, 46, 47, 54, 58, 68

Sierra Madre Oriental, 36, 46, 74
Simmons, Marc, 81–82
Sinaloa, 38, 43, 52, 78, 233n56
Slave raids, 76, 78–79, 236n109
Sombrerete (Villa de Llerena), 55, 77
Sonora, 40, 50, 52, 53, 54, 74, 75, 174; conquest of, 78, 192
Soto, Hernando de, 70, 72, 73, 93, 230–31n19
Southwest, 50–53
Spanish Armada, 83
Spanish conquerors and conquest: administrative structure of, 17–18; and alienation, 19, 200, 203; altepetl as conceived by, 120, 122, 124–25, 254n87; analogies with own society drawn by, 30–31, 91–92, 105, 120, 198–99, 200; astonishment and awe by, 15, 23–24, 27, 35, 96; and Aztlan, 40, 187–88, 191, 192, 198; "Chichimeca" term used by, 6, 33, 39, 40, 55; "civilization" concept of, 15, 19, 21–22, 23, 34–35, 191–92, 210n2; and colonial knowledge, 38–39; consolidation of Nuevo México by, 17, 35, 194; credence to Nahua narratives by, 5–6, 27, 75–76, 93–94, 175–86, 184, 190, 191–92; destruction and massacres by, 5–6, 18, 63, 69, 173, 258n1; documentary sources on, 89–91; English and French competitors of, 64, 83, 231n20; indigenous seen as savages by, 20, 33, 34–35; indigenous troops as allies of, 3, 6, 40, 55, 59, 66, 68, 72–73, 76, 77–78, 119, 184–85, 192, 193, 201, 261n57; influence of cross-cultural interaction on, 3, 9, 10, 24, 39, 59, 92, 173, 175–76, 187–88, 194, 197, 201; medieval legends as influence on, 7, 89, 91–93, 96, 175; and Mesoamerica, 22, 62, 199, 214n36; and Mexico-Tenochtitlan, 5, 15, 19, 20, 27, 28, 34, 35, 216n65; and Moctezuma, 22, 23, 32, 62–63, 214n36, 217n81; and Náhuatl, 110–11, 248n16; naming practices of, 15–16, 25–27, 215n50; Nueva España conceptualized by, 5, 15–16, 18–19, 24, 25–26, 30–31, 32, 33, 184, 199; popular culture as influence on, 92; population of colonists, 64–65, 238n126; and quest for precious metals, 64, 68, 76–77, 81, 92; religious views of, 20–22, 191–92, 199–200; resettlement of natives by, 76, 236–37n111; routes of conquest by, 3, 16–17, 40, 44–45, 49, *158–59*, *164*, 191–92; search for Copala by, 78, 185; view of Nuevo México by, 187–88, 192, 194, 198, 199. *See also* Nuevo México expeditions
Stampa, Carrera, 114
Stoler, Ann Laura, 9–10

Tafur, Pedro, 93
Taínos, 21
Tamaulipas, 44, 46, 50, 63
Tambiah, Stanley, 121, 122
Tamime, 56, 57, 58, 229n111
Tamoanchan, 123, 193
Tangaxoan II, 63
Tanoan language, 52
Tapia, Andrés de, 28, 62
Tarahumaras, 52, 54
Tarascan plateau, 64–65, 231n34
Tarascans, 231n24, 238n119; as allies of Spanish troops, 55, 76, 77–78, 185, 192; state of, 45–46, 47, 63, 68
Taussig, Michael, 195
Taylor, Walter, 48
Tehuacán, 44
Tehuantepec, 37, 63
Téllez, Fernão, 103
Tello, Antonio, 49, 66, 232n35
Tena, Rafael, 117
Tenochtitlan, 50, 189; archeological recoveries from, 28, 216n62; and Aztlan, 125–32, 186–87, 188–89; city layout of, 28–29; Cortés on, 15, 24, 27; geography of, 27–28; as hegemonic center, 15, 30, 32, 67, 132; map of, *163,* 187–88; and migration stories, 125, 131; pictorial history of, 56, 131, *138, 145, 147, 168, 169*; population of, 29, 216n72; rulership in, 19–20, 22–23, 132; size of, 28, 29–30; Spanish arrival in, 5, 15, 19, 27, 28,

Tenochtitlan (*continued*)
34, 35, 216n65; Spanish conquest and destruction of, 5–6, 18, 63; temple-pyramids in, 28, 63, 216n62, 258n148
Teocalli de la Guerra Sagrada, 131, *150*, *151*, 187, 258n149
Teocolhuacan/Teoculhuacan, 1, 129
Teotihuacan, 45, 48, 108–109, 129, 193
Teotlalpan, 119
Tepanecas, 121, 123, 130, 132
Tepehuanes, 54, 76
Tetzcoco, 28, 30, 116, 121, 130, 132
Teuchichimecas, 56, 57, 228n106
Thomas, Nicholas, 9
Tieve, Diego de, 103
Tiguex uprising (1540–41), 73, 235n89
Tira de Tepechpan, 114, 131, *138*
Tizaapan, 130–31
Tlacopan, 28, 30, 121, 132, *162*
Tlatelolco, 28, 29, 125, 132, *153*
Tlatocáyotl, 121, 130, 132, 192
Tlatoque, 23, 55, 120, 132
Tlaxcala, 22, 23, 31, 62, 132, *172*. See also Puebla-Tlaxcala Valley
Tlaxcala Codex, 184, 192
Tlaxcalans, 59, 66, 72, 76, 184, 233n56
Tlaxcaltecas, 55, 81, 123, 130, 132
Todorov, Tzvetan, 197
Tolosa, Juan de, 76
Los toltecas en tierras chichimecas (Hers), 57
Toltecs, 57, 58, 128, 130; culture of, 49–50, 56, 57, 119, 128–29; migration by, 123, 247n6; state of, 47, 129, 130
Toluca, 37, 110
Tonalá, 68, 238n119
Topia (Topira), 71, 78, 185, 238n122
Topilci (Topiltzin Quetzalcóatl), 129
Toponyms: about, 15; of Nueva España, 5, 15–16, 18–19, 24, 25–26, 30–31, 32, 33, 199; of Nuevo México, 6, 15–16, 26–27, 32, 61, 80, 178, 191, 199; place-naming practices, 25–31
Torquemada, Juan de, 18, 49, 118, 128, 182
Torres, Luis de, 31

Toscanelli, Paolo, 103
Totolimpanecas, 130
Totomihuaques, 115, 130
Totonteac, 72, 74, 76
Tovar, Juan de, 116
Tovar, Pedro, 73
Tovar manuscript, 115–16
Transculturation, 11–12, 203–204; Nuevo México and, 60, 198, 204. *See also* Cross-cultural interaction
Tratado de antigüedades mexicanas, 117
Tribute, 30, 32, 67, 121
Triple Alliance (*Excan Tlatoloyan*), 30, 67, 115, 30, 132, 192
Tula, 45, 47–48, 58, 128–29
Tula Xicocotitlan, 128–29
Tylor, Edward, 40, 206n9
Tzintzuntzan, 68

Ulloa, Francisco de, 97
Ulloa, Lope de, 83
Ulúa, 31, 213n19
Undreiner, George J., 74
United States, 51, 225n72, 225n74
Unos anales históricos de la nación mexicano (Anales de Tlatelolco), 117
Urdiñola, Francisco de, 81
Uto-Aztecan language family, 43, 52, 246n3

Valdivia, Pedro de, 93
Valley of Mexico, 2, 57–58, 110, 121, *162*; about, 27–28, 215–16n59; cities and towns in, 30, 130; climatic changes in, 48; and migration narratives, 176, 179; Spanish astonishment at, 35, 96
Vargas Zapata, Diego de, 86
Vázquez de Coronado, Francisco, 105; expeditions of, 7, 17, 33, 72–74, 84, *164*, 174, 184; and Niza excursion, 61, 71, 72, 230n4; and seven cities legend, 100, 106; traditional historiography on, 61–62
Vázquez de Tapia, Bernardino, 215n56
Veinte y un libros rituales y monarquía indiana (Torquemada), 118
Velasco, Gasco de, 85

Velasco, Luis de, 61, 78, 81–82, 236–37n111
Velázquez, Diego, 98, 99, 102
Veracruz, 18, 31, 34, 63
Villagrá, Gaspar de, 82, 174, 182, 240n148, 259n21; on Aztec/Mexicas migration, 178–84
Villamanrique, marqués de, 80–81
Vucub Ziván, 109, 247n10

Wagner, Henry R., 74
Wallerstein, Immanuel, 43
Weber, David J., 75
Weber, Max, 206n9
Weigand, Phil, 58
Western Mexico sub-area, 43
Wissler, Clark, 40
Wittfogel, Karl (*Oriental Despotism*), 122
Wolf, Eric, 4
Worsley, Peter, 194–95

Xalisco, 67, 69
Xaltepec, 76
Xaltocan, 130
Xiuhámatl, 113–14
Xochimilco, 121, 123, 130, 131
Xólotl, 57, 130

Yaqui, 54
Yucatan, 25, 31
Yunge Oweenge (San Gabriel), 85, 241n172

Zacatecas, 46, 47, 48, 49, 50, 129, *164*, 188; indigenous revolts in, 69, 76, 237n112; silver mines in, 76–77, 81
Zacateco Indians, 54, 55, 76, 77
Zacateco-Guahichil rebellion (1561), 77
Zacatula, 63
Zárate Salmerón, Gerónimo de, 70, 81
Zemes, 21, 199, 200
Zuazo, Alonso, 30, 213–14n31
Zumárraga, Juan de, 61, 117
Zúñiga y Acevedo, Gaspar de, 82, 83
Zuñis, 52, 60–61, 79
Zutacapan, 84
Zuyuano political order, 108–10, 119

www.ingramcontent.com/pod-product-compliance
Lightning Source LLC
Chambersburg PA
CBHW080438170426
43195CB00017B/2814